german

DeMYSTiFieD

Demystified Series

Accounting Demystified
Advanced Calculus Demystified
Advanced Physics Demystified
Advanced Statistics Demystified
Algebra Demystified
Alternative Energy Demystified
Anatomy Demystified
asp.net 2.0 Demystified
Astronomy Demystified
Audio Demystified
Biology Demystified
Biotechnology Demystified
Business Calculus Demystified
Business Math Demystified
Business Statistics Demystified
C++ Demystified
Calculus Demystified
Chemistry Demystified
Circuit Analysis Demystified
College Algebra Demystified
Corporate Finance Demystified
Databases Demystified
Data Structures Demystified
Differential Equations Demystified
Digital Electronics Demystified
Earth Science Demystified
Electricity Demystified
Electronics Demystified
Engineering Statistics Demystified
Environmental Science Demystified
Everyday Math Demystified
Fertility Demystified
Financial Planning Demystified
Forensics Demystified
French Demystified
Genetics Demystified
Geometry Demystified
Home Networking Demystified
Investing Demystified
Italian Demystified
Java Demystified
JavaScript Demystified
Lean Six Sigma Demystified
Linear Algebra Demystified

Macroeconomics Demystified
Management Accounting Demystified
Math Proofs Demystified
Math Word Problems Demystified
MATLAB ® Demystified
Medical Billing and Coding Demystified
Medical Terminology Demystified
Meteorology Demystified
Microbiology Demystified
Microeconomics Demystified
Nanotechnology Demystified
Nurse Management Demystified
OOP Demystified
Options Demystified
Organic Chemistry Demystified
Personal Computing Demystified
Pharmacology Demystified
Physics Demystified
Physiology Demystified
Pre-Algebra Demystified
Precalculus Demystified
Probability Demystified
Project Management Demystified
Psychology Demystified
Quality Management Demystified
Quantum Mechanics Demystified
Real Estate Math Demystified
Relativity Demystified
Robotics Demystified
Sales Management Demystified
Signals and Systems Demystified
Six Sigma Demystified
Spanish Demystified
sql Demystified
Statics and Dynamics Demystified
Statistics Demystified
Technical Analysis Demystified
Technical Math Demystified
Trigonometry Demystified
uml Demystified
Visual Basic 2005 Demystified
Visual C# 2005 Demystified
xml Demystified

german
DeMYSTiFieD

Ed Swick

New York   Chicago   San Francisco   Lisbon   London   Madrid   Mexico City
Milan   New Delhi   San Juan   Seoul   Singapore   Sydney   Toronto

Trademarks: McGraw-Hill, the McGraw-Hill Publishing logo, Demystified, and related trade dress are trademarks or registered trademarks of The McGraw-Hill Companies and/or its affiliates in the United States and other countries and may not be used without written permission. All other trademarks are the property of their respective owners. The McGraw-Hill Companies is not associated with any product or vendor mentioned in this book.

8 9 10 11 12 13 14 15 16 17 18 19 20   DOC/DOC   1 9 8 7 6 5 4 3 2 1 0

ISBN 978-0-07-147561-7
MHID   0-07-147561-3
Library of Congress Control Number: 2006046906

Maps created by Douglas Norgord, Geographic Techniques.

McGraw-Hill books are available at special quantity discounts to use as premiums and sales promotions or for use in corporate training programs. To contact a representative, please e-mail us at bulksales@mcgraw-hill.com.

CONTENTS

1" />

Contents

vii

CHAPTER 7 **Irregularities in Present Tense Verbs**   **103**
Present Tense Verb Irregularities   103
Inseparable Verb Prefixes   106
Colors   109
Common/Professional Titles   111
QUIZ   114

CHAPTER 8 **Talking About Location**   **117**
Using the Verb *Kommen*   118
Telling Time   121
Using the Verbs *Gehen* and *Fahren*   122
Using the Verbs *Wohnen* and *Leben*   123
Word Order   124
Some Coordinating Conjunctions   125
Using the Verbs *Wissen* and *Kennen*   126
Infinitives Ending in *-ieren*   127
Separable Verb Prefixes   128
Accusative Case   130
Accusative Pronouns   133
QUIZ   135

CHAPTER 9 **Talking About the Past**   **137**
Possessive Adjectives   137
Regular Past Tense   140
Irregular Past Tense   142
Accusative Case Prepositions   147
Plurals   150
QUIZ   153

CHAPTER 10 **Time and Calendar**   **157**
More Irregular Verbs in the Present and Past Tenses   158
Dative Case   160
Dative Pronouns   162
More About Word Order   164
Cardinal Numbers Twenty and Above   165
More About Telling Time   166

Contents

CHAPTER 18   **Using the Passive Voice**   **327**
More About the Passive Voice   327
Modal Auxiliaries in the Passive Voice   329
Sich Lassen and the Passive Voice   333
Adjective Endings with *Ein-* Words   335
Professions   339
QUIZ   342

CHAPTER 19   **Using the Subjunctive Mood**   **345**
Subjunctive Mood   345
Indirect Discourse   350
Foreign Words in German   356
More Idioms   357
QUIZ   358

CHAPTER 20   **Expressing Wishes and Conditions**   **363**
Expressing Wishes with the Subjunctive   363
Subjunctive with *Als Ob*   365
Expressing Conditions with the Subjunctive   366
Irregular Verbs in the Subjunctive   368
Being Polite in the Subjunctive   369
Infinitive Clauses   369
QUIZ   375
PART FOUR TEST   381

FINAL EXAM   391

APPENDIX A: **Principal Parts of Irregular Verbs**   403
APPENDIX B: **Prepositions and Their Required Cases**   415

English-German Dictionary   417

German-English Dictionary   427

Answer Key   437

Index   **471**

ACKNOWLEDGMENT

With much gratitude to Stefan Feyen for all his help and suggestions.

INTRODUCTION

You've decided to learn German. Or you want to refresh the German skills you learned in the past. Or perhaps you're currently in a German class and you need some extra help with difficult concepts. Whatever your goal might be for learning German, *German Demystified* will efficiently guide you on your way.

Taking the mystery out of German is an important step in the learning process. Students need to know that the study of German is not as formidable a challenge as they might have thought. For one thing, English and German are sister languages that were separated in the early years by the migration of one Germanic group—the Anglo-Saxons—from the Continent to England. In the centuries that have passed since that migration, the Continental language and the language spoken in England evolved in two different ways. But, despite the separation of the two languages by geography and the passage of time, much in them remains similar.

There are many words in both German and English that are identical or that show an obvious kinship. The spelling of the words or even their modern pronunciation may be somewhat different, but the fact that they belong to the same family is quite clear. Here are just a few examples:

German	English
braun	*brown*
bringen	*to bring*
Bruder	*brother*
finden	*to find*
Haus	*house*
kommen	*to come*
Kuh	*cow*
Mann	*man*

Much of the grammar is also similar. All European languages have irregularities, especially with verbs. However, learning the irregularities of German verbs can be less of a task, because German and English have some similarities in how verbal irregularities occur. For example, both languages often have the same irregular vowel change from the present to the past tense.

German	English
kommen—kam	*to come—came*
sehen—sah	*to see—saw*
trinken—trank	*to drink—drank*

This alone is an enormous advantage for the English speaker who wishes to learn German.

How to Use This Book

Demystifying German goes beyond recognizing the similarities between German and English. This book will provide a clear and straightforward approach to understanding German grammatical concepts, including uncomplicated explanations of new material, a variety of examples that illustrate that material, and numerous vehicles for practicing what is learned. In this book you will also find key vocabulary. Vocabulary terms are presented both in short lists and in context within example phrases and sentences.

German Demystified can be used in two ways. You can begin with Chapter 1 and work your way through the chapters in progression. You can also use this book in a modular way by using the Table of Contents and Index to locate particular areas of German that you want to study.

This book features two kinds of practice: oral and written. It's important to understand that one form of practice is no more important than the other. They are different in form but function together in the development of German skills. Language is both a spoken and written entity; therefore, oral practice is obviously necessary when learning a new language, but written practice provides time to think about grammatical concepts and vocabulary meaning. Written practice allows the student time to ponder and analyze what is being learned and is the way in which one records knowledge and evaluates progress. Both forms of practice will be important for you as you proceed through this book.

Below is an illustration of how the oral practices in this book are structured. They are not merely lists of words or of random sentences to be practiced aloud. Instead, the oral practices contain paradigms that illustrate a concept important to the language. Let's look at an example of an oral practice in English providing paradigms that illustrate pronouns used as direct objects.

Practice saying the following list of sentences out loud.

We visited them in March.

We visited her in March.

We visited him in March.

I visited you in March.

She visited us in March.

You visited me in March.

The written practices will appear in various forms. In some instances you will be asked to complete a sentence by inserting new words. For example, an English exercise with pronouns changing from their subjective form to their objective form would look like this:

Rewrite the following sentence using the correct forms of the pronouns provided in parentheses.

Thomas met _____ at the theater.

(I) *Thomas met me at the theater.*

(she) *Thomas met her at the theater.*

(he) *Thomas met him at the theater.*

(we) *Thomas met us at the theater.*

Other forms of written practice include verb conjugations, multiple-choice exercises, and writing original sentences.

You will occasionally find tables in this book. They are used to highlight special information and to remind you of a concept that is important to keep in mind. For example:

German does not capitalize adjectives that refer to a country:

die **deutsche** Fahne	*the **German** flag*
der **amerikanische** Tourist	*the **American** tourist*
der **italienische** Wagen	*the **Italian** car*

Each chapter ends with a quiz that will help you to evaluate your understanding of the material covered. The quizzes are open-book quizzes—you should use the content of the chapter as a resource for determining the correct answers. A good suggestion is to achieve a score of at least 80 percent before going on to the next chapter.

After every five chapters, you will have a Part Test. There are four parts to the book, and the Part Tests are, therefore, named Part One Test, Part Two Test, Part Three Test, and Part Four Test. It is suggested that you consider these tests closed-book tests in order to check your comprehension of the concepts in each part. You should get a score of at least 75 percent in a Part Test before moving on to the next part.

The last test in this book is the Final Exam. It consists of questions that are drawn from all four parts of the book. This exam contains 100 questions, and a good score on the Final Exam would be 75 percent or above.

At the end of the book, there is an Answer Key, which provides the correct answers for all Quizzes, Part Tests, and the Final Exam. In the case of questions that require you to provide an original sentence as your answer, you will be provided with sample answers for comparison.

If you work diligently but at a pace that is comfortable for you, your efforts will result in success and the language of German will be demystified.

Übung macht den Meister. *Practice makes perfect.*

PART ONE

GETTING STARTED

CHAPTER 1

German Pronunciation

In this chapter you will learn:

German Alphabet

There really isn't a German alphabet just like there really isn't an English alphabet. The Germans do what English speakers do: They use the Latin alphabet and add a few extra characters of their own for good measure. There are only four extra characters in

German, and all the other letters are the same as used in the English language. However, there is a difference between German and English pronunciation of the letters.

You must remember that the letters of the alphabet are merely signals of pronunciation possibilities. In all languages there are nuances of the same sound, and often one letter stands for all those nuances. Consider the English vowel *a*. Its name is *ay*, but it is pronounced differently in various words. For example: f*a*ther, b*a*d, b*a*ll, and t*a*pe. Unlike *a*, sometimes the name of a letter gives absolutely no clue as to its pronunciation, such as the English consonant *w*. It is called *double u,* but makes a sound completely different from that. You'll discover that there are a few instances when the German name of a letter does the same thing.

There are various pronunciations for single letters in German as well. Fortunately, they are not as numerous as in English, and, for the most part, German spelling consistently gives the information needed to pronounce words accurately.

Following is the complete alphabet with the German name of each letter, the sound each letter makes, and a sample German word using that letter with its pronunciation and meaning.

Letter	Name	Sounds Like	German Example Word (German Pronunciation)	English Meaning
A a	ah	**m**a**m**a	las (lahss)	*read*
B b	bay	**B**ob	Boot (bote)	*boat*
C c	tsay	i**ts**	Cent (tsent)	*cent*
D d	day	**d**ad	dann (dunn)	*then*
E e	ay	s**ay**	Tee (tay)	*tea*
F f	eff	**f**i**f**e	finden (fin-den)	*to find*
G g	gay	**g**o**gg**le	geben (gay-ben)	*to give*
H h	hah	**h**ope	Haus (house)	*house*
I i	ee	k**ee**p	Igel (ee-gel)	*hedgehog*
J j	yawt	**y**awn	ja (yah)	*yes*
K k	kah	**k**i**ck**	kalt (kult)	*cold*
L l	ell	**l**u**ll**	Laus (louse)	*louse*
M m	emm	**m**o**m**	Maus (mouse)	*mouse*
N n	enn	**n**oo**n**	nein (nine)	*no*
O o	oh	**o**nly	oder (oh-duh)	*or*
P p	pay	**p**i**p**e	parken (par-ken)	*to park*
Q q	koo	**q**uite	Quark (kvahrk)	*curd cheese*

(When pronounced in a German word, the **k** sound of the letter **q** is followed by the **v** sound.)

R r	air	**r**oar	Ruhm (room)	*fame*

(There is no English equivalent for this pronunciation of **r**. See "Some Special Pronunciation Rules" in this chapter for further explanation.)

S s	**ess**	zealous	Sessel (zes-sel)	*armchair*

(At the beginning of a word **s** is pronounced like a **z**.)

T t	**tay**	tot	Teil (tile)	*part*
U u	**oo**	moon	U-Bahn (oo-bahn)	*subway*
V v	**fow**	for	Volkswagen (fohlks-vah-gen)	*Volkswagen*
W w	**vay**	vivid	wild (villt)	*wild*
X x	**ix**	taxi	Taxi (tahk-see)	*taxi*
Y y	**uepsilon**	mystic	physisch (fuez-ish)	*physical*

(With this letter, the lips are pursed to say **oo**, but the voice is saying **ee**. The result is this special vowel sound **ue**. For further explanation, see the explanation for **Ü ü** later in this chapter.)

Z z	**tset**	its	Zelt (tsellt)	*tent*

Oral Practice

Say each word out loud. Look at the pronunciation on the right to check your accuracy.

	German	**English**	**German Pronunciation**
1.	faul	*lazy*	(fowl)
2.	Sau	*sow*	(zow)
3.	Mauer	*wall*	(mow-uh)
4.	Eisen	*iron*	(eye-zen)
5.	Meister	*master*	(my-stuh)
6.	schnell	*fast*	(shnell)
7.	stellen	*to put*	(shtel-len)
8.	sterben	*to die*	(shtair-ben)
9.	Sitz	*seat*	(zits)
10.	sitzen	*to sit*	(zit-sen)
11.	Spiel	*game*	(shpeel)
12.	spielen	*to play*	(shpee-len)
13.	wiegen	*to weigh*	(vee-gen)
14.	Wagen	*car*	(vah-gen)

15.	schlagen	*hit*	(shlah-gen)
16.	Zeit	*time*	(tsite)
17.	Zimmer	*room*	(tsim-muh)
18.	Donner	*thunder*	(dawn-uh)
19.	Tanne	*fir tree*	(tuh-neh)
20.	Tante	*aunt*	(tahn-teh)

Special Characters

The next three special characters in the German alphabet have an umlaut over them. These dots over the vowels indicate a shift in the normal pronunciation of those letters.

The first letter is very much like the letter **E e** illustrated previously.

Ä ä   **ay**   say   spät (shpayt)   *late*

The following letter does not have an English equivalent sound. It is similar to the vowel **e** as it is pronounced in the English word *her*. The letter combination **er** will stand for its pronunciation here.

Ö ö   **er**   were   schön (sh**ern**)   *nice, pretty*

The next letter is pronounced like the sound **oo** with the lips tightly pursed, but the voice is saying **ee**. It is the same pronunciation for the letter **Y y** illustrated previously. The vowel combination **ue** will stand for its pronunciation. It is similar to a French **u** as in **sud** (*south*).

Ü ü   **ue**   sure   über (**ue**-buh)*over*

Vowel with Umlaut	Sound	Vowel with No Umlaut	Sound
Ä ä	**ay**	**A a**	**ah**
Ö ö	**er**	**O o**	**oh**
Ü ü	**ue** (like French)	**U u**	**oo**

The following letter is a combination of an **s** and a **z** treated as a single letter. It does not have a capitalized form and is used in place of a double **s** (**ss**) after long vowel sounds, and diphthongs.

ß   ess-tset   less   weiß (vice)   *white*

Compare the use of the **ß** following a long vowel and **ss** following a short vowel.

aß (ahs—long *ah*) *ate*   passen (puhs-sen—short *uh*) *to fit*

Oral Practice

Say each word out loud. Look at the pronunciation on the right to check your accuracy.

German	English	German Pronunciation
1. älter	*older*	(**el**-tuh)
2. fällt	*falls*	(fellt)
3. löst	*solves*	(**l**erst)
4. böse	*angry*	(**ber**-zeh)
5. Flüsse	*rivers*	(**flu**es-eh)
6. klug	*smart*	(klook)
7. lügen	*to lie*	(**lue**-gen)
8. groß	*big*	(gross)
9. Grüße	*greetings*	(**grue**-seh)
10. Kasse	*cashier*	(kuhs-eh)

Consonant Combinations

The following letter combinations stand for a specific sound different from a single consonant. You will notice that some have an English equivalent.

1. **Ch** stands for the sound of the friction of air at the back of the throat much like the **ch** sound in the Scottish word *loch*. For example: **ich** means *I* and is pronounced **eech**. The italicized consonants *ch* will stand for this sound.

2. **Chs** in the middle of a word is pronounced like English *x*. For example, **Sachsen** means *Saxony* and is pronounced **zahx-en**.

3. **Ck** is pronounced like the English *ck*. For example, **schicken** means *to send* and is pronounced **shick-en**.

4. A final **g** is pronounced as a **k** or the guttural *ch* (see Number 1, in this list). For example, **klug** means *smart* and is pronounced **klook**. The word for *king* is **König** and is pronounced **ker-ni*ch*** or **ker-nik**.

5. **H** that follows a vowel at the end of a syllable is not pronounced. For example, **gehen** means *to go* and is pronounced **gay-en**.

6. With **pf**, both the **p** and the **f** are sounded in the pronunciation. For example, **pfiff** means *whistle* and is pronounced **pfiff**.

7. **Sch** is like the English combination *sh*. For example: **Schule** means *school* and is pronounced **shoo-leh**.

8. Two consonant combinations—**sp** and **st**—add the sound **sh** to their pronunciation. For example, **Sport** means *sports* and is pronounced **shport**. **Still** means *quiet* and is pronounced **shtill**.

9. **Th** exists in German, but it is pronounced like a **t**. For example, the German noun **Theater** means *theater*, but it is pronounced **tay-ah-tuh**.

10. **Tsch** sounds like the English combination *ch*. For example, **Tschechien** means *Czech Republic* and is pronounced **che*ch*-ee-en**.

11. **Tz** is pronounced as it is in English. For example, **letzte** means *last* and is pronounced **letz-teh**.

Oral Practice

Say each word out loud. Look at the pronunciation on the right to check your accuracy.

German	English	German Pronunciation
1. sprechen	*to speak*	(shpre*ch*-en)
2. Stadt	*city*	(shtaht)

3. setzen	*to set*	(zet-zen)
4. schrecken	*to scare*	(shreck-en)
5. Thema	*topic*	(tay-mah)
6. Tisch	*table*	(tish)
7. Käfig	*cage*	(kay-fi**ch**)
8. sehen	*to see*	(zay-en)
9. Pförtner	*doorman*	(pfert-nuh)
10. sechs	*six*	(zex)

Vowel Combinations

The following vowel combinations stand for a single sound but, in most cases, have a sound different from a single vowel.

1. **Aa** is pronounced as a long **ah**. For example, **Haar** means *hair* and is pronounced **hahr**.

2. **Au** is pronounced together as **ow**. For example, **kaufen** means *to buy* and is pronounced **cow-fen**.

3. **Äu** is pronounced **oi**. For example, **Fräulein** means *miss/young lady* and is pronounced **froi-line**.

4. **Ee** has a long **ay** sound. For example, **Tee** means *tea* and is pronounced **tay**.

5. **Ei** is pronounced **eye**. For example, **mein** means *my* and is pronounced **mine**.

6. **Eu** is also pronounced **oi**. For example, **Freude** means *joy* and is pronounced **froi-deh**.

7. **Ie** is pronounced **ee**. For example, **sieht** means *sees* and is pronounced **zeet**.

8. **Oo** has a long **oh** sound. For example, **Boot** means *boat* and is pronounced **bote**.

Oral Practice

Say each word out loud. Look at the pronunciation on the right to check your accuracy.

	German	English	German Pronunciation
1.	Eule	*owl*	(oi-leh)
2.	teilen	*to share*	(ty-len)
3.	schrieb	*wrote*	(shreep)
4.	Kaufmann	*businessman*	(cowf-munn)
5.	Seemann	*seaman*	(zay-munn)
6.	Säule	*column*	(zoi-leh)
7.	fährt	*drives*	(fairt)
8.	Saar	*the Saar*	(zahr)
9.	Freundin	*girlfriend*	(froin-din)
10.	Boote	*boats*	(bote-eh)

Some Special Pronunciation Rules

The final **-e** on a German word is pronounced **eh**. Be careful not to pronounce it **ah** or **uh**. For example, **Tante** means *aunt* and is pronounced **tahn-teh**. **Beste** means *best* and is pronounced **bess-teh**.

In the German-speaking world of Germany, Austria, and Switzerland, there are two distinct ways of pronouncing **r**. One way is the rolled **r** as is heard in Italian or Russian. The other is the so-called guttural **r** that is a sound made near the back of the tongue. In German the guttural sound is used when the **r** is located at the beginning of a word. For example, **rot** means *red* and is pronounced **rote**, with a guttural sound distinctly similar to a French **r**. When this letter is at the end of a syllable or word, particularly in the combination **er**, it sounds more like **uh** and does not resemble an **r**. It is similar to a final **r** in British English. For example, **Zucker** means *sugar* and is pronounced **tsoo-kuh**.

When a **b** or a **d** is located at the end of a prefix or word, they are pronounced **p** and **t** respectively. For example, **starb** means *died* and is pronounced **shtahrp**. The word **abfahren** means *to depart* and is pronounced **ahp-fahr-en**. The noun **Land** means *country* and is pronounced **lunt**. The word **Kind** means *child* and is pronounced **kint**.

SHORT AND LONG VOWELS

Vowels tend to be pronounced short before a double consonant and long before a single consonant or a consonant preceded by **h**. Let's look at some examples.

German	German Pronunciation	English
lassen	(luhs-sen) long	*to let*
lasen	(lah-zen) short	*read*
stehlen	(shtay-len) long	*to steal*
stellen	(shtel-len) short	*to put*
gib	(geep) long	*give*
Mitte	(mit-teh) short	*middle*
Hof	(hofe) long	*court, yard*
hoffen	(haw-fen) short	*to hope*
tun	(toon) long oo	*to do*
Suppe	(zoo-peh) short oo	*soup*

In English the combination *oo* may look the same in many words, but that vowel combination has two pronunciations. For example, long *oo—moon, soon*; and short *oo—look, shook*. When learning German, however, English speakers tend to use the long **oo** sound for all words that have the vowel **u**. But the short and long **oo** sounds must be distinguished in German, as well.

Oral Practice

Say each word out loud. Look at the pronunciation on the right to check your accuracy.

German	English	German Pronunciation
1. stören	*to disturb*	(ster-ren)
2. gelacht	*laughed*	(geh-lah*ch*t)
3. Kaffee	*coffee*	(kah-fay)
4. Brötchen	*roll*	(brert-*ch*en)
5. Schlange	*snake*	(shlahng-eh)
6. jünger	*younger*	(y**ue**ng-uh)
7. floh	*fled*	(flow)
8. Sprüche	*sayings*	(shpr**ue***ch*-eh)

9. gelb   *yellow*   (gelp)
10. Band   *ribbon*   (bunt)

German Cognates

Cognates are words that are identical or very similar in two languages. And that can be problematic, because English speakers sometimes pronounce the German cognate with the English pronunciation. Here are some example words in German with their pronunciations and the English equivalents. Take special note of the German pronunciations.

German	German Pronunciation	English
Auto	(ow-toe)	*auto*
Adresse	(ah-dres-seh)	*address*
effektiv	(ay-feck-teef)	*effective*
Konflikt	(kone-flickt)	*conflict*
minus	(mee-noos)	*minus*
Präsident	(pray-zee-dent)	*president*
Problem	(proe-blame)	*problem*
Service	(zare-veese)	*service*

Many words that end in *-tion* in English also do in German. But that syllable is pronounced **-tsee-own** in German.

Position	(poe-zee-tsee-own)	*position*
Konstitution	(kone-stee-too-tsee-own)	*constitution*

Perhaps you have already noticed that all German nouns—whether proper or common—are capitalized. Here are a few more examples:

German	German Pronunciation	English
Name	(nah-meh)	*name*
Berlin	(bare-leen)	*Berlin*
Kapitalist	(kah-pee-tah-leest)	*capitalist*
Amerika	(ah-mare-ee-kah)	*America*

Oral Practice

Pronounce the following German words out loud without looking at the pronunciations. Then check the correct pronunciation that is provided.

German	English	German Pronunciation
1. Pilot	*pilot*	(pee-lote)
2. Professor	*professor*	(pro-fes-suh)
3. attraktiv	*attractive*	(ah-trahk-teef)
4. komisch	*funny*	(koe-mish)
5. Tür	*door*	(**tuer**)
6. Kanada	*Canada*	(kah-nah-dah)
7. halten	*to hold*	(hul-ten)
8. blind	*blind*	(blint)
9. Dialekt	*dialect*	(dee-ah-lekt)
10. Alpen	*Alps*	(ahl-pen)
11. Fenster	*window*	(fenn-stuh)
12. schreiben	*to write*	(shry-ben)
13. Diplomat	*diplomat*	(dee-ploh-maht)
14. laufen	*to run*	(low-fen)
15. Bier	*beer*	(beer)

QUIZ

Pronounce the following German words out loud. Check your accuracy by using the Answer Key at the back of this book to see the correct pronunciation.

German	English
1. fahren	*to drive*
2. spielen	*to play*
3. Kommunist	*communist*
4. Frau	*woman*

5.	Kreide	*chalk*
6.	Buch	*book*
7.	allein	*alone*
8.	spülen	*to rinse*
9.	tanzen	*to dance*
10.	Mutter	*mother*

CHAPTER 2

People and Names

In this chapter you will learn:

German Names

People

Definite Articles

Conjugation of German Verbs

Places

Greetings

German Names

The United States consists of people from many lands, and one of those lands is Germany. For over two centuries Germans have come to this country with their culture, their traditions, and their names. Consequently, you may find that you already know many German names.

Some names are considered traditional or maybe even called old-fashioned. But just like in English, as time goes by, old-fashioned names come back into vogue. Here are just a few:

Für Jungen *For Boys*	**Für Mädchen** *For Girls*
Gerhardt	Luise
Reinhardt	Gretchen
Helmut	Angelika
Werner	Frieda
Heinrich	Waltraud

In Germany today you will encounter a variety of names, some that come from other cultures, and some that are currently in fashion but will gradually lose their popularity and be replaced by a new trend. For example:

Für Jungen *For Boys*	**Für Mädchen** *For Girls*
Erik	Gudrun
Boris	Tanja
Christoph	Natascha
Felix	Angela
Nils	Iris

Oral Practice

Practice saying the following list of sentences out loud. Then for the last sentence, fill in the blank with your own name.

Mein Name ist Gerhardt.	*My name is Gerhardt.*
Mein Name ist Frieda.	*My name is Frieda.*
Mein Name ist Boris.	*My name is Boris.*
Mein Name ist Tanja.	*My name is Tanja.*
Mein Name ist _____.	*My name is _____.*

ASKING SOMEONE'S NAME

When you ask for someone's name, you say:

Was ist Ihr Name?   *What is your name?*

Interestingly, German has another way of asking for or for giving someone's name. The verb **heißen** is used in these sentences. This verb means *to be called*. When you use it in a sentence, it will have the same translation as **Mein Name ist _____**.

What is your Name?   **My name is Marianne.**

Was ist Ihr Name?   Mein Name ist Marianne.

Wie heißen Sie?   Ich heiße Marianne.

Oral Practice

Practice asking someone's name and telling what your name is.

Wie heißen Sie?   *What is your name?*

Ich heiße Helmut.   *My name is Helmut.*

Ich heiße Luise.   *My name is Luise.*

Ich heiße Werner.   *My name is Werner.*

Ich heiße Gudrun.   *My name is Gudrun.*

Ich heiße _____.   *My name is _____.*

Notice that in the question **Wie heißen Sie?** the verb has an **-en** ending. In the answer **Ich heiße...**, the verb has an **-e** ending. This difference is important and will be explained fully a little later. For now, use **heißen** in the question and **heiße** in the answer.

GERMAN TITLES

Just as in English, Germans use a title with their last names in formal situations or when providing official information about themselves. The word for *Mr.* before a man's last name is **Herr**, and the word for *Ms.*, *Mrs.*, or *Miss* before a woman's last name is **Frau**. There is another feminine title: **Fräulein** (*Miss*). German tends to shy away from using this title, and all women, married or single, are addressed with **Frau**. Let's look at some example sentences in the following Oral Practice section.

Oral Practice

Practice saying the following list of sentences out loud. At the end of the series of sentences, provide your own last name.

Wie heißen Sie, bitte?	*What is your name, please?*
Ich heiße Braun. Werner Braun.	*My name is Braun. Werner Braun.*
Guten Tag, Herr Braun.	*Hello, Mr. Braun.*
Ich heiße Schiller. Tanja Schiller.	*My name is Schiller. Tanja Schiller.*
Guten Tag, Frau Schiller.	*Hello, Ms. Schiller.*
Ich heiße Schneider. Friedrich Schneider.	*My name is Schneider. Friedrich Schneider.*
Guten Tag, Herr Schneider.	*Hello, Mr. Schneider.*
Ich heiße Keller. Marianne Keller.	*My name is Keller. Marianne Keller.*
Guten Tag, Frau Keller.	*Hello, Mrs. Keller.*
Ich heiße _____. _____ _____.	*My name is _____. _____ _____.*
Guten Tag, (Herr/Frau) _____.	*Hello, (Mr./Mrs.) _____.*

Written Practice 1

Using the names in parentheses, write the two ways you can give your name. For example:

(Albert)   Ich heiße Albert. _____   Mein Name ist Albert.

1. (Martin)   _____ .   _____ .
2. (Tina)   _____ .   _____ .
3. (Herr Schäfer) _____ .   _____ .
4. (Frau Kamps)   _____ .   _____ .
5. (Boris Becker) _____ .   _____ .

6. (Maria Schell)   _____ .   _____ .

7. (Professor Bach)   _____ .   _____ .

8. (Doktor Berg)   _____ .   _____ .

9. (Iris)   _____ .   _____ .

10. (*your own name*)   _____ .   _____ .

People

Since English and German are related languages, it's no surprise that there are many words in both languages that resemble one another. These words are called cognates. English and German share a variety of cognates absorbed from other sources as well.

Many cognates refer to people. For example:

der Artist	*artist; performer*	der Mechaniker	*mechanic*
der Boss	*boss*	der Pilot	*pilot*
der Diplomat	*diplomat*	der Professor	*professor*
der Clown	*clown*	der Reporter	*reporter*
der Kapitalist	*capitalist*	der Student	*student*
der Mann	*man*	der Vater	*father*

The German words in this list are used only to describe men. English speakers tend to avoid using words that specify a gender role, but German is different. The makeup of the language requires specifying gender, therefore many nouns add the suffix **-in** to signal that the person described is female. Let's look at some feminine nouns or nouns that refer to women. Some of them will have the suffix **-in**.

die Artistin	*artist; performer*	die Mutter	*mother*
die Dame	*lady*	die Pilotin	*pilot*
die Frau	*woman*	die Professorin	*professor*
die Kapitalistin	*capitalist*	die Reporterin	*reporter*
die Lehrerin	*teacher*	die Sängerin	*singer*
die Mechanikerin	*mechanic*	die Studentin	*student*

If you know the feminine form of a word ends in **-in**, simply remove the suffix and you will have the masculine form of that word. For example:

Feminine	Masculine
die Lehrerin	der Lehrer
die Sängerin	der Sänger

Written Practice 2

Change each of the following masculine nouns to feminine nouns and include the definite article.

1. der Diplomat _____
2. der Student _____
3. der Artist _____
4. der Kommunist _____
5. der Mechaniker _____
6. der Optimist _____
7. der Pilot _____
8. der Manager _____

Definite Articles

Feminine nouns use **die** (*the*) as their definite article, and masculine nouns use **der** (*the*). German also has a third gender: neuter. The definite article for neuter nouns or inanimate objects is **das** (*the*), for example, **das Haus** (*the house*). But many German nouns are considered masculine, feminine, or neuter even though they are not referring to males, females, or inanimate objects. For example:

Masculine		Feminine		Neuter	
der Wagen	*car*	die Lampe	*lamp*	das Baby	*baby*
der Schuh	*shoe*	die Schule	*school*	das Kind	*child*
der Arm	*arm*	die Hand	*hand*	das Mädchen	*girl*

This concept of gender, although not difficult, is new to English speakers and requires some getting used to. Be patient with it, and it will gradually fall in line for you. Just accept the fact that you have to be aware of three forms of the definite article (**der, die, das**) and not just one as in English (*the*).

When you ask *who* someone is, you use **wer** (**Wer ist das?** *Who is that?*). The answer always begins with **Das ist...** (*That is . . .*).

Das ist...   der Lehrer.

                              die Lehrerin.

                              das Kind.

                              das Mädchen.

                              der Professor.

                              die Mutter.

                              Erik.

                               Frau Schneider.

Oral Practice

Practice saying the following list of sentences out loud.

Wer ist das?	*Who is that?*
Das ist der Lehrer.	*That is the teacher.*
Wer ist das?	*Who is that?*
Das ist die Professorin.	*That is the professor.*
Wer ist das?	*Who is that?*
Das ist der Student.	*That is the student.*
Wer ist das?	*Who is that?*
Das ist der Pilot.	*That is the pilot.*
Wer ist das?	*Who is that?*
Das ist die Mutter.	*That is the mother.*
Wer ist das?	*Who is that?*
Das ist der Vater.	*That is the father.*
Wer ist das?	*Who is that?*
Das ist Professor Schäfer.	*That is Professor Schäfer.*

Wer ist das?	*Who is that?*
Das ist Frau Kamps.	*That is Frau Kamps.*

Now practice saying these sentences out loud.

Wie heißt der Herr?	*What is the gentleman's name?*
Der Herr heißt Schneider. Konrad Schneider.	*The gentleman's name is Schneider. Konrad Schneider.*
Wie heißt die Dame?	*What is the lady's name?*
Die Dame heißt Bauer. Angela Bauer.	*The lady's name is Bauer. Angela Bauer.*
Wie heißt die Studentin?	*What is the student's name?*
Die Studentin heißt Tanja.	*The student's name is Tanja.*
Wie heißt der Reporter?	*What is the reporter's name?*
Der Reporter heißt Herr Bach.	*The reporter's name is Mr. Bach.*
Wie heißt das Baby?	*What is the baby's name?*
Das Baby heißt Gudrun.	*The baby's name is Gudrun.*
Wie heißt das Kind?	*What is the child's name?*
Das Kind heißt Felix.	*The child's name is Felix.*

Conjugation of German Verbs

You have probably noticed that **heißt** in the previous sentences looks a little different from what it looked like in earlier examples (**heiße**). When it is used with a word that describes a person other than the speaker, its form is **heißt**. For example:

Sie heißen	*you are called (your name is)*
ich heiße	*I am called (my name is)*
das Kind heißt	*the child is called (the child's name is)*
der Mann heißt	*the man is called (the man's name is)*
die Dame heißt	*the lady is called (the lady's name is)*
der Lehrer heißt	*the teacher is called (the teacher's name is)*

This change of endings on a verb is called a conjugation. There are conjugations in English, but they are simpler in form than German conjugations. Most English verbs add an -*s* in the third person singular of the present tense, and the plural forms of other persons have no added ending.

I speak, you speak, he speak**s**, we speak, they speak

I learn, you learn, he learn**s**, we learn, they learn

Only the verb *to be* is more complicated:

I am, you are, he is, we are, they are

The difference of the endings on **heißen** is part of the German conjugation. Verb conjugations will be taken up fully later in this book.

Oral Practice

Practice saying the following list of sentences out loud.

Wie heißen Sie?	*What is your name?*
Ich heiße Tina.	*My name is Tina.*
Mein Vater heißt Karl.	*My father's name is Karl.*
Wie heißen Sie?	*What is your name?*
Ich heiße Robert.	*My name is Robert.*
Mein Vater heißt Gerhardt.	*My father's name is Gerhardt.*
Wie heißen Sie?	*What is your name?*
Ich heiße Wilhelm.	*My name is Wilhelm.*
Mein Vater heißt Wilhelm.	*My father's name is Wilhelm.*

Written Practice 3

Write the question that asks a person's name. Then write responses to that question with the names shown in parentheses. For example:

(Karl) _Wie heißen Sie?_____

_Ich heiße Karl._____

1. (Angela) _____?

_____.

2. (Herr Bauer) _____?

_____.

3. (Thomas) _____?

_____.

4. (Frau Kamps) _____?

_____.

5. (Gudrun Klein) _____?

_____.

Places

Many cities and countries have similar names in both English and German. Let's look at a few.

German	English
Amerika	*America*
Berlin	*Berlin*
Dänemark	*Denmark*
England	*England*
Hamburg	*Hamburg*
Hannover	*Hanover*
Kanada	*Canada*
Mexiko	*Mexico*
Paris	*Paris*
Polen	*Poland*
Rom	*Rome*
Warschau	*Warsaw*

The word for *German* is **Deutsch**. The English word *Dutch* is a similar word but refers to the Netherlands and not to Germany. The word for *Germany* is **Deutschland**. And a German city that may not be recognized by its German spelling is **München** (*Munich*).

German words for two general locations are **hier** and **da** (or **dort**), which mean respectively *here* and *there*. A sentence that gives someone's location is composed of a subject, the verb **ist**, and the location, usually following the preposition **in**.

Herr Bauer ist...   in Berlin.

                           in Mexiko.

                           in Frankfurt.

                           in Amerika.

                           hier.

                           dort.

Now that you know some countries and cities, you can begin to ask where (**wo**) someone is.

Oral Practice

Practice saying the following list of sentences out loud.

Wo ist Herr Schneider?	*Where is Mr. Schneider?*
Herr Schneider ist in Deutschland.	*Mr. Schneider is in Germany.*
Wo ist Professor Gelb?	*Where is Professor Gelb?*
Professor Gelb ist in Amerika.	*Professor Gelb is in America.*
Wo ist der Lehrer?	*Where is the teacher?*
Der Lehrer ist in Paris.	*The teacher is in Paris.*
Wo ist die Studentin?	*Where is the student?*
Die Studentin ist in Berlin.	*The student is in Berlin.*
Wo ist das Kind?	*Where is the child?*
Das Kind ist hier.	*The child is here.*
Wo ist der Vater?	*Where is the father?*

Der Vater ist da.	*The father is there.*
Wo ist die Reporterin?	*Where is the reporter?*
Die Reporterin ist in Warschau.	*The reporter is in Warsaw.*
Wo ist Frau Bauer?	*Where is Mrs. Bauer?*
Frau Bauer ist in Dänemark.	*Mrs. Bauer is in Denmark.*

Written Practice 4

Use the nouns in parentheses that refer to a person to ask where someone is. Then use the noun that refers to a place to answer the question. For example:

(Martin/Berlin) *Wo ist Martin?*
Martin ist in Berlin.

1. (das Kind/hier) _____?
   _____.

2. (mein Vater/dort) _____?
   _____.

3. (Erik/Deutschland) _____?
   _____.

4. (Thomas/da) _____?
   _____.

5. (Iris/München) _____?
   _____.

Greetings

You now know three interrogative words: **wer** (*who*), **wie** (*how*), and **wo** (*where*). In the expression **Wie heißt der Mann?** we translate **wie** as *what* (*What is the man's name?*). Actually, in German you're saying: *How is the man called?*

The phrase **Wie geht's?** (*How are you?*) is a very common expression in German. For example:

Guten Tag, Thomas. Wie geht's?	*Hello, Thomas. How are you?*
Gut, danke.	*Fine, thanks.*
Guten Tag, Tanja. Wie geht's?	*Hello, Tanja. How are you?*
Gut, danke.	*Fine, thanks.*
Guten Tag, Felix. Wie geht's?	*Hello, Felix. How are you?*
Gut, danke.	*Fine, thanks.*
Guten Tag, Gudrun. Wie geht's?	*Hello, Gudrun. How are you?*
Gut, danke.	*Fine, thanks.*

Although **Guten Tag** means literally *good day*, it is also used during the day to say *hello*. In the morning, you say **Guten Morgen** (*good morning*). In the evening, you say **Guten Abend** (*good evening*). And late at night, when you're about to go to bed, you say **Gute Nacht** (*good night*).

Oral Practice

In the following section you'll find some common exchanges between two people meeting on the street. Practice saying these brief dialogues out loud.

Guten Tag, Herr Schneider.	*Good day, Mr. Schneider.*
Guten Tag, Wilhelm. Wie geht's?	*Hello, Wilhelm. How are you?*
Gut, danke.	*Fine, thanks.*

And two more people:

Guten Morgen, Frau Benz.	*Good morning, Ms. Benz.*
Guten Morgen, Karl. Wie geht's?	*Hello, Karl. How are you?*
Gut, danke.	*Fine, thanks.*

And two more people:

Guten Abend, Doktor Bauer.	*Good evening, Dr. Bauer.*
Guten Abend, Tina. Wie geht's?	*Hello, Tina. How are you?*
Gut, danke.	*Fine, thanks.*

At bedtime you say:

Gute Nacht, Herr Dorf.	*Good night, Mr. Dorf.*
Gute Nacht, Nils.	*Good night, Nils.*

Written Practice 5

Write a greeting to the people whose names are given in parentheses. Note the time of day indicated. For bedtime, write the appropriate phrase.

1. in the morning (Onkel Peter) _____.
2. in the evening (Herr Schneider) _____.
3. in the afternoon (Frau Keller) _____.
4. bedtime (Martin) _____.

When saying good-bye to someone, use the phrase **Auf Wiedersehen** (*till I see you again*). It is sometimes said without **auf**: just **Wiedersehen**. And occasionally you'll hear **Auf Wiederschauen**. In casual conversation, you can use the word **Tschüs** (*so long*).

Oral Practice

Practice saying the following brief dialogues out loud.

Guten Tag, Frau Bach.	*Hello, Ms. Bach.*
Guten Tag, Felix. Wie geht's?	*Hello, Felix. How are you?*
Gut, danke.	*Fine, thanks.*
Auf Wiedersehen, Felix.	*Good-bye, Felix.*
Auf Wiedersehen, Frau Bach.	*Good-bye, Ms. Bach.*

Two more people:

Guten Morgen, Helmut.	*Good morning, Helmut.*
Guten Morgen, Luise. Wie geht's?	*Good morning, Luise. How are you?*
Gut, danke.	*Fine, thanks.*

| Auf Wiederschauen, Luise. | *Good-bye, Luise.* |
| Auf Wiederschauen, Helmut. | *Good-bye, Helmut.* |

Two more people:

Guten Abend, Karl.	*Good evening, Karl.*
Guten Abend, Natascha. Wie geht's?	*Good evening, Natascha. How are you?*
Gut, danke.	*Fine, thanks.*
Tschüs, Natascha.	*So long, Natascha.*
Tschüs, Karl.	*So long, Karl.*

Written Practice 6

Greet each person and ask how he or she is. Translate the English expressions in parentheses into German to form your sentences. For example:

(good day/Karl) *Guten Tag, Karl.*

Wie geht's?

1. (good day/Helga) _____ .

_____ ?

2. (good morning/Thomas) _____ .

_____ ?

3. (good evening/Tanja) _____ .

_____ ?

4. (good day/Herr Bach) _____ .

_____ ?

5. (good morning/Rita) _____ .

_____ ?

6. (good evening/Frau Kamps) _____ .

_____ ?

QUIZ

Write the feminine forms of the masculine nouns provided, using the definite articles. For example:

der Professor *die Professorin* _____

1. der Lehrer _____
2. der Reporter _____

Using the names provided in parentheses, write the two ways that you tell someone your name. For example:

(Karl) *Mein Name ist Karl.* _____
Ich heiße Karl. _____

3. (Gudrun) _____.

   _____.

4. (Felix) _____.

   _____.

Using the name in parentheses, ask who someone is and give the answer. For example:

(Martin) *Wer ist das?* _____
Das ist Martin. _____

5. (Tanja) _____?

   _____.

Use the nouns in parentheses that refer to a person to ask where someone is. Then use the nouns that refer to a place to answer the questions. For example:

(der Mann/London) *Wo ist der Mann?* _____

Der Mann ist in London. _____

6. (der Pilot/Polen) _____?

_____.

7. (die Frau/Rom) _____?

_____.

Circle the letter of the word or phrase that best completes each sentence.

8. _____ ist das?

   (a) Helmut   (c) Name

   (b) Wer   (d) Heißen

9. Das Mädchen heißt _____.

   (a) Herr   (c) Angela

   (b) Frau   (d) Erik

10. Wie geht's? Gut, _____.

   (a) Morgen   (c) hier

   (b) danke   (d) wer

CHAPTER 3

Asking Questions

In this chapter you will learn:

Asking Questions with *Wer*

Wer ist das? You already know what that question means: *Who is that?* The answer will always be a person. Let's meet some new people, so you can begin forming questions about them.

der Bruder	*brother*	der Junge	*boy*
die Schwester	*sister*	das Mädchen	*girl*
der Freund	*friend*	der Onkel	*uncle*
die Freundin	*friend; girlfriend*	die Tante	*aunt*
der Großvater	*grandfather*	der Sohn	*son*
die Großmutter	*grandmother*	die Tochter	*daughter*

Notice the gender of the previous nouns and the use of the definite articles **der**, **die**, and **das**. Except for **das Mädchen**, the masculine and feminine nouns happen to conform to the sexual gender of the person. Remember that that will not always be the case.

Indefinite Articles

Just as in English, German has indefinite articles. In English, the indefinite articles are *a* and *an*. In German, they are **ein** and **eine**. Use **ein** with all masculine and neuter nouns, and use **eine** with all feminine nouns. For example:

der Lehrer	*the teacher*	ein Lehrer	*a teacher*
das Haus	*the house*	ein Haus	*a house*
die Lehrerin	*the teacher*	eine Lehrerin	*a teacher*

Possessive Adjective *Mein*

The same endings are used with the possessive adjective **mein** (*my*). Use **mein** with all masculine and neuter nouns, and use **meine** with all feminine nouns. For example:

der Wagen	*the car*	mein Wagen	*my car*
das Kind	*the child*	mein Kind	*my child*
die Lampe	*the lamp*	meine Lampe	*my lamp*

In a response to the question **Wer ist das?** (*Who is that?*), the definite article, indefinite article, or the possessive adjective **mein** can be used.

Wer ist das?
Das ist die Lehrerin.

Das ist ein Freund.

Das ist meine Tante.

Oral Practice

Practice asking who someone is and answering each question out loud.

Wer ist das?	*Who is that?*
Das ist ein Freund.	*That is a friend.*
Wer ist das?	*Who is that?*
Das ist eine Freundin.	*That is a friend.*
Wer ist das?	*Who is that?*
Das ist mein Bruder.	*That is my brother.*
Wer ist das?	*Who is that?*
Das ist meine Schwester.	*That is my sister.*
Wer ist das?	*Who is that?*
Das ist mein Onkel.	*That is my uncle.*
Wer ist das?	*Who is that?*
Das ist meine Tante.	*That is my aunt.*
Wer ist das?	*Who is that?*
Das ist mein Großvater.	*That is my grandfather.*
Wer ist das?	*Who is that?*
Das ist meine Tochter.	*That is my daughter.*

Yes or No Questions

You can respond to many questions with **ja** or **nein** (*yes* or *no*). Notice that the questions that require a **ja** or **nein** answer begin with a verb and the verb is followed by a subject (**das**). In the following examples the verb used is **ist**, followed by **das**. It's the same word order we use in English for such questions. For example:

Ist das ein Professor?	*Is that a professor?*
Ja, das ist ein Professor.	*Yes, that is a professor.*
Ist das eine Schule?	*Is that a school?*
Ja, das ist eine Schule.	*Yes, that is a school.*

When you negate an answer with **nein**, you must use the negative **kein** (*not a, not any, none*), which follows the verb **ist** in the sentence. Use the following pattern when answering questions in the positive (**ja**) or in the negative (**nein**).

Ist das ein _____?   Ja, das ist ein _____.   Nein, das ist kein _____.

For example:

Ist das ein Haus?	*Is that a house?*
Nein, das ist kein Haus.	*No, that is not a house.*
Das ist ein Museum.	*That is a museum.*
Ist das eine Lampe?	*Is that a lamp?*
Nein, das ist keine Lampe.	*No, that is not a lamp.*
Das ist eine Vase.	*That is a vase.*

However, if a definite article (**der**, **die**, **das**) or a possessive pronoun precedes a noun that is negated, **nicht** is used in place of **kein**.

Ist das der Lehrer?

Ja, das ist der Lehrer.	*Yes, that is the teacher.*
Nein, das ist nicht der Lehrer.	*No, that is not the teacher.*

Ist das Ihr Bruder?

Ja, das ist mein Bruder.	*Yes, that is my brother.*
Nein, das ist nicht mein Bruder.	*No, that is not my brother.*

Written Practice 1

Answer each question in the negative using **nein** and **nicht**. For example:

Ist der Mann zu Hause? _Nein, der Mann ist nicht zu Hause._

1. Ist Werner in der Schweiz? _____.
2. Ist der Junge Ihr Bruder? _____.
3. Ist das Mädchen Ihre Schwester? _____.
4. Ist die Bibliothek hier? _____.
5. Ist der Park weit von hier? _____.

Oral Practice

Practice saying each question and answer out loud.

Ist das der Onkel?	*Is that the uncle?*
Ja, das ist der Onkel.	*Yes, that is the uncle.*
Nein, das ist nicht der Onkel. Das ist der Großvater.	*No, that is not the uncle. That is the grandfather.*
Ist das ein Freund?	*Is that a friend?*
Ja, das ist ein Freund.	*Yes, that is a friend.*
Nein, das ist kein Freund. Das ist mein Bruder.	*No, that is not a friend. That is my brother.*
Ist das die Großmutter?	*Is that the grandmother?*
Ja, das ist die Großmutter.	*Yes, that is the grandmother.*
Nein, das ist nicht die Großmutter. Das ist meine Tante.	*No, that is not the grandmother. That is my aunt.*
Ist das eine Freundin?	*Is that a friend?*
Ja, das ist eine Freundin.	*Yes, that is a friend.*
Nein, das ist keine Freundin. Das ist meine Schwester.	*No, that is not a friend. That is my sister.*

Using *Oder* for Differentiation

When you add the word **oder** (*or*) to questions, you can ask for a differentiation between two people or things.

Ist das eine Schule oder ein Museum?	*Is that a school or a museum?*
Das ist ein Museum.	*That is a museum.*
Ist das der Bruder oder der Sohn?	*Is that the brother or the son?*
Das ist der Bruder.	*That is the brother.*
Ist das Gudrun oder Tanja?	*Is that Gudrun or Tanja?*
Das ist Tanja.	*That is Tanja.*
Ist das eine Professorin oder eine Lehrerin?	*Is that a professor or a teacher?*
Das ist eine Lehrerin.	*That is a teacher.*

Written Practice 2

For each of the pairs of words in parentheses, write a question asking to differentiate between the two people or things. Answer with either one of the words in the pair. For example:

(Karl/Helmut) Ist das Karl oder Helmut?

Das ist Karl.

1. (ein Professor/ein Lehrer) _____?

_____.

2. (der Vater/der Großvater) _____?

_____.

3. (eine Lampe/eine Vase) _____?

_____.

4. (Frau Bauer/Frau Schäfer) _____?

_____.

Asking Questions with *Was*

Was ist das? (*What is that?*) This question asks *what* something is and, therefore, inquires about inanimate objects. Let's become acquainted with some objects, so you can begin forming questions with **was** (*what*).

das Auto	ein Auto	*car*
das Buch	ein Buch	*book*
das Gymnasium	ein Gymnasium	*secondary school*
das Heft	ein Heft	*notebook*
das Sweatshirt	ein Sweatshirt	*sweatshirt*
der Bleistift	ein Bleistift	*pencil*
der Computer	ein Computer	*computer*
der Fluss	ein Fluss	*river*
der Kuli	ein Kuli	*ballpoint pen*
der Park	ein Park	*park*
die Bibliothek	eine Bibliothek	*library*
die Stadt	eine Stadt	*city*
die Uhr	eine Uhr	*clock*
die Wohnung	eine Wohnung	*apartment*
die Zeitung	eine Zeitung	*newspaper*

The response to the question **Was ist das?** (*What is that?*) will follow **Das ist...** and can be composed of a noun modified by a definite article, indefinite article, or the possessive adjective **mein**, as shown here:

Das ist...	*der Park.*
	die Zeitung.
	ein Sweatshirt.
	eine Uhr.
	mein Kuli.
	meine Wohnung.

Oral Practice

Practice asking these questions and giving the answers out loud.

Ist das ein Buch oder ein Heft?	*Is that a book or a notebook?*
Das ist ein Buch.	*That is a book.*
Ist das eine Bibliothek oder ein Gymnasium?	*Is that a library or a secondary school?*
Das ist eine Bibliothek.	*That is a library.*
Was ist das?	*What is that?*
Das ist mein Computer.	*That is my computer.*
Was ist das?	*What is that?*
Das ist meine Zeitung.	*That is my newspaper.*
Was it das?	*What is that?*
Das ist ein Fluss.	*That is a river.*
Was ist das?	*What is that?*
Das ist eine Uhr.	*That is a clock.*
Ist das eine Wohnung?	*Is that an apartment?*
Ja, das ist eine Wohnung.	*Yes, that is an apartment.*
Nein, das ist keine Wohnung. Das ist ein Haus.	*No, that is not an apartment. That is a house.*
Ist das ein Bleistift?	*Is that a pencil?*
Ja, das ist ein Bleistift.	*Yes, that is a pencil.*
Nein, das ist kein Bleistift. Das ist ein Kuli.	*No, that is not a pencil. That is a ballpoint pen.*
Ist das eine Stadt.	*Is that a city?*
Ja, das ist eine Stadt.	*Yes, that is a city.*

Asking Questions with *Wo*

Wo ist...? (*Where is . . . ?*) When asked *where* someone or something is, you can respond with a city or country name. Or you might use the expression **weit von hier** (*far from here*). In its negated form it's **nicht weit von hier** (*not far from here*). You can use **zu Hause** to say that someone is *at home*. In its negated form you say **nicht zu Hause** (*not at home*). For example:

Wo ist Herr Weber?	*Where is Mr. Weber?*
Herr Weber ist in Deutschland.	*Mr. Weber is in Germany.*
Wo ist das Gymnasium?	*Where is the secondary school?*
Das Gymnasium ist weit von hier.	*The secondary school is far from here.*
Wo ist der Park?	*Where is the park?*
Der Park ist nicht weit von hier.	*The park is not far from here.*
Wo ist Frau Bach?	*Where is Ms. Bach?*
Frau Bach ist zu Hause.	*Ms. Bach is at home.*

A response to the question **Wo ist...?** (*Where is . . .?*) consists of any phrase that shows location. Many such phrases begin with the preposition **in**.

Die Frau ist...	in Amerika.
	in London.
	zu Hause.
	nicht zu Hause.
	dort.
Mein Haus ist...	in Berlin.
	hier.
	da.
	weit von hier.
	nicht weit von hier.

Oral Practice

Practice asking these questions and giving the answers out loud.

Wo ist der Pilot?	*Where is the pilot?*
Der Pilot ist in Hannover.	*The pilot is in Hanover.*
Wo ist die Bibliothek?	*Where is the library?*

Die Bibliothek ist weit von hier.	*The library is far from here.*
Wo ist das Museum?	*Where is the museum?*
Das Museum ist nicht weit von hier.	*The museum is not far from here.*
Wo ist Professor Kamps?	*Where is Professor Kamps?*
Professor Kamps ist zu Hause.	*Professor Kamps is at home.*
Ist Frau Kamps zu Hause?	*Is Ms. Kamps at home?*
Ja, Frau Kamps ist zu Hause.	*Yes, Ms. Kamps is at home.*
Nein, Frau Kamps ist nicht zu Hause. Frau Kamps ist in Berlin.	*No, Ms. Kamps is not at home. Ms. Kamps is in Berlin.*
Ist Ihre Tante zu Hause?	*Is your aunt at home?*
Ja, meine Tante ist zu Hause.	*Yes, my aunt is at home.*
Nein, meine Tante ist nicht zu Hause. Meine Tante ist in Polen.	*No, my aunt is not at home. My aunt is in Poland.*

Written Practice 3

Write a question asking about the word or phrase in parentheses. Remember that **Wer ist das?** is used when referring to a person, **Was ist das?** refers to an object, and **Wo ist _____?** is used when referring to a place. For example:

(mein Vater) _Wer ist das?_ _____

(das Haus) _Was ist das?_ _____

(Berlin) _Wo ist Berlin?_ _____

1. (der Pilot) _____?

2. (mein Bruder) _____?

3. (die Bibliothek) _____?

4. (Tante Ingrid) _____?

5. (München) _____?

Possessive Adjective *Ihr*

Until now you have used only the possessive adjective **mein**. Use the possessive adjective **Ihr** to say *your*. Notice that **Ihr** is always written with a capital **i**. And like **eine** and **meine**, **Ihr** will have an **-e** ending with feminine nouns (**Ihre Mutter**).

Masculine	Feminine	Neuter
der Sohn	die Schwester	das Heft
ein Sohn	eine Schwester	ein Heft
mein Sohn	meine Schwester	mein Heft
Ihr Sohn	Ihre Schwester	Ihr Heft

Let's look at some example sentences with **Ihr**.

Ist das Ihr Wagen oder mein Wagen?	*Is that your car or my car?*
Das ist Ihr Wagen.	*That is your car.*
Ist das Ihre Zeitung oder meine Zeitung?	*Is that your newspaper or my newspaper?*
Das ist Ihre Zeitung.	*That is your newspaper.*
Ist das Ihr Heft oder mein Heft?	*Is that your notebook or my notebook?*
Das ist Ihr Heft.	*That is your notebook.*

Oral Practice

Practice asking these questions and giving the answers out loud.

Wo ist Ihr Vater?	*Where is your father?*
Mein Vater ist zu Hause.	*My father is at home.*
Wo ist Ihre Schwester?	*Where is your sister?*
Meine Schwester ist in Hamburg.	*My sister is in Hamburg.*
Wo ist Ihre Großmutter?	*Where is your grandmother?*
Meine Großmutter ist in Rom.	*My grandmother is in Rome.*
Ist Ihr Onkel in Berlin?	*Is your uncle in Berlin?*
Nein, mein Onkel ist nicht in Berlin. Mein Onkel ist in Heidelberg.	*No, my uncle is not in Berlin. My uncle is in Heidelberg.*

Ist Ihre Freundin zu Hause?	*Is your girlfriend at home?*
Nein, meine Freundin ist nicht zu Hause. Meine Freundin ist in Amerika.	*No, my girlfriend is not at home. My girlfriend is in America.*
Ist Ihr Auto hier?	*Is your car here?*
Nein, mein Auto ist weit von hier.	*No, my car is far from here.*

Written Practice 4

Ask the question whether something or someone is here with each of the words in parentheses. Use **Ihr** or **Ihre** appropriately. For example:

(Haus) Ist Ihr Haus hier? (Is your house here?)
(Lampe) Ist Ihre Lampe hier? (Is your lamp here?)

1. (Schwester) _____?
2. (Vater) _____?
3. (Tante) _____?
4. (Wagen) _____?
5. (Schule) _____?

About the German-Speaking World

The three major countries that use German as the official language or one of the official languages are:

Deutschland   *Germany*   Österreich   *Austria*   die Schweiz   *Switzerland*

Notice that **die Schweiz** is always said with the definite article much the same way that English says *the Netherlands* or *the Ukraine*. When you say that you are in Switzerland, the definite article changes: **in der Schweiz**. This does not occur with Germany and Austria: **in Deutschland** and **in Österreich**.

As German speakers travel about the three German-speaking countries, they communicate with little difficulty. There are regional pronunciations and local dialects, but since everyone is taught **Hochdeutsch** (*High German*) in the educational system, everyone has command of the standard language. Dialects are usually limited to a community or small region.

If someone comes from Germany, his or her nationality is described like this:

Der Mann ist Deutscher.	*The man is German.*
Die Frau ist Deutsche.	*The woman is German.*

If someone comes from Austria, you say:

Mein Onkel ist Österreicher.	*My uncle is Austrian.*
Meine Tante ist Österreicherin.	*My aunt is Austrian.*

If someone comes from Switzerland, you say:

Der Lehrer ist Schweizer.	
Die Lehrerin ist Schweizerin.	*The teacher is Swiss.*

If someone comes from the United States, he or she is called **Amerikaner**:

Ihr Freund ist Amerikaner.	*Your friend is an American.*
Ist Ihre Freundin Amerikanerin?	*Is your girlfriend an American?*

Oral Practice

Practice asking these questions and giving the answers out loud.

Wo ist Ihr Freund?	*Where is your friend?*
Mein Freund ist in der Schweiz.	*My friend is in Switzerland.*
Ist Ihr Freund Schweizer?	*Is your friend Swiss?*
Nein, mein Freund ist kein Schweizer. Mein Freund ist Deutscher.	*No, my friend is not Swiss. My friend is German.*
Wo ist Ihre Lehrerin?	*Where is your teacher?*
Meine Lehrerin ist in Österreich.	*My teacher is in Austria.*
Ist Ihre Lehrerin Österreicherin?	*Is your teacher Austrian?*
Ja, meine Lehrerin ist Österreicherin.	*Yes, my teacher is Austrian.*
Wo ist Ihre Tante?	*Where is your aunt?*
Meine Tante ist in Bern.	*My aunt is in Bern.*
Ist Ihre Tante Schweizerin?	*Is your aunt Swiss?*
Nein, meine Tante ist keine Schweizerin. Meine Tante ist Deutsche.	*No, my aunt is not Swiss. My aunt is German.*

Written Practice 5

Complete each sentence with any appropriate word or phrase. For example:

Mein Freund ist *Schweizer.* _____

1. Ist das ein Museum oder _____?
2. Wo ist _____?
3. Der Mann ist mein _____?
4. _____ ist das?
5. Ist die Frau Ihre Mutter oder _____?
6. Die Dame ist eine _____.
7. Mein Bruder ist in _____.
8. _____ ist nicht weit von hier.
9. _____ heißt Professor Schmidt.
10. Ist das Ihre _____?

QUIZ

Write each noun with **ein**, **mein**, and **Ihr**. For example:

das Haus   *ein Haus* _____   *mein Haus* _____   *Ihr Haus* _____

1. das Auto   _____   _____   _____
2. die Bibliothek _____   _____   _____
3. das Mädchen _____   _____   _____

Write two answers to each question, one with **ja** and the other with **nein** and **nicht** or **nein** and **kein**. For example:

Ist der Mann Deutscher?

Ja, der Mann ist Deutscher.

Nein, der Mann ist kein Deutscher.

4. Ist Ihr Professor in Deutschland?

_____.

_____.

5. Ist Ihre Freundin Österreicherin?

_____.

_____.

Using **wer**, **was**, **wie**, or **wo**, write a question about the word or phrase in bold print in each of the sentences. For example:

Der Mann heißt **Helmut**.

Wie heißt der Mann?

6. Mein Onkel ist **in der Schweiz**.

_____.

7. Das ist **die Bibliothek**.

_____.

Circle the letter of the word or phrase that best completes each sentence.

8. Der _____ ist mein Freund.

  (a) Dame   (c) Mädchen

  (b) Kind   (d) Junge

9. Wo ist _____ Bleistift?

    (a) mein   (c) eine

    (b) Ihre   (d) das

10. Ist das ein Haus _____ ein Museum?

    (a) oder   (c) in der

    (b) in   (d) was

CHAPTER 4

Describing People and Things

In this chapter you will learn:

Using the Verb *Sein*

An infinitive is the unconjugated form of a verb that expresses the action of the verb but does not indicate the person (first, second, or third) or number (singular or plural) doing the action. The English infinitive for **sein** is *to be*. The German infinitive for *to be* is **sein**.

In Chapter 2, you were introduced to the third person singular conjugation (**ist**) of the infinitive **sein** (*to be*).

Was ist das? *What is that?*   Das ist mein Buch. *That is my book.*

But just like English, German has other conjugations of that verb. In English they are:

	Singular	**Plural**
First person	I am	we are
Second person	you are	you are
Third person	he is	they are
		she is
		it is

Pronouns

The German pronouns fall into the categories of singular and plural like English, and they likewise are distinguished by being first, second, or third person pronouns. Let's look at the conjugation of **sein** to see what happens to this verb when conjugated with the various pronouns.

Conjugation of the verb **sein** in the present tense:

	Singular		**Plural**	
First person	ich bin	*I am*	wir sind	*we are*
Second person	du bist	*you are*	ihr seid	*you are*
	Sie sind	*you are*	Sie Sind	*you are*
Third person	er ist	*he is*	sie sind	*they are*
	sie ist	*she is*		
	es ist	*it is*		

After looking at this chart, you are undoubtedly aware of the frequent use of the pronoun *you*. Long ago, English included *thou* and *ye* among the words that mean *you*. Today, English speakers use only the pronoun *you* as both the singular and plural forms of the word and make no distinctions between formal or informal usage. German is different.

German makes a distinction between people with whom you are on a formal basis (strangers, your boss, a store clerk, a police officer, and so on), and those with whom you are on an informal basis (children, family members, friends).

When you are on a formal basis with one person or a group of people, you use the pronoun **Sie**. For example, when asking a stranger's name, you say:

Wie heißen Sie?	*What is your name?*

When you are speaking to two or more strangers, you ask:

Wie heißen Sie?	*What are your names?*

There is no difference between the singular and the plural for **Sie** in German.

But when you speak to children, family members, or friends, use the pronoun **du** (this is actually the counterpart of the old English word *thou*). **Du** is singular. You use it when speaking to one person:

Wie heißt du?	*What is your name?*

The plural of **du** is **ihr**. Use this pronoun when speaking informally to two or more people:

Wie heißt ihr?	*What are your names?*

The verb **sein** functions much like the English verb *to be* within sentences. Let's look at some example questions and answers using **sein** conjugated with the three forms of the pronoun *you*.

Sind Sie zu Hause?	*Are you at home?*
Ja, ich bin zu Hause.	*Yes, I am at home.*

or

Ja, wir sind zu Hause.	*Yes, we are at home.*
Bist du in Berlin?	*Are you in Berlin?*
Nein, ich bin nicht in Berlin.	*No, I am not in Berlin.*
Seid ihr in der Schweiz?	*Are you in Switzerland?*
Ja, wir sind in der Schweiz.	*Yes, we are in Switzerland.*

Oral Practice

Practice saying the following list of sentences out loud.

Ich bin Amerikaner.	*I am an American.*
Ich bin Amerikanerin.	*I am an American.*
Bist du Deutscher?	*Are you German?*
Sind Sie Deutsche?	*Are you German?*
Wo seid ihr?	*Where are you?*
Wir sind in Deutschland.	*We are in Germany.*
Sie sind nicht weit von hier.	*They are not far from here.*
Wo ist Ihr Vater?	*Where is your father?*
Er ist in Hamburg.	*He is in Hamburg.*
Wo ist Ihre Freundin?	*Where is your girlfriend?*
Sie ist in Österreich.	*She is in Austria.*
Wo ist Ihr Heft?	*Where is your notebook.*
Es ist zu Hause.	*It is at home.*

Written Practice 1

Provide the conjugated forms for the verb **sein** with the pronouns and nouns below.

1. ich _____
2. sie (*they*) _____
3. du _____
4. sie (*she*) _____
5. ihr _____
6. Ihr Bruder _____
7. die Studentin _____
8. er _____
9. es _____
10. wir _____

Using the Verb *Heißen*

Let's look at the conjugation of the verb *heißen* in the present tense. As discussed in Chapter 2, this verb is used to tell what someone's name is. It literally means *to be called* but is most often translated as *one's name is*. For example:

Ich heiße Martin.	*My name is Martin.*
ich heiße	wir heißen
du heißt	ihr heißt
Sie heißen	Sie heißen
er, sie, es heißt	sie heißen

Notice that the pronouns **er**, **sie**, and **es** are used like their English counterparts (*he*, *she*, and *it*) to refer, respectively, to a male, a female, and an inanimate object. In German you also use **er** with all masculine nouns, **sie** with all feminine nouns, and **es** with all neuter nouns. For example:

Ist der Wagen neu?	*Is the car (masculine) new?*
Ja, **er** ist neu.	*Yes, it is new.*
Ist die Lampe neu?	*Is the lamp (feminine) new?*
Ja, **sie** ist neu.	*Yes, it is new.*
Ist das Kind krank?	*Is the child (neuter) sick?*
Ja, **es** ist krank.	*Yes, he/she is sick.*

The plural of **er**, **sie**, and **es** is **sie** (*they*). Perhaps it seems confusing at first that **sie** (*she, it*) and **sie** (*they*) look identical. But Germans have no trouble distinguishing these two pronouns: One is singular, and the other is plural, so the verb conjugations are different, making it clear which pronoun is being used.

In addition, there is the pronoun **Sie** (formal, singular, or plural *you*). Once again, there is no confusion in using this pronoun, because the context of a conversation or a text tells how it is being used.

Oral Practice

Practice saying the following list of sentences out loud.

Ist sie eine Freundin?	*Is she a friend?*
Sind sie in der Schweiz?	*Are they in Switzerland?*
Sind Sie Deutscher, Herr Bauer?	*Are you German, Mr. Bauer?*
Sie ist zu Hause.	*She is at home.*
Sie sind in Heidelberg.	*They are in Heidelberg.*
Sie sind der Professor.	*You are the professor.*
Die Vase? Wo ist sie?	*The vase? Where is it?*
Der Kuli? Wo ist er?	*The ballpoint? Where is it?*
Das Buch? Wo ist es?	*The book? Where is it?*

To avoid any possibility of confusion in this book, the pronoun **sie** will be identified as either **sie** *s.* (singular = *she; it*) or **sie** *pl.* (plural = *they*) where necessary. The pronoun **Sie** (*you*) is always capitalized and is, therefore, easily identifiable.

Remember, if you use a singular noun as the subject of the verb **sein**, use the conjugation form **ist**: **mein Vater ist**, **das Mädchen ist**, and so on.

Written Practice 2

Change the phrases in bold print below to the appropriate pronouns: **er**, **sie** *s.*, **es**, or **sie** *pl.* For example:

Der Mann ist mein Freund. _Er ist mein Freund._

1. **Mein Wagen** ist hier. _____ .
2. Ist **die Wohnung** da? _____ ?
3. **Das Haus** ist weit von hier. _____ .
4. Wo ist **Ihr Kind**? _____ ?
5. **Thomas und Karl** sind zu Hause. _____ .
6. Wo ist **meine Mutter**? _____ ?

Write the appropriate pronoun substitution using **er, sie** *s.*, **es**, or **sie** *pl.* for the following nouns.

7. Ihre Tante _____

8. Ihr Haus _____

9. mein Bleistift _____

10. mein Sohn _____

11. ein Onkel _____

12. eine Vase _____

13. ein Mädchen _____

14. das Wetter _____

15. Martin und Tanja _____

Some Useful Adjectives

Now that you've learned how to conjugate the verb **sein**, it's time to add some adjectives to your vocabulary. Adjectives modify or describe nouns and are useful in telling what someone or something is like. Here are some examples:

alt	*old*	krank	*sick*
gesund	*healthy*	kurz	*short*
glücklich	*happy*	lang	*long*
groß	*big, large*	neu	*new*
gut	*good*	rot	*red*
interessant	*interesting*	schlecht	*bad*
jung	*young*	schwarz	*black*
klein	*little, small*	weiß	*white*

When using words like these as predicate adjectives (adjectives that follow the verb) in German, place the adjective at the end of the sentence. For example:

Ist Ihr Haus groß?	*Is your house big?*
Nein, mein Haus ist klein.	*No, my house is little.*
Ist der Bleistift kurz oder lang?	*Is the pencil short or long?*
Der Bleistift ist kurz.	*The pencil is short.*

The rule is the same when adjectives describe pronouns.

Ich bin alt.	*I am old.*
Du bist jung.	*You are young.*
Er ist krank.	*He is sick.*
Sie ist interessant.	*She is interesting.*
Es ist neu.	*It is new.*
Wir sind glücklich.	*We are happy.*
Ihr seid gesund.	*You are healthy.*
Sie Sind schön.	*They are pretty.*

Oral Practice

Practice saying the following list of sentences out loud.

Der Lehrer ist gut.	*The teacher is good.*
Die Professorin ist interessant.	*The professor is interesting.*
Meine Großmutter ist alt.	*My grandmother is old.*
Mein Wagen ist rot.	*My car is red.*
Ist Ihr Haus weiß?	*Is your house white?*
Sind sie jung?	*Are they young?*
Das Wetter ist schlecht.	*The weather is bad.*
Der Kuli ist neu.	*The ballpoint is new.*
Ist das Museum alt?	*Is the museum old?*
Ich bin jung.	*I am young.*
Du bist klein, Felix.	*You are little, Felix.*

Written Practice 3

Rewrite the sentences with the adjectives provided in parentheses.

1. Ist Ihr Vater alt?

   (jung) _____?

   (krank) _____?

   (gesund) _____?

2. Das Buch ist alt.

   (interessant) _____.

   (neu) _____.

   (schwarz) _____.

3. Wir sind alt.

   (klein) _____.

   (groß) _____.

   (krank) _____.

Written Practice 4

Rewrite the questions filling in the first blanks with the words in parentheses and the second with their opposites. For example:

   (alt) Ist er _____*alt*_____ oder _____*jung*___?

1. (neu) Ist das Haus _____ oder _____?
2. (krank) Ist sie _____ oder _____?
3. (schlecht) Ist das Wetter _____ oder _____?
4. (kurz) Ist mein Bleistift _____ oder _____?
5. (jung) Sind Karl und Max _____ oder _____?
6. (groß) Ist das Museum _____ oder _____?
7. (weiß) Ist Ihr Haus _____ oder _____?
8. (gesund) Ist meine Schwester _____ oder _____?
9. (lang) Ist der Kuli _____ oder _____?
10. (klein) Ist das Kind _____ oder _____?

Asking Questions with *Wann* and *Warum*

You have learned how to form questions with **wer**, **was**, **wie**, and **wo**. Two more useful interrogatives are **wann** (*when*) and **warum** (*why*). They function the same as the other interrogatives do: A question begins with the interrogative and is followed by the verb.

Wer ist das?	***Who is*** *that?*
Was ist das?	***What is*** *that?*
Wie geht's?	***How are*** *you?*
Wo sind Gudrun und Sonja?	***Where are*** *Gudrun and Sonja?*
Wann ist die Party?	***When is*** *the party?*
Warum bist du zu Hause?	***Why are*** *you at home?*

The answer to a question beginning with **wann** will provide a moment in time.

heute	*today*	nächste Woche	*next week*
morgen	*tomorrow*	am Montag	*on Monday*

Oral Practice

Practice saying the following list of sentences out loud.

Wann ist die Party?	*When is the party?*
Die Party ist heute.	*The party is today.*
Die Party ist morgen.	*The party is tomorrow.*
Die Party ist nächste Woche.	*The party is next week.*
Die Party ist am Montag.	*The party is on Monday.*
Wann ist das Examen?	*When is the exam?*
Das Examen ist heute.	*The exam is today.*
Das Examen ist morgen.	*The exam is tomorrow.*
Das Examen ist nächste Woche.	*The exam is next week.*
Das Examen ist am Montag.	*The exam is on Monday.*

The answer to a question beginning with **warum** will provide a reason for an action and will begin with the conjunction **denn** (*because*). For example:

Warum ist Erik zu Hause?   *Why is Erik at home?*

Erik ist zu Hause, **denn** er ist krank.   *Erik is at home, because he is sick.*

Written Practice 5

Change each sentence into a question. Use the word or phrase in bold print as a guide for which interrogative word to use (**wann**, **warum**, or **wer**). For example:

> **Mein Professor** ist in Mannheim.
> *Wer ist in Mannheim?*
> _____

1. Das Examen ist **nächste Woche**.

   _____?

2. **Meine Tochter** ist in der Schweiz.

   _____?

3. Die Party ist **morgen**.

   _____?

4. Thomas und Helga sind in Bonn, **denn sie sind krank**.

   _____?

5. Mein Großvater ist zu Hause, **denn er ist alt**.

   _____?

6. **Ich** bin morgen in Deutschland.

   _____?

7. Wir sind **am Montag** in Leipzig.

   _____?

8. **Ihr** seid gesund.

   _____?

9. Das Examen ist **heute**.

_____?

10. Das Kind ist zu Hause, **denn es ist sehr klein**.

_____?

Oral Practice

Practice saying the following list of sentences out loud.

Warum ist Iris zu Hause?	*Why is Iris at home?*
Iris ist zu Hause, denn sie ist krank.	*Iris is at home, because she is sick.*
Warum bist du zu Hause?	*Why are you at home?*
Ich bin zu Hause, denn ich bin krank.	*I am at home, because I am sick.*
Warum ist er zu Hause?	*Why is he at home?*
Er ist zu Hause, denn er ist krank.	*He is home, because he is sick.*
Warum ist das Mädchen zu Hause?	*Why is the girl at home?*
Das Mädchen ist zu Hause, denn es ist krank.	*The girl is at home, because she is sick.*
Warum sind wir zu Hause?	*Why are we at home?*
Ihr seid zu Hause, denn ihr seid krank.	*You are at home, because you are sick.*
Thomas! Erik! Warum seid ihr zu Hause?	*Thomas! Erik! Why are you at home?*
Wir sind zu Hause, denn wir sind krank.	*We are at home, because we are sick.*
Warum sind Sie zu Hause, Herr Brenner?	*Why are you at home, Mr. Brenner?*
Ich bin zu Hause, denn ich bin krank.	*I am at home, because I am sick.*

Written Practice 6

Write an answer to each question, using the information provided in parentheses.
For example:

> (sein krank) Warum ist Martin zu Hause?
> *Martin ist zu Hause, denn er ist krank.*

1. (sein krank) Warum sind Tanja und Maria in Berlin?

   _____.

2. (nächste Woche) Wann ist das Examen?

   _____.

3. (sein krank) Warum bist du zu Hause, Erik?

   _____.

4. (am Montag) Wann ist das Konzert?

   _____.

Asking *Wie geht's?*

The expression **Wie geht's?** contains a contraction. The verb **geht** is followed by an
apostrophe and the letter **s**. That apostrophe and **s** are the contraction of the pronoun
es. In its full form you would say: **Wie geht es?**

A response to this question might be: **Gut, danke.** But if you're not feeling well,
you can say: **Schlecht** (*bad*). And you ask: **Und Ihnen?** (*And you?*) to inquire about
someone else's health. In a conversation between two people, the phrases may look
like this:

Guten Abend, Herr Meier.	*Good evening, Mr. Meier.*
Guten Abend, Frau Keller. Wie geht's?	*Hello, Mrs. Keller. How are you?*
Gut, danke. Und Ihnen?	*Fine, thanks. And you?*
Sehr gut.	*Very well.*

Or the conversation could look like this:

Guten Morgen, Frau Benz.	*Good morning, Mrs. Benz.*
Guten Morgen, Professor Braun. Wie geht's?	*Hello, Professor Braun. How are you?*
Schlecht. Und Ihnen.	*Bad. And you?*
Sehr gut. Danke.	*Very well. Thanks.*

Oral Practice

Practice saying the following list of sentences out loud.

Guten Tag, Herr Bauer. Wie geht's?	*Hello, Mr. Bauer. How are you?*
Sehr schlecht.	*Very bad.*
Nicht schlecht.	*Not bad.*
Nicht gut. Und Ihnen?	*Not well. And you?*
Sehr gut. Und Ihnen?	*Very well. And you?*

Cardinal Numbers One to Ten

Cardinal numbers express the numerical value of a number: one, two, ten, one hundred, and so forth. In German the first ten cardinal numbers, including zero, are:

null	*zero*	sechs	*six*
eins	*one*	sieben	*seven*
zwei	*two*	acht	*eight*
drei	*three*	neun	*nine*
vier	*four*	zehn	*ten*
fünf	*five*		

In mathematical equations, use the following words:

+	plus *or* und	*plus; and*
−	minus *or* weniger	*minus; less*
=	ist	*is*
?	wie viel	*how much*

In sentences they look like this:

Wie viel ist zwei plus drei?	*How much is two plus three?*
Zwei plus drei ist fünf.	*Two plus three is five.*
Wie viel ist acht und eins?	*How much is eight and one?*
Acht und eins ist neun.	*Eight and one is nine.*
Wie viel ist zehn minus vier?	*How much is ten minus four?*
Zehn minus vier ist sechs.	*Ten minus four is six.*
Wie viel ist sieben weniger fünf?	*How much is seven minus five?*
Sieben weniger fünf ist zwei.	*Seven minus five is two.*

Oral Practice

Practice saying the following list of sentences out loud.

Drei plus eins ist vier.	*Three plus one is four.*
Acht und zwei ist zehn.	*Eight and two is ten.*
Neun minus neun ist null.	*Nine minus nine is zero.*
Sechs weniger fünf ist eins.	*Six minus five is one.*
Wie viel ist drei und sieben?	*How much is three and seven?*

Now change the following equations into words out loud. The correct version is shown on the right.

$8 - 7 = 1$	Acht weniger (minus) sieben ist eins.
$3 + 3 = ?$	Wie viel ist drei plus (und) drei?
$9 - 5 = 4$	Neun weniger (minus) fünf ist vier.
$10 + 0 = ?$	Wie viel ist zehn plus (und) null?
$6 + 1 = 7$	Sechs plus (und) eins ist sieben.
$4 + 2 = ?$	Wie viel ist vier plus (und) zwei?

Written Practice 7

Change the following equations into words.

1. 4 + 5 = 9 _____.
2. 8 − 6 = ? _____?
3. 10 − 3 = 7 _____.

QUIZ

Write the appropriate form of **heißen** for the subjects provided. For example:

Sie _heißen_____

1. wir _____ ich _____
2. du _____ ihr _____

Write the appropriate form of **sein** for the subjects provided. For example:

Sie _sind_____

3. ich _____ ihr _____
4. er _____ du _____

In the blanks provided, replace the nouns given with the pronoun **er**, **sie** *s.*, or **es**. For example:

der Mann _er_____

5. die Frau _____
6. das Haus _____
7. der Lehrer _____

Circle the letter of the word or phrase that best completes each sentence.

8. Mein Vater ist _____ alt.

    (a) klein   (c) dort

    (b) nicht   (d) jung

9. Warum _____ ihr heute zu Hause?

    (a) sein   (c) ist

    (b) seid   (d) sind

10. _____ ist die nächste Party?

    (a) Wer   (c) Sehr

    (b) Denn   (d) Wann

CHAPTER 5

Indicating Possession

In this chapter you will learn:

Using the Verb Haben

Definite Article Die

Possessive Adjectives Dein *and* Euer

Using Kein

Household Objects

Using the Verb *Haben*

Another important German verb is **haben** (*to have*). And like **sein** and **heißen**, **haben** requires special conjugational endings with the various pronouns. Let's see what these endings look like.

The conjugation of **haben** in the present tense:

ich habe	*I have*	wir haben	*we have*
du hast	*you have*	ihr habt	*you have*
Sie haben	*you have*	Sie haben	*you have*
er hat	*he has*	sie haben	*they have*
sie hat	*she has*		
es hat	*it has*		
wer hat	*who has*		
der Mann hat	*the man has*		

Written Practice 1

Conjugate the verb **haben** with the nouns and pronouns provided below.

1. Tina und Benno _____

2. sie *s.* _____

3. sie *pl.* _____

4. ihr _____

5. meine Tochter _____

6. du _____

7. die Fahrkarten _____

8. Sie _____

9. es _____

10. mein Schreibtisch _____

To use **haben**, one must *have* something. Here are some handy words that a person can have:

das Bier	*beer*	die CD	*CD*
das Brot	*bread*	die CDs	*CDs*
das Geld	*money*	die Fahrkarten	*tickets (bus, train, etc.)*
der Fahrplan	*schedule, timetable*	die Milch	*milk*
die Bluse	*blouse*	die Schlüssel	*keys*

In sentences with **haben**, these nouns can look like this:

Haben Sie das Brot?	*Do you have the bread?*
Thomas hat das Geld.	*Thomas has the money.*
Wir haben eine CD.	*We have a CD.*
Wer hat meine Schlüssel?	*Who has my keys?*

Definite Article *Die*

You'll notice in the previous list of nouns that the plural words (**die CDs**, **die Fahrkarten**, and **die Schlüssel**) are used with the definite article **die**. However, these words may not be feminine nouns. They are plural, and all plural nouns use the definite article **die**—no matter what their gender is in the singular.

Oral Practice

Practice saying the following list of sentences out loud.

Hast du das Geld?	*Do you have the money?*
Ja, ich habe das Geld.	*Yes, I have the money.*
Habt ihr die Fahrkarten?	*Do you have the tickets?*
Ja, wir haben die Fahrkarten.	*Yes, we have the tickets.*
Wer hat das Bier?	*Who has the beer?*
Mein Vater hat das Bier.	*My father has the beer.*
Sie hat meine Bluse.	*She has my blouse.*
Haben Sie die Milch?	*Do you have the milk?*
Robert hat den Fahrplan.	*Robert has the schedule.*

Did you notice that **der Fahrplan** changed to *den* **Fahrplan** in the example sentence? This occurs with all *masculine* nouns when they are used as direct objects, in this case following the verb **haben**. This will be explained fully in Chapter 8.

Naturally, the verb **haben** can be used with other nouns that you have learned previously, and they can be used with definite articles, indefinite articles, **mein**, or **Ihr**.

Written Practice 2

Rewrite each sentence, replacing the nouns with the ones in parentheses.

1. Hast du die Bluse?

   (die CDs) _____?

   (das Geld) _____?

   (ein Heft) _____?

2. Ich habe die Bluse.

   (die Fahrkarten) _____.

   (der Fahrplan) _____.

   (das Brot) _____.

Oral Practice

Practice saying the following list of sentences out loud.

Wer hat meine CDs?	*Who has my CDs?*
Haben Sie Ihre Fahrkarten?	*Do you have your tickets?*
Tina hat eine Zeitung.	*Tina has a newspaper.*
Wir haben ein Haus in Berlin.	*We have a house in Berlin.*
Was hat das Kind?	*What does the child have?*
Es hat ein Sweatshirt.	*He/She (The child) has a sweatshirt.*
Herr Benz, Ich habe Ihr Buch.	*Mr. Benz, I have your book.*

Written Practice 3

Ask the people shown in parentheses what they have. **Was haben Sie?** is used if the relationship is formal. Use **Was hast du?** if it is informal singular. And if the relationship is informal plural, **Was habt ihr?** is used.

1. (Tante Gerda) _____?

2. (Bruder) _____?

3. (Vater und Mutter) _____?

4. (Professor Keller) _____?

5. (eine Freundin) _____?

6. (Frau Schneider) _____?

Possessive Adjectives *Dein* and *Euer*

You are already quite aware that German has three forms of *you*: **du**, **ihr**, and **Sie**. German also has three forms of the possessive adjective *your*. Until now, you have used only **Ihr**, which is the formal *your* and refers to the pronoun **Sie** (the formal *you*). The pronouns **du** and **ihr** have their own possessive adjectives, shown below.

Pronoun (*you*)	Masculine and Neuter	Feminine and Plural
du	dein	deine
ihr	euer	eure
Sie	Ihr	Ihre

Just as you must know which pronoun to use (**du**, **ihr**, or **Sie**), you must also know which possessive adjective to use (**dein**, **euer**, or **Ihr**), depending on the relationship you have with a person—formal or informal. For example:

Formal:

Herr Bauer, haben Sie Ihre Fahrkarten? *Mr. Bauer, do you have your tickets?*

Informal, singular:

Tanja, hast du dein Heft? *Tanja, do you have your notebook?*

Informal, plural:

Robert und Tina, habt ihr eure *Robert and Tina, do you have your*
Schlüssel? *keys?*

Written Practice 4

Using the names of the people in parentheses, ask whether it is their desk. Use **dein**, **euer**, or **Ihr**. For example:

(Herr Bauer) _Herr Bauer, ist das Ihr Schreibtisch?_

1. (Doktor Keller) _____?
2. (Tanja) _____?
3. (Tante Gerda) _____?
4. (Albert und Tina) _____?
5. (Frau Schäfer) _____?

Oral Practice

Practice saying the following list of sentences out loud.

Hast du dein Sweatshirt?	*Do you have your sweatshirt?*
Ja, ich habe mein Sweatshirt.	*Yes, I have my sweatshirt.*
Haben Sie Ihr Buch?	*Do you have your book?*
Ja, ich habe mein Buch.	*Yes, I have my book.*
Habt ihr eure Fahrkarten?	*Do you have your tickets?*
Nein, Thomas hat die Fahrkarten.	*No, Thomas has the tickets.*
Wer hat einen Fahrplan?	*Who has a schedule?*
Er hat einen Fahrplan.	*He has a schedule.*
Wir haben einen Fahrplan.	*We have a schedule.*
Wer hat eine CD?	*Who has a CD?*
Sie hat eine CD.	*She has a CD.*
Sie haben eine CD.	*They have a CD.*

As you probably noticed in the previous sentences, just as **der Fahrplan** changes to *den* **Fahrplan** when it follows **haben**, **ein Fahrplan** changes to **ein*en* Fahrplan**.

Written Practice 5

Provide the appropriate forms of **dein**, **euer**, and **Ihr** for the nouns provided. For example:

Lehrer	_dein_	_euer_	_Ihr_
1. der Tisch			
2. die Treppe			
3. das Sofa			
4. die CDs			
5. der Fahrplan			

When you want to know *how many* or *how much* of something someone has, you ask **wie viel**. It's the same expression used in a mathematical equation: *Wie viel* **ist zwei plus sieben?** Let's look at **wie viel** as it's used in sentences with the verb **haben**.

Wie viel Fahrkarten haben Sie?	*How many tickets do you have?*
Ich habe vier Fahrkarten.	*I have four tickets.*
Wie viel CDs hat Marianne?	*How many CDs does Marianne have?*
Marianne hat zehn CDs.	*Marianne has ten CDs.*

You need to be aware that with the English infinitive *to have*, it is most common to form a question with *do*: *Do you* **have your tickets?** *How many books* **does** *he* **have?** German forms all such questions with the verb preceding the subject: *Haben* **Sie Ihre Fahrkarten?** **Wie viel CDs** *hat er?* In German the equivalent of a verb such as *do* is never added to a question.

It is common to use **wie viele** with plural nouns. But **wie viel** is also correct, so this form can be used with both singular and plural nouns.

wie viele Fahrkarten (plural)	*how many tickets*
wie viel Fahrkarten (plural)	*how many tickets*
wie viel Geld (singular)	*how much money*

Oral Practice

Practice saying the following list of sentences out loud.

Wie viel(e) Schlüssel haben Sie?	*How many keys do you have?*
Ich habe vier Schlüssel.	*I have four keys.*
Wie viel Geld hat dein Bruder?	*How much money does your brother have?*
Wie viel(e) Fahrkarten habt ihr?	*How many tickets do you have?*
Wir haben drei Fahrkarten.	*We have three tickets.*
Wie viel(e) CDs haben wir?	*How many CDs do we have?*
Ihr habt neun CDs.	*You have nine CDs.*
Wie viel Brot hat eure Mutter?	*How much bread does your mother have?*
Wie viel Milch hat dein Sohn?	*How much milk does your son have?*
Wie viel Bier hast du?	*How much beer do you have?*

You can use the word **viel(e)** alone. It means *much* or *many* and it answers the question **wie viel**. Use **viel** with singular nouns, use **viele** with plural nouns. For example:

Ich habe viel Geld.	*I have a lot of (much) money.*
Sie hat viele CDs.	*She has a lot of (many) CDs.*

Written Practice 6

With each word provided in parentheses, write a question with **wie viel(e)** and an answer with **viel(e)**. Follow the pattern of the example.

(Brot) Wie viel Brot habt ihr? How much bread do you have?
Wir haben viel Brot. We have a lot of bread.

1. (Milch) _____?
   _____.

2. (CDs) _____?
   _____.

3. (Geld) _____?

_____.

4. (Fahrkarten) _____?

_____.

5. (Schlüssel) _____?

_____.

Using *Kein*

This is a word that you encountered in Chapter 3 that means *not any*, *not a*, or *no*: **kein Brot** (*no bread*), **keine Fahrkarten** (*not any tickets*). It functions like *mein* or *dein* and is a replacement for **nicht ein** (*not a*). But unlike **ein**, **kein** can be used in the plural (**keine Schlüssel**—*no keys*). Like **nicht** it is a negative.

Masculine and Neuter	**Feminine and Plural**
dein	deine
mein	meine
kein	keine

In sentences, **kein** looks like this:

Hast du ein Auto?	*Do you have a car?*
Nein, ich habe kein Auto.	*No, I have no car. (No, I don't have a car.)*
Hat Benno eine Schwester?	*Does Benno have a sister?*
Nein, er hat keine Schwester.	*No, he has no sister.*

Oral Practice

Practice saying the following list of sentences out loud.

Habt ihr Geld?	*Do you have money?*
Nein, wir haben kein Geld.	*No, we have no money.*
Hast du viel Brot?	*Do you have a lot of bread?*

Nein, ich habe kein Brot.	*No, I have no bread.*
Haben Sie viele Schlüssel?	*Do you have many keys?*
Nein, ich habe keine Schlüssel.	*No, I have no keys.*
Hat dein Bruder viele Fahrkarten?	*Does your brother have many tickets?*
Nein, mein Bruder hat keine Fahrkarten.	*No, my brother has no tickets.*

Written Practice 7

Rewrite the sentences, filling in the blanks with the appropriate forms of the words in parentheses. Remember that the feminine and plural will require an **-e** ending.

1. Wer hat _____ Geld? *Who has money?* _____

   (mein) _____ ?

   (viel) _____ ?

   (kein) _____ ?

2. Martin hat _____ Schlüssel. *Martin has _____ keys.*

   (euer) _____ .

   (viel) _____ .

   (kein) _____ .

3. Wo ist _____ Freundin? *Where is _____ girlfriend?*

   (dein) _____ ?

   (Ihr) _____ ?

   (euer) _____ ?

Written Practice 8

Using **kein**, write a negative answer to each question. Remember to provide the appropriate endings to **kein** when necessary. For example:

Haben Sie ein Heft? *Nein, ich habe kein Heft.* _____

1. Habt ihr Brot? _____.
2. Hat Frau Keller meine Schlüssel? _____.
3. Haben Sie das Geld? _____.
4. Hat das Kind die Milch? _____.
5. Hat deine Schwester die Bluse? _____.
6. Haben Sie viele Zimmer? _____.
7. Hat Robert meine CDs? _____.
8. Hat dein Vater das Bier? _____.

Household Objects

In a German household you'll find many of the same objects that you'd find in a house anywhere. Some of these are:

das Bild	*picture*	der Teppich	*carpet*
der Boden	*floor*	der Tisch	*table*
das Fenster	*window*	die Treppe	*stairway*
der Schreibtisch	*desk*	die Tür	*door*
das Sofa	*sofa*	die Zimmer (*pl.*)	*rooms*
der Stuhl	*chair*		

These words can be used in sentences such as:

Ist die Tür groß oder klein?	*Is the door big or little?*
Wo ist dein Fenster?	*Where is your window?*
Der Boden ist weiß.	*The floor is white.*
Der Tisch und der Stuhl sind dort.	*The table and the chair are there.*
Ist euer Sofa alt?	*Is your sofa old?*
Der Teppich ist rot und lang.	*The carpet is red and long.*
Ist die Treppe kurz?	*Is the stairway short?*
Mein Bild ist schlecht.	*My picture is bad.*
Ist Ihr Schreibtisch neu?	*Is your desk new?*
Wie viele Zimmer habt ihr?	*How many rooms do you have?*

Written Practice 9

Rewrite the sentences, filling in the blanks with the words in parentheses. Change the verbs from singular to plural or plural to singular as needed.

1. Wo ist _____?

   (das Sofa) _____?

   (der Stuhl und der Schreibtisch) _____?

2. Die Zimmer haben _____ Fenster.

   (ein) _____.

   (kein) _____.

3. _____ ist sehr klein.

   (der Tisch) _____.

   (die Zimmer) _____.

QUIZ

Fill in each blank with the appropriate conjugation of the verb **haben**, using the subject nouns and pronouns provided. For example:

der Mann _____*hat*_____

1. wir _____ ich _____

2. er _____ du _____

Provide the appropriate forms of **dein**, **euer**, **Ihr**, and **kein** for the nouns given. Then place an X on the blank to identify the noun as singular or plural. For example:

					sing.	plur.
Lehrer	*dein*	*euer*	*Ihr*	*kein*	X	
3. die Tante	____	____	____	____	____	____
4. der Computer	____	____	____	____	____	____
5. die Fahrkarten	____	____	____	____	____	____

Using **kein**, write a negative answer to each question. Provide the appropriate endings to **kein** where necessary. For example:

Haben Sie ein Heft? _Nein, ich habe kein Heft._

6. Hast du ein Sofa? _____ .

7. Hat Herr Bauer eine Tochter? _____ .

Circle the letter of the word or phrase that best completes each sentence.

8. Wo ist _____ Schwester?

    (a) Ihr   (c) deine

    (b) keine   (d) mein

9. Wie _____ Geld hat Onkel Heinrich?

    (a) euer   (c) heißt

    (b) hier   (d) viel

10. Nein, _____ ist nicht gut.

    (a) das Bild   (c) die Fahrkarten

    (b) die Zimmer   (d) die CDs

PART ONE TEST

Pronounce the following words and phrases out loud. Check your accuracy in the Answer Key.

1. Flugzeug
2. heißen
3. ihr seid
4. meine Tochter
5. Frau Schäfer

Write the correct form of **heißen** needed for each of the subject nouns and pronouns provided.

6. er _____
7. wir _____
8. ich _____
9. du _____
10. ihr _____

Using the words or phrases in bold as a signal for which interrogative to use, ask questions with **wer, was, wann, wo,** or **warum.**

11. Das ist **mein Computer**. _____?
12. Onkel Peter ist **in der Schweiz**. _____?
13. **Wir** haben kein Geld. _____?
14. Sie ist zu Hause, **denn sie ist sehr krank**. _____?
15. Das Examen ist **nächste Woche**. _____?
16. **Euer Bruder** ist sehr jung. _____?
17. Meine Freundin ist **zu Hause**. _____?
18. Robert hat **ein Auto**. _____?
19. Das Konzert ist **am Montag**. _____?
20. Tina und Marianne sind **in Hannover**. _____?

Write the appropriate forms of **ein**, **Ihr**, and **kein** for each of the following nouns.

21. der Wagen _____ _____ _____
22. die Treppe _____ _____ _____
23. das Haus _____ _____ _____
24. mein Vater _____ _____ _____
25. eure Milch _____ _____ _____

Using **nicht**, answer each question in the negative. For example:

Ist das Ihr Haus? _Nein, das ist nicht mein Haus._____

26. Ist das Ihre Schwester? _____.
27. Ist das Fenster groß? _____.
28. Ist deine Tante in Berlin? _____.

In each blank provided, write the pronoun that is the appropriate replacement for the phrase given, using **er**, **sie** *s.*, **es**, or **sie** *pl.*

29. der Stuhl _____
30. die Schlüssel _____
31. die Treppe _____
32. das Sofa _____
33. Karl und Tina _____

Rewrite the sentences filling in the first blanks with the words in parentheses and the second with their opposites. For example:

(alt) Ist er ____alt____ oder ____jung____?

34. (klein) Ist das Haus _____ oder _____?
35. (neu) Ist das Auto _____ oder _____?

Answer each question in the negative using **kein**. For example:

Haben Sie ein Buch? _Nein, ich habe kein Buch._

36. Hat Erik viel Geld? _____ .

37. Habt ihr die Fahrkarten? _____ .

38. Hast du Brot? _____ .

Circle the letter of the word or phrase that best completes each sentence.

39. _____ ist das?

    (a) Marianne   (c) Name

    (b) Wer   (d) Heißen

40. Das Mädchen heißt _____ .

    (a) Herr   (c) Angela

    (b) Frau   (d) Erik

41. _____ Name ist Tina.

    (a) Das   (c) Junge

    (b) Wer   (d) Mein

42. Mein Bruder ist nicht _____ .

    (a) die Schweiz   (c) die Lehrerin

    (b) zu Hause   (d) Österreicherin

43. Nein, die Bibliothek ist _____ weit von hier.

    (a) in   (c) was

    (b) nicht   (d) ja

44. _____ ist die Professorin?

    (a) Wo   (c) Wie

    (b) Der   (d) Nein

45. _____ ist das?

    (a) Was   (c) Nein

    (b) Ja   (d) Oder

46. Das Museum ist weit von _____.

    (a) wo

    (b) das

    (c) nicht zu Hause

    (d) hier

47. Danke, sehr gut. Und _____?

    (a) Ihnen

    (b) Herr

    (c) morgen

    (d) Guten Abend

48. Sind _____ in der Schweiz?

    (a) ihr

    (b) ich

    (c) wir

    (d) sie *s.*

49. Zehn weniger acht ist _____.

    (a) eins

    (b) zwei

    (c) minus

    (d) plus

50. Nicht _____. Und Ihnen?

    (a) schlecht

    (b) Danke

    (c) dort

    (d) zu Hause

PART TWO

USING VERBS

CHAPTER 6

Actions in the Present Tense

In this chapter you will learn:

Using the Verb Werden

Pronoun Es

Present Tense

Cardinal Numbers Eleven to Twenty

Using the Verb *Werden*

The verb **werden** means *to become* or *to get* and has a unique conjugation that should be learned early, because this verb has a high-frequency use. Its conjugation looks like this:

ich werde	*I become*	wir werden	*we become*
du wirst	*you become*	ihr werdet	*you become*
Sie werden	*you become*	Sie werden	*you become*
er wird	*he becomes*	sie werden	*they become*
sie wird	*she becomes*		
es wird	*it becomes*		
wer wird	*who becomes*		
was wird	*what becomes*		

Werden can be used to tell what profession someone wants to join—what someone whats to *become*. For example:

| Mein Bruder wird Professor. | *My brother is becoming a professor.* |
| Wird Ihre Tochter Lehrerin? | *Is your daughter becoming a teacher?* |

Oral Practice

Practice saying the following list of sentences out loud.

Ich werde Krankenschwester.	*I am becoming a nurse.*
Wirst du Arzt?	*Are you becoming a physician?*
Er wird Zahnarzt.	*He is becoming a dentist.*
Wird sie auch Ärztin?	*Is she becoming a physician, too?*
Werden Sie Lehrer?	*Are you becoming a teacher?*
Die Kinder werden Fußballspieler.	*The children are becoming soccer players.*

In addition, you can use a variety of adjectives that tell how someone's or something's condition is changing. Some of these adjectives are:

böse	*angry*	kalt	*cold*
dunkel	*dark*	kühl	*cool*
glücklich	*happy*	müde	*tired*
heiß	*hot*	spät	*late*
hell	*bright*	warm	*warm*

Written Practice 1

The words in parentheses describe a person, an occupation, and a second person. Write a sentence that says that the first person is becoming that occupation. Write that the second person is also (**auch**) becoming that occupation. For example:

(Karl/Lehrer/er)

Karl wird Lehrer.

Er wird auch Lehrer.

1. (deine Tochter/Lehrerin/meine Schwester)

    _____.

    _____.

2. (Erik/Zahnarzt/Sie *pl.*)

    _____.

    _____.

3. (die Kinder/Fußballspieler/er)

    _____.

    _____.

Written Practice 2

For each statement on the left, choose a statement on the right that logically follows.

1. Es ist spät. _____   a. Guten Morgen.

2. Es wird hell. _____   b. Nein, ich bin nicht müde.

3. Ich bin müde. _____   c. Ich gehe nach Hause.

4. Der Mann ist sehr krank. _____   d. Nein, ich habe kein Geld.

5. Wie alt ist das Mädchen? _____   e. Er wird wieder gesund.

6. Es wird sehr kalt. _____   f. Deutsch auch.

7. Wir lernen Spanisch. _____   g. Neunzehn Jahre alt.

8. Kaufst du ein Auto? _____   h. Nein, mit dem Zug.

9. Schläfst du? _____   i. Das Wetter ist schlecht.

10. Fährst du mit dem Bus? _____   j. Hier ist ein Bett.

Pronoun *Es*

In English there are impersonal expressions used which have the pronoun *it* as their subject. In these expressions an invisible entity is causing something to happen. That entity is *it*.

> It is raining again.
>
> It got dark early.
>
> It was terribly hot yesterday.

The cause for the rain, the darkness, and the heat is *it*. German does the same thing with **es** (*it*) and frequently uses **werden** in such expressions. Let's look at some examples.

Es wird kalt.	*It is getting cold.*
Es wird hell.	*It is becoming bright.*
Es wird spät.	*It is getting late.*

You can also use other subjects with the verb **werden** to tell what a person or thing is becoming.

Mein Onkel wird böse.	*My uncle is becoming angry.*
Ihre Wirtin wird müde.	*Your landlady is getting tired.*
Thomas und Erik werden glücklich.	*Thomas and Erik are becoming happy.*
Der Ofen wird heiß.	*The oven is getting hot.*

Oral Practice

Practice saying the following list of sentences out loud.

Wird es wieder kalt?	*Is it getting cold again?*
Ja, es wird wieder sehr kalt.	*Yes, it is getting very cold again.*
Wird es wieder heiß?	*Is it getting hot again?*
Ja, es wird wieder sehr heiß.	*Yes, it is getting very hot again.*
Werdet ihr müde, Kinder?	*Are you getting tired, children?*

Nein, wir werden nicht müde.	*No, we are not getting tired.*
Es wird spät. Es ist zehn Uhr.	*It is getting late. It is ten o'clock.*
Werden Sie krank, Herr Müller?	*Are you getting sick, Mr. Mueller?*
Nein, ich werde gesund.	*No, I am getting healthy.*
Warum wirst du wieder böse?	*Why are you getting angry again?*

Written Practice 3

Complete the sentence with each of the adjectives in parentheses.

Es wird wieder _____.

1. (kalt) _____.
2. (kühl) _____.
3. (hell) _____.
4. (dunkel) _____.
5. (heiß) _____.

Present Tense

You have already encountered the present tense of four verbs: **heißen**, **sein**, **haben**, and **werden**.

	heißen	sein	haben	werden
ich	heiße	bin	habe	werde
du	heißt	bist	hast	wirst
er	heißt	ist	hat	wird
wir	heißen	sind	haben	werden
ihr	heißt	seid	habt	werdet
sie	heißen	sind	haben	werden

Perhaps you can already see the pattern developing in these four conjugations. Except for **sein** and **werden**, these verbs have the same specific ending that occurs with each pronoun. In summary, those endings are:

ich	-e	wir	-en
du	-st	ihr	-t
er	-t	sie	-en

(The pronoun **er** in this list represents the endings required for **sie** *s.* and **es** as well as for all singular nouns. The pronoun **sie** in this list is plural and represents **Sie** and all plural nouns.)

The basic form of a German verb is the infinitive. Most German infinitives end in **-en**. Here are just a few examples:

fragen	*to ask*	lernen	*to learn*
gehen	*to go*	sagen	*to say*
hören	*to hear*	schreiben	*to write*
kaufen	*to buy*	spielen	*to play*
kommen	*to come*	suchen	*to look for*

When you conjugate a verb in the present tense, you remove the infinitive ending **-en** and add the conjugational endings as illustrated above. For example:

	lernen (lern-)	**schreiben (schreib-)**	**kommen (komm-)**
ich	lerne	schreibe	komme
du	lernst	schreibst	kommst
er	lernt	schreibt	kommt
wir	lernen	schreiben	kommen
ihr	lernt	schreibt	kommt
sie	lernen	schreiben	kommen

Written Practice 4

Conjugate each of the following verbs with the subjects provided.

	hören	**suchen**	**fragen**
ich	_____	_____	_____
du	_____	_____	_____
er	_____	_____	_____
wir	_____	_____	_____
ihr	_____	_____	_____

sie   _____   _____   _____

Tina   _____   _____   _____

Oral Practice

Practice saying the following list of sentences out loud.

Lernst du Deutsch?	*Are you learning German?*
Ja, ich lerne Deutsch und Spanisch.	*Yes, I am learning German and Spanish.*
Was lernt deine Schwester?	*What is your sister learning?*
Meine Schwester lernt auch Deutsch.	*My sister is learning German, too.*
Die Kinder schreiben auf deutsch.	*The children write in German.*
Wir schreiben auch auf deutsch.	*We are writing in German, too.*
Wer geht nach Hause?	*Who is going home?*
Die Kinder gehen nach Hause.	*The children are going home.*
Spielt ihr Fußball?	*Do you play soccer?*
Ja, wir spielen gut Fußball.	*Yes, we play soccer well.*

Perhaps you've noticed that the English translation of some of the examples is not word for word. This is due in part to the complexity of English. The English present tense has three forms. German has one. Let's take a closer look at this.

A Habit, a Frequent Action:

I write in German.   Ich schreibe auf deutsch.

An Action in Progress or Incomplete:

I am writing in German.   Ich schreibe auf deutsch.

An Emphatic Statement:

I do write in German.   Ich schreibe auf deutsch.

And when you ask a question in English, you begin the question with the verb if it is an action in progress or incomplete. If the question relates to a habit or a frequent action, you begin the question with a form of *do*. In German both types of questions begin with the verb.

Do you write in German?	Schreibst du auf deutsch?
Are you writing in German?	Schreibst du auf deutsch?

These translation differences occur in the other tenses as well.

USING AN UMLAUT

Some verbs have an irregularity in the present tense: They require the addition of an umlaut in the second person singular (**du**) and the third person singular (**er**). This occurs mostly with verbs that have the vowel **-a-** in the stem. Here are some examples with **fahren** (*to drive*; *to travel*), **fallen** (*to fall*), **schlafen** (*to sleep*), and **tragen** (*to carry*; *to wear*).

	fahren	**fallen**	**schlafen**	**tragen**
ich	fahre	falle	schlafe	trage
du	fährst	fällst	schläfst	trägst
er	fährt	fällt	schläft	trägt
wir	fahren	fallen	schlafen	tragen
ihr	fahrt	fallt	schlaft	tragt
sie	fahren	fallen	schlafen	tragen

IDENTIFYING LOCATION

To say that someone or something is *at home*, use the expression **zu Hause**. Use the expression **nach Hause** (*home, homeward*) to say someone is going home. Use **wo** to ask *where* a location is. And use **wohin** to ask *where* someone is going.

Wo ist er?	*Where is he?*
Er ist zu Hause.	*He is at home.*
Wohin fährt er?	*Where is he driving?*
Er fährt nach Hause.	*He is driving home.*

Oral Practice

Practice saying the following list of sentences out loud.

Wohin fahren Sie?	*Where are you driving?*
Ich fahre nach Hause.	*I am driving home.*
Wohin fährst du, Hans?	*Where are you driving, Hans?*
Ich fahre nach Deutschland.	*I am driving to Germany.*
Wohin fährt Herr Weber?	*Where is Mr. Weber driving?*
Er fährt nach Dortmund.	*He is driving to Dortmund.*
Wir fahren nach Heidelberg.	*We are driving to Heidelberg.*
Fahrt ihr nach Köln?	*Are you driving to Cologne?*
Sie fahren nach Dänemark.	*They are driving to Denmark.*
Ist Hans müde?	*Is Hans tired?*
Ja, er ist sehr müde und fällt ins Bett.	*Yes, he is very tired and falls into bed.*
Sind die Kinder müde?	*Are the children tired?*
Ja, sie sind sehr müde und fallen ins Bett.	*Yes, they are very tired and fall into bed.*
Wer schläft im Park?	*Who is sleeping in the park?*
Ein Freund schläft im Park.	*A friend is sleeping in the park.*
Schläfst du im Park?	*Do you sleep in the park?*
Nein, ich schlafe zu Hause.	*No, I sleep at home.*
Trägst du einen Hut?	*Do you wear a hat?*
Nein, ich trage keinen Hut.	*No, I do not wear a hat.*

Written Practice 5

Using the pronouns or nouns given, write questions that ask whether someone is traveling *by bus* (**mit dem Bus**) or *by train* (**mit dem Zug**). For example:

(Hans) *Fährt Hans mit dem Bus oder mit dem Zug?*

1. (du) _____?

2. (sie *s.*) _____?

3. (Sie) _____?

4. (Herr Weber) _____?

5. (sie *pl.*) _____?

6. (er) _____?

7. (die Kinder) _____?

Written Practice 6

Answer each of the following questions in the affirmative using **ja**. For example:

Hast du einen Bruder? *Ja, ich habe einen Bruder.*

1. Schreibt Herr Mann ein Buch? _____.

2. Hört ihr die Musik? _____.

3. Tragen Sie einen Hut? _____.

Now answer each question in the affirmative using **ja** and in the negative using **nein** and **nicht**. For example:

Seid ihr zu Hause? *Ja, wir sind zu Hause.*
Nein, wir sind nicht zu Hause.

4. Sind wir in Österreich? _____.

   _____.

5. Fahren Sie mit dem Bus? _____.

   _____.

6. Schläft Onkel Peter im Park? _____.

   _____.

7. Fallen die Kinder ins Bett? _____.

   _____.

8. Kommt ihr nach Hause? _____.

   _____.

Cardinal Numbers Eleven to Twenty

You already know the numbers from zero to ten. Here are the numbers from eleven to twenty.

elf	*eleven*	sechzehn	*sixteen*
zwölf	*twelve*	siebzehn	*seventeen*
dreizehn	*thirteen*	achtzehn	*eighteen*
vierzehn	*fourteen*	neunzehn	*nineteen*
fünfzehn	*fifteen*	zwanzig	*twenty*

Notice that the final **-s** in the number **sechs** is dropped when it becomes **sechzehn**. And the number **sieben** drops the second syllable when it becomes **siebzehn**.

Let's look at these numbers in some example sentences.

Meine Wirtin hat elf Kinder.	*My landlady has eleven children.*
Martin kauft vierzehn Fahrkarten.	*Martin is buying fourteen tickets.*
Mein Bruder ist zwanzig Jahre alt.	*My brother is twenty years old.*

Oral Practice

Practice saying the following list of sentences out loud.

Wie viel Kinder habt ihr?	*How many children do you have?*
Wir haben zehn Kinder.	*We have ten children.*
Wer hat fünfzehn Kinder?	*Who has fifteen children?*
Herr Benz hat fünfzehn Kinder.	*Mr. Benz has fifteen children.*
Kaufen Sie einen Schlüssel?	*Are you buying a key?*
Ich kaufe zwölf Schlüssel.	*I am buying twelve keys.*
Wie viel CDs kaufst du?	*How many CDs are you buying?*
Ich kaufe neunzehn CDs.	*I am buying nineteen CDs.*
Wie alt bist du?	*How old are you?*
Ich bin sechzehn Jahre alt.	*I am sixteen years old.*
Wie alt sind Karl und Tina?	*How old are Karl and Tina?*
Karl ist elf Jahre alt und Tina ist siebzehn.	*Karl is eleven years old and Tina is seventeen.*

Wie viel ist zwanzig minus sechs?	*How much is twenty minus six?*
Zwanzig minus sechs ist vierzehn.	*Twenty minus six is fourteen.*
Wie viel ist dreizehn plus sieben?	*How much is thirteen plus seven?*
Dreizehn plus sieben ist zwanzig.	*Thirteen plus seven is twenty.*

Written Practice 7

Using the information in parentheses, tell how old someone or something is. For example:

(die Schule/10) *Die Schule ist zehn Jahre alt.*

1. (die Kinder/13) _____ .
2. (das Museum/15) _____ .
3. (du/20) _____ .

QUIZ

1. Write the present tense conjugation of the following verbs using the subjects provided.

	werden	**suchen**	**spielen**
ich	_____	_____	_____
du	_____	_____	_____
er	_____	_____	_____
wir	_____	_____	_____
ihr	_____	_____	_____
Sie	_____	_____	_____
die Kinder	_____	_____	_____

In this exercise you will see a person, an occupation, and a second person in parentheses. Say that the first person is becoming that occupation. Say that the second person is also (**auch**) becoming that occupation. For example:

(Hans/Lehrer/ich) *Hans wird Lehrer.*

Ich werde auch Lehrer.

2. (mein Bruder/Arzt/du) _____.

_____.

3. (Sie/Krankenschwester/ich) _____.

_____.

4. Write the present tense conjugation of the following verbs with the subjects provided.

	fahren	schlafen	tragen
ich	_____	_____	_____
du	_____	_____	_____
er	_____	_____	_____
ihr	_____	_____	_____
die Kinder	_____	_____	_____

Answer each question in the affirmative using **ja** and in the negative using **nein** and **kein**. For example:

Hast du ein Buch? *Ja, ich habe ein Buch.*

Nein, ich habe kein Buch.

5. Trägst du eine Bluse? _____.

_____.

6. Kaufen Sie die Fahrkarten? _____.

_____.

Write a question for each person in parentheses asking about the person's age and then write an answer that gives the age. For example:

(Hans/11) *Wie alt ist Hans?*

Hans ist elf Jahre alt.

7. (Iris/12) _____?

_____.

8. (dein Sohn/19) _____?

_____.

Circle the letter of the word or phrase that best completes each sentence.

9. Es _____ sehr warm.

   (a) sind   (c) wird

   (b) hat   (d) wieder

10. Werden Sie _____?

   (a) nach Hause   (c) Ärztin

   (b) trägt   (d) heute

CHAPTER 7

Irregularities in Present Tense Verbs

In this chapter you will learn:

Present Tense Verb Irregularities

Inseparable Verb Prefixes

Colors

Common/Professional Titles

Present Tense Verb Irregularities

There are a few more unique aspects of the German present tense that must be discussed. You are already aware that some present tense conjugations require an umlaut over the vowel **-a-** in the second and third person singular (**du fährst, er**

fährt). Only one verb requires an umlaut over the vowel **-o-**: **stoßen** (*to punch*; *to kick*).

ich stoße	wir stoßen
du stößt	ihr stoßt
er stößt	sie stoßen

Notice that there is not an **-st** ending on the second person singular **du stößt**. When the stem of a verb ends with **-s, -ss, -ß, -z,** or **-tz,** only a **-t** is added:

heißen	*to be called*	du heißt	*you are called*
passen	*to fit*	du passt	*you fit*
reisen	*to travel*	du reist	*you travel*
reizen	*to annoy*	du reizt	*you annoy*
schützen	*to protect*	du schützt	*you protect*

Some verbs in the present tense have another kind of irregularity in the conjugation of the second and third person singular. Many verbs that have the vowel **-e-** in the stem change that vowel to **-i-** or **-ie-**. Let's look at some examples of verbs that change the stem vowel **-e-** to **-i-**.

	essen (*to eat*)	**sprechen** (*to speak*)	**nehmen** (*to take*)
ich	esse	spreche	nehme
du	isst	sprichst	nimmst
er	isst	spricht	nimmt
wir	essen	sprechen	nehmen
ihr	esst	sprecht	nehmt
sie	essen	sprechen	nehmen

Now let's look at some examples of verbs that change the stem vowel to **-ie-**.

	lesen (*to read*)	**sehen** (*to see*)	**stehlen** (*to steal*)
ich	lese	sehe	stehle
du	liest	siehst	stiehlst
er	liest	sieht	stiehlt
wir	lesen	sehen	stehlen
ihr	lest	seht	stehlen
sie	lesen	sehen	stehlen

Refer to Appendix A for a complete list of irregular verbs.

Oral Practice

Practice saying the following list of sentences out loud.

Was nimmst du?	*What are you taking (having)?*
Ich nehme eine Tasse Kaffee.	*I am taking a cup of coffee.*
Was nimmt Johannes?	*What is Johannes taking?*
Er nimmt eine Tasse Tee.	*He is taking a cup of tea.*
Was nehmen Sie, Herr Müller?	*What are you taking, Mr. Mueller?*
Ich nehme ein Glas Milch.	*I am taking a glass of milk.*
Was essen Sie?	*What are you eating?*
Ich esse ein Butterbrot.	*I am eating a sandwich.*
Was isst dein Sohn?	*What is your son eating?*
Mein Sohn isst Eis.	*My son is eating ice cream.*
Was liest du, Hans?	*What are you reading, Hans?*
Ich lese die Zeitung.	*I am reading the newspaper.*
Was liest Andrea?	*What is Andrea reading?*
Andrea liest einen Brief.	*Andrea is reading a letter.*
Wer sieht den Mann?	*Who sees the man?*
Wir sehen den Mann.	*We see the man.*
Was stiehlt der Mann?	*What does the man steal?*
Er stiehlt eine Tasche.	*He steals a purse.*
Der Mann ist ein Dieb.	*The man is a thief.*

Written Practice 1

Write the present tense conjugation of the following verbs with the pronouns provided.

	sprechen	**sehen**
ich	_____	_____
du	_____	_____
er	_____	_____

	sprechen	**sehen**
wir	_____	_____
ihr	_____	_____
sie	_____	_____

There is another aspect of spelling to be considered. If a verb stem ends in **-d** or **-t**, an **-e-** will follow the stem before the conjugational endings for the second person singular and plural and the third person singular are added. For example:

	finden (*to find*)	**warten** (*to wait*)
ich	finde	warte
du	findest	wartest
er	findet	wartet
wir	finden	warten
ihr	findet	wartet
sie	finden	warten

Inseparable Verb Prefixes

Prefixes alter the meaning of verbs. English does this primarily with verbs that are derived from Latin: *press*—de*press*, com*press*, sup*press*, and so on. But German uses prefixes extensively with a wide variety of verbs. One type of prefix is the inseparable prefix—prefixes that do not separate from the verb when the verb is conjugated. These prefixes are: **be-, emp-, ent-, er-, ge-, ver-,** and **zer-**. These prefixes change the meaning of the verb.

For example, **kaufen** means *to buy*; **ver**kaufen means to *sell*. **Suchen** means *to look for*; **be**suchen means *to visit*. The change in meaning, however, does not affect the conjugation of these verbs.

	verkaufen	**besuchen**
ich	verkaufe	besuche
du	verkaufst	besuchst
er	verkauft	besucht
wir	verkaufen	besuchen
ihr	verkauft	besucht
sie	verkaufen	besuchen

Here are a few commonly used verbs that have an inseparable prefix.

bestellen	*to order* (*food, etc.*)		
empfinden	*to feel*	gehören	*to belong to*
entsetzen	*to horrify*	verstehen	*to understand*
erwarten	*to expect, await*	zerstören	*to destroy*

Oral Practice

Practice saying the following list of sentences out loud.

Sprechen Sie Deutsch?	*Do you speak German?*
Ja, ich spreche und verstehe Deutsch.	*Yes, I speak and understand German.*
Sprichst du Arabisch?	*Do you speak Arabic?*
Nein, ich spreche Italienisch.	*No, I speak Italian.*
Wer spricht Russisch?	*Who speaks Russian?*
Frau Wolkow spricht Russisch.	*Ms. Volkov speaks Russian.*
Was verkaufst du?	*What are you selling?*
Ich verkaufe mein Auto.	*I am selling my car.*
Robert kauft es.	*Robert is buying it.*
Was bestellst du?	*What are you ordering?*
Ich bestelle ein Glas Bier.	*I am ordering a glass of beer.*
Mein Freund bestellt eine Tasse Tee.	*My friend is ordering a cup of tea.*
Der Film entsetzt meine Mutter.	*The movie horrifies my mother.*
Verstehen Sie die Dame?	*Do you understand the lady?*
Nein, ich verstehe sie nicht.	*No, I do not understand her.*

Written Practice 2

Rewrite the following sentences, changing the verb in bold print to the verb provided in parentheses. Note the change in meaning of the sentences.

1. Er **sieht** meine Freundin. (*He sees my girlfriend.*)

   (besuchen *to visit*) _____.

   (erwarten *to expect*) _____.

   (verstehen *to understand*) _____.

   (finden *to find*) _____.

2. Erik **hat** die Schlüssel. (*Erik has the keys.*)

   (sehen *to see*) _____.

   (suchen *to look for*) _____.

   (stehlen *to steal*) _____.

   (verkaufen *to sell*) _____.

Oral Practice

Practice saying the following list of sentences out loud.

Lernen Sie Deutsch?	*Are you learning German?*
Sprechen Sie Deutsch?	*Do you speak German?*
Verstehen Sie Deutsch?	*Do you understand German?*
Lesen Sie Deutsch?	*Do you read German?*
Schreiben Sie Deutsch?	*Do you write German?*
Das Buch gehört Robert.	*The book belongs to Robert.*
Die CDs gehören Robert.	*The CDs belong to Robert.*
Der Hut gehört Tina.	*The hat belongs to Tina.*
Die Schlüssel gehören Tina.	*The keys belong to Tina.*
Was suchst du?	*What are you looking for?*
Ich suche ein Buch.	*I am looking for a book.*
Was schreibst du?	*What are you writing?*
Ich schreibe einen Brief.	*I am writing a letter.*

Colors

You already know the colors **schwarz**, **weiß**, and **rot**. Here are a few more:

braun	*brown*	grün	*green*
gelb	*yellow*	rosa	*pink*
grau	*gray*		

When you use a color as a predicate adjective after **sein** or **werden**, it requires no ending. However, when a color or any other adjective modifies many singular subject nouns directly, it requires an **-e** ending. The only exception is **rosa**. It makes no changes. Adjectives that end in **-el** will also make a change, by dropping the **e** when an ending is added: **dunkel—dunkle**. Let's look at some examples.

Mein Wagen ist rot.	*My car is red.*
Der rote Wagen ist neu.	*The red car is new.*
Ihre Bluse ist grün.	*Her blouse is green.*
Ihre grüne Bluse ist sehr alt.	*Her green blouse is very old.*
Die Tasse ist gelb.	*The cup is yellow.*
Die gelbe Tasse ist nicht hier.	*The yellow cup is not here.*
Die Vase ist rosa.	*The vase is pink.*
Wo ist die rosa Vase?	*Where is the pink vase?*

Oral Practice

Practice saying the following list of sentences out loud.

Die braune Jacke ist neu.	*The brown jacket is new.*
Das weiße Haus ist in Washington.	*The White House is in Washington.*
Der alte Herr ist mein Vater.	*The old gentleman is my father.*
Das kleine Glas ist für Tina.	*The little glass is for Tina.*
Ist der junge Mann ein Freund?	*Is the young man a friend?*
Ist die rosa Bluse für deine Mutter?	*Is the pink blouse for your mother?*
Ist der grüne Hut neu oder alt?	*Is the green hat new or old?*
Das große Buch ist ein Wörterbuch.	*The big book is a dictionary.*

Written Practice 3

Fill in the blanks with the adjectives provided in parentheses.

1. (klein) Das _____ Mädchen ist meine Tochter.

2. (weiß) Meine _____ Bluse ist nicht alt.

3. (dunkel) Es wird sehr _____ .

4. (jung) Ist Ihr Onkel _____ oder alt?

5. (neu) Wo ist die _____ Tasse?

6. (grau) Der _____ Hut ist nicht hier.

7. (deutsch) Die _____ Frau kauft eine Tasse Kaffee.

Written Practice 4

Look at each statement on the left. Then place the letter of the statement on the right that logically follows. Not all letters will be used.

1. Wer stiehlt das Geld? _____
2. Sie kauft eine neue Bluse. _____
3. Hans spricht Russisch. _____
4. Was liest du? _____
5. Ist der neue BMW rot? _____
6. Sie bestellt eine Tasse Tee. _____
7. Erik nimmt ein Glas Milch. _____
8. Lesen Sie ein Buch? _____
9. Ist die Tasse grau? _____
10. Sie spricht Arabisch. _____

a. Er ist elf Jahre alt.
b. Ich verstehe sie nicht.
c. Der Dieb.
d. Nein, sie ist weiß.
e. Ist sie gelb?
f. Ich nehme ein Butterbrot.
g. Thomas bestellt Bier.
h. Er versteht es auch.
i. In der Schweiz.
j. Ein Buch.
k. Nein, ich lese eine Zeitung.
l. Nein, er ist grün.

Common/Professional Titles

Most titles are similar in both English and German. There are common titles that refer to everyone, and other titles that designate someone's profession. For example:

Common Titles:

Herr Meier	*Mr. Meier*
Frau Meier	*Ms. Meier, Mrs. Meier, Miss Meier*

Professional Titles:

Doktor Bauer ist Arzt.	*Dr. Bauer is a physician.*
Doktor Keller ist Ärztin.	*Dr. Keller is a physician (female).*
Doktor Schmidt ist Zahnarzt.	*Dr. Schmidt is a dentist.*
Professor Benz schreibt ein Buch.	*Professor Benz is writing a book.*

When addressing someone with a common title (**Herr**, **Frau**), just use the title and the last name.

Guten Tag, Herr Schröder.	*Hello, Mr. Schroeder.*
Gute Nacht, Frau Kamps.	*Good night, Ms. Kamps.*

When someone has a professional title, use both the common and professional titles together.

Guten Abend, Herr Doktor.	*Good evening, doctor.*
Auf Wiedersehen, Frau Doktor.	*Good-bye, doctor.*
Guten Tag, Herr Professor.	*Good afternoon, professor.*
Guten Morgen, Frau Professor.	*Good morning, professor.*

And if a doctor or professor has a wife, she, too, can be addressed with the professional title.

Wiederschauen, Frau Doktor.	*Good-bye, ma'am (wife of the doctor).*
Wiedersehen, Frau Professor.	*Good-bye, ma'am (wife of the professor).*

Written Practice 5

Complete each sentence by filling in the blanks with any appropriate word or phrase.

1. Meine Mutter liest _____.
2. Die Kinder spielen im _____.
3. Der alte Mann _____ Englisch und Deutsch.
4. Ich habe kein Geld. Ich kann es nicht _____.
5. Der Dieb _____ meine Tasche.
6. Ist _____ heiß oder kalt?
7. Es ist _____. Wo ist die Lampe?
8. Siehst du _____?
9. Guten _____, Frau Doktor.
10. Der _____ Hut ist sehr alt.
11. Ist euer Vater _____?
12. Ist der neue Wagen braun oder _____?
13. Ich finde _____.
14. Martin _____ ein Butterbrot und ein Glas Milch.
15. Die _____ gehören Tina.

Written Practice 6

Form a question about each sentence by changing the words or phrases in bold print to **wer, was, wann, wo, wohin, wie viel, wie alt,** or **warum.** For example:

Martin kauft **ein Heft**.

Was kauft Martin? _____

1. **Angela** besucht eine Freundin in Berlin.

_____?

2. Mein Vater fährt **nach Österreich**.

_____?

3. Die Kinder finden **eine alte Uhr**.

   _____?

4. Sie trägt ein Sweatshirt, **denn es ist sehr kalt**.

   _____?

5. Meine Tochter ist **zwölf Jahre alt**.

   _____?

6. Ich gehe **heute** in die Stadt.

   _____?

7. Zwei Jungen spielen Tennis **im Park**.

   _____?

8. Der Professor hat **achtzehn** Schlüssel.

   _____?

9. Er fährt mit dem Bus **nach Hause**.

   _____?

10. Karin liest **einen Brief**.

    _____?

11. **Die Kinder** warten im Park.

    _____?

12. Erik hat **kein** Geld.

    _____?

13. Sonja versteht **Russisch und Italienisch**.

    _____?

14. Ich lese das Buch, **denn es ist sehr interessant**.

    _____?

15. Onkel Heinz trägt **einen Hut**.

    _____?

QUIZ

1. Write the present tense conjugation of the following verbs using the pronouns provided.

	reisen	**sehen**	**sprechen**	**verstehen**
ich	_____	_____	_____	_____
du	_____	_____	_____	_____
er	_____	_____	_____	_____
wir	_____	_____	_____	_____
ihr	_____	_____	_____	_____
sie	_____	_____	_____	_____

Rewrite each sentence below, changing the italicized verbs to the ones provided in parentheses.

2. Andrea *kauft* eine neue Bluse.

(suchen) _____?

(verkaufen) _____?

(finden) _____?

(sehen) _____?

3. *Hast* du das Buch?

(verstehen) _____?

(lesen) _____?

(finden) _____?

(stehlen) _____?

Answer each of the following questions with any appropriate statement.

4. Was kaufen die Kinder?

_____.

5. Wohin reisen Sie?

_____.

6. Warum trägt Ihr Sohn ein Sweatshirt?

_____.

Circle the letter of the word or phrase that best completes each sentence.

7. Das _____ ist sehr groß.

   (a) Lehrer   (c) Wörterbuch

   (b) Kinder   (d) Brief

8. Andrea _____ sehr gut Tennis.

   (a) spielt   (c) habt

   (b) hat   (d) verkauft

9. Der schlechte Film _____ meine Frau.

   (a) spricht   (c) zu Hause

   (b) nach Hause   (d) entsetzt

10. Die Touristen fahren _____ .

   (a) mit dem Zug   (c) neu

   (b) zu Hause   (d) interessante

CHAPTER 8

Talking About Location

In this chapter you will learn:

Using the Verb *Kommen*

The verb **kommen** (*to come*) is a high-frequency verb. In the present tense this verb has no irregularities.

ich komme	*I come*	wir kommen	*we come*
du kommst	*you come*	ihr kommt	*you come*
er kommt	*he comes*	sie kommen	*they come*

When you want to know where someone comes from, ask:

Woher kommen Sie?	*Where do you come from?*
Woher kommst du?	*Where do you come from?*
Woher kommt ihr?	*Where do you come from?*
Woher kommt dieser Mann?	*Where does this man come from?*
Woher kommt diese Frau?	*Where does this woman come from?*

Use the preposition **aus** (*out*; *from*) to reply to this with the name of a city, a country, or a continent.

Wir kommen aus Wien.	*We come from Vienna.*
Ich komme aus England.	*I am from England.*
Er kommt aus Asien.	*He comes from Asia.*

Oral Practice

Practice saying the following list of sentences out loud.

Woher kommen Sie?	*Where do you come from?*
Ich komme aus Amerika.	*I come from America.*
Woher kommt dieser Herr?	*Where does this gentleman come from?*
Er kommt aus Schweden.	*He comes from Sweden.*
Woher kommt diese Dame?	*Where does this lady come from?*
Sie kommt aus Düsseldorf.	*She comes from Düsseldorf.*
Kommt der Student aus China?	*Does the student come from China?*

Nein, er kommt aus Japan. *No, he comes from Japan.*

Kommen diese Leute aus Asien? *Do these people come from Asia?*

Nein, sie kommen aus Afrika. *No, they come from Africa.*

Nein, sie kommen aus Australien. *No, they come from Australia.*

Nein, sie kommen aus Nordamerika. *No, they come from North America.*

Nein, sie kommen aus Südamerika. *No, they come from South America.*

The pronoun **man** means *one* or *you* when it refers to people in general. It is commonly used with **kommen**.

Wie kommt man zum Theater? *How does one (do you) get to the theater?*

Wie kommt man zum Park? *How does one get to the park?*

Written Practice 1

Rewrite each sentence, changing the subject in bold print to the pronoun **man**. For example:

> Verstehen **Sie** das?
>
> *Versteht man das?*
> _____

1. Warum fahrt **ihr** mit der Straßenbahn?

   _____?

2. Wie kommen **deine Eltern** vom Rathaus zum Bahnhof?

   _____?

3. Wisst **ihr**, wohin Gudrun reist?

   _____?

4. Hier sprechen **die Leute** Deutsch.

   _____.

Oral Practice

Practice saying the following list of sentences out loud.

Wie kommt man zum Bahnhof?	*How do you (does one) get to the train station?*
Man kommt mit dem Bus zum Bahnhof.	*You get to the train station by bus.*
Wie kommt man zum Rathaus?	*How do you get to city hall?*
Man kommt mit der Straßenbahn zum Rathaus.	*You get to city hall by streetcar.*
Wie kommt man zur Kunsthalle?	*How do you get to the art museum?*
Man kommt mit dem Bus zur Kunsthalle.	*You get to the art museum by bus.*
Wie kommt man nach Berlin?	*How do you get to Berlin?*
Man kommt mit dem Zug nach Berlin.	*You get to Berlin by train.*
Wie kommt man nach Kanada?	*How do you get to Canada?*
Man kommt mit dem Flugzeug nach Kanada.	*You get to Canada by airplane.*
Kommst du mit dem Auto nach Paris?	*Are you coming to Paris by car?*
Ja, ich komme mit dem Auto nach Paris.	*Yes, I am coming to Paris by car.*

Written Practice 2

Write the present tense conjugation of **kommen** with the following pronouns and nouns.

ich	_____	wir	_____
du	_____	ihr	_____
er	_____	sie	_____
man	_____	dieser Herr	_____
die Kinder	_____	diese Dame	_____

Written Practice 3

Using the words in parentheses, answer the questions. For example:

Woher kommst du? (Bonn) *Ich komme aus Bonn.*

1. Woher kommt Herr Braun? (London)

   _____.

2. Woher kommt der Amerikaner? (New York)

   _____.

3. Woher kommt die Österreicherin? (Wien)

   _____.

4. Woher kommt Frau Benz? (Deutschland)

   _____.

5. Woher kommt diese Dame? (Italien)

   _____.

Telling Time

When telling time, place the hour number in front of the word **Uhr**. For example, **Es ist drei Uhr** means *It is three o'clock*. When telling at what time something occurs, precede the phrase with the preposition *um*. For example, **Er kommt um drei Uhr nach Hause** means *He comes home at three o'clock*.

There are numerous phrases that can be used with the verb **kommen**. Let's look at a few of them.

Er kommt spät.	*He comes late.*
Um sechs Uhr kommt er von der Arbeit.	*At six o'clock he comes from work.*
Ich komme in einer halben Stunde.	*I will come in a half hour.*
Wir kommen in zwei Wochen.	*We are coming in two weeks.*
Wer kommt ins Zimmer?	*Who is coming into the room?*
Er kommt in den Himmel.	*He is going to heaven.*
Er kommt in die Hölle.	*He is going to hell.*

Oral Practice

Practice saying the following list of sentences out loud.

Kommt er spät zur Party?	*Is he coming to the party late?*
Ja, er kommt sehr spät zur Party.	*Yes, he is coming very late to the party.*
Kommt sie immer spät?	*Does she always come late?*
Ja, sie kommt immer zu spät.	*Yes, she always comes too late.*
Mein Vater kommt immer um sechs Uhr von der Arbeit.	*My father always comes from work at six o'clock.*
Um wie viel Uhr kommst du von der Arbeit?	*What time do you come from work?*
Ich komme sehr spät von der Arbeit.	*I come from work very late.*
Wann kommen Sie zum Bahnhof?	*When are you coming to the train station?*
Ich komme in einer halben Stunde.	*I am coming in a half hour.*
Martin kommt in einer Stunde.	*Martin is coming in an hour.*
Wann kommt ihr zur Party?	*When are you coming to the party?*
Wir kommen um sechs Uhr zur Party.	*We are coming to the party at six o'clock.*
Wann kommst du nach Hause?	*When are you coming home?*
Ich komme in zwei Wochen nach Hause.	*I am coming home in two weeks.*
Wer kommt nächste Woche?	*Who is coming next week?*
Tante Gerda kommt nächste Woche.	*Aunt Gerda is coming next week.*
Kommst du zu Fuß?	*Are you coming on foot?*

Using the Verbs *Gehen* and *Fahren*

Both **gehen** and **fahren** can be translated as *to go*. However, **gehen** is more precisely *to go on foot* and **fahren** *to travel* or *to drive* by some form of transportation (**Bus, Zug, Straßenbahn**, and so forth). English does not have to be so specific when using the verb *to go*:

What time are you going to school?   (It could be on foot. It could be by bus.)

When are you going to Berlin?   (It could be by train or airplane.)

German prefers to be specific:

Um wie viel Uhr gehst du   *What time are you going to school?*
  zur Schule?   *(on foot)*

Wann fährst du nach Berlin?   *When are you going to Berlin?*
                                      (by a form of motorized transportation)

And when the distance is great and you're going to travel by airplane, you use the
verb **fliegen** (*to fly*).

Wohin fliegt ihr nächste Woche?   *Where are you flying (going) next week?*

Wir fliegen nächste Woche   *We are flying (going) to China next week.*
  nach China.

Using the Verbs *Wohnen* and *Leben*

The verbs **wohnen** and **leben** can be translated as *to live*, but the former means *to
reside* somewhere, and the latter means to *be alive*. Let's look at some example
sentences.

Wo wohnen Sie, Herr Bauer?   *Where do you live, Mr. Bauer?*

Ich wohne in Hamburg.   *I live in Hamburg.*

Mein Großvater lebt noch.   *My grandfather is still living.*

Oral Practice

Practice saying the following list of sentences out loud.

Wo wohnen Sie jetzt?   *Where do you live now?*

Ich wohne jetzt in Freiburg.   *I live in Freiburg now.*

Wo wohnt Ihre Tochter?   *Where does your daughter live?*

Meine Tochter wohnt jetzt in Bonn. *My daughter lives in Bonn now.*

Lebt Ihr Großvater noch?	*Is your grandfather still living?*
Ja, er lebt noch, aber er ist sehr alt.	*Yes, he is still living, but he is very old.*
Lebt Ihre Großmutter noch?	*Is your grandmother still living?*
Nein, sie lebt nicht mehr.	*No, she is no longer living.*
Wann gehst du zum Bahnhof?	*When are you going to the train station?*
Ich gehe um neun Uhr zum Bahnhof.	*I am going to the train station at nine o'clock.*
Wann fährt er zum Rathaus?	*When is he going to city hall?*
Er fährt morgen zum Rathaus.	*He is going to city hall tomorrow.*
Fliegt ihr nach Europa?	*Are you flying to Europe?*
Ja, wir fliegen nach Europa.	*Yes, we are flying to Europe.*
Von Frankfurt nach München fahren wir mit dem Auto.	*We are going by car from Frankfurt to Munich.*
Von Hamburg nach Berlin fahren wir mit dem Zug.	*We are going by train from Hamburg to Berlin.*
Vom Bahnhof zum Rathaus fahren wir mit der Straßenbahn.	*From the train station to city hall we are going by streetcar.*
Wohin fahren diese Leute?	*Where are these people going?*

Word Order

When a word or phrase other than the subject begins a sentence, the verb precedes the subject. For example:

Wir fahren nach Hamburg. (subject followed by verb)

but

Heute *fahren wir* nach Hamburg. (verb followed by subject)

Ich fahre mit der Straßenbahn. (subject followed by verb)

but

Vom Bahnhof zum Rathaus *fahre ich* mit der Straßenbahn. (verb followed by subject)

Written Practice 4

Rewrite each sentence, starting it with the word or phrase in parentheses and changing the word order accordingly. For example:

Ich gehe zur Schule. (heute) _Heute gehe ich zur Schule._

1. Die Touristen reisen nach Italien. (morgen) _____ .
2. Wir sehen viele Kinder. (im Park) _____ .
3. Ich bestelle ein Glas Bier. (im Restaurant) _____ .
4. Sie fahren mit dem Auto. (vom Rathaus zur Schule) _____ .
5. Mein Vater fliegt nach Australien. (heute) _____ .

Some Coordinating Conjunctions

You have already encountered four important conjunctions: **und** (*and*), **oder** (*or*), **denn** (*because*), and **aber** (*but*). These are called coordinating conjunctions because they combine two sentences (clauses) into one.

Karl liest ein Buch **und** Marianne schreibt einen Brief.	*Karl reads a book, **and** Marianne writes a letter.*
Gehen wir zum Rathaus, **oder** gehen wir zum Bahnhof?	*Are we going to city hall, **or** are we going to the train station?*
Er trägt ein Sweatshirt, **denn** es wird sehr kalt.	*He is wearing a sweatshirt, **because** it is getting very cold.*
Der Mann lebt noch, **aber** er ist sehr alt.	*The man is still living, **but** he is very old.*

NOTICE: *The German conjunction **und** does not require a comma to separate the two clauses as do the other coordinating conjunctions.*

Using the Verbs *Wissen* and *Kennen*

These two verbs mean *to know*, but the former means *to have knowledge*, and the latter means *to be acquainted with*. The verb **wissen** has an irregular conjugation in the present tense. Let's compare the conjugations of these two verbs.

	wissen	**kennen**
ich	weiß	kenne
du	weißt	kennst
er	weiß	kennt
wir	wissen	kennen
ihr	wisst	kennt
sie	wissen	kennen

In sentences, these two verbs are used like this:

Wissen Sie, wo Herr Bauer wohnt?	*Do you know where Mr. Bauer lives?*
Nein, das weiß ich nicht.	*No, I do not know that.*
Kennst du Frau Meier?	*Do you know Ms. Meier?*
Ja, ich kenne sie gut.	*Yes, I know her well.*

Oral Practice

Practice saying the following list of sentences out loud.

Weißt du, wo meine Schlüssel sind?	*Do you know where my keys are?*
Nein, das weiß ich nicht.	*No, I do not know.*
Weiß man, wer da wohnt?	*Does anyone know who lives there?*
Ich weiß, wer da wohnt.	*I know who lives there.*
Erik wohnt da. Kennst du Erik?	*Erik lives there. Do you know Erik?*
Nein, ich kenne Erik nicht.	*No, I do not know Erik.*
Kennen Sie diese Frau?	*Do you know this woman?*
Ja, ich kenne sie. Das ist Frau Kamps.	*Yes, I know her. That is Ms. Kamps.*
Sie wohnt in Bonn, aber Herr Kamps wohnt in Leipzig.	*She lives in Bonn, but Mr. Kamps lives in Leipzig.*

Written Practice 5

Complete the sentences by filling in the blanks with the appropriate verbs: **gehen** or **fahren**, **wohnen** or **leben**, **wissen** or **kennen**. Conjugate the verbs accordingly.

1. Meine Eltern _____ jetzt in Freiburg.
2. _____ Ihre Großmutter noch?
3. Wir _____ den Mann nicht. Wie heißt er?
4. Er _____ mit dem Zug nach Rom.
5. Herr Benz _____ in der Schillerstraße.
6. Wohin _____ du?
7. _____ Sie, wo Frau Schneider wohnt?
8. Ich _____ zum Rathaus. Es ist nicht weit von hier.
9. Warum _____ ihr zu Fuß?
10. _____ Sie meine Eltern nicht?

Infinitives Ending in *-ieren*

There is a large category of verbs that end in **-ieren**. These verbs tend to come from foreign sources, and in many instances English speakers can recognize the meanings of such verbs at first glance. For example:

arrangieren	*to arrange*	marschieren	*to march*
diskutieren	*to discuss*	organisieren	*to organize*
fotografieren	*to photograph*	probieren	*to try, to taste*
imitieren	*to imitate*	spazieren	*to stroll*
immigrieren	*to immigrate*	studieren	*to study*

These verbs are always regular in the present tense.

	diskutieren	**studieren**
ich	diskutiere	studiere
du	diskutierst	studierst
er	diskutiert	studiert
wir	diskutieren	studieren
ihr	diskutiert	studiert
sie	diskutieren	studieren

Though you will encounter many such verbs in German, there are a few German verbs that look like **-ieren** verbs but are not. This distinction will become important in the next few chapters when you begin working with other tenses. The present tense of these verbs is conjugated the same, but it is in the various past tenses that the verbs will differ from regular **-ieren** verbs. One such German verb that is not an **-ieren** verb is **verlieren** (*to lose*).

ich verliere	wir verlieren
du verlierst	ihr verliert
er verliert	sie verlieren

Written Practice 6

Combine each string of words as a sentence, conjugating the verbs appropriately. For example:

ich/suchen/mein/Schlüssel *Ich suche meine Schlüssel.* _____

1. wir/fotografieren/das Rathaus _____.
2. Martin/verlieren/das Geld _____.
3. ich/studieren/Deutsch/und/Russisch _____.
4. die Kinder/probieren/den Pudding _____.
5. diese Leute/spazieren/im Park _____.

Separable Verb Prefixes

In Chapter 7 you were introduced to inseparable prefixes. There are also numerous separable prefixes that are derived from two large groups of words: prepositions and adverbs. Here are some examples of separable prefixes: **an-, auf-, aus-, ein-, mit-, um-, vor-,** and **zu-.** Some example verbs with these prefixes are:

ankommen	*to arrive*	mitgehen	*to go along*
aufmachen	*to open*	umsteigen	*to transfer (to other transportation)*
ausgeben	*to spend*	vorstellen	*to introduce*
einsteigen	*to get on (transportation)*	zumachen	*to close*

There are many other separable prefixes, but you can quickly identify them by the position of the stress in the verb. If the stress is on the prefix (**áufmachen**), the prefix is separable. If the stress is on the stem of the verb (**besúchen**), the prefix is inseparable. When a verb with a separable prefix is conjugated in the present tense, the prefix separates from the verb and is placed at the end of the sentence. For example:

aufmachen (*to open*)

Ich mache das Fenster **auf**.	*I open the window.*
Du machst das Fenster **auf**.	*You open the window.*
Er macht das Fenster **auf**.	*He opens the window.*
Wir machen das Fenster **auf**.	*We open the window.*
Ihr macht das Fenster **auf**.	*You open the window.*
Sie machen das Fenster **auf**.	*They open the window.*
Wer macht das Fenster **auf**?	*Who is opening the window?*

ausgeben (*to spend*)

Ich gebe zu viel Geld **aus**.	*I spend too much money.*
Du gibst zu viel Geld **aus**.	*You spend too much money.*
Er gibt zu viel Geld **aus**.	*He spends too much money.*
Wir geben zu viel Geld **aus**.	*We spend too much money.*
Ihr gebt zu viel Geld **aus**.	*You spend too much money.*
Sie geben zu viel Geld **aus**.	*They spend too much money.*
Wer gibt zu viel Geld **aus**?	*Who spends too much money?*

Written Practice 7

Write the present tense conjugation of each of the following verbs.

	ankommen	einsteigen	vorstellen
ich	_____	_____	_____
du	_____	_____	_____
er	_____	_____	_____
wir	_____	_____	_____

	ankommen	einsteigen	vorstellen
ihr	_____	_____	_____
sie	_____	_____	_____

Accusative Case

The subject of a German sentence is in the nominative case. For example:

Der Mann ist alt.	*The man is old.*
Meine Lampe ist neu.	*My lamp is new.*
Wo ist **dein Sweatshirt**?	*Where is your sweatshirt?*
Ihre Kinder haben keine CDs.	*Your children do not have any CDs.*

Direct objects are in the accusative case. The direct object in a sentence is the word that receives the action of the verb. Ask *what* or *whom* of the verb to identify the direct object. For example:

I buy a new blouse.	(*What* do I buy?) (*a new blouse* = direct object)
I know this woman.	(*Whom* do I know?) (*this woman* = direct object).

It works the same in German.

Ich kaufe eine neue Bluse.	(*Was* kaufe ich?) (**eine neue Bluse** = direct object)
Ich kenne diese Frau.	(*Wen* kenne ich?) (**diese Frau** = direct object)

It's important to be able to identify a direct object, because in German, masculine nouns used as direct objects make a declensional change. Let's compare the nominative and accusative cases of masculine nouns.

Nominative	Accusative
der Mann	den Mann
ein Lehrer	einen Lehrer
kein Freund	keinen Freund
mein Tisch	meinen Tisch
Ihr Wagen	Ihren Wagen

As you can plainly see, the modifier (**der**, **ein**, **kein**, **mein**, **Ihr**) of a masculine noun requires an **-en** ending when it is used in the accusative case, that is, when it is used with a direct object. Now compare masculine nouns used as subjects of sentences and as direct objects of sentences.

Subjects—Nominative Case

Mein Lehrer wohnt in Heidelberg.	*My teacher lives in Heidelberg.*
Wo ist Ihr Wagen?	*Where is your car?*

Direct Objects—Accusative Case

Kennen Sie meinen Lehrer?	*Do you know my teacher?*
Ein Freund kauft Ihren Wagen.	*A friend buys your car.*

But with feminine, neuter, and plural nouns, there is no declensional change from the nominative case to the accusative case.

Subjects—Nominative Case

Meine Tante ist sehr alt.	*My aunt is very old.*
Wo ist das Heft?	*Where is the notebook?*
Die Schlüssel sind in der Tasche.	*The keys are in the purse.*

Direct Objects—Accusative Case

Morgen besuche ich meine Tante.	*Tomorrow I will visit my aunt.*
Robert verliert das Heft.	*Robert loses the notebook.*
Iris findet die Schlüssel.	*Iris finds the keys.*

Oral Practice

Practice saying the following list of sentences out loud.

Kennen Sie meine Eltern?	*Do you know my parents?*
Nein, ich kenne sie nicht.	*No, I do not know them.*
Ich stelle meinen Vater und meine Mutter vor.	*I introduce my father and my mother.*
Kennst du den Amerikaner?	*Do you know the American?*
Ja, ich kenne den Amerikaner.	*Yes, I know the American.*

Er wohnt in Cleveland, aber studiert in Hamburg.	*He lives in Cleveland but is studying in Hamburg.*
Ich stelle den Amerikaner vor.	*I introduce the American.*
Wann kommt Herr Schneider an?	*When does Mr. Schneider arrive?*
Ich weiß nicht. Ich frage meinen Mann.	*I do not know. I will ask my husband.*
Wir steigen in den Bus ein und fahren nach Hause.	*We get on the bus and go home.*
In der Schillerstraße steigen wir um.	*We transfer at Schiller Street.*
Wo steigt ihr ein?	*Where do you get on?*
Wir steigen in der Hauptstraße ein.	*We get on on Main Street.*
Wo steigen sie um?	*Where do they transfer?*
Sie steigen in der Waldstraße um.	*They transfer on Wald Street.*
Hans, machst du das Fenster auf?	*Hans, are you opening the window?*
Ja, es ist sehr heiß heute.	*Yes, it is very hot today.*
Wer macht die Tür zu?	*Who closes the door?*
Meine Eltern machen die Tür zu.	*My parents close the door.*
Wir gehen zum Bahnhof.	*We are going to the train station.*
Mein Bruder geht mit.	*My brother is going along.*

Written Practice 8

Rewrite the sentences using the nouns in parentheses. These will be direct objects and will require the accusative case.

1. Kennen Sie _____?

(mein Onkel) _____?

(diese Dame) _____?

(der Professor) _____?

(das Mädchen) _____?

2. Dieser Mann kauft _____.

(ein Wagen) _____.

(mein Haus) _____ .

(Ihre CDs) _____ .

(der Teppich) _____ .

Accusative Pronouns

Just as masculine nouns change in the accusative case when they are used as direct objects, so do most pronouns. In English it looks like this, for example:

Subject: He learns German.

Direct Object: Do you know **him**?

German pronouns act in the same way.

Subject Pronouns—Nominative Case	Direct Object Pronouns—Accusative Case
ich	mich
du	dich
er	ihn
sie *s.*	sie
es	es
wir	uns
ihr	euch
sie *pl.*	sie
Sie	Sie
wer	wen
was	was

In sentences they look like this:

Der Mann kennt mich nicht.	*The man does not know me.*
Der Mann kennt dich nicht.	*The man does not know you.*
Der Mann kennt ihn nicht.	*The man does not know him.*
Der Mann kennt sie nicht.	*The man does not know her.*
Der Mann kennt uns nicht.	*The man does not know us.*
Der Mann kennt euch nicht.	*The man does not know you.*

Der Mann kennt sie nicht.	*The man does not know them.*
Der Mann kennt Sie nicht.	*The man does not know you.*
Wen kennt der Mann?	*Whom does the man know?*
Was sieht der Mann?	*What does the man see?*

When you replace a noun with a pronoun, it must be the same gender and case as the noun. For example:

Eine Frau kommt.	*A woman is coming.*
Sie kommt.	*She is coming.*
Sehen Sie den Mann?	*Do you see the man?*
Sehen Sie **ihn**?	*Do you see him?*

Written Practice 9

Rewrite the sentences using the nouns or pronouns in parentheses. These will be direct objects and will require the accusative case.

1. Wer verkauft _____?

   (mein Wagen) _____?

   (ein Hut) _____?

   (die Fahrkarten) _____?

   (das Auto) _____?

   (es) _____?

2. Kennt ihr _____?

   (meine Eltern) _____?

   (der Lehrer) _____?

   (die Leute) _____?

   (mein Freund) _____?

   (er) _____?

QUIZ

Rewrite each sentence as a question. Use the phrases in bold print as signals to use
wo, **wohin**, or **woher**. For example:

> Er geht **nach Hause**. _Wohin geht er?_ _____

1. Die Kinder spielen **im Park**. _____?
2. Mein Onkel kommt **aus Italien**. _____?
3. Morgen fahren die Touristen **nach Polen**. _____?

Rewrite the sentence with the words in parentheses.

4. Meine Eltern fotografieren _____ .

   (die Kinder) _____ .

   (dieser Mann) _____ .

   (Ihr Bruder) _____ .

   (diese Frau) _____ .

   (wir) _____ .

Provide the accusative case form of each word or phrase.

5. (mein Vater) _____

   (ich) _____

   (du) _____

   (Ihr Zahnarzt) _____

   (er) _____

   (sie _s._) _____

   (keine Schule) _____

   (wir) _____

   (ihr) _____

   (diese Leute) _____

Circle the letter of the word or phrase that best completes each sentence.

6. Es ist elf Uhr! Du kommst zu _____!

   (a) nach Hause   (c) Hause

   (b) spät   (d) vom Bahnhof

7. _____ versteht Sie nicht.

   (a) Man   (c) Den Mann

   (b) Diese Leute   (d) Wir

8. Um wie viel _____ kommt er von der Arbeit?

   (a) Stunde   (c) Uhr

   (b) in einer halben Stunde   (d) zehn Uhr

9. _____ siehst du im Park?

   (a) Wen   (c) Eine junge Frau

   (b) Der alte Mann   (d) Ein Bus

10. Ich _____ die junge Amerikanerin vor.

   (a) gehe   (c) steige

   (b) komme   (d) stelle

CHAPTER 9

Talking About
the Past

In this chapter you will learn:

Possessive Adjectives

Regular Past Tense

Irregular Past Tense

Accusative Case Prepositions

Plurals

Possessive Adjectives

You have already encountered some of the possessive adjectives. Each possessive adjective has a subject pronoun counterpart, from which it is derived. Here is a complete list:

Subject Pronoun	Possessive Adjective
ich	mein
du	dein
er	sein
sie *s.*	ihr
es	sein
wir	unser
ihr	euer
sie *pl.*	ihr
Sie	Ihr
wer	wessen

Except for **wessen** (*whose*), a feminine or masculine ending is required in the accusative case: **mein, meine, meinen/sein, seine, seinen/unser, unsere, unseren**, and so forth. In sentences, the possessive adjectives look like this:

Ich verliere mein Buch.	*I lose my book.*
Du verlierst dein Buch.	*You lose your book.*
Er verliert sein Buch.	*He loses his book.*
Sie verliert ihr Buch.	*She loses her book.*
Es (Das Kind) verliert sein Buch.	*He/She (The child) loses his/her book.*
Wir verlieren unser Buch.	*We lose our book.*
Ihr verliert euer Buch.	*You lose your book.*
Sie verlieren ihr Buch.	*They lose their book.*
Sie verlieren Ihr Buch.	*You lose your book.*
Wessen Buch verlieren sie?	*Whose book do they lose?*

Masculine, feminine, and neuter nouns use **sein**, **ihr**, and **sein** (*his*, *her*, *its*) as their possessive adjectives. All plural nouns use **ihr** (*their*).

Der Mann verkauft sein Haus.	*The man sells his house.*
Die Frau verkauft ihren Wagen.	*The woman sells her car.*
Das Mädchen verkauft sein Buch.	*The girl sells her book.*
Diese Leute verkaufen ihre Autos.	*These people sell their cars.*

Oral Practice

Practice saying the following list of sentences out loud.

Wir diskutieren unser Problem.	*We discuss our problem.*
Das ist aber auch mein Problem.	*But that is my problem, too.*
Der Student macht seine Tür auf.	*The student opens his door.*
Die Ärztin macht ihr Fenster zu.	*The physician closes her window.*
Wessen Wagen kaufen Sie?	*Whose car are you buying?*
Ich kaufe seinen Wagen.	*I am buying his car.*
Wessen Haus kauft ihr?	*Whose house are you buying?*
Wir kaufen ihr Haus.	*We are buying her house.*
Wessen Kleider verkauft ihr?	*Whose clothes are you selling?*
Wir verkaufen unsere Kleider.	*We are selling our clothes.*
Wessen Bücher verkauft der Chef?	*Whose books is the boss selling?*
Der Chef verkauft seine Bücher.	*The boss is selling his books.*

Written Practice 1

Answer each question with the possessive adjective provided in parentheses. For example:

Wessen Buch hast du? (mein) _Ich habe mein Buch._ _____

1. Wessen Kleider findest du? (sein) _____.
2. Wessen Freundin kennst du? (ihr) _____.
3. Wessen Wagen kauft ihr? (euer) _____.
4. Wessen Kind siehst du? (mein) _____.
5. Wessen Milch nimmt er? (dein) _____.
6. Wessen Eltern wohnen in Leipzig? (Ihr) _____.
7. Wessen Chef weiß nichts? (unser) _____.

Written Practice 2

For each sentence, change the possessive adjective in bold print to the one in parentheses. For example:

Er findet **sein** Buch.
(ihr) Er findet ihr Buch.

1. Ich besuche **meine** Eltern in München.

   (Ihr) _____ .

   (euer) _____ .

   (unser) _____ .

2. Wer findet **ihren** Bleistift?

   (mein) _____ ?

   (sein) _____ ?

   (unser) _____ ?

Regular Past Tense

German, just like English, has both a regular past tense formation and an irregular past tense formation. The regular past tense adds the suffix **-te** to the stem of the verb plus the appropriate conjugational endings. This is similar to how English adds the suffix *-ed* to a verb to form the past tense (*look—looked*, *jump—jumped*, and so forth).

To form the regular past tense in German, drop the infinitive ending **-en** and add the endings **-te**, **-test**, **-te**, **-ten**, **-tet**, and **-ten**. Let's look at some regular verbs in the past tense.

	bestellen (*ordered*)	**studieren** (*studied*)	**lernen** (*learned*)	**zumachen** (*closed*)
ich	bestell**te**	studier**te**	lern**te**	mach**te** zu
du	bestell**test**	studier**test**	lern**test**	mach**test** zu
er	bestell**te**	studier**te**	lern**te**	mach**te** zu
wir	bestell**ten**	studier**ten**	lern**ten**	mach**ten** zu
ihr	bestell**tet**	studier**tet**	lern**tet**	mach**tet** zu
sie	bestell**ten**	studier**ten**	lern**ten**	mach**ten** zu

In the past tense the first person singular (**ich**) and the third person singular (**er**) will always have the same ending. And the rules for using separable and inseparable prefixes apply in the past tense just as they do in the present tense.

Written Practice 3

Conjugate the following verbs in the past tense.

	fragen	**gehören**	**vorstellen**
ich	_____	_____	_____
du	_____	_____	_____
er	_____	_____	_____
wir	_____	_____	_____
ihr	_____	_____	_____
sie	_____	_____	_____
wer	_____	_____	_____

Oral Practice

Practice saying the following list of sentences out loud.

Wo lerntest du Deutsch?	*Where did you learn German?*
Ich lernte in Berlin Deutsch.	*I learned German in Berlin.*
Wohntest du in Berlin?	*Did you live in Berlin?*
Ja, ich wohnte zwei Jahre in Berlin.	*Yes, I lived in Berlin for two years.*
Studiertest du in Berlin?	*Did you study in Berlin?*
Nein, ich studierte an der Universität in Hamburg.	*No, I studied at the university in Hamburg.*
Wo spieltet ihr Tennis?	*Where did you play tennis?*
Wir spielten Tennis im Park.	*We played tennis in the park.*
Wo hörtet ihr Radio?	*Where did you listen to the radio?*

Wir hörten Radio im Wohnzimmer.	*We listened to the radio in the living room.*
Wen fragtest du?	*Whom did you ask?*
Ich fragte den Chef.	*I asked the boss.*
Warum verkauftest du diese Kleider?	*Why did you sell these clothes?*
Ich verkaufte die Kleider, denn sie sind alt.	*I sold the clothes, because they are old.*
Wo arbeiteten Sie?	*Where did you work?*
Ich arbeitete in der Stadt.	*I worked in the city.*

Remember that a verb stem that ends in **-d** or **-t** will add an extra **-e-** before the conjugational endings, as illustrated by **Ich arbeitete** in the previous sentence.

Irregular Past Tense

Some English verbs do not form the past tense with the suffix *-ed*. These verbs are irregular and form the past tense by means of a vowel change. For example, in the case of the verb *to go*, a completely new verb is formed—*went*. Some examples of these English verbs are:

Infinitive	Past Tense
to go	went
to speak	spoke
to stand	stood
to write	wrote

German does the same thing. The irregular past tense is formed by a vowel change, and the appropriate conjugational endings are added to the verb. Here are some commonly used irregular verbs in the third person singular (**er**) past tense.

Infinitive	Past Tense	Meaning
ausgeben	gab aus	*spent*
bleiben	blieb	*stayed*
einsteigen	stieg ein	*got on (transportation)*
essen	aß	*ate*
fahren	fuhr	*drove*

Infinitive	Past Tense	Meaning
finden	fand	*found*
fliegen	flog	*flew*
gehen	ging	*went*
heißen	hieß	*was called*
kommen	kam	*came*
lesen	las	*read*
schreiben	schrieb	*wrote*
sehen	sah	*saw*
sprechen	sprach	*spoke*
stehlen	stahl	*stole*
tragen	trug	*carried; wore*
verstehen	verstand	*understood*

See Appendix A for a complete list of irregular verbs.

When conjugated with the various persons, irregular verbs add the endings **-**, **-st**, **-**, **-en**, **-t**, and **-en** to the stem of the irregular past tense. Notice that the **ich** and **er** forms have no endings added.

	verstehen (*understood*)	gehen (*went*)	ausgeben (*spent*)
ich	verstand	ging	gab aus
du	verstandest	gingst	gabst aus
er	verstand	ging	gab aus
wir	verstanden	gingen	gaben aus
ihr	verstandet	gingt	gabt aus
sie	verstanden	gingen	gaben aus

Again, take note of **du verstandest** and **ihr verstandet** in this list to see how the extra **-e-** is added when a verb stem ends in **-d** or **-t**.

Written Practice 4

Conjugate the following irregular verbs in the past tense with the subjects provided.

	fahren	kommen	fliegen
ich	_____	_____	_____
du	_____	_____	_____

	fahren	**kommen**	**fliegen**
er	_____	_____	_____
wir	_____	_____	_____
ihr	_____	_____	_____
sie	_____	_____	_____
dieser Mann	_____	_____	_____

A few verbs not only make a vowel change but also add the **-te**, **-test**, **-tet**, or **-ten** suffixes in the irregular past tense. For example:

	wissen (*knew*)	**kennen** (*was acquainted*)	**nennen** (*named*)
ich	wusste	kannte	nannte
du	wusstest	kanntest	nanntest
er	wusste	kannte	nannte
wir	wussten	kannten	nannten
ihr	wusstet	kanntet	nanntet
sie	wussten	kannten	nannten

Just as in the present tense, the past tense in English begins most *yes* or *no* questions with a form of *to do. Did you understand him? Did you see your Friend?* In German such questions begin with the verb. **Verstandest du ihn? Sahen Sie Ihren Freund?** In questions that begin with an interrogative (**wie lange**, **wo**, and so forth), the verb and subject follow the interrogative word. **Wo wohnten diese Leute?** *Where did these people live?*

Oral Practice

Practice saying the following list of sentences out loud.

Wie lange blieben Sie in der Stadt?	*How long did you stay in the city?*
Ich blieb zwei Tage in der Stadt.	*I stayed in the city for two days.*
Wer blieb zu Hause?	*Who stayed home?*
Seine Kinder blieben zu Hause.	*His children stayed home.*
Was schrieb der Chef?	*What did the boss write?*
Der Chef schrieb drei Briefe.	*The boss wrote three letters.*

Wusstet ihr, wo die Leute wohnten?	*Did you know where the people lived?*
Ja, wir wussten, wo sie wohnten.	*Yes, we knew where they lived.*
Wussten Sie, was Thomas sah?	*Did you know what Thomas saw?*
Nein, wir wussten nicht, was er sah.	*No, we did not know what Thomas saw.*
Kamst du mit dem Flugzeug?	*Did you come by airplane?*
Nein, ich kam mit dem Auto.	*No, I came by car.*
Wohin gingen sie?	*Where did they go?*
Sie gingen zum Bahnhof.	*They went to the train station.*
Sie fuhren mit dem Zug nach Bern.	*They went to Bern by train.*
Kannten Sie diese Leute?	*Did you know these people?*
Ja, ich kannte sie gut.	*Yes, I knew them well.*
Kanntest du unseren Chef?	*Did you know our boss?*
Nein, ich kannte ihn nicht.	*No, I did not know him.*

Three important verbs need to be considered individually because of the extensive role they play in the German language. These verbs are **haben**, **sein**, and **werden**. Each one is irregular in the present tense and likewise irregular in the past tense. Their past tense conjugations follow:

	haben (*had*)	sein (*was/were*)	werden (*became*)
ich	hatte	war	wurde
du	hattest	warst	wurdest
er	hatte	war	wurde
wir	hatten	waren	wurden
ihr	hattet	wart	wurdet
sie	hatten	waren	wurden

Oral Practice

Practice saying the following list of sentences out loud.

Hatten Sie ein Problem?	*Did you have a problem?*
Nein, ich hatte kein Problem.	*No, I did not have a problem.*
Was hatten die Leute?	*What did the people have?*

Die Leute hatten viele Fragen.	*The people had a lot of questions.*
Wo warst du gestern?	*Where were you yesterday?*
Ich war gestern in der Stadt.	*I was in the city yesterday.*
Wer war im Restaurant?	*Who was in the restaurant?*
Mein Chef war im Restaurant.	*My boss was in the restaurant.*
Wann wurde es so kalt?	*When did it become (get) so cold?*
Es wurde gestern so kalt.	*It became (got) so cold yesterday.*
Wer wurde die neue Chefin?	*Who became the new boss?*
Frau Benz wurde die neue Chefin.	*Ms. Benz became the new boss.*

Written Practice 5

Write the past tense of the following regular and irregular verbs in the third person singular (**er**) conjugation.

essen	_____	lesen	_____
sagen	_____	sprechen	_____
bleiben	_____	heißen	_____
haben	_____	gehen	_____
sein	_____	warten	_____
arbeiten	_____	werden	_____
finden	_____	wissen	_____
verstehen	_____	ankommen	_____

Written Practice 6

Rewrite the following sentences putting them in the past tense.

1. Ich komme mit dem Bus.

   _____.

2. Es wird heute sehr kalt.

   _____.

3. Warum esst ihr im Wohnzimmer?

_____?

4. Meine Tochter studiert an einer Universität in Amerika.

_____.

5. Wo steigen wir um?

_____?

6. Die Männer zerstören das alte Haus.

_____.

7. Wen siehst du im Wohnzimmer?

_____?

8. Der Chef diskutiert die Probleme.

_____.

9. Ich bin immer krank.

_____.

10. Weißt du, wer die Bücher verkauft?

_____?

Accusative Case Prepositions

The accusative case of nouns and pronouns is used not only with direct objects but also when a noun or pronoun is the object of an accusative preposition. The accusative prepositions are as follows:

bis	_until_; _as far as_	ohne	_without_
durch	_through_	wider	_against_ (poetic older form)
für	_for_	um	_around_
gegen	_against_		

Prepositions are not always used in the same way in every language. The definitions of the prepositions illustrated above are only their general meanings. But their translations can differ when used in a specific sense. For example, **um** means _around_. However, when using it to express at what time something occurs, **um** then means _at_.

um die Ecke   _around the corner_   um sechs Uhr   _at six o'clock_

The preposition **bis** is used alone with names of places, words that express time, and adverbs. In other sentences **bis** is combined with another preposition. For example:

Er reiste bis Leipzig.	*He was traveling as far as Leipzig.*
Sie blieb bis Montag hier.	*She stayed here until Monday.*
Ich war bis gestern Abend da.	*I was there until last evening.*

but

Er blieb bis **zu** seinem Tod in Bonn.	*He stayed in Bonn until his death.*
Sie gingen bis **zum** Rathaus.	*They went as far as city hall.*

Oral Practice

Practice saying the following list of sentences out loud.

Was hatte Onkel Peter?	*What did Uncle Peter have?*
Er hatte ein Geschenk für seinen Sohn.	*He had a gift for his son.*
Er hatte ein Geschenk für ihn.	*He had a gift for him.*
Er kaufte ein Geschenk für seine Tochter.	*He bought a gift for his daughter.*
Er kaufte ein Geschenk für sie.	*He bought a gift for her.*
Gegen wen sprach der Chef?	*Whom did the boss speak against?*
Er sprach gegen diese Leute.	*He spoke against these people.*
Er sprach gegen sie.	*He spoke against them.*
Er sprach auch gegen mich.	*He also spoke against me.*
Wir fuhren durch einen Tunnel.	*We drove through a tunnel.*
Wir fuhren bis Heidelberg.	*We drove as far as Heidelberg.*
Kamen Sie ohne Ihre Kinder?	*Did you come without your children?*
Ja, ich kam ohne sie.	*Yes, I came without them.*
Die Kunsthalle ist um die Ecke.	*The art museum is around the corner.*

Written Practice 7

Rewrite each sentence with the words in parentheses.

1. Ich fand eine neue Lampe für _____.

   (du) _____.

   (mein Freund) _____.

   (sie *s.*) _____.

   (Ihr Chef) _____.

2. Diese Frau hatte nichts gegen _____. (**nichts** = *nothing*)

   (ich) _____.

   (wir) _____.

   (Ihre Chefin) _____.

   (Sie) _____.

3. Robert kam ohne _____.

   (das Geld) _____.

   (er) _____.

   (sie *pl.*) _____.

   (sein Vater) _____.

4. Er ging ohne _____ zum Park.

   (sein Freund) _____.

   (du) _____.

   (wir) _____.

   (ihr Onkel) _____.

   (ihr) _____.

   (seine Kinder) _____.

5. Die Amerikaner fuhren bis _____.

   (Hamburg) _____.

   (München) _____.

   (Polen) _____.

   (gestern Abend) _____.

   (elf Uhr) _____.

Plurals

English plurals are, for the most part, quite simple to form. Most end in *-s*. German has a few plurals that end in **-s** as well. But these are foreign words such as: **die Parks**, **die Hotels**, **die Autos**. The majority of German nouns form their plurals in a variety of patterns. Let's look at some of these patterns.

MASCULINE NOUNS

If a noun ends in **-er**, **-en**, or **-el**, it will not have an added ending but may add an umlaut to a vowel in the word.

der Lehrer	becomes	die Lehrer	*teachers*
der Wagen	becomes	die Wagen	*cars*
der Mantel	becomes	die Mäntel	*coats*

Many other masculine nouns form the plural with an **-e** or **umlaut** + **-e**.

der Brief	becomes	die Briefe	*letters*
der Bleistift	becomes	die Bleistifte	*pencils*
der Bahnhof	becomes	die Bahnhöfe	*train stations*

FEMININE NOUNS

Most feminine nouns end in **-(e)n** in their plural forms.

die Stunde	becomes	die Stunden	*hours*
die Frau	becomes	die Frauen	*women*

Feminine nouns formed with the suffix **-in** add **-nen** in the plural.

die Studentin	becomes	die Studentinnen	*students*
die Chefin	becomes	die Chefinnen	*bosses*

NEUTER NOUNS

If a noun ends in a suffix that forms a diminutive (**-chen** or **-lein**), no ending is added to form the plural.

das Mädchen	becomes	die Mädchen	*girls*
das Röslein	becomes	die Röslein	*little roses*

Many nouns with one syllable form the plural by adding **-er** or **umlaut + -er**.

das Haus	becomes	die Häuser	*houses*
das Kind	becomes	die Kinder	*children*
das Land	becomes	die Länder	*countries*

These rules are generalizations about the formation of plurals. Many nouns break the rules. Some masculine nouns use an **-en** or **-er** ending to form the plural.

der Student	becomes	die Studenten	*students*
der Mann	becomes	die Männer	*men*

Some feminine nouns add an **umlaut** but no suffix to form the plural.

die Mutter	becomes	die Mütter	*mothers*
die Tochter	becomes	die Töchter	*daughters*

Some neuter nouns add the suffix **-e** to form the plural.

das Gedicht	becomes	die Gedichte	*poems*
das Element	becomes	die Elemente	*elements*

The only true way to be certain of the plural formation of a noun is to check it in a dictionary. In time and with experience, you will come to use plurals automatically, just as you know in English that *children* is the plural of *child* or that *geese* is the plural of *goose*.

Written Practice 8

Form the plurals of the following nouns. Write each one with the definite article.

1. das Buch ＿＿＿＿＿＿＿＿＿＿＿＿＿＿＿＿

2. der Arm ＿＿＿＿＿＿＿＿＿＿＿＿＿＿＿＿＿

3. der Vater ＿＿＿＿＿＿＿＿＿＿＿＿＿＿＿＿

4. die Schwester ＿＿＿＿＿＿＿＿＿＿＿＿＿＿

5. der Boden ＿＿＿＿＿＿＿＿＿＿＿＿＿＿＿

6. das Rathaus ＿＿＿＿＿＿＿＿＿＿＿＿＿＿

7. der Himmel ＿＿＿＿＿＿＿＿＿＿＿＿＿＿

8. die Ärztin ＿＿＿＿＿＿＿＿＿＿＿＿＿＿＿

9. das Kleid ＿＿＿＿＿＿＿＿＿＿＿＿＿＿＿

10. die Tante ＿＿＿＿＿＿＿＿＿＿＿＿＿＿＿

11. der Bruder ＿＿＿＿＿＿＿＿＿＿＿＿＿＿

12. das Heft ＿＿＿＿＿＿＿＿＿＿＿＿＿＿＿

13. die Zeitung ＿＿＿＿＿＿＿＿＿＿＿＿＿＿

14. der Tisch ＿＿＿＿＿＿＿＿＿＿＿＿＿＿＿

15. der Teppich ＿＿＿＿＿＿＿＿＿＿＿＿＿＿

16. die Lampe ＿＿＿＿＿＿＿＿＿＿＿＿＿＿＿

Oral Practice

Practice saying the following list of sentences out loud.

Hattest du nur eine Lampe?	*Did you only have one lamp?*
Nein, ich hatte viele Lampen.	*No, I had a lot of lamps.*
Hatten Sie nur einen Wagen?	*Did you only have one car?*
Nein, ich hatte zwei Wagen.	*No, I had two cars.*
Hattet ihr nur einen Bruder?	*Did you only have one brother?*
Nein, wir hatten vier Brüder.	*No, we had four brothers.*

Wie viele Schwestern hattest du?	*How many sisters did you have?*
Ich hatte nur eine Schwester.	*I only had one sister.*
Wie viele Bücher hatte Erik?	*How many books did Erik have?*
Er hatte nur ein Buch.	*He only had one book.*
Wie viele Fahrkarten hatte Tina?	*How many tickets did Tina have?*
Sie hatte nur eine Fahrkarte.	*She only had one ticket.*
Wie viele Briefe hattet ihr?	*How many letters did you have?*
Wir hatten nur einen Brief.	*We only had one letter.*

QUIZ

Answer each question with the possessive adjective in parentheses. For example:

Wessen Haus ist das? (mein) _Das ist mein Haus._ _____

1. Wessen Fahrkarten haben Sie? (unser) _____ .
2. Wessen Zeitung las Gudrun? (mein) _____ .
3. Wessen Freund besuchte Erik? (sein) _____ .

Rewrite the sentence below, replacing the possessive adjective in bold print with the ones provided in parentheses.

4. Herr Schmidt verkaufte **seinen** Wagen.

(mein) _____ .

(dein) _____ .

(ihr) _____ .

(euer) _____ .

(unser) _____ .

Write the past tense conjugations for the following verbs using the subjects provided.

5.   **bestellen**   **ausgeben**   **sein**

ich   _____   _____   _____

du   _____   _____   _____

er   _____   _____   _____

wir   _____   _____   _____

ihr   _____   _____   _____

sie   _____   _____   _____

die Leute   _____   _____   _____

Change the following present tense questions into the past tense.

6. Wer macht die Tür auf?

_____?

7. Verstehst du, was er sagt?

_____?

Rewrite the sentence below, filling in the blank with the words in parentheses. Make any necessary changes to pronouns or word endings.

8. Die Touristen hatten ein Geschenk für _____.

(ich) _____.

(er) _____.

(meine Tante) _____.

(dein Sohn) _____.

(sie *s.*) _____.

(ihre Eltern) _____.

Circle the letter of the word or phrase that best completes each sentence.

9. Tante Gerda _____ Angelika Geli.

(a) wartete   (c) ging mit

(b) nannte   (d) geht

10. Wer _____ das interessante Buch?

(a) las   (c) verkaufen

(b) verkauften   (d) last

CHAPTER 10

Time and Calendar

In this chapter you will learn:

More Irregular Verbs in the Present and Past Tenses

There are several other important verbs that are irregular. They have a high-frequency use in German and should be identified early. Some of these irregular verbs have a vowel change and add the suffixes **-te**, **-test**, **-ten**, and **-tet**. Look at the examples below (note only the third person singular conjugation is shown here).

Present and Past Tense

Infinitive		Present Tense		Past Tense	
bringen	*to bring*	bringt	*brings*	brachte	*brought*
denken	*to think*	denkt	*thinks*	dachte	*thought*
rennen	*to run*	rennt	*runs*	rannte	*ran*
senden	*to send*	sendet	*sends*	sandte	*sent*

Other irregular verbs are:

Infinitive		Present Tense		Past Tense	
anfangen	*to begin*	fängt an	*begins*	fing an	*began*
anrufen	*to telephone*	ruft an	*telephones*	rief an	*telephoned*
brechen	*to break*	bricht	*breaks*	brach	*broke*
fallen	*to fall*	fällt	*falls*	fiel	*fell*
fressen*	*to eat*	frisst	*eats*	fraß	*ate*
geben	*to give*	gibt	*gives*	gab	*gave*
helfen	*to help*	hilft	*helps*	half	*helped*
laufen	*to run*	läuft	*runs*	lief	*ran*
liegen	*to lay*	liegt	*lies*	lag	*lay*
nehmen	*to take*	nimmt	*takes*	nahm	*took*
schneiden	*to cut*	schneidet	*cuts*	schnitt	*cut*
stehen	*to stand*	steht	*stands*	stand	*stood*
tun	*to do*	tut	*does*	tat	*did*
vergessen	*to forget*	vergisst	*forgets*	vergaß	*forgot*

Oral Practice

Practice saying the following list of sentences out loud.

Der Metzger brachte das Fleisch.	*The butcher brought the meat.*
Der Hund fraß das Fleisch.	*The dog ate the meat.*

*This verb is used with animals only.

Der Ausländer nahm das Fleisch.	*The foreigner took the meat.*
Niemand schnitt das Fleisch.	*No one cut the meat.*
Er dachte an Frau Keller.	*He thought about Ms. Keller.*
Sie rief Frau Keller an.	*She telephoned Ms. Keller.*
Ich sandte Frau Keller ein Geschenk.	*I sent Ms. Keller a gift.*
Wer gab Frau Keller ein Geschenk?	*Who gave Ms. Keller a gift?*
Niemand half Frau Keller.	*No one helped Ms. Keller.*
Niemand vergaß Frau Keller.	*No one forgot Ms. Keller.*
Der Metzger rennt wieder zur Polizei.	*The butcher is running to the police again.*
Wann fängt der Film an?	*When does the movie start?*
Meine Kusine brach sich den linken Arm.	*My cousin broke her left arm.*
Oma fiel auf den rechten Arm.	*Granny fell on her right arm.*
Der Hund liegt unter dem Tisch.	*The dog is lying under the table.*
Was tust du? Warum stehst du hinter der Tür?	*What are you doing? Why are you standing behind the door?*
Ich tue nichts.	*I am not doing anything.*

Written Practice 1

Conjugate the following verbs in the present tense with the pronouns provided.

	denken	**anfangen**	**helfen**
ich	_____	_____	_____
du	_____	_____	_____
er	_____	_____	_____

	brechen	**fallen**	**vergessen**
du	_____	_____	_____
er	_____	_____	_____
wir	_____	_____	_____

Conjugate the following verbs in the past tense with the pronouns provided.

	fallen	bringen	stehen
ich	_____	_____	_____
er	_____	_____	_____
wir	_____	_____	_____

	rennen	anrufen	schneiden
ich	_____	_____	_____
du	_____	_____	_____
ihr	_____	_____	_____

Dative Case

You have already encountered the nominative case, which identifies the subject of a sentence, and the accusative case, which identifies the direct object of a sentence and which is used following accusative prepositions. The dative case identifies the indirect object of a sentence.

When you ask *to whom* or *for whom* with the subject and verb of a sentence, you can identify the indirect object. For example:

I gave Karl a gift. (*To whom* did I give a gift?) The indirect object is *Karl*.

I bought Tina a flower. (*For whom* did I buy a flower?) The indirect object is *Tina*.

The indirect object in a German sentence will be in the dative case. In the accusative case, only masculine nouns make a declensional change. In the dative case, all nouns make a declensional change. Let's compare the nominative, accusative, and dative cases of the three genders and the plural forms.

	Masculine	Feminine	Neuter	Plural
nom	der Mann	die Frau	das Kind	die Kinder
acc	den Mann	die Frau	das Kind	die Kinder
dat	dem Mann	der Frau	dem Kind	den Kindern

Any determiner (**der**, **mein**, **kein**, **dieser**, etc.) used in the dative case will have the same dative endings illustrated above, for example: **einem Mann**, **diesem Mann**,

keinem Mann; **dieser Frau, meiner Frau, Ihrer Frau**; **einem Kind, deinem Kind, unserem Kind**; **diesen Kindern, seinen Kindern, keinen Kindern**. Take note that a dative plural noun that does not have an **-n** ending will add that ending: **Kinder*n***. In sentences, the dative case looks like this:

Ich gab **dem Mann** ein Geschenk.   *I gave **the man** a gift.*

Ich kaufte **meiner Frau** eine Blume.   *I bought **my wife** a flower.*

Written Practice 2

Rewrite the nouns provided on the left in the dative case with **ihr**, **mein**, and **dies-**. For example:

der Mann	*ihrem Mann*	*meinem Mann*	*diesem Mann*
der Metzger	_____	_____	_____
die Wohnung	_____	_____	_____
das Land	_____	_____	_____
die Bücher	_____	_____	_____
die Uhr	_____	_____	_____

Oral Practice

Practice saying the following list of sentences out loud.

Was gibst du dem Ausländer?	*What are you giving the foreigner?*
Ich gebe dem Ausländer eine Fahrkarte.	*I give the foreigner a ticket.*
Was gaben Sie Ihrer Tante?	*What did you give your aunt?*
Ich gab meiner Tante eine Rose.	*I gave my aunt a rose.*
Was kauftet ihr den Männern?	*What did you buy the men?*
Wir kauften den Männern Bier.	*We bought the men beer.*
Wir senden unserem Freund einen Brief.	*We send our friend a letter.*

Wir sandten deiner Tochter ein Paket.	*We sent your daughter a package.*
Wer sandte den Studenten neue Bücher?	*Who sent the students new books?*

Dative Pronouns

German pronouns also have a dative case formation.

Nominative Case	Dative Case
ich	mir
du	dir
er	ihm
sie *s.*	ihr
es	ihm
wir	uns
ihr	euch
sie *pl.*	ihnen
Sie	Ihnen
wer	wem

Use the dative pronouns when the pronouns are indirect objects in a sentence. For example:

Ich gebe **dir** eine Blume.	*I give **you** a flower.*
Ich kaufe **ihr** eine Tasse Tee.	*I buy **her** a cup of tea.*

Oral Practice

Practice saying the following list of sentences out loud.

Wem geben Sie die Bücher?	*To whom are you giving the books?*
Ich gebe ihm die Bücher.	*I give him the books.*
Was bringst du deiner Lehrerin?	*What are you bringing for your teacher?*
Ich bringe ihr ein Geschenk.	*I bring her a gift.*
Wem schreiben Sie diesen Brief?	*To whom are you writing this letter?*

Ich schreibe Ihnen diesen Brief.	*I am writing this letter to you.*
Er sandte mir eine Postkarte.	*He sent me a postcard.*
Er sandte dir eine Ansichtskarte.	*He sent you a picture postcard.*
Er sandte uns ein Telegramm.	*He sent us a telegram.*
Er sandte euch ein Geschenk.	*He sent you a gift.*
Er sandte ihnen vier Briefe.	*He sent them four letters.*

Written Practice 3

Rewrite the sentences below, filling in the blanks with the words in parentheses.
Make the appropriate declensional changes.

1. Der Metzger gab _____ ein Geschenk.

    (ich) _____ .

    (du) _____ .

    (sie *pl.*) _____ .

    (mein Sohn) _____ .

    (meine Söhne) _____ .

    (die Ausländerin) _____ .

2. Wer schreibt _____ einen Brief?

    (sie *s.*) _____ ?

    (wir) _____ ?

    (Sie) _____ ?

    (ihr) _____ ?

    (die Polizei) _____ ?

    (Ihre Kinder) _____ ?

3. Was sendet er _____?

    (wir) _____ ?

    (sie *pl.*) _____ ?

    (ihr) _____ ?

    (Sie) _____ ?

    (ich) _____ ?

More About Word Order

In German if the indirect object and the direct object of a sentence are both nouns, the indirect object will precede the direct object.

Wir geben dem Lehrer einen Kuli.   *We give the teacher a ballpoint pen.*

If the indirect object is a pronoun and the direct object is a noun, the indirect object will precede the direct object.

Wir geben ihm einen Kuli.   *We give him a ballpoint pen.*

However, when the direct object is a pronoun, the direct object will precede the indirect object, whether the indirect object is a noun or a pronoun.

Wir geben ihn dem Lehrer.   *We give it to the teacher.*

Wir geben ihn ihm.   *We give it to him.*

Written Practice 4

Rewrite each sentence twice. In the first sentence, change the indirect object to a pronoun. In the second sentence, change both the indirect object and the direct object to a pronoun. For example:

Sie gab dem Lehrer ein Geschenk.

Sie gab ihm ein Geschenk.

Sie gab es ihm.

1. Robert schrieb seiner Frau einen Brief.

   _____.

   _____.

2. Ich kaufte meinem Sohn ein Auto.

   _____.

   _____.

3. Senden Sie Ihren Eltern neue Bücher?

   _____?

   _____?

4. Gudrun brachte ihrer Freundin ein Heft.

_____.

_____.

5. Wir verkauften den Männern die Kleider.

_____.

_____.

Cardinal Numbers Twenty and Above

In earlier times, the number twenty-four was said as _four and twenty_. (Do you remember the nursery rhyme that begins, "Four and twenty blackbirds baked in a pie . . ."?) That approach to numbers over twenty still exists in German. Let's become familiar with such numbers.

20	zwanzig	21	einundzwanzig
30	dreißig	32	zweiunddreißig
40	vierzig	43	dreiundvierzig
50	fünfzig	54	vierundfünfzig
60	sechzig	65	fünfundsechzig
70	siebzig	76	sechsundsiebzig
80	achtzig	87	siebenundachtzig
90	neunzig	98	achtundneunzig
100	(ein)hundert	900	neunhundert
340	dreihundertvierzig	672	sechshundertzweiundsiebzig
1 000	(ein)tausend	4 000	viertausend
1 000 000	eine Million	3 000 000	drei Millionen
1 000 000 000	eine Milliarde	1 000 000 000 000	eine Billion

German numbers are always written as one word; however, they tend to be shown as numerals and not as words. Notice that the German word **Billion** means _trillion_ in U.S. English. **Milliarde** means _billion_.

More About Telling Time

You already know the expression used to tell time on the hour.

Es ist acht Uhr.   *It is eight o'clock.*

Er kommt um neun Uhr.   *He comes at nine o'clock.*

Just as in English, German has a variety of ways to express certain times on the clock. There are three ways of expressing the quarter hour.

3:15   Es ist drei Uhr fünfzehn.

        Es ist Viertel nach drei. (**das Viertel** = *quarter*)

        Es ist ein Viertel vier.

Notice the third expression, which says that the time is one quarter before the next hour—**vier** (*four*).

On the half hour, you say:

6:30   Es ist sechs Uhr dreißig.

        Es ist halb sieben.

Notice the second expression, which says that the time is halfway to the next hour—**sieben** (*seven*).

On the three-quarters of the hour, you say:

9:45   Es ist neun Uhr fünfundvierzig.

        Es ist Viertel vor zehn.

        Es ist drei Viertel zehn.

Notice the second and third time expressions, which say that the time is on the way to the next hour—**zehn** (*ten*).

Now look at some varied examples of time.

12:05   Es ist zwölf Uhr fünf.

        Es ist fünf (Minuten) nach zwölf.

1:10   Es ist ein Uhr zehn.

          Es ist zehn (Minuten) nach eins.

2:22   Es ist zwei Uhr zweiundzwanzig.

          Es ist zweiundzwanzig (Minuten) nach zwei.

4:35   Es ist vier Uhr fünfunddreißig.

          Es ist fünf Minuten nach halb fünf.

10:48   Es ist zehn Uhr achtundvierzig.

          Es ist zwölf Minuten vor elf.

German does not use A.M. or P.M. Instead, the twenty-four-hour clock is used. For example:

0.05	null Uhr fünf	*12:05 A.M.*
4.15	vier Uhr fünfzehn	*4:15 A.M.*
6.30	sechs Uhr dreißig	*6:30 A.M.*
13.00	dreizehn Uhr	*1:00 P.M.*
15.30	fünfzehn Uhr dreißig	*3:30 P.M.*
24.00	vierundzwanzig Uhr	*12:00 midnight*

German uses a period to separate the hour from the minutes: *2.30 two-thirty.*

Written Practice 5

Complete the phrases that express the times shown on the left.

1. (6.30) Es ist _____ sieben.
2. (9.35) Es ist neun Uhr _____ .
3. (12.55) Es ist fünf Minuten vor _____ .
4. (2.15) Es ist _____ nach zwei.
5. (11.30) Es ist halb _____ .

6. (4.45) Es ist vier Uhr _____.

7. (3.55) Es ist fünf Minuten _____ _____.

Ordinal Numbers

Ordinal numbers are those that can be used as adjectives. In English most ordinal numbers end in *-th*: *eighth*, *sixteenth*, *hundredth*, and so forth. In German the numbers through nineteen end in **-te**. From twenty and above, they end in **-ste**. For example:

5th	fünfte	*fifth*	20th	zwanzigste	*twentieth*
10th	zehnte	*tenth*	31st	einunddreißigste	*thirty-first*
14th	vierzehnte	*fourteenth*	99th	neunundneunzigste	*ninety-ninth*

Just like English, German has a few irregular ordinals. They are:

1st	erste	*first*
3rd	dritte	*third*
7th	siebte	*seventh*

In sentences German ordinals look like this:

Das erste Gedicht heißt *Rote Rosen*.	*The first poem is called* Red Roses.
Unser dritter Sohn ist in Mannheim.	*Our third son is in Mannheim.*
Sie ist am Dreiundzwanzigsten geboren.	*She was born on the twenty-third.*

When the ordinals are used to express dates, they follow **am** (the contraction of **an** + **dem** = **am**): **am vierten Mai** (*on the fourth of May*).

Days and Months

Let's look at the days of the week and the months of the year in German. Notice how much they resemble their English equivalents. First, **Wochentage** (*days of the week*):

Sonntag	*Sunday*	Donnerstag	*Thursday*
Montag	*Monday*	Freitag	*Friday*
Dienstag	*Tuesday*	Samstag	*Saturday*
Mittwoch	*Wednesday*	(*or*) Sonnabend	*Saturday*

Now, **Monate** (*months*):

Januar	*January*	Juli	*July*
Februar	*February*	August	*August*
März	*March*	September	*September*
April	*April*	Oktober	*October*
Mai	*May*	November	*November*
Juni	*June*	Dezember	*December*

All days of the week and months of the year are masculine: **der Montag**, **der Oktober**.

Use **am** (**an** + **dem**) to say *on* a day of the week: **am Freitag** (*on Friday*). Use **im** (**in** + **dem**) to say *in* a month of the year.

Robert kommt am Sonntag.	*Robert is coming on Sunday.*
Sie ist im Juli geboren.	*She was born in July.*

Oral Practice

Practice saying the following list of sentences out loud.

Wann kommt dein Cousin zu Besuch?	*When is your cousin coming for a visit?*
Er kommt am Dienstag zu Besuch.	*He is coming on Tuesday for a visit.*
Wann seid ihr wieder in Mannheim?	*When are you in Mannheim again?*
Wir sind am Mittwoch wieder in Mannheim.	*We are back in Mannheim again on Wednesday.*
Wann ist das Kind geboren?	*When was the child born?*
Das Kind ist im Februar geboren.	*The child was born in February.*
Wann sind die Zwillinge geboren?	*When were the twins born?*
Die Zwillinge sind im Juni geboren.	*The twins were born in June.*

Wann bist du geboren?	*When were you born?*
Ich bin im Dezember geboren.	*I was born in December.*
Ich bin am elften Mai geboren.	*I was born on the eleventh of May.*
Sie ist am ersten September geboren.	*She was born on the first of September.*
Sie sind am dritten Oktober geboren.	*They were born on the third of October.*
Wer ist am Achtundzwanzigsten geboren?	*Who was born on the twenty-eighth?*
Unsere Tochter ist am Achtundzwanzigsten geboren.	*Our daughter was born on the twenty-eighth.*

Use **im Jahre** to express in what year something occurs.

Er ist im Jahre 1992 geboren.	*He was born in 1992.*

(1812 = achtzehnhundertzwölf)

Im Jahre 2000 wohnte sie noch in Bonn.	*In 2000 she still lived in Bonn.*

(2000 = zweitausend)

Written Practice 6

Rewrite each sentence, filling in the blank with the dates provided in parentheses. Change the cardinal number to the appropriate ordinal number.

1. Er besuchte uns am _____ März.

   (1) _____.

   (3) _____.

   (9) _____.

   (15) _____.

   (27) _____.

2. Ihr Sohn ist am _____ Juli geboren.

(30) _____ .

(31) _____ .

(2) _____ .

(7) _____ .

(12) _____ .

Sports and Hobbies

Germans are very much into fitness. They belong to gyms and athletic leagues and participate in various sports. **Welche Sportart treiben Sie?** (*What sport do you participate in?*) is what is said to ask what sport someone is pursuing. You can answer with: **Ich spiele...** (*I play . . .*) and name the sport.

Oral Practice

Practice saying the following list of sentences out loud.

Welche Sportart treiben Sie?	*What sport do you participate in?*
Ich spiele Fußball.	*I play soccer.*
Welche Sportart treibst du, Monika?	*What sport do you participate in, Monica?*
Ich spiele Basketball.	*I play basketball.*
Welche Sportart treibt ihr?	*What sport do you participate in?*
Wir spielen Eishockey.	*We play hockey.*
Wir spielen Golf.	*We play golf.*
Wir spielen Handball.	*We play handball.*
Wir spielen Tischtennis.	*We play table tennis.*
Was macht ihr gern?	*What do you like to do?*
Wir spielen gern Schach.	*We like to play chess.*
Was machst du gern, Thomas?	*What do you like to do, Thomas?*

Ich schwimme gern.	*I like swimming.*
Was machen Sie gern, Herr Benz?	*What do you like to do, Mr. Benz?*
Ich fahre gern Rad.	*I like biking.*
Ich laufe gern Ski.	*I like skiing.*
Ich lese gern.	*I like reading.*
Ich wandere gern.	*I like hiking.*
Ich sammele Briefmarken.	*I collect stamps.*
Mein Hobby ist Basteln.	*My hobby is doing handicrafts.*

Use the word **gern** after a verb to say what you *like* doing.

Ich spiele gern Tennis.	*I like playing tennis.*
Wir tanzen gern.	*We like dancing.*

Written Practice 7

Using the phrases in parentheses, write sentences that tell what you like to do. For example:

(Briefe schreiben) _Ich schreibe gern Briefe._ _____

1. (Schach spielen) _____.
2. (wandern) _____.
3. (schimmen) _____.
4. (Golf spielen) _____.
5. (Rad fahren) _____.
6. (Ski laufen) _____.
7. (lesen) _____.

QUIZ

1. Write the present tense conjugation of the following verbs with the pronouns provided.

	laufen	**fressen**	**geben**
ich	_____	_____	_____
du	_____	_____	_____
er	_____	_____	_____

Write the past tense conjugation of the following verbs with the pronouns provided.

	denken	**anfangen**	**helfen**
ich	_____	_____	_____
du	_____	_____	_____
er	_____	_____	_____

2. Rewrite each noun in the dative case using **kein**, **Ihr**, and **dies-**.

	kein	**Ihr**	**dies-**
das Fenster	_____	_____	_____
die Kinder	_____	_____	_____
die Treppe	_____	_____	_____
der Besuch	_____	_____	_____
die Leute	_____	_____	_____

3. Rewrite the following sentence using the dative case for the pronouns provided in parentheses.

Sie geben _____ drei Fahrkarten.

(ich) _____ .

(du) _____ .

(er) _____ .

(sie *s.*) _____ .

(ihr) _____ .

4. Rewrite each sentence twice. In the first sentence, change the indirect object to a pronoun. In the second sentence, change both the indirect object and the direct object to a pronoun. For example:

Sie gab dem Lehrer ein Geschenk.
Sie gab ihm ein Geschenk. _____
Sie gab es ihm. _____

Iris schrieb ihrem Mann einen Brief.

_____ .

_____ .

Sie gaben den Kindern neue Kulis.

_____ .

_____ .

Write out the times in sentences. For example:

3:00 *Es ist drei Uhr.* _____

5. 12.30 _____ .

6. 9.45 _____ .

7. 1.15 _____ .

8. Rewrite the following sentence, filling in the blank with the date as provided by the numbers in parentheses.

> Ich bin am _____ Februar geboren.
>
> (1) _____ .
>
> (3) _____ .
>
> (7) _____ .
>
> (16) _____ .
>
> (28) _____ .

Circle the letter of the word or phrase that best completes each sentence.

9. Der Film fängt um _____ Uhr an.

   (a) neunzehn   (c) zweiundzwanzigsten

   (b) einundzwanzigste   (d) spät

10. Ist dein _____ Basteln?

   (a) Basketball   (c) Radfahren

   (b) Handball   (d) Hobby

Write the present tense forms of the following verbs with the pronouns provided.

1. werden

   ich _____

   du _____

   er _____

   wir _____

2. anfangen

   ich _____

   du _____

   er _____

   wir _____

3. sehen

   ich _____

   du _____

   er _____

   wir _____

4. fahren

   ich _____

   du _____

   er _____

   ihr _____

5. stehlen

   ich _____

   du _____

   er _____

   ihr _____

6. mitgehen

   ich _____

   du _____

   er _____

   ihr _____

Write the past tense conjugation of the following verbs with the pronouns provided.

7. fahren

ich _____

du _____

er _____

wir _____

8. besuchen

ich _____

du _____

er _____

wir _____

9. helfen

ich _____

du _____

er _____

wir _____

10. gehen

ich _____

du _____

wir _____

ihr _____

11. sein

ich _____

du _____

wir _____

ihr _____

12. haben

ich _____

du _____

wir _____

ihr _____

Use the words or phrases in bold print as signals for the kind of question you should form from each sentence. Change the word or phrase in bold print to **wer, wen, wem, was, wann, wo,** or **wohin**. For example:

Martin kauft **ein Heft**.
Was kauft Martin?

13. Erik besuchte **eine Freundin** in Berlin.

_____?

14. Meine Eltern fahren **nach Mannheim**.

_____?

15. Sie fand **eine alte Uhr**.

_____?

16. Ich gehe **heute** nach Hause.

_____?

17. Tina gab **mir** einen Kuli.

_____?

18. Er fährt mit dem Bus **nach Hause**.

_____?

19. Karin liest **einen Brief**.

_____?

20. Die Kinder warten **im Park**.

_____?

Fill in the blanks with the appropriate verb: **gehen** or **fahren**, and **wissen** or **kennen**. Conjugate the verb accordingly.

21. Ich _____ die Frau nicht. Wie heißt sie?

22. Wir _____ mit dem Zug nach Paris.

23. Warum _____ du zu Fuß?

24. _____ Sie, wo Herr Bauer wohnt?

25. _____ Sie meine Eltern nicht?

Rewrite each sentence with the direct objects in parentheses.

26. Seine Freunde fotografieren _____.

    (die Kinder) _____.

    (dieser Mann) _____.

    (wir) _____.

27. Wer verkauft _____?

    (ein Hut) _____?

    (das Auto) _____?

    (es) _____?

28. Kennen Sie _____?

    (meine Eltern) _____?

    (der Lehrer) _____?

    (er) _____?

Provide the accusative case and dative case forms of each word or phrase.

	Accusative Case	**Dative Case**
29. meine Mutter	_____	_____
30. der Zahnarzt	_____	_____
31. die Kinder	_____	_____
32. sein Heft	_____	_____
33. diese Bücher	_____	_____

Rewrite the following sentences changing them from the present tense to the past tense.

34. Wer macht das Fenster auf?

    _____?

35. Sie fliegen nach Asien.

    _____.

36. Verstehst du, was sie fragt?

    _____.

Rewrite each sentence, filling in the blank with the correct forms of the pronouns provided.

37. Sie gab _____ drei Zeitungen.

   (ich) _____.

   (du) _____.

   (er) _____.

   (sie *s.*) _____.

38. Was sandten sie _____?

   (wir) _____?

   (ihr) _____?

   (Sie) _____?

   (sie *pl.*) _____?

Rewrite each sentence twice. In the first sentence, change the indirect object to a pronoun. In the second sentence, change both the indirect object and the direct object to a pronoun. For example:

   Sie gab dem Lehrer ein Geschenk.
   Sie gab ihm ein Geschenk.
   Sie gab es ihm.

39. Gibst du diesem Mann eine Zeitung?

   _____?

   _____?

40. Thomas sandte seinen Eltern einen Brief.

   _____.

   _____.

41. Ich kaufte meiner Freundin eine Blume.

   _____.

   _____.

Rewrite the sentence below, filling in the blank with the dates as provided by the numbers in parentheses.

42. Das Kind is am _____ März geboren.

(1) _____.

(3) _____.

(7) _____.

(9) _____.

(27) _____.

(30) _____.

Circle the letter of the word or phrase that best completes each sentence.

43. Es _____ sehr warm.

    (a) sind   (c) wird

    (b) hat   (d) wieder

44. Ich _____ Robert, wo das Restaurant ist.

    (a) frage   (c) werde

    (b) spiele   (d) wird

45. _____ fahren Sie morgen?

    (a) Heute   (c) Wer

    (b) Wohin   (d) Zu Hause

46. _____ siehst du im Park?

    (a) Wen   (c) Eine junge Frau

    (b) Der alte Mann   (d) Ein Bus

47. Ich _____ die junge Dame vor.

    (a) gehe   (c) steige

    (b) komme   (d) stelle

48. Das _____ ist sehr groß.

    (a) Lehrer   (c) Haus

    (b) Kinder   (d) Brief

49. Meine Eltern fahren _____.

    (a) mit dem Zug   (c) neu

    (b) zu Hause   (d) Berlin

50. Das _____ Glas war sehr alt.

    (a) neu   (c) schwarz und weiß

    (b) schlecht   (d) gelbe

PART THREE

LOTS MORE ABOUT VERBS

CHAPTER 11

More Talking About the Past

In this chapter you will learn:

Present Perfect Tense

So far in this book, you have learned the formation of the German simple past tense. That tense is used primarily in written language. In spoken language, events in the past are expressed, for the most part, in the present perfect tense.

The English present perfect tense consists of the conjugation of *to have* plus a past participle: *I have listened*, *they have spoken*, and so on. The German present perfect tense is formed similarly.

The verb **haben** is conjugated in the present tense and is accompanied by a past participle. Participles of regular verbs have the following structure: **ge-** + **verb stem** + **t**. For example:

fragen:
ge + frag + t = **gefragt**   er hat gefragt   *he has asked*

machen:
ge + mach + t = **gemacht**   er hat gemacht   *he has made*

If the infinitive has a separable prefix, that prefix will precede the **ge-** prefix of the participle. For example:

zumachen:
zu + ge + mach + t = **zugemacht**   er hat zugemacht   *he has closed*

And if the infinitive has an inseparable prefix, that prefix replaces the **ge-** prefix of the participle. For example:

besuchen:
be + such + t = **besucht**   er hat besucht   *he has visited*

erwarten:
er + wart + et = **erwartet**   er hat erwartet   *he has expected*

If the stem of the verb ends in **-d** or **-t**, add an **-e-** before the final **-t**, as in **erwart*e*t**.

Verbs that end with **-ieren** never have a **ge-** prefix added to the participle. For example:

studieren   er hat studiert   *he has studied*

diskutieren   er hat diskutiert   *he has discussed*

Written Practice 1

Conjugate the following regular verbs in the present perfect tense with the pronouns provided.

	lachen	versuchen	vorstellen
ich	_____	_____	_____
du	_____	_____	_____
er	_____	_____	_____
wir	_____	_____	_____
ihr	_____	_____	_____
sie	_____	_____	_____

IRREGULAR PAST PARTICIPLES

German has a long list of irregular past participles. If an irregular verb has no prefix, the participle will begin with the prefix **ge-** and most often end in **-en**. If the verb has a separable prefix, that prefix will precede the **ge-** prefix of the participle. And if the verb has an inseparable prefix, that prefix replaces the **ge-** prefix of the participle. Let's look at some examples of irregular past participles.

Verbs Without a Prefix

essen	gegessen	er hat gegessen	*he has eaten*
finden	gefunden	er hat gefunden	*he has found*
geben	gegeben	er hat gegeben	*he has given*
lesen	gelesen	er hat gelesen	*he has read*
schreiben	geschrieben	er hat geschrieben	*he has written*
sehen	gesehen	er hat gesehen	*he has seen*
singen	gesungen	er hat gesungen	*he has sung*
sprechen	gesprochen	er hat gesprochen	*he has spoken*
stehlen	gestohlen	er hat gestohlen	*he has stolen*
trinken	getrunken	er hat getrunken	*he has drunk*

Notice that **essen** requires a **g** after the **ge-** prefix of the participle.

Verbs with a Separable Prefix

ansehen	*to look at*	angesehen	er hat angesehen	*he has looked at*
ausgeben	*to spend*	ausgegeben	er hat ausgegeben	*he has spent*

| aussprechen | *to pronounce* | ausgesprochen | er hat ausgesprochen | *he has pronounced* |
| mitnehmen | *to take along* | mitgenommen | er hat mitgenommen | *he has taken along* |

Verbs with an Inseparable Prefix

besitzen	*to possess*	besessen	er hat besessen	*he has possessed*
erhalten	*to receive*	erhalten	er hat erhalten	*he has received*
versprechen	*to promise*	versprochen	er hat versprochen	*he has promised*
verstehen	*to understand*	verstanden	er hat verstanden	*he has understood*

Irregular Participles Ending in *-t*

absenden	*to dispatch*	abgesandt	er hat abgesandt	*he has dispatched*
erkennen	*to recognize*	erkannt	er hat erkannt	*he has recognized*
kennen	*to be acquainted*	gekannt	er hat gekannt	*he has been acquainted*
nennen	*to name*	genannt	er hat genannt	*he has named*
senden	*to send*	gesandt	er hat gesandt	*he has sent*
wissen	*to know*	gewusst	er hat gewusst	*he has known*

Be aware that you will encounter verbs whose participles will look like their infinitives. For example:

Infinitive		**Participle**	
erhalten	*to obtain*	hat erhalten	*has obtained*
bekommen	*to receive*	hat bekommen	*has received*

Written Practice 2

Conjugate the following irregular verbs in the present perfect tense with the pronouns provided.

	sprechen	**versprechen**	**aussprechen**
ich	_____	_____	_____
du	_____	_____	_____
er	_____	_____	_____
wir	_____	_____	_____
ihr	_____	_____	_____
sie	_____	_____	_____

	wissen	beschreiben (*describe*)	aussehen (*look like*)
ich	_____	_____	_____
du	_____	_____	_____
er	_____	_____	_____
wir	_____	_____	_____
ihr	_____	_____	_____
sie	_____	_____	_____

Although German verbs in the present perfect tense can be translated by the English present perfect tense, the English tendency is to use the simple past tense. For example:

Ich habe ihn besucht.

I have visited him. (present perfect)

I visited him. (simple past)

Therefore, where it sounds appropriate, the English past tense will be used in this book to translate the German present perfect tense.

A NOTE ABOUT WORD ORDER: *The verb **haben** is positioned in a present perfect sentence with the subject just as it would be in any other tense. But the past participle in the present perfect tense is always the last element of a sentence.*

Wir **haben** zwei lange Gedichte **gelernt.** *We **learned** two long poems.*

Look at that structure in the Oral Practice that follows.

Oral Practice

Practice saying the following list of sentences out loud.

Haben Sie die Musik gehört?   *Did you hear the music?*

Ja, ich habe die schöne Musik gehört.   *Yes, I heard the pretty music.*

Nein, ich habe nichts gehört.   *No, I heard nothing.*

Niemand hat die Musik gehört.	*No one heard the music.*
Hast du seinen Roman gelesen?	*Did you read his novel?*
Ja, ich habe ihn gelesen.	*Yes, I read it.*
Nein, ich habe ihn noch nicht gelesen.	*No, I still have not read it.*
Was hat er gekauft?	*What did he buy?*
Er hat nichts gekauft.	*He did not buy anything.*
Karin hat ihr Fahrrad verkauft.	*Karin sold her bicycle.*
Wie lange habt ihr auf mich gewartet?	*How long have you waited for me?*
Wir haben eine Stunde auf dich gewartet.	*We waited an hour for you.*
Haben Sie noch nicht gegessen?	*Have you not eaten yet?*
Nein, ich habe noch nicht gegessen.	*No, I have not eaten yet.*
Ich bin sehr hungrig. Und ich habe Durst.	*I am very hungry. And I am thirsty.*
Die alte Frau hat krank ausgesehen.	*The old woman looked sick.*
Robert hat meine Tasche gefunden.	*Robert found my purse.*
Die Kinder haben nichts verstanden.	*The children understood nothing.*
Aber er hat langsam gesprochen.	*But he spoke slowly.*

Written Practice 3

Rewrite the following present tense sentences changing them to the present perfect tense. For example:

Er kauft einen Hut. <u>Er hat einen Hut gekauft.</u>

1. Was sagst du? _____?

2. Wir lernen Deutsch. _____.

3. Die Kinder spielen gern im Park. _____.

4. Sehen Sie meinen Sohn? _____?

5. Wir erhalten drei Briefe von ihnen. _____ .

6. Robert wohnt in der Hauptstadt. _____ .

7. Hört ihr die schöne Musik? _____ ?

8. Die Männer zerstören das alte Haus. _____ .

9. Ich sende euch ein kleines Paket. _____ .

10. Wer arrangiert die Musik? _____ ?

11. Er verspricht es. _____ .

12. Was liest du? _____ ?

13. Gudrun nimmt mein Fahrrad. _____ .

14. Was stiehlt der Dieb? _____ ?

15. Niemand versteht dich. _____ .

Present Participles

English present participles are used extensively to express an action in progress or an incomplete action.

She was *combing* her hair.   They were *sitting* in the dark.

Although German also has present participles, they are not used in conjugations like English present participles. German present participles are used as modifiers.

A present participle is formed quite simply by adding **-d** to an infinitive: **fahren— fahren*d*, singen—singen*d*, schlafen—schlafen*d*.** When a present participle modifies a noun, it requires an adjective ending.

das schlafende Kind	*the sleeping child*
der fahrende Sänger	*the traveling (wandering) minstrel*
die singende Frau	*the singing woman*

As illustrated earlier, past participles are used in the structure of the present perfect tense. But, like present participles, they can also be used as modifiers. For example:

ein gebrochener Mensch	*a broken man*
das geschriebene Wort	*the written word*
ein gesuchter Wissenschaftler	*a much sought-after scientist*

Verbs That Take the Dative

German has a concept that does not exist in English: a category of verbs that require an object in the dative case. The translation of a sentence that has a dative verb in it appears in English to have a direct object. But in German, that object is not a direct object. It is a dative object.

Ich glaube **dem Mann** nicht.	*I do not believe **the man**.*

In the English sentence *the man* is a direct object. But **dem Mann** is in the dative case, because **glauben** is a dative verb. Other dative verbs are:

dienen	*to serve*	gehören	*to belong to*
folgen	*to follow*	helfen	*to help*
gefallen	*to please; like*	imponieren	*to impress*

The verbs **gefallen** and **gehören** are used in a special way. In the case of **gefallen**, the verb is used to express liking something. In English the structure is *subject + like + direct object*:

I + like + the book.	My mother + likes + the new car.

But the German structure is different, because the literal sentence is *something is pleasing to someone.*

Das Buch gefällt mir.	*(The book pleases me.) I like the book.*
Der neue Wagen gefällt meiner Mutter.	*(The new car pleases my mother.) My mother likes the new car.*

The verb **gehören** is also followed by the dative case. Unlike English, the preposition *to* is not needed for the meaning in German.

Das gehört mir.	*The book belongs to me.*
Der neue Wagen gehört meiner Mutter.	*The new car belongs to my mother.*

All dative verbs can be used in all the tenses. For example:

Ich glaube dem Mann nicht.	*I do not believe the man.*
Ich glaubte dem Mann nicht.	*I did not believe the man.*
Ich habe dem Mann nicht geglaubt.	*I did not believe the man.*
Wir helfen unserer Tante.	*We help our aunt.*
Wir halfen unserer Tante.	*We helped our aunt.*
Wir haben unserer Tante geholfen.	*We have helped our aunt.*

Oral Practice

Practice saying the following list of sentences out loud.

Hast du ihm nicht geglaubt?	*Did you not believe him?*
Nein, ich habe ihm niemals geglaubt.	*No, I have never believed him.*
Wem habt ihr geholfen?	*Whom did you help?*
Wir haben unserer Kusine geholfen.	*We helped our cousin.*
Sein Singen hat mir sehr imponiert.	*His singing really impressed me.*
Ihr Tanzen hat uns sehr imponiert.	*Her dancing really impressed us.*
Niemand hat dem König gedient.	*No one served the king.*
Wer dient der Königin?	*Who is serving the queen?*
Der Mann folgt uns.	*The man is following us.*
Nein. Niemand folgt uns.	*No. No one is following us.*
Wie gefällt dir mein Fahrrad?	*How do you like my bike?*
Es gefällt mir gut.	*I like it a lot.*
Gehört Ihnen dieser Roman?	*Does this novel belong to you?*
Nein, er gehört mir nicht.	*No, it does not belong to me.*
Dieser Roman gehört meiner Kusine.	*This novel belongs to my cousin.*

Prepositions That Take the Dative

The dative case is used for indirect objects and follows dative verbs. It is also required for objects of dative prepositions. The dative prepositions are:

aus	*out*; *from*	nach	*after*
außer	*except*	seit	*since*
gegenüber	*opposite*; *across from*	von	*from*
mit	*with*	zu	*to*
bei	*by*; *at* (for example, living at someone's house)		

The preposition **gegenüber** follows a pronoun and can follow or precede a noun. If the noun refers to a person, it tends to follow the noun.

Wir sitzen einer schönen Frau gegenüber.	*We sit across from a pretty woman.*
Wir sitzen ihr gegenüber.	*We sit across from her.*
Wir wohnen gegenüber der Bibliothek.	*We live across from the library.*

The other dative prepositions precede both nouns and pronouns. In sentences, the dative prepositions look like this:

Die Mädchen kamen aus dem Theater.	*The girls came out of the theater.*
Niemand hörte es außer meinem Freund.	*No one heard it except my friend.*
Tina hat bei ihrer Tante gewohnt.	*Tina lived at her aunt's house.*
Ich habe mit dem Hund gespielt.	*I played with the dog.*
Nach der Oper gingen wir nach Hause.	*After the opera we went home.*
Seit zwei Stunden wartet er im Flur.	*He has been waiting in the hallway for two hours.*
Ich fahre von Hamburg nach Bremen.	*I drive from Hamburg to Bremen.*
Fährt diese Straßenbahn zum Bahnhof?	*Does this streetcar go to the train station?*

When going home, or to a city, country, or continent, use **nach** to mean *to*.

Wir fahren nach Deutschland.	*We are going to Germany.*
Wir fahren nach Hause.	*We are going home.*

Use **nach** with the dative case to mean *after*.

nach dem Konzert	*after the concert*	nach einer Stunde	*after an hour*

Oral Practice

Practice saying the following list of sentences out loud.

Die Kinder kommen aus der Schule.	*The children are coming out of the school.*
Wer kommt aus der Bibliothek?	*Who is coming out of the library?*
Niemand kommt aus der Bibliothek.	*No one is coming out of the library.*
Niemand versteht mich außer Karl.	*No one understands me except Karl.*
Niemand besucht mich außer meinem Onkel.	*No one visits me except my uncle.*
Niemand hilft mir außer dir.	*No one helps me except you.*
Sie hat bei uns gewohnt.	*She lived at our house.*
Habt ihr bei euren Eltern gewohnt?	*Did you live at your parents' house?*
Nein, wir haben bei Freunden gewohnt.	*No, we lived with friends.*
Mit wem hat er getanzt?	*With whom did he dance?*
Er hat mit der schönen Studentin getanzt.	*He danced with the pretty student.*
Sie half mir nach der Arbeit.	*She helped me after work.*
Sie halfen mir nach dem Fußballspiel.	*They helped me after the soccer game.*
Ich wohne seit März in Darmstadt.	*I have been living in Darmstadt since March.*
Ich bin seit drei Wochen hier.	*I have been here for three weeks.*
Das ist ein Geschenk von der Königin.	*That is a gift from the queen.*
Ich habe es vom König erhalten.	*I received it from the king.*
Um wie viel Uhr gehst du zur Schule?	*What time do you go to school?*
Um wie viel Uhr ging er zur Arbeit?	*What time did he go to work?*

It is common to form contractions with the prepositions **von** and **zu**.

von + dem   →   **vom**

zu + dem   →   **zum**

zu + der   →   **zur**

Written Practice 4

Rewrite each sentence with the nouns or pronouns provided in parentheses. Apply the dative case appropriately.

1. Der Ausländer hat mit _____ gesprochen.

   (die Kinder) _____.

   (meine Tante) _____.

   (der König) _____.

   (ich) _____.

   (wir) _____.

   (sie *pl.*) _____.

2. Gudrun wohnt seit April bei _____.

   (ihre Eltern) _____.

   (meine Schwester) _____.

   (ein Freund) _____.

   (er) _____.

   (sie *s.*) _____.

   (ich) _____.

3. Sie bekommt einen Brief von _____.

   (ihre Eltern) _____.

   (ein Ausländer) _____.

   (dein Bruder) _____.

   (du) _____.

   (ihr) _____.

Geography

In this book you have already encountered several geographical regions and cities. Let's take a look at a few more.

Afrika	*Africa*	die Erdteile	*the continents*
Asien	*Asia*	Europa	*Europe*
Australien	*Australia*	Mittelamerika	*Central America*
die Antarktis	*Antartica*	Nordamerika	*North America*
die Erde	*the Earth*	Südamerika	*South America*

Oral Practice

Practice saying the following list of sentences out loud.

Wo liegt Deutschland?	*Where is Germany located?*
Deutschland liegt in Europa.	*Germany is located in Europe.*
Liegt Hamburg im Norden oder Süden?	*Is Hamburg located in the north or the south?*
Hamburg liegt im Norden.	*Hamburg is located in the north.*
Wo liegt Belgien?	*Where is Belgium located?*
Belgien liegt im Westen.	*Belgium is located in the west.*
Wo liegt Bulgarien?	*Where is Bulgaria located?*
Bulgarien liegt im Osten.	*Bulgaria is located in the east.*
Ist Griechenland im Norden?	*Is Greece in the north?*
Nein, Griechenland ist im Süden.	*No, Greece is in the south.*
Andere europäische Länder sind:	*Other European countries include:*
Estland	*Estonia*
Frankreich	*France*
Großbritannien	*Great Britain*
Irland	*Ireland*
Lettland	*Latvia*
Litauen	*Lithuania*
die Niederlande	*the Netherlands*

Norwegen	*Norway*
Portugal	*Portugal*
Rumänien	*Romania*
Russland	*Russia*
die Slowakei	*Slovakia*
Spanien	*Spain*
Tschechien	*Czech Republic*
Ukraine	*Ukraine*
Weißrussland	*White Russia*

Written Practice 5

Combine each country and capital in a sentence. Use the example sentence as your pattern. Notice the usage of a final possessive **-s** on the country name.

(Deutschland, Berlin) *Die Hauptstadt Deutschlands ist Berlin.*

1. (Frankreich, Paris) _____.
2. (Italien, Rom) _____.
3. (Russland, Moskau) _____.
4. (Norwegen, Oslo) _____.
5. (Polen, Warschau) _____.
6. (Spanien, Madrid) _____.
7. (Tschechien, Prag) _____.
8. (Griechenland, Athen) _____.
9. (Japan, Tokio) _____.
10. (Österreich, Wien) _____.

QUIZ

1. Write the present perfect tense conjugation for the following verbs with the pronouns provided.

	dienen	**verkaufen**	**vorstellen**
ich	_____	_____	_____
du	_____	_____	_____
er	_____	_____	_____
wir	_____	_____	_____
ihr	_____	_____	_____
sie	_____	_____	_____

2. Provide the past participle for the following verbs.

sagen	_____	trinken	_____
imponieren	_____	erkennen	_____
gehören	_____	aussehen	_____
schreiben	_____	helfen	_____
essen	_____	glauben	_____
tun	_____	stehlen	_____
lesen	_____	besitzen	_____

3. Write the present, past, and present perfect conjugations of each of the following verbs with the pronouns provided. For example:

fragen

ich	_frage_	_fragte_	_habe gefragt_
du	_fragst_	_fragtest_	_hast gefragt_

finden

ich	_____	_____	_____
du	_____	_____	_____

ausgeben

du _____   _____   _____

er _____   _____   _____

Using the appropriate form of the dative case, rewrite each sentence filling in the blank with the words in parentheses.

4. Warum glaubt er _____ nicht?

(sein Bruder) _____?

(diese Dame) _____?

(die Männer) _____?

(ich) _____?

(wir) _____?

5. Ich habe gestern mit _____ gesprochen.

(deine Kusine) _____.

(der König) _____.

(er) _____.

(sie *s.*) _____.

(sie *pl.*) _____.

Circle the letter of the word or phrase that best completes each sentence.

6. Warum hat der Mann so _____ gesprochen?

  (a) niemals   (c) gefallen

  (b) schnell   (d) gestern

7. Ich habe dreißig Minuten _____ dich gewartet.

  (a) heute   (c) getan

  (b) vom   (d) auf

8. Habt ihr diesen Roman _____?

  (a) mit einem Freund   (c) schreibt

  (b) gelesen   (d) zu euren Eltern

9. Meine Wirtin hat mit meinem Sohn _____ .

   (a) gespielt   (c) verstanden

   (b) aufgemacht   (d) erkannt

10. Der neue Manager steht unserem Chef _____ .

   (a) gegenüber   (c) von

   (b) bei   (d) außer

CHAPTER 12

Important Details

In this chapter you will learn:

Present Perfect Tense with *Sein*

German has a concept in the present perfect tense that no longer exists in English. Certain German verbs require **sein** as their auxiliary in the present perfect tense rather than **haben**. In an earlier form of English, the same thing occurred with the verb *to be*. Consider this line from the Bible: *The Lord is come.* Today, that would be said as: *The Lord has come.*

When **sein** is the auxiliary in the present perfect tense, the past participles still have the same regular and irregular formations as those with **haben**. For example:

reisen		**fahren**	
ich bin gereist	*I have traveled*	ich bin gefahren	*I have driven*
du bist gereist	*you have traveled*	du bist gefahren	*you have driven*
er ist gereist	*he has traveled*	er ist gefahren	*he has driven*
wir sind gereist	*we have traveled*	wir sind gefahren	*we have driven*
ihr seid gereist	*you have traveled*	ihr seid gefahren	*you have driven*
sie sind gereist	*they have traveled*	sie sind gefahren	*they have driven*

Of course, the question is: How do you know when to use **haben** and when to use **sein**? In general, use **haben** with verbs that are transitive, that is, verbs that take a direct object.

Er hat den Roman gelesen. *He read the novel.* (*Novel* is the direct object.)

And use **sein** with verbs of motion, that is, verbs whose action requires movement from one place to another. For example:

Er ist nach Deutschland gefahren. *He drove to Germany.* (Shows movement from an original location to Germany.)

It is possible to test for verbs of motion by giving a command with the verb. If the action can be carried out without moving the feet from one place to another, the verb is probably transitive and will use **haben** as its auxiliary. For example:

Sing. Read a book. Keep the money.

But if the feet have to move to carry out the action of the verb, the verb is probably a verb of motion and will use **sein** as its auxiliary. For example:

Run. Go home. Fly to Munich.

Sein is also used with verbs that show a change of physical state or a state over which a person has no direct control.

Er ist in Amerika gestorben.	*He died in America.* (Dying is a change of physical state and is one over which a person has no control.)

It is also possible to test for this usage of **sein** by giving a command with the verb. If there is no tangible action of the verb and it describes a state or condition, the verb will probably use **sein** as its auxiliary. For example:

Be nice.   Become a doctor.   Don't die.

You have already encountered many verbs in the present and past tenses that use **sein** as the auxiliary in the present perfect tense. Let's look at some conjugations in the third person singular.

Regular Verbs

folgen	er ist gefolgt	*he has followed*
marschieren	er ist marschiert	*he has marched*
reisen	er ist gereist	*he has traveled*
spazieren	er ist spaziert	*he has strolled*

Irregular Verbs

ankommen	er ist angekommen	*he has arrived*
bleiben	er ist geblieben	*he has stayed*
einsteigen	er ist eingestiegen	*he has gotten on (transportation)*
fahren	er ist gefahren	*he has driven*
fallen	er ist gefallen	*he has fallen*
fliegen	er ist geflogen	*he has flown*
gehen	er ist gegangen	*he has gone*
kommen	er ist gekommen	*he has come*
laufen	er ist gelaufen	*he has run*
mitgehen	er ist mitgegangen	*he has gone along*
rennen	er ist gerannt	*he has run*
sterben	er ist gestorben	*he has died*
umsteigen	er ist umgestiegen	*he has transferred*

NOTE: *Remember that the German present perfect tense tends to be translated into English in the simple past tense. But the example sentences above were translated into English in the present perfect tense to emphasize that **sein** means* to have *in this conjugation.*

Written Practice 1

Write the present perfect tense conjugation of the following verbs with the pronouns provided.

	spazieren	kommen	umsteigen
ich	_____	_____	_____
du	_____	_____	_____
er	_____	_____	_____
wir	_____	_____	_____
ihr	_____	_____	_____
sie	_____	_____	_____

	bleiben	sterben	folgen
ich	_____	_____	_____
du	_____	_____	_____
er	_____	_____	_____
wir	_____	_____	_____
ihr	_____	_____	_____
sie	_____	_____	_____

Oral Practice

Practice saying the following list of sentences out loud.

Wann kommt dein Vater?	*When is your father coming?*
Er ist schon gekommen.	*He has already come.*
Wann kommen deine Eltern?	*When are your parents coming?*
Sie sind schon gekommen.	*They have already come.*
Wir sind in der Hauptstraße eingestiegen.	*We got on on Main Street.*
Wir sind am Marktplatz ausgestiegen.	*We got off at the market square.*
Wie lange seid ihr da geblieben?	*How long did you stay there?*
Wir sind den ganzen Tag da geblieben.	*We stayed there the whole day.*
Wohin ist Tina geflogen?	*Where did Tina fly?*

Sie ist nach Tokio geflogen.	*She flew to Tokyo.*
Sie ist gestern angekommen.	*She arrived yesterday.*
Lebt der Kranke noch?	*Is the patient still alive?*
Nein, er ist leider gestorben.	*No, unfortunately he died.*
Wohnen Ihre Eltern noch in Bonn?	*Do your parents still live in Bonn?*
Nein, sie sind vor einem Jahr gestorben.	*No, they died a year ago.*
Wann ist er nach Norwegen gereist?	*When did he travel to Norway?*
Er ist vor drei Tagen nach Norwegen gereist.	*He traveled to Norway three days ago.*

A Special Use of *Vor*

Use **vor** with the dative case to express how much time *ago* something occurred.

vor einer Woche	*a week ago*	vor einem Tag	*one day ago*
vor zwei Wochen	*two weeks ago*	vor zehn Tagen	*ten days ago*
vor einem Monat	*a month ago*	vor einem Jahr	*one year ago*
vor drei Monaten	*three months ago*	vor elf Jahren	*eleven years ago*

The verbs **sein** and **werden** are important verbs and must be looked at separately. They both use **sein** as their auxiliary in the present perfect tense, because these verbs describe a state: *to be* and *to become*. Their conjugations look like this in the present perfect tense:

sein		**werden**	
ich bin gewesen	*I have been*	ich bin geworden	*I have become*
du bist gewesen	*you have been*	du bist geworden	*you have become*
er ist gewesen	*he has been*	er ist geworden	*he has become*
wir sind gewesen	*we have been*	wir sind geworden	*we have become*
ihr seid gewesen	*you have been*	ihr seid geworden	*you have become*
sie sind gewesen	*they have been*	sie sind geworden	*they have become*

A third important verb to discuss is **haben**. It is a transitive verb and therefore uses **haben** in its present perfect tense conjugation.

ich habe gehabt	*I have had*	wir haben gehabt	*we have had*
du hast gehabt	*you have had*	ihr habt gehabt	*you have had*
er hat gehabt	*he has had*	sie haben gehabt	*they have had*

Use the contraction im (**in** + **dem**) with the four seasons of the year (**die vier Jahreszeiten**). All seasons are masculine.

im Winter	*in the winter*	im Sommer	*in the summer*
im Frühling	*in the spring*	im Herbst	*in the fall/autumn*

Oral Practice

Practice saying the following list of sentences out loud.

Wo sind Sie gewesen, Herr Benz?	*Where were you, Mr. Benz?*
Ich bin in Frankreich gewesen.	*I was in France.*
Ich habe meine Verwandten besucht.	*I visited my relatives.*
Es ist schon kalt geworden.	*It has already become cold.*
Ja, das Wetter im Winter ist immer kalt.	*Yes, the weather in winter is always cold.*
Haben Sie einen warmen Mantel?	*Do you have a warm coat?*
Ich habe lange in diesem Klima gelebt.	*I have lived a long time in this climate.*
Ich habe immer einen warmen Mantel gehabt.	*I have always had a warm coat.*
Ist Ihr Sohn krank gewesen?	*Was your son sick?*
Ja, er hat eine Erkältung bekommen.	*Yes, he caught a cold.*
Er ist sehr krank gewesen.	*He was very sick.*
Er ist nicht zur Schule gegangen.	*He did not go to school.*
Er ist vier Tage zu Hause geblieben.	*He stayed home four days.*
Meine Tochter ist im Sommer krank gewesen.	*My daughter was sick in the summer.*
Im Frühling ist die ganze Familie nach Belgien gereist.	*In the spring the whole family traveled to Belgium.*
Im Herbst ist die ganze Familie nach Irland geflogen.	*In the fall the whole family flew to Ireland.*

Written Practice 2

Rewrite the following present tense sentences changing them to the present perfect tense.

1. Ich bin sehr müde. _____ .
2. Wird deine Schwester wieder gesund? _____ ?
3. Der Zug kommt um elf Uhr zehn an. _____ .
4. Die Kinder bleiben in der Stadt. _____ .
5. Die Touristen gehen zum Rathaus. _____ .
6. Meine Eltern gehen im Park spazieren. _____ .
7. Wir haben Hunger. _____ .
8. Wohin fährst du? _____ ?
9. Die Jungen laufen zum Marktplatz. _____ .
10. Sie haben kein Geld. _____ .

Expressing Hunger and Thirst with *Haben*

When talking about *hunger* or *thirst*, it is possible to use the German adjectives **hungrig** and **durstig**. However, a more commonly used expression uses **haben** with the noun form of both words.

Ich habe Hunger.	*I am hungry.*
Ich habe Durst.	*I am thirsty.*

Accusative-Dative Prepositions

You have already encountered prepositions that take the accusative case and prepositions that take the dative case in this book. There is another category of prepositions that can take either the accusative case or the dative case. These prepositions are:

an	*at; to; on*	über	*over, above; about*
auf	*on*	unter	*under; among*

hinter	*behind*	vor	*before, in front of*
in	*in, into*	zwischen	*between*
neben	*next to*		

This use of two cases may seem confusing at first glance, but there is a simple explanation for it. If the preposition is used with the accusative case, it is being used to show motion to a place. If the preposition is used with the dative case, it is being used to show a location. For example:

Showing Motion to a Place—Accusative

Ich hänge ein Bild an die Wand.	*I hang a picture on the wall.*
Ich lege das Buch auf den Tisch.	*I lay the book on the table.*
Ich laufe hinter die Tür.	*I run behind the door.*
Ich gehe in die Schule.	*I go into the school.*
Ich setze mich neben den Lehrer.	*I seat myself next to the teacher.*
Ich hänge ein Bild über den Tisch.	*I hang a picture over the table.*
Ich lege Papier unter den Stuhl.	*I lay paper under the chair.*
Ich stelle eine Stehlampe vor das Klavier.	*I place a floor lamp in front of the piano.*
Ich stelle einen Stuhl zwischen die Tische.	*I place a chair between the tables.*

Showing Location—Dative

Ein Bild hängt an der Wand.	*A picture is hanging on the wall.*
Das Buch liegt auf dem Tisch.	*The book is lying on the table.*
Ich stehe hinter der Tür.	*I stand behind the door.*
Ich bin in der Schule.	*I am in the school.*
Ich sitze neben dem Lehrer.	*I am sitting next to the teacher.*
Ein Bild hängt über dem Tisch.	*A picture is hanging over the table.*
Papier liegt unter dem Stuhl.	*Paper is lying under the chair.*
Eine Stehlampe steht vor dem Klavier.	*A floor lamp is standing in front of the piano.*
Ein Stuhl steht zwischen den Tischen.	*A chair stands between the tables.*

There is a tendency in German to use a more specific word for the English verb *to put*. If you are putting something in a horizontal position, you should use **legen** (*to lay*). If you are putting something in a vertical position, you should use **stellen** (*to place upright*). Use the accusative case with these two verbs and the accusative-dative prepositions.

Er legt das Heft auf das Bett.	*He lays the notebook on the bed.*

If you use **stellen** in this sentence instead of **legen**, it will mean that he is propping up the notebook so it can stand on one edge.

Er stellt die Vase auf das Klavier.	*He places the vase on the piano.*

If you use **legen** in this sentence instead of **stellen**, it will mean that he is laying the vase on its side.

When persons or objects are already located in a horizontal or vertical position use **liegen** (*to lie, be situated*) and **stehen** (*to stand*) respectively, with the dative case. For example:

Das Heft liegt auf dem Bett.	*The notebook is lying on the bed.*
Die Vase steht auf dem Klavier.	*The vase is standing on the piano.*

Notice that **legen** and **stellen** are regular verbs and **liegen** and **stehen** are irregular verbs. Let's look at the principal parts of their conjugations in the three tenses you know.

Present:	er legt	er stellt	er liegt	er steht
Past:	er legte	er stellte	er lag	er stand
Present Perfect:	er hat gelegt	er hat gestellt	er hat gelegen	er hat gestanden

Oral Practice

Practice saying the following list of sentences out loud.

Warum läuft der Hund an die Tür?	*Why is the dog running to the door?*
Jemand steht an der Tür und klopft.	*Someone is standing at the door and knocking.*

Ich habe mich ans Fenster gesetzt.	*I seated myself at the window.*
Ich habe mich zwischen die Jungen gesetzt.	*I seated myself between the boys.*
Ich habe die Kleider in den Schrank gehängt.	*I hung up the clothes in the wardrobe.*
Ich habe den Tisch neben das Sofa gestellt.	*I placed the table next to the sofa.*
Der Brief hat unter dem Stuhl gelegen.	*The letter lay under the chair.*
Sie hat den Brief auf den Tisch gelegt.	*She laid the letter on the table.*
Das neue Hotel ist neben dem Rathaus.	*The new hotel is next to city hall.*
Die Touristen haben vor dem Rathaus gestanden.	*The tourists stood in front of city hall.*
Wohin hat sie den Regenschirm gestellt?	*Where did she put the umbrella?*
Sie hat den Regenschirm hinter den Schrank gestellt.	*She put the umbrella behind the wardrobe.*
Karin hängt das Poster über das Bett.	*Karin hangs the poster over the bed.*
Was hängt über deinem Bett?	*What hangs above your bed?*
Über meinem Bett hängt ein Poster.	*A poster hangs above my bed.*
Frau Kamps legt das Baby aufs Bett.	*Ms. Kamps lays the baby on the bed.*
Wer schläft auf dem Bett?	*Who is sleeping on the bed?*
Das Baby schläft auf dem Bett.	*The baby is sleeping on the bed.*

Did you notice the words **ans** and **aufs** in these sentences? Certain prepositions can form contractions. You have already encountered a few. Let's add to that list. The following prepositions combine with **das** in the accusative case.

ans	(an + das)
aufs	(auf + das)
ins	(in + das)

In certain contexts the rules of movement to a place and location do not apply with these prepositions. For example, **warten auf** means *to wait for* and requires the use of the accusative case. But there is no actual movement of a person or object. With such verb and preposition combinations, the appropriate case must be memorized. Let's look at some of these verb and preposition combinations. The letter A designates the use of the accusative case, and the letter D designates the use of the dative case.

warten auf A	Ich warte auf ihn.	*I am waiting for him.*
glauben an A	Er glaubt an Gott.	*He believes in God.*
denken an A	Sie denkt an ihre Mutter.	*She thinks about her mother.*
sich verlieben in A	Ich verliebe mich in sie.	*I fall in love with her.*
sein unter D	Er war unter den Gästen.	*He was among the guests.*
reden über A	Sie redet über das Problem.	*She talks about the problem.*

When you encounter a new verb with one of the accusative-dative prepositions, check in a dictionary to determine which case to use.

The preposition **entlang** follows a noun and is used in the accusative case to indicate motion down the middle of a place or *along* a location.

Wir sind den Fluss entlang gegangen.   *We went along the river.*

But when **entlang** is used in combination with **an**, the case needed is the dative case. Its meaning is then *alongside* a place.

Wir sind am Fluss entlang gegangen.   *We went alongside the river.*

Written Practice 3

Rewrite each sentence filling in the blank with the words in parentheses.

Er geht an _____.
(die Tür) *Er geht an die Tür.*

1. Wir haben eine Stunde auf _____ gewartet.

   (er) _____.

   (du) _____.

(dieser Ausländer) _____.

(unsere Wirtin) _____.

(die Diplomaten) _____.

(ihr) _____.

2. Ich denke niemals an _____ .

(diese Probleme) _____.

(meine Arbeit) _____.

(unser König) _____.

(sie *s*.) _____.

(Sie) _____.

(sie *pl*.) _____.

Other Verb Prefixes

You are already aware of the separable and inseparable prefixes. There are a few other prefixes that are sometimes separable and sometimes inseparable. They are:

	Separable		**Inseparable**	
durch-	dúrchfallen	*to fail*	durchfáhren	*to drive through*
hinter-	N/A		hinterlássen	*to leave behind*
über-	überhängen	*to hang over*	übertréiben	*to exaggerate*
um-	úmkommen	*to die*	umármen	*to embrace*
unter-	únterbringen	*to put up, accommodate*	unterbréchen	*to interrupt*
voll-	vólltanken	*to fill up the tank*	vollénden	*to complete*
wider-	wíderspiegeln	*to reflect*	widerstéhen	*to resist*
wieder-	wíederkehren	*to return*	wiederhólen	*to repeat*

When the accent is on the prefix of the verb, the prefix is separable: **dúrchfallen—er fällt durch** (*he fails*). When the accent is on the stem of the verb, the prefix is inseparable: **übertréiben—er übertréibt** (*he exaggerates*).

Written Practice 4

Write the present, past, and present perfect conjugations of the following verbs with the pronouns provided. For example:

haben

er ___ *hat* _____ *hatte* _____ *hat gehabt* _____

1. unterbrechen

   ich _____

   du _____

   ihr _____

2. widerspiegeln

   er _____

   wir _____

   du _____

Subordinating Conjunctions

Subordinating conjunctions introduce a clause that, when stated alone, does not make complete sense. For example:

Er hat gesagt, dass es spät wurde.   *He said that it was getting late.*

The subordinate clause *that it was getting late* does not make complete sense on its own. In German the subordinating conjunction (which in this sentence would be **dass** [*that*]) is the signal that there will be a word order change in the sentence: The conjugated verb will be the last element in the sentence. Notice the position of the conjugated verb in the following subordinate clauses.

Ich weiß, dass er kein Geld **hat**.   *I know that he has no money.*

Er schreibt, dass seine Mutter   *He writes that his mother has died.*
   gestorben **ist**.

Some of the commonly used subordinating conjunctions are:

als	*when* (past tense)	während	*while*
ob	*whether, if*	wenn	*when(ever)*
nachdem	*after*		

In sentences, they look like this:

Erik fragt, ob die Kinder Hunger haben.	*Erik asks whether the children are hungry.*
Ich besuche Martin, wenn ich in Bern bin.	*I visit Martin whenever I am in Bern.*
Als wir in Stuttgart waren, gingen wir oft ins Theater.	*When we were in Stuttgart, we often went to the theater.*
Nachdem das Baby gegessen hat, haben die Eltern Karten gespielt.	*After the baby ate, the parents played cards.*
Tina hat die Dokumente gefunden, während wir in Paris gewesen sind.	*Tina found the documents while we were in Paris.*

Written Practice 5

Complete each sentence with the clauses provided. For example:

Er schreibt, dass…

Die Kinder lernen jetzt Deutsch.

Er schreibt, dass die Kinder jetzt Deutsch lernen.

1. Sie wissen nicht, dass…

    Es ist wieder sehr kalt geworden.

    _____.

    Onkel Peter ist vor zwei Tagen gestorben.

    _____.

2. Niemand fragt, ob…

    Sie wohnen noch in Freiburg.

    _____.

    Wir glauben ihnen.

    _____.

3. Sie hat ihre Tasche verloren, während…

   Sie ist in Schweden gewesen.

   _____.

   Sie hat mit den Kindern gespielt.

   _____.

4. Die Königin fragt, ob…

   Der König ist noch in Frankreich.

   _____.

   Ihre Kinder sind schon nach Italien gereist.

   _____.

   Die alte Frau hat Hunger gehabt.

   _____.

   Der Wissenschaftler hat den Leuten geholfen.

   _____.

Food and Beverages

You already know how to use the verbs **essen** and **trinken**. Now you need some food and beverages to use them with. And remember, when you order food and beverages, use the verb **bestellen**.

das Essen	*food*	die Getränke	*beverages*
die Bratwurst	*roasted sausage*	das Pils	*lager beer*
die Erbsen	*peas*	der Wein	*wine*
der Fisch	*fish*	das Wasser	*water*
das Hähnchen	*chicken*	die Coca	*Coca-Cola*
die Kartoffeln	*potatoes*	die Cola	*Coca-Cola*
der Käse	*cheese*	der Sekt	*(German) champagne*
der Kohl	*cabbage*	der Schinken	*ham*
das Rindfleisch	*beef*	das Obst	*fruit*
das Gemüse	*vegetables*		

Oral Practice

Practice saying the following list of sentences out loud. Then restate the sentences using the vocabulary in the preceding list.

Ich esse gern Bratwurst und Käse.	*I like eating roasted sausage and cheese.*
Er trinkt gern Wein oder Sekt.	*He likes drinking wine or champagne.*
Ich habe nur Gemüse bestellt.	*I only ordered vegetables.*

QUIZ

1. Write the present perfect conjugation of the following verbs with the pronouns provided.

	gehen	marschieren	umsteigen
ich	_____	_____	_____
du	_____	_____	_____
er	_____	_____	_____
wir	_____	_____	_____

	ankommen	reisen	folgen
ich	_____	_____	_____
du	_____	_____	_____
ihr	_____	_____	_____
sie *pl.*	_____	_____	_____

2. In the blanks provided write the auxiliary **haben** if the verb is transitive or write the auxiliary **sein** if the verb is intransitive or is a verb of motion.

_____	gelaufen	_____	gesehen
_____	gesprochen	_____	gelernt
_____	mitgegangen	_____	gekommen

_____ diskutiert		_____ gestorben	
_____ verstanden		_____ gewusst	
_____ geschrieben		_____ versprochen	
_____ geworden		_____ gewesen	
_____ gehabt		_____ getrunken	
_____ geblieben		_____ abgesandt	

3. Write the accusative and dative forms of the following words and phrases.

	Accusative	Dative
(ich)	_____	_____
(du)	_____	_____
(er)	_____	_____
(sie _s._)	_____	_____
(wir)	_____	_____
(ihr)	_____	_____
(sie _pl._)	_____	_____
(dieser Ausländer)	_____	_____
(das Mädchen)	_____	_____
(die Musik)	_____	_____
(viele Romane)	_____	_____

4. Rewrite the sentence below filling in the blank with the words in parentheses.

Er ist vor _____ angekommen.

(ein Tag) _____.

(drei Wochen) _____.

(eine Woche) _____.

(eine Minute) _____.

(ein Jahr) _____.

(zwei Jahre) _____.

5. Rewrite the sentence below with the subordinate clauses provided.

    Mein Bruder schreibt, dass…
    Seine Frau ist Ärztin geworden.

    _____.

    Er hat ein Haus in der Hauptstadt gekauft.

    _____.

    Unser Onkel kommt im Februar zu Besuch.

    _____.

    Niemand hat seinen neuen Roman gelesen.

    _____.

Circle the letter of the word or phrase that best completes each sentence.

6. Der alte Herr ist _____ gestorben.

    (a) noch   (c) morgen

    (b) leider   (d) ins Wohnzimmer

7. Wir haben die _____ Musik gehört.

    (a) schöne   (c) dienen

    (b) alt   (d) langsam

8. Ich bin _____ in Russland gewesen.

    (a) während   (c) vor

    (b) niemand   (d) niemals

9. Niemand hat _____ bestellt.

    (a) ins Wohnzimmer   (c) an die Tür

    (b) dem Chef   (d) den Wein

10. Mein Großvater liegt auf _____.

    (a) dem Bett   (c) im Flur

    (b) das Wohnzimmer   (d) den Schrank

CHAPTER 13

Talking About the Future

In this chapter you will learn:

Future Tense

You have already been using a form of the future tense, because German—like English—can use a present tense conjugation to infer the future tense. This is particularly true when there is an adverb in the sentence indicating the future.

Wir gehen **morgen** in die Stadt.   *We are going to the city **tomorrow**.*

But there is another way to express the future tense. Just as English has a future tense auxiliary (*shall*, *will*), German uses **werden** as its future tense auxiliary. The future tense structure is quite simple: Conjugate **werden** in the present tense and end the sentence with an infinitive. For example:

Ich werde meine Tante besuchen.   *I will visit my aunt.*

Wirst du ihm helfen?   *Will you help him?*

Sie werden in Polen bleiben.   *They will stay in Poland.*

Written Practice 1

Write the following verbs in the future tense with the pronouns provided.

	fahren	**aufmachen**	**beschreiben**
ich			
du			
er			
wir			

	haben	**sein**	**werden**
ich			
er			
ihr			
sie *pl.*			

Since the future tense is composed of **werden** plus an infinitive, you need not be concerned with whether a verb is regular or irregular or whether it has a prefix or not.

Regular verb:	Sie wird fragen.	*She will ask.*
Irregular verb:	Sie wird sprechen.	*She will speak.*
Separable prefix:	Sie wird zumachen.	*She will close.*
Inseparable prefix:	Sie wird bekommen.	*She will receive.*

Oral Practice

Practice saying the following list of sentences out loud.

Werden Sie Ihrem Freund helfen?	*Will you help your friend?*
Ja, ich werde ihm helfen.	*Yes, I will help him.*
Nein, ich werde ihm nicht helfen.	*No, I will not help him.*
Wird Frau Bauer die Kinder mitnehmen?	*Will Ms. Bauer take the children along?*
Ja, sie wird die Kinder mitnehmen.	*Yes, she will take the children along.*
Nein, sie wird sie nicht mitnehmen.	*No, she will not take them along.*
Werden sie lachen oder weinen?	*Will they laugh or cry?*
Sie werden wahrscheinlich lachen.	*They will probably cry.*
Sie werden ein bisschen weinen.	*They will cry a little.*
Was wirst du tun?	*What will you do?*
Ich werde einen Job suchen.	*I will look for a job.*
Was werdet ihr tun?	*What will you do?*
Wir werden unsere Verwandten suchen.	*We will look for our relatives.*

Written Practice 2

Rewrite the future tense sentences below as present tense sentences using **morgen** to infer the future tense. For example:

Ich werde das alte Haus verkaufen.
Morgen verkaufe ich das alte Haus.

1. Sie wird ein Glas Rotwein bestellen.

   _____.

2. Die Familie wird drei Briefe erhalten.

   _____.

3. Der Vater wird wieder weinen.

   _____.

4. Die Ausländer werden am Marktplatz umsteigen.

_____

5. Wirst du wieder nach Portugal fliegen?

_____

6. Er wird den interessanten Roman lesen.

_____

7. Die Kinder werden unter dem Tisch spielen.

_____

Negatives

Like English, German can only have one negative in a sentence. The double negative is not an option. Let's look at some examples.

Ich verstehe **nichts**.	_I **do not** understand **anything**._ _(I understand **nothing**.)_
Er fuhr **nicht** in die Stadt.	_He **did not** drive to the city._
Wir haben **keine** Zeit.	_We have **no** time._
Niemand hat ihm geholfen.	_**No one** helped him._
Er hat mich **niemals** verstanden.	_He **never** understood me._

NOTE: _The adverb **niemals** is often said as **nie**._

Adverbs of Time, Manner, and Place

German has special rules for using adverbial expressions when more than one adverb will appear in a sentence. Adverbs of time will appear first, adverbs of manner second, and adverbs of place last. First, let's look at these adverbs individually.

When adverbs of time alone are used in a sentence, they follow the conjugated verb.

Ich fahre **heute** in die Stadt.   *I am driving to the city **today**.*

Sie hat **jetzt** keine Zeit.   *She has no time **now**.*

When adverbs of manner alone are used in a sentence, they follow the conjugated verb.

Ich fahre **mit dem Bus**.   *I am going **by bus**.*

Der Vater kommt **mit dem Auto**.   *The father comes **by car**.*

When adverbs of place alone are used in a sentence, they follow the conjugated verb.

Ich fahre **nach Berlin**.   *I am driving **to Berlin**.*

Der Vater kommt **ins Wohnzimmer**.   *The father comes **into the living room**.*

But when more than one adverb is used in a sentence, the adverbs must appear in the assigned order: time, manner, then place.

Wir fahren **nach Hamburg**.   *We are traveling **to Hamburg**.*

Wir fahren **morgen** nach Hamburg.   ***Tomorrow** we are traveling to Hamburg.*

Wir fahren morgen **mit dem Zug**   *Tomorrow we are traveling **by train** to*
nach Hamburg.   *Hamburg.*

Written Practice 3

Rewrite each sentence, each time adding the adverbs provided in parentheses.

1. Ich komme mit der Straßenbahn.

    (nach Hause) _____ .

    (heute) _____ .

2. Wir sind mit dem Zug gereist.

    (in die Schweiz) _____ .

    (vor einer Woche) _____ .

Genitive Case

The genitive case is the last of the four German cases. Its primary function is to show possession much the way the English 's or the preposition *of* does.

Whose book is it?	*It is my brother's book.*
Whose father is he?	*He is the father* of *the bride.*

German achieves the possessive meaning by using the genitive case. Let's look at the genitive as it compares to the other cases.

The genitive case of nouns with the definite article:

	Masculine	**Feminine**	**Neuter**	**Plural**
nom	der Mann	die Frau	das Kind	die Kinder
acc	den Mann	die Frau	das Kind	die Kinder
dat	dem Mann	der Frau	dem Kind	den Kindern
gen	**des** Mannes	**der** Frau	**des** Kindes	**der** Kinder

Other determiners in the genitive case will have the same endings as the definite articles. For example:

eines Mannes	meiner Frau	dieses Kindes	ihrer Kinder
deines Mannes	seiner Frau	keines Kindes	unserer Kinder

In sentences, the genitive case looks like this:

Das Auto des Mannes ist sehr alt.	*The man's car is very old.*
Kennst du den Sohn dieser Frau?	*Do you know this woman's son?*
Der Hund meines Kindes ist braun.	*My child's dog is brown.*
Der Onkel der Kinder ist gestorben.	*The children's uncle has died.*

Notice that the possessor follows the person or object possessed.

However, when using a possessive form of a person's name or a thing, use only a final **-s** (no apostrophe, as in English), and the possessor precedes the object possessed.

Peters Wagen	*Peter's car*
Deutschlands Grenzen	*Germany's borders*

Oral Practice

Practice saying the following list of sentences out loud.

Wessen Handschuhe hast du?	*Whose gloves do you have?*
Ich habe die Handschuhe des Lehrers.	*I have the teacher's gloves.*
Ich habe die Handschuhe meiner Schwester.	*I have my sister's gloves.*
Ich habe die Handschuhe des Kindes.	*I have the child's gloves.*
Wessen Wagen wird er kaufen?	*Whose car will he buy?*
Er wird den Wagen der Ärztin kaufen.	*He will buy the physician's car.*
Er wird den Wagen seines Freundes kaufen.	*He will buy his friend's car.*
Er wird den Wagen einer Freundin kaufen.	*He will buy a girlfriend's car.*
Wessen Verwandten wird sie helfen?	*Whose relatives will she help?*
Sie wird den Verwandten ihres Mannes helfen.	*She will help her husband's relatives.*
Sie wird den Verwandten meiner Wirtin helfen.	*She will help my landlady's relatives.*
Sie wird den Verwandten der Gäste helfen.	*She will help the guests' relatives.*
Ist das das Fahrrad deines Bruders?	*Is that your brother's bicycle?*
Ja, das ist sein Fahrrad.	*Yes, that is his bicycle.*
Nein, das ist das Fahrrad meiner Schwester.	*No, that is my sister's bicycle.*
Ist das der Enkel deiner Nachbarin?	*Is that your neighbor's grandchild?*
Ja, das ist ihr Enkel.	*Yes, that is her grandchild.*
Nein, das ist der Enkel eines Gasts.	*No, that is a guest's grandchild.*
Die Enkelin meines Chefs ist Studentin.	*My boss's granddaughter is a student.*

Written Practice 4

Write the dative and genitive forms for the following phrases.

	Dative	**Genitive**
das Fahrrad	_____	_____
die Leute	_____	_____
mein Schrank	_____	_____
seine Nachbarin	_____	_____
unsere Gäste	_____	_____
der Handschuh	_____	_____
die Handschuhe	_____	_____
ein Roman	_____	_____
eine Bratwurst	_____	_____
der Turm	_____	_____
die Burg	_____	_____
die Kaufhäuser	_____	_____
deine Geschwister	_____	_____
der Dom	_____	_____

There is a tendency to use an **-es** ending in the genitive case of masculine and neuter singular nouns when those nouns are of one syllable.

des Kindes   *child's*   des Mannes   *man's*

But it is also correct to add only **-s**.

des Kinds   *child's*   des Manns   *man's*

Nouns that end in **s**, **ss**, **ß**, **z**, or **tz** add **-es**.

des Hauses   *house's*   des Schmerzes   *pain's*

Masculine and neuter singular nouns that have more than one syllable but do not end in **s** add only **-s**.

des Bahnhofs   *train station's*   des Lehrers   *teacher's*

Pronouns do not have a genitive form. Instead, possessive adjectives are used to show possession. You encountered these in Chapter 9.

mein	*my*	ihr	*her*	ihr	*their*
dein	*your*	unser	*our*	Ihr	*your*
sein	*his/its*	euer	*your*	wessen	*whose*

The possessive **wessen** does not show a gender or case change, unlike the other possessive adjectives.

Oral Practice

Practice saying the following list of sentences out loud.

Wird dein Bruder da arbeiten?	*Will your brother work there?*
Nein, der Bruder meines Freunds wird da arbeiten.	*No, my friend's brother will work there.*
Wird seine Tante da arbeiten?	*Will his aunt work there?*
Nein, die Tante einer Nachbarin wird da arbeiten.	*No, a neighbor's aunt will work there.*
Werden eure Geschwister da arbeiten?	*Will your brothers and sisters work there?*
Nein, die Geschwister des Chefs werden da arbeiten.	*No, the boss's brothers and sisters will work there.*
Werden Ihre Gäste mitkommen?	*Will your guests come along?*
Nein, die Gäste meines Bruders werden mitkommen.	*No, my brother's guests will come along.*
Wird ihre Kusine mitkommen?	*Will her cousin come along?*
Nein, die Kusine einer Freundin wird mitkommen.	*No, a girlfriend's cousin will come along.*
Wirst du hier aussteigen?	*Will you get off here?*
Nein, ich werde am Bahnhof aussteigen.	*No, I will get off at the train station.*
Nein, ich werde vor der Bank aussteigen.	*No, I will get off in front of the bank.*
Nein, ich werde vor dem Café aussteigen.	*No, I will get off in front of the café.*

Past Perfect Tense

In the present perfect tense, the action of the verb started in the past and ended in the present.

He has worked here all day.

In the past perfect tense, the action of the verb started in the past and ended in the past.

He had worked here until his death last year.

In German the only conjugational difference between the present perfect and the past perfect is the tense used for the auxiliaries **haben** and **sein**. In the present perfect tense, the auxiliary is conjugated in the present tense.

Present Perfect Tense

Ich habe es gesehen.	*I saw it.*	Ich bin schnell gelaufen.	*I ran fast.*
Du hast es gesehen.	*You saw it.*	Du bist schnell gelaufen.	*You ran fast.*
Er hat es gesehen.	*He saw it.*	Er ist schnell gelaufen.	*He ran fast.*
Wir haben es gesehen.	*We saw it.*	Wir sind schnell gelaufen.	*We ran fast.*
Ihr habt es gesehen.	*You saw it.*	Ihr seid schnell gelaufen.	*You ran fast.*
Sie haben es gesehen.	*They saw it.*	Sie sind schnell gelaufen.	*They ran fast.*

In the past perfect tense, the auxiliary is conjugated in the past tense.

Past Perfect Tense

Ich hatte es gesehen.	*I had seen it.*	Ich war schnell gelaufen.	*I had run fast.*
Du hattest es gesehen.	*You had seen it.*	Du warst schnell gelaufen.	*You had run fast.*
Er hatte es gesehen.	*He had seen it.*	Er war schnell gelaufen.	*He had run fast.*
Wir hatten es gesehen.	*We had seen it.*	Wir waren schnell gelaufen.	*We had run fast.*
Ihr hattet es gesehen.	*You had seen it.*	Ihr wart schnell gelaufen.	*You had run fast.*
Sie hatten es gesehen.	*They had seen it.*	Sie waren schnell gelaufen.	*They had run fast.*

The change from the present perfect tense to the past perfect tense does not influence other aspects of verb conjugations: prefixes or regularity and irregularity of conjugation.

Written Practice 5

Change the following present perfect tense sentences to the past perfect tense.

1. Robert hat mir ein Geschenk gegeben.

   _____.

2. Wir sind zum Park gegangen.

   _____.

3. Hast du mit dem kleinen Hund gespielt?

   _____.

4. Warum bist du so böse gewesen?

   _____.

5. Unsere Gäste sind in der Stadt geblieben.

   _____.

Accusative Reflexive Pronouns

Reflexive pronouns are those that reflect back to the subject of the sentence. In other words, they refer to the person who is the subject of the sentence. For example:

Same Person	**Different Persons**
Tom hurt himself.	*Tom* hurt *her.*
We bought ourselves some candy.	*We* bought *them* some candy.

The German accusative reflexive pronouns are:

Subject Pronoun	**Reflexive Pronoun**
ich	mich
du	dich
er	sich
sie *s.*	sich
es	sich
wir	uns
ihr	euch
sie *pl.*	sich
Sie	sich

Subject Pronoun	Reflexive Pronoun
wer	sich
was	sich
man	sich

When the direct object or the object of an accusative preposition are the same person as the subject of the sentence, use a reflexive pronoun.

Same Person

Ich frage mich, wo sie ist.   *I ask myself (wonder) where she is.*

Different Persons

Ich frage ihn, wo sie ist.   *I ask him where she is.*

Written Practice 6

Rewrite the following sentence with the new subjects provided in parentheses. Change the reflexive pronoun appropriately.

1. Er wird sich in einer Stunde rasieren.

(ich) _____.

(du) _____.

(wir) _____.

(ihr) _____.

(sie *pl.*) _____.

Some verbs require a reflexive pronoun to complete their meaning. Consider the English verb *to enjoy oneself.* You cannot say *I enjoy.* The meaning is not complete. You have to add the reflexive pronoun to make sense: *I enjoy myself.* German has similar verbs. For example:

sich beeilen	*to hurry*	sich irren	*to be mistaken*
sich freuen auf	*to look forward to*	sich verlieben in	*to be in love with*
sich freuen über	*to be happy about/with*		

When in the infinitive form, reflexive verbs are preceded by **sich**. These verbs are incomplete if the reflexive pronoun does not accompany them. Notice that **sich**

freuen is used with two different prepositions. With **auf**, the verb means *to look forward to*. With **über**, the verb means *to be happy about*.

Wir freuen uns schon auf deine Party.	*We are already looking forward to your party.*
Sie freute sich über das Geschenk.	*She was happy about the gift.*

This verb can also be used without a preposition.

Ich freue mich, dass dein Mann jetzt gesund ist.	*I am happy that your husband is well now.*

Oral Practice

Practice saying the following list of sentences out loud.

Ich wasche die Kinder.	*I wash the children.*
Ich wasche mich.	*I wash myself.*
Ich setze mich an den Tisch.	*I seat myself at the table.*
Thomas setzte sich an den Tisch.	*Thomas seated himself at the table.*
Thomas rasierte sich langsam.	*Thomas shaved (himself) slowly.*
Rasierst du dich jetzt?	*Are you shaving now?*
Irrst du dich wieder?	*Are you wrong again?*
Das Kind hat sich aufs Sofa gelegt.	*The child lay down on the sofa.*
Oma wird sich aufs Sofa legen.	*Granny will lie down on the sofa.*
Wir beeilen uns.	*We hurry.*
Er hat sich beeilt.	*He hurried.*
Ich werde mich beeilen.	*I will hurry.*
Ich freue mich über das Geschenk.	*I am happy with the gift.*
Ich freue mich auf das Wochenende.	*I am looking forward to the weekend.*
Er hat sich in Tina verliebt.	*He fell in love with Tina.*
In wen hattest du dich verliebt?	*Whom had you fallen in love with?*
Er kaufte Handschuhe für ihn.	*He bought gloves for him.*
Er kaufte Handschuhe für sich.	*He bought gloves for himself.*

Written Practice 7

Make sentences by conjugating the following verb phrases in the present tense with the pronouns provided. Use the appropriate reflexive pronoun.

	sich beeilen	**sich rasieren schnell**
ich	_____.	_____.
du	_____.	_____.
er	_____.	_____.
wir	_____.	_____.
wer	_____?	_____?

	sich irren	**sich freuen über das Buch**
ich	_____.	_____.
sie *s.*	_____.	_____.
sie *pl.*	_____.	_____.
ihr	_____.	_____.
man	_____.	_____.

Written Practice 8

Change each sentence to the future tense. Replace the subjects with the words provided in parentheses. For example:

Sie schreibt einen Brief.

(du) *Du wirst einen Brief schreiben.* _____

1. Die Kinder waschen sich.

   (du) _____.

   (er) _____.

   (ich) _____.

2. Ich steige hier aus.

   (er) _____.

   (ihr) _____.

   (sie *pl.*) _____.

3. Er arbeitet in Bonn.

(ich) _____ .

(du) _____ .

(wer) _____ ?

More Subordinating Conjunctions

You already know a variety of interrogative words: **wer, wen, wem, wessen, was,
wo, wohin, woher, wie, wann,** and **warum.** These same words can function as
subordinating conjunctions, which means that the conjugated verb in the subordinate clause will be the last element. Compare the following interrogative words
used in both a question and a subordinate clause.

Wer ist das?	*Who is that?*
Sie fragt mich, wer das ist.	*She asks me who that is.*
Was haben sie gekauft?	*What did they buy?*
Weißt du, was sie gekauft haben?	*Do you know what they bought?*
Wo wohnt Herr Bauer?	*Where does Mr. Bauer live?*
Wir wissen, wo Herr Bauer wohnt.	*We know where Mr. Bauer lives.*
Wann hat er den Brief bekommen?	*When did he get the letter?*
Ich weiß nicht, wann er den Brief bekommen hat.	*I do not know when he got the letter.*
Wie alt ist ihre Tochter?	*How old is her daughter?*
Niemand weiß, wie alt ihre Tochter ist.	*No one knows how old her daughter is.*

You can use all interrogative words as subordinating conjunctions.

Things Around the City

When visiting a German city, you will see many of the same sights whether the city is located in the north, south, east, or west. Let's become familiar with some of things you'll see in a city.

das Kaufhaus	*department store*	der Zirkus	*circus*
das Kino	*movie theater*	der Zoo	*zoo*
das Motorrad	*motorcycle*	die Apotheke	*drugstore* (prescriptions)
das Schiff	*ship*	die Besichtigung	*tour; sightseeing*
das Stadtzentrum	*city center, downtown*	die Brücke	*bridge*
der Ausflug	*excursion*	die Burg	*castle*
der Dom	*cathedral*	die Drogerie	*drugstore* (general products)
der Flughafen	*airport*	die Hafenrundfahrt	*trip around harbor*
der Hafen	*harbor*	die Post	*post office*
der Hauptbahnhof	*main railroad station*	die Sehenswürdigkeiten	*sights*
der Laden	*shop, small store*	die Stadtmauer	*city wall*
der Turm	*tower*	die Stadtrundfahrt	*trip around the city*
der Verkehr	*traffic*	die Tour	*tour*

Let's look at a few example sentences.

Wir werden eine Stadtrundfahrt machen.	*We are going to take a trip around the city.*
Die Touristen machen morgen eine Tour.	*The tourists are going on a tour tomorrow.*
Morgen machen wir einen Ausflug.	*We are going on an excursion tomorrow.*
Die Besichtigung des Doms fängt um neun Uhr an.	*The tour of the cathedral starts at nine o'clock.*
Im Hafen sehen wir viele Schiffe aus dem Ausland.	*In the harbor we see many ships from foreign countries.*
Von der Brücke sehen wir das ganze Stadtzentrum.	*From the bridge we see the entire downtown.*
Ich fotografiere die alte Burg und den Turm.	*I photograph the old castle and the tower.*

QUIZ

Change the sentences conjugated in the present tense to the future tense with the pronouns provided.

Ich komme mit.

Er _wird mitkommen._

Wir _werden mitkommen._

1. Ich bestelle ein Bier.

   Du _____.

   Wir _____.

   Sie *pl.* _____.

2. Er verspricht nichts.

   Sie *s.* _____.

   Ihr _____.

   Man _____.

3. Write the accusative, dative, and genitive declensions for each of the following phrases.

	Accusative	**Dative**	**Genitive**
meine Gäste	_____	_____	_____
ihr Handschuh	_____	_____	_____
seine Enkelin	_____	_____	_____
das Kaufhaus	_____	_____	_____

4. Rewrite the following sentence with the pronouns provided in parentheses. Change the reflexive pronoun appropriately.

   Wann hat er sich gewaschen?

   (du) _____?

   (sie *s.*) _____?

   (wir) _____?

(ihr) _____?

(Sie) _____?

5. Change the following questions to subordinate clauses using the phrase provided.

Ich weiß nicht, ...

Wo haben meine Verwandten gearbeitet?

_____.

Warum warten die Jungen vor der Bank?

_____.

Wie lange wird sie noch arbeiten?

_____.

Woher kommen diese Ausländer?

_____.

Wie heißen diese Gäste?

_____.

6. Conjugate the following verbs in the present perfect tense and the past perfect tense with the pronouns provided.

	sich beeilen	**aussteigen**	**arbeiten**
sie *s.*	_____	_____	_____
	_____	_____	_____
wir	_____	_____	_____
	_____	_____	_____
ihr	_____	_____	_____
	_____	_____	_____

Circle the letter of the word or phrase that best completes each sentence.

7. Die Tochter _____ wird in Amerika arbeiten.

   (a) der Sohn   (c) meines Freundes

   (b) für den Sohn   (d) auf den Freund

8. Wir freuen uns schon _____ das Wochenende.

   (a) auf   (c) gegen

   (b) zu   (d) entlang

9. Ist _____ des Mannes jung oder alt?

   (a) die Frau   (c) das Mädchen

   (b) der Dame   (d) dem Kind

10. _____ Familie hatten sie besucht?

   (a) Wessen   (c) Der

   (b) Ihr   (d) Meiner

CHAPTER 14

Review of Verb Tenses

In this chapter you will learn:

Comparing German and English Verb Tenses

Key Verbs: Haben, Sein, *and* Werden

Genitive Prepositions

Dative Reflexive Pronouns

Some Special Masculine Nouns

Modal Auxiliaries

Comparing German and English Verb Tenses

In general, we can say that German and English tenses are used in much the same way. But let's review those few differences that do exist.

PRESENT TENSE

The English present tense has three versions: the habitual, the progressive or incomplete, and the emphatic. German has one present tense form.

Die Kinder lernen Deutsch.

The children learn German.

The children are learning German.

The children do learn German.

This variety of English tenses in the present occurs in the other tenses as well. In German there is only one form.

PAST TENSES

When telling something that occurred in the past, German primarily uses the simple past tense in written language and the present perfect tense in spoken language. English tends to prefer the simple past tense.

Written Language:
Sie lernten Deutsch. *They learned German.*

Spoken Language:
Sie haben Deutsch gelernt. *They learned German.*

But when emphasizing what began in the past and ends in the future, use the present perfect tense.

Wir haben lange gearbeitet. *We have worked long.*

When emphasizing what began in the past and ended in the past, use the past perfect tense.

Wir hatten lange gearbeitet. *We had worked long.*

FUTURE TENSE

The German future tense resembles the English future tense in great degree. Both can use a present tense conjugation to infer the future tense, usually with an accompanying adverbial expression that indicates the future.

Wir fahren morgen nach Bremen.   *We are driving to Bremen tomorrow.*

And both use an auxiliary with an infinitive to show an action in the future tense.

Ich werde in Bonn studieren.   *I will study in Bonn.*

There is another future tense to consider: the future perfect tense. This identifies an action that begins and ends in the future.

Er wird es schon gelesen haben.   *He will already have read it.*

This tense consists of a conjugation of **werden** followed by a past participle and either **haben** or **sein**.

Er wird es gefunden haben.   *He will have found it.*
Sie wird gegangen sein.   *She will have gone.*

The use of **haben** or **sein** in this tense depends upon the past participle. With transitive verbs, use **haben**. With intransitive verbs and verbs of motion, use **sein**.

Key Verbs: *Haben, Sein*, and *Werden*

You have undoubtedly noticed how significant these three verbs are in German conjugations. Let's review:

HABEN

Haben is used as a transitive verb that means *to have*.

Ich habe neun CDs.   *I have nine CDs.*

It is also used as the auxiliary of transitive verbs in the perfect tenses.

Ich habe es verstanden.   *I understood it.*
Ich hatte es verkauft.   *I had sold it.*
Ich werde es gelernt haben.   *I will have learned it.*

SEIN

Sein is used alone as an intransitive verb that means *to be*.

Sie ist meine Schwester.   *She is my sister.*

It is also the auxiliary of intransitive verbs and verbs of motion in the perfect tenses.

Sie ist gestorben.   *She has died.*

Sie war Lehrerin geworden.   *She had become a teacher.*

Sie wird gefahren sein.   *She will have driven.*

WERDEN

Werden is used as an intransitive verb that means *to become*.

Tina wird Ärztin.   *Tina is becoming a physician.*

It is also the auxiliary of the future tense.

Tina wird Professorin werden.   *Tina will become a professor.*

Tina wird es gefunden haben.   *Tina will have found it.*

In addition, **werden** is the auxiliary of the passive voice, which will be taken up in Chapter 17.

Oral Practice

Practice saying the following list of sentences out loud.

Ich freue mich auf ihren Besuch.   *I am looking forward to her visit.*

Wir freuten uns auf ihren Besuch.   *We looked forward to her visit.*

Hast du dich auf das Examen gefreut?   *Did you look forward to the exam?*

Er wird sich auf den Ausflug freuen.   *He will be looking forward to the excursion.*

Ich komme allein.	*I am coming alone.*
Sie kam mit einer Flasche Wein.	*She came with a bottle of wine.*
Seid ihr mit einem Freund gekommen?	*Did you come with a friend?*
Wir werden allein kommen.	*We will come alone.*
Ein Fremder ist im Garten.	*A stranger is in the garden.*
Niemand war in der Küche.	*No one was in the kitchen.*
Wer ist im Keller gewesen?	*Who was in the cellar?*
Unser Nachbar wird in den Vereinigten Staaten sein.	*Our neighbor will be in the United States.*

Written Practice 1

Conjugate the following verbs in the tenses in bold print with the pronouns provided.

		aussteigen		**versprechen**
pres	er	_____	wir	_____
past	er	_____	wir	_____
pres perf	er	_____	wir	_____
past perf	er	_____	wir	_____
fut	er	_____	wir	_____
fut perf	er	_____	wir	_____

		besuchen		**sich rasieren**
pres	du	_____	ich	_____
past	du	_____	ich	_____
pres perf	du	_____	ich	_____
past perf	du	_____	ich	_____
fut	du	_____	ich	_____
fut perf	du	_____	ich	_____

In the following conjugations use the pronoun provided for each line.

		wohnen		**verstehen**
pres	ich	_____	ich	_____
past	du	_____	du	_____
pres perf	er	_____	er	_____
past perf	wir	_____	wir	_____
fut	ihr	_____	ihr	_____
fut perf	sie _pl._	_____	sie _pl._	_____

Genitive Prepositions

Just like the accusative and dative cases, the genitive case has certain high-frequency prepositions.

(an)statt	_instead of_	während	_during_
trotz	_inspite of, despite_	wegen	_because of_

In sentences, these prepositions look like this:

Er kauft einen Hut (an)statt eines Hemdes.	_He buys a hat instead of a shirt._
Trotz des Wetters fahren sie nach Bremen.	_Despite the weather they drive to Bremen._
Während des Krieges wohnte er in London.	_During the war he lived in London._
Sie bleibt wegen des Schnees zu Hause.	_She stays home because of the snow._

These prepositions are sometimes used in the dative case in the colloquial language.

Oral Practice

Practice saying the following list of sentences out loud.

Statt einer Postkarte schickt er mir einen Brief.	*Instead of a postcard, he sends me a letter.*
Statt eines Briefes schickt sie mir ein Telegramm.	*Instead of a letter she sends me a telegram.*
Trotz des Regens gehen wir zum Park.	*Despite the rain we go to the park.*
Trotz des Schnees gehen wir in die Stadt.	*Despite the snow we go to the city.*
Während des Sommers fliegt sie nach Italien.	*During the summer she flies to Italy.*
Während des Frühlings fliegt er nach Norwegen.	*During the spring he flies to Norway.*
Wegen des Krieges bleiben sie zu Hause.	*Because of the war they stay at home.*
Wegen eines Gewitters bleiben sie zu Hause.	*Because of a thunderstorm they stay at home.*

Written Practice 2

Write each phrase with the genitive prepositions provided.

1. wegen

    ein Examen _____

    diese Besichtigung _____

    die Touristen _____

2. während

    ein Krieg _____

    das Gewitter _____

    der Tag _____

3. trotz

    der Schnee _____

    seine Geschwister _____

    eine Nachbarin _____

4. anstatt

    die Handschuhe _____

    eine Küche _____

    diese Flaschen _____

Dative Reflexive Pronouns

Just as there are accusative reflexive pronouns, there are also dative reflexive pronouns. Dative reflexive pronouns are used when an indirect object, an object of a dative verb, or an object of a dative preposition is the same person or thing that is the subject of the sentence. The dative reflexive pronouns are:

Subject Pronoun	Reflexive Pronoun
ich	mir
du	dir
er	sich
sie *s.*	sich
es	sich
wir	uns
ihr	euch
sie *pl.*	sich
Sie	sich
wer	sich
was	sich
man	sich

Here are some example sentences.

Ich kaufe mir eine Flasche Bier.	*I buy myself a bottle of beer.*
Er hilft sich so gut er kann.	*He helps himself as well as he can.*
Robert spricht mit sich selbst.	*Robert is talking to himself.*

Certain personal activities (washing, combing the hair, putting on clothes, and so on) tend to use a dative reflexive pronoun followed by a direct object in German, where in English there is only a direct object.

Wir waschen **uns die Hände**.	*We wash **our hands**.*

Notice that German uses a definite article with the direct object, where English uses a possessive pronoun.

The phrase *to break* (**sich brechen**) as in a limb or other body part is a special phrase in German. It requires a dative reflexive pronoun and a direct object.

Sie bricht **sich die Hand**.	*She breaks **her hand**.*

Oral Practice

Practice saying the following list of sentences out loud.

Wer spricht mit sich selbst?	*Who is talking to himself?*
Der alte Mann spricht mit sich selbst.	*The old man is talking to himself.*
Was tust du?	*What are you doing?*
Ich putze mir die Zähne.	*I am brushing my teeth.*
Ich kämme mir die Haare.	*I am combing my hair.*
Das Kind wäscht sich die Hände.	*The child is washing his hands.*
Sie zieht sich einen Mantel an.	*She is putting on a coat.*
Ziehst du dir eine Jacke an?	*Are you putting on a jacket?*
Nein, ich ziehe mir einen Regenmantel an.	*No, I am putting on a raincoat.*
Haben Sie sich das Bein gebrochen?	*Did you break your leg?*
Nein, ich habe mir den Arm gebrochen.	*No, I broke my arm.*
Er hat sich den Finger gebrochen.	*He broke his finger.*

Written Practice 3

Exchange the subject and the object in each sentence with the new subjects and objects provided. Make any necessary changes to the reflexive pronouns. For example:

Sie bricht sich die Hand.

(du/der Arm) *Du brichst dir den Arm.*

1. Er zieht sich einen Mantel an.

(sie *s.*/die Jacke) _____ .

(ich/der Regenmantel) _____ .

(du/das Sweatshirt) _____ .

2. Er hat sich die Fahrkarten gekauft.

(wir/eine Flasche Wein) _____ .

(ihr/die Handschuhe) _____ .

(sie *pl.*/ein Roman) _____ .

3. Er hat sich den Arm gebrochen.

(ich/der Finger) _____ .

(sie *pl.*/die Finger) _____ .

(du/die Beine) _____ .

Written Practice 4

Rewrite the following sentence with the words in parentheses. Change the reflexive pronouns appropriately. For example:

Er kauft sich ein Sweatshirt.

(ich) *Ich kaufe mir ein Sweatshirt.*

1. Ich habe mir die Hände gewaschen.

(er) _____ .

(ihr) _____ .

(die Männer) _____ .

(wir) _____ .

(du) _____ .

Some Special Masculine Nouns

Certain masculine nouns have a special declension. These nouns are words that require an **-n** or **-en** ending in the declension. They tend to be old words, words that end in the vowel **-e**, and foreign words with the accent on the last syllable. Here are some sample words:

Old Words		Words Ending in -e		Foreign Words	
der Herr	*gentleman*	der Junge	*boy*	der Soldat	*soldier*
der Mensch	*human*	der Löwe	*lion*	der Sozialist	*socialist*
der Held	*hero*	der Knabe	*boy*	der Elefant	*elephant*
der Graf	*count, earl*	der Matrose	*sailor*	der Musikant	*musician*

When these words decline, they require an **-(e)n** ending and in the plural they end in **-(e)n** also. For example:

nom	der Mensch	der Löwe	der Elefant
acc	den Mensch**en**	den Löw**en**	den Elefant**en**
dat	dem Mensch**en**	dem Löw**en**	dem Elefant**en**
gen	des Mensch**en**	des Löw**en**	des Elefant**en**

Plural nominative: die Mensch**en**, die Löw**en**, die Elefant**en**.

Notice that the genitive case does not require an **-s** ending in this declension.

Written Practice 5

1. Decline each noun phrase in the accusative, dative, and genitive cases.

	der Held	**der Junge**	**der Soldat**
acc	_____	_____	_____
dat	_____	_____	_____
gen	_____	_____	_____

2. **der Affe**   **der Prinz**   **der Diplomat**
   (*monkey*)   (*prince*)   (*diplomat*)

acc _____ _____ _____

dat _____ _____ _____

gen _____ _____ _____

Modal Auxiliaries

A modal auxiliary is a conjugated verb that works together with an infinitive. When a modal auxiliary is used, the infinitive is placed at the end of the sentence. The modal auxiliaries color the meaning of the verb in the sentence by telling what obligation, permission, or ability the doer of the action has. Let's meet the modal auxiliaries.

dürfen	*may, to be allowed*	müssen	*must, to have to*
können	*can, to be able to*	sollen	*should, to be supposed to*
mögen	*to like; may*	wollen	*to want*

IN THE PRESENT TENSE

With most of the modal auxiliaries, there is a difference in the present tense between the verb stem in the singular conjugation and the stem in the plural conjugation.

	dürfen	**können**	**mögen**
ich	darf	kann	mag
du	darfst	kannst	magst
er	darf	kann	mag
wir	dürfen	können	mögen
ihr	dürft	könnt	mögt
sie	dürfen	können	mögen

	müssen	**sollen**	**wollen**
ich	muss	soll	will
du	musst	sollst	willst
er	muss	soll	will
wir	müssen	sollen	wollen
ihr	müsst	sollt	wollt
sie	müssen	sollen	wollen

In sentences, the modal auxiliaries look like this:

Darf ich diese Zeitung nehmen?	*May I take this newspaper?*
Niemand kann ihn verstehen.	*No one can understand him.*
Ich mag Butter nicht.	*I do not like butter.*
Wir müssen den Kindern helfen.	*We have to help the children.*
Was soll man tun?	*What should one do?*
Er will sich die Zähne putzen.	*He wants to brush his teeth.*

Oral Practice

Practice saying the sentences in the following list out loud.

Das darf man nicht tun.	*You (One) should not do that.*
Ihr dürft nicht Auto fahren.	*You are not allowed to drive a car.*
Können Sie mich hören?	*Can you hear me?*
Nein, ich kann nichts hören.	*No, I cannot hear anything.*
Das mag wohl sein.	*That may well be.*
Sie mögen mehr als zehn Jahre alt sein.	*They may be more than ten years old.*
Sie müssen heute Briefe schreiben.	*They have to write letters today.*
Der Mann muss sehr krank sein.	*The man must be very sick.*
Ihr sollt jetzt fleißig arbeiten.	*You should work diligently now.*
Der Diplomat soll schwer krank sein.	*The diplomat is supposed to be seriously ill.*
Was wollen Sie tun?	*What do you want to do?*
Ich will mir die Hände waschen.	*I want to wash my hands.*

IN THE PAST TENSE

When conjugated in the past tense, the modal auxiliaries look like regular verbs and never have an umlaut, even if there is one in the infinitive.

	dürfen	**können**	**mögen**
ich	durfte	konnte	mochte
du	durftest	konntest	mochtest
er	durfte	konnte	mochte
wir	durften	konnten	mochten
ihr	durftet	konntet	mochtet
sie	durften	konnten	mochten

	müssen	**sollen**	**wollen**
ich	musste	sollte	wollte
du	musstest	solltest	wolltest
er	musste	sollte	wollte
wir	mussten	sollten	wollten
ihr	musstet	solltet	wolltet
sie	mussten	sollten	wollten

IN THE PERFECT TENSES

In the perfect tenses, all the modal auxiliaries use **haben** as their auxiliary. And as participles they look like regular verbs but never have an umlaut.

er hat gedurft	*he has been allowed*	er hat gemusst	*he has had to*
er hat gekonnt	*he was able to*	er hat gesollt	*he was supposed to*
er hat gemocht	*he has liked*	er hat gewollt	*he has wanted*

But the present perfect conjugation illustrated here is used only when there is no other verb in the sentence.

Mein Bruder hat es nicht gekonnt.	*My brother was not able to.*
Das habe ich nicht gewollt.	*I did not want that.*

Modal auxiliaries are intended to be used in conjunction with other infinitives. You have seen that in the present and past tenses, the second verb (an infinitive) in the sentence appears at the end of that sentence, unlike English.

Ich will eine Flasche Bier **trinken**.	*I want **to drink** a bottle of beer.*
Ich wollte eine Flasche Bier **trinken**.	*I wanted **to drink** a bottle of beer.*

In the perfect and future tenses, however, this requires a new structure: a double infinitive. When the same sentences are stated in the perfect or future tenses, the infinitive of the modal auxiliary is the last element in the sentence and forms a double-infinitive structure with the second verb. A past participle is not used in the perfect tenses.

Ich habe eine Flasche Bier **trinken wollen**.	*I wanted to drink a bottle of beer.*
Ich werde eine Flasche Bier **trinken wollen**.	*I will **want to drink** a bottle of beer.*

Oral Practice

Practice saying the following list of sentences out loud.

Was hast du tun wollen?	*What did you want to do?*
Ich habe ins Kino gehen wollen.	*I wanted to go to the movies.*
Hast du mitkommen können?	*Were you able to go along?*
Nein, ich habe arbeiten müssen.	*No, I had to work.*
Wohin habt ihr gehen sollen?	*Where were you supposed to go?*
Wir haben zum Hotel gehen sollen.	*We were supposed to go to the hotel.*
Das darfst du nicht tun.	*You may not do that.*
Ich habe das niemals tun dürfen.	*I have never been allowed to do that.*
Ich habe niemals tanzen können.	*I have never been able to dance.*

The modal auxiliary **mögen** (*to like; may*) is used frequently in another form: **möchte** (*would like*). It is a polite replacement for **wollen** (*to want*).

Ich möchte bitte eine Tasse Tee.	*I would like a cup of tea, please.*
Wir möchten nach Südamerika fliegen.	*We would like to fly to South America.*

Written Practice 6

Make complete sentences by conjugating the following phrases with the pronouns provided. Use the tenses shown in bold.

1. wollen einen Roman lesen

   pres   Ich   _____.

   past   Ich   _____.

   pres perf Wir   _____.

   fut   Wir   _____.

2. können sehr gut Schach spielen

   pres   Du   _____.

   past   Du   _____.

   pres perf Ihr   _____.

   fut   Ihr   _____.

3. müssen ein bisschen warten

   pres   Sie *s.* _____.

   past   Sie *s.* _____.

   pres perf Sie *pl.* _____.

   fut   Sie *pl.* _____.

4. sollen fleißig arbeiten

   pres   Ich   _____.

   past   Er   _____.

   pres perf Wir   _____.

   fut   Man   _____.

Written Practice 7

Rewrite the following sentences in the past and present perfect tenses.

1. Die Kinder können gut Klavier spielen.

   _____.

   _____.

2. Ich muss jeden Tag fleißig arbeiten.

   _____.

   _____.

3. Du sollst dir die Hände waschen.

   _____.

   _____.

4. Sie mag kein Eis.

   _____.

   _____.

5. Hier kann man umsteigen.

   _____.

   _____.

6. Ihr müsst den Nachbarn helfen.

   _____.

   _____.

QUIZ

1. Conjugate the following verbs in the tenses shown with the pronouns provided.

		schicken	waschen	aussteigen
pres	ich	_____	_____	_____
past	du	_____	_____	_____
pres perf	er	_____	_____	_____
past perf	wir	_____	_____	_____
fut	ihr	_____	_____	_____
fut perf	sie	_____	_____	_____

2. In the blank provided, write the letter that identifies the case required by each preposition: a = accusative, d = dative, a–d = accusative or dative, and g = genitive.

mit	_____	von	_____
wegen	_____	zu	_____
in	_____	trotz	_____
anstatt	_____	auf	_____
während	_____	durch	_____
für	_____	statt	_____
gegen	_____	bis	_____
neben	_____		

Rewrite each sentence using the words in parentheses.

3. Wegen _____ mussten wir zu Hause bleiben.

(das Gewitter) _____.

(der Regen) _____.

(diese Arbeit) _____.

4. Statt _____ hat Erik uns helfen müssen.

(mein Bruder) _____.

(unsere Geschwister) _____.

(dieser Matrose) _____.

Using the words in parentheses change the subject and reflexive pronoun in each sentence.

Ich kaufte mir einen Wagen.

(er) *Er kaufte sich einen Wagen.*

5. Ich putze mir die Zähne.

(man) _____.

(die Kinder) _____.

(meine Tochter) _____.

(wir) _____.

(du) _____.

6. Ich habe mir einen warmen Mantel angezogen.

(du) _____.

(sie *s.*) _____.

(Sie) _____.

(niemand) _____.

(Tina) _____.

7. Write the accusative, dative, and genitive forms of the following nouns.

	die Kirche	**ein Held**	**die Gäste**
nom	_____	_____	_____
acc	_____	_____	_____
dat	_____	_____	_____
gen	_____	_____	_____

8. Write the present and past tense conjugations of the following modal auxiliaries with the pronouns provided.

		dürfen	**können**	**mögen**
pres	ich	_____	_____	_____
past	ihr	_____	_____	_____

		wollen	**sollen**	**müssen**
pres	er	_____	_____	_____
past	wir	_____	_____	_____

Change each of the following present tense sentences to the present perfect and the future tenses.

9. Kannst du dieses Gedicht verstehen?

_____?

_____?

10. Meine Nachbarin soll ihre Pflicht tun.

_____.

_____.

CHAPTER 15

Linking Ideas Together

In this chapter you will learn:

Relative Pronouns

Relative pronouns are used to link two sentences having a common element together. For example:

The girls play soccer.   The girls attend this school.

In these two sentences, the common element is, of course, *the girls*. The two sentences can be combined into one by changing one of the instances of *the girls* to a relative pronoun. In this case, the relative pronoun is *that*. *That* is used to add pertinent information about the antecedent (the word to which the relative pronoun refers). The result is:

The girls *that* attend this school play soccer.

English has more than one kind of relative pronoun. *Who* and *which* are used to provide additional but nonessential information about the antecedent.

The man, *who* happens to be my friend, lost the election.
An election, *which* is rare in these parts, will be tomorrow.

English also has an elliptical relative pronoun—that is, a relative pronoun that does not appear in a relative clause, but is understood.

The person they arrested was a drifter. (The person *that* they arrested was a drifter.)

German relative pronouns are the definite articles (**der**, **die**, **das**). They are used like subordinating conjunctions, which means that the conjugated verb is the last element in the clause. The relative pronouns must conform to the gender and number of their antecedents. For example:

der Mann, der...	*the man, who . . .*	das Kind, das...	*the child, who . . .*
die Frau, die...	*the woman, who . . .*	die Leute, die...	*the people, who . . .*

But, in addition to being the same gender and number of the antecedent, the relative pronoun can be of any case: nominative, accusative, dative, or genitive. It depends upon on how the relative pronoun is used in the relative clause: as the subject of the clause, as the direct object, as the object of a preposition, and so forth. For example:

der Mann, **der** in Bonn wohnt (subject)	*the man **that** lives in Bonn*
der Mann, **den** Tina kennt (direct object)	*the man **that** Tina knows*
der Mann, **mit dem** sie tanzt (dative prep.)	*the man **that** she dances **with*** *(the man **with whom** she dances)*

Before we look at a variety of sentences with relative clauses, let's look at the declension of the relative pronouns, paying particular attention to the few occasions in which the declension differs from the definite article.

	Masculine	Feminine	Neuter	Plural	
nom	der	die	das	die	*that, who, which*
acc	den	die	das	die	*that, whom, which*
dat	dem	der	dem	denen	*that, whom, which*
gen	dessen	deren	dessen	deren	*whose*

Now let's look at some example sentences. Notice how the relative pronoun conforms to the gender and number of its antecedent and is in the case needed for its function within the relative clause.

Der Lehrer, der in der Nähe wohnt, hat in England studiert.	*The teacher, who lives in the vicinity, studied in England.*
Kennen Sie die Studentin, die die Touristen fotografieren?	*Do you know the student that the tourists are photographing?*
Er findet das Buch, von dem der Professor gesprochen hat.	*He finds the book that the professor spoke about.*
Ich besuche meine Verwandten, deren Sohn im Irak ist.	*I visit my relatives whose son is in Iraq.*

Oral Practice

Practice saying the following list of sentences out loud.

Welches Haus hast du gekauft?	*Which house did you buy?*
Das Haus, das in der Hauptstraße steht.	*The house that is on Main Street.*
Das Haus, in dem Bach gewohnt hatte.	*The house that Bach had lived in.*
Wo ist der Politiker, den sie interviewen wollen?	*Where is the politician that they want to interview?*
Wo sind die Rockstars, mit denen sie sprechen wollen?	*Where are the rock stars with whom they want to speak?*

Wo ist die Tänzerin, über die er einen Artikel schreiben will?	*Where is the dancer that he wants to write an article about?*
Welche Gedichte willst du lernen?	*Which poems do you want to learn?*
Die Gedichte, von denen mein Lehrer sprach.	*The poems that my teacher talked about.*
Die Gedichte, die auf deutsch geschrieben sind.	*The poems that are written in German.*
Das sind die Briefmarken, die Karl mir gegeben hat.	*These are the stamps that Karl gave me.*
Das ist der Regenschirm, den Oma in Bonn gekauft hat.	*That is the umbrella that Granny bought in Bonn.*
Das ist das Wörterbuch, unter dem ich das Geld gefunden habe.	*That is the dictionary under which I found the money.*
Das ist die Dame, deren Tochter Tänzerin werden will.	*That is the lady whose daughter wants to become a dancer.*

Written Practice 1

Rewrite each sentence, changing the antecedent in bold print to the ones in parentheses and making any necessary changes.

Wo ist **das Haus**, das Erik kaufen will?

(der Hut) _Wo ist der Hut, den Erik kaufen will?_

1. Ich habe **die Bücher**, die du verloren hast.

   (das Heft) _____.

   (ein Regenschirm) _____.

   (die Flasche) _____.

   (der Artikel) _____.

2. Robert besucht **die Tänzerin**, deren Vater Diplomat gewesen ist.

   (der Matrose) _____.

   (die Ausländer) _____.

   (eine Dame) _____.

   (das Mädchen) _____.

3. Wo fandest du **das Geld**, nach dem der Polizist fragte?

(die Schlüssel) _____?

(der Wagen) _____?

(der Ausländer) _____?

(das Mädchen) _____?

(die Tasche) _____?

4. **Das Mädchen**, das ich in Freiburg traf, wohnt jetzt in Wien.

(der Soldat) _____.

(die Touristen) _____.

(die Tänzerin) _____.

(das Kind) _____.

(der Polizist) _____.

5. **Das Kind**, dessen Schwester gestorben ist, will nicht mitgehen.

(die Kinder) _____.

(der Junge) _____.

(die Tänzerin) _____.

(das Mädchen) _____.

(der Student) _____.

More About Modal Auxiliaries

As you know, modal auxiliaries in the perfect and future tenses form a double-infinitive structure.

Er hat es nicht verstehen können.   *He was not able to understand it.*

Wir werden zu Hause bleiben müssen.   *We will have to stay at home.*

But when a modal auxiliary in a double-infinitive structure is used in a subordinate clause, there is a matter of word order to be considered: The conjugated auxiliary (**haben** or **werden**) of a double-infinitive structure will directly precede the double infinitive. For example:

Er sagt, dass er es nicht **hat** verstehen können.	*He says that he was not able to understand it.*
Weißt du, ob wir zu Hause **werden** bleiben müssen?	*Do you know whether we will have to stay at home?*

Written Practice 2

Complete each phrase with the sentences provided. Employ the appropriate word order.

1. Die Mutter sagt, dass...

   Sie hat die Kinder gut erziehen wollen.

   _____.

   Ihr Sohn wird Soldat werden müssen.

   _____.

   Die Kinder haben kein Bier trinken dürfen.

   _____.

2. Ich weiß nicht, warum...

   Tina hat das Klavier nicht spielen können.

   _____.

   Du wirst nach Belgien reisen sollen.

   _____.

   Die Tänzerin wird in Bremen tanzen wollen.

   _____.

Double Infinitives

There is a short list of other verbs that can serve as the auxiliaries of infinitives and that, in the perfect and future tenses, form a double-infinitive structure. These verbs are: **lassen**, **sehen**, **hören**, **helfen**, and **lernen**. Let's look at some examples with one of these verbs.

Ich lasse den Wagen reparieren.	*I have the car repaired.*
Ich ließ den Wagen reparieren.	*I had the car repaired.*
Ich habe den Wagen reparieren lassen.	*I have had the car repaired.*
Ich werde den Wagen reparieren lassen.	*I will have the car repaired.*

Oral Practice

Practice saying the following list of sentences out loud.

Haben Sie das Radio reparieren lassen?	*Did you have the radio repaired?*
Nein, ich habe es noch nicht reparieren lassen.	*No, I have not had it repaired yet.*
Hast du die Kinder im Garten spielen sehen?	*Did you see the children playing in the garden?*
Ja, ich habe sie im Garten spielen sehen.	*Yes, I saw them playing in the garden.*
Haben Sie Ihren Sohn singen hören?	*Did you hear your son singing?*
Ja, ich habe ihn schon singen hören.	*Yes, I already heard him singing.*
Wirst du deinem Bruder im Garten arbeiten helfen?	*Will you help your brother work in the garden?*
Ja, ich werde ihm im Garten arbeiten helfen.	*Yes, I will help him work in the garden.*
Sie wird schwimmen lernen.	*She will learn to swim.*
Er wird tanzen lernen.	*He will learn to dance.*
Wir werden Ski laufen lernen.	*We will learn to ski.*

Written Practice 3

Conjugate each verb phrase in the tenses shown with the pronouns provided.

		können es reparieren	**hören sie sprechen**
pres	ich	_____	_____
past	ich	_____	_____
pres perf	wir	_____	_____
fut	wir	_____	_____

		lassen ein Hemd machen	**wollen ihn interviewen**
pres	Sie	_____	_____
past	Sie	_____	_____
pres perf	er	_____	_____
fut	er	_____	_____

Prepositions and Inanimates

A preposition can be followed by most nouns or an animate pronoun.

Ich sprach mit dem Herrn.   *I spoke with the gentleman.*

Ich sprach mit ihm.   *I spoke with him.*

But when a pronoun represents an inanimate object, it forms a special structure with a preposition: a prepositional adverb. The structure of a prepositional adverb in German is **da-** plus the preposition. For example:

dafür   *for it*   damit   *with it*   davon   *from it*

When a preposition begins with a vowel, use **dar-** plus the preposition.

darauf   *on it; for it*   daraus   *from it*   darin   *in it; therein*

Let's compare a few examples with animates and inanimates.

Animate:

Er wartet auf den Matrosen.   *He is waiting for the sailor.*

Er wartet auf ihn.   *He is waiting for him.*

Inanimate:

Er wartet auf den Zug.   *He is waiting for the train.*

Er wartet darauf.   *He is waiting for it.*

Something similar occurs when asking questions with prepositions and inanimate pronouns. In this case, use **wo-** plus the preposition.

womit   *with what*   worin   *in what*   wovon   *of what*

When a preposition begins with a vowel, use **wor-** plus the preposition.

worauf   *on what*   woraus   *out of what*   worin   *in what; in which*

Let's look at some example sentences.

Animate:

Von wem sprecht ihr?   *About whom are you speaking?*

Über wen schreibt der Mann?   *About whom is the man writing?*

Inanimate:

Wovon sprecht ihr?   *About what are you speaking?*

Worüber schreibt der Mann?   *About what is the man writing?*

Oral Practice

Practice saying the following list of sentences out loud.

Von wem hast du es bekommen?   *From whom did you get it?*

Ich habe es von einem Fremden   *I got it from a stranger.*
bekommen.

Wovon habt ihr gesprochen?   *What were you talking about?*

Wir haben von dem Gewitter   *We talked about the thunderstorm.*
gesprochen.

Worüber freute sie sich?	*What was she happy about?*
Sie freute sich über den Artikel.	*She was happy about the article.*
Worauf freuen sich die Kinder?	*What are the children looking forward to?*
Sie freuen sich auf das Wochenende.	*They are looking forward to the weekend.*
Wofür interessiert er sich?	*What is he interested in?*
Er interessiert sich für Sport.	*He is interested in sports.*
Womit hat er kommen wollen?	*By what did he want to come?*
Er hat mit dem Bus kommen wollen.	*He wanted to come by bus.*

Written Practice 4

Rewrite each prepositional phrase twice, changing the nouns to pronouns, once as a replacement for the prepositional phrase and once as a question.

vor dem Haus	*davor*	*wovor*
an einen Freund	*an ihn*	*an wen*
1. mit seinem Chef		
2. mit dem Zug		
3. von der Erde		
4. in seine Freundin		
5. in der Stadt		
6. am Tisch		
7. gegen die Leute		
8. gegen die Tür		
9. aus dem Wohnzimmer		
10. nach seiner Tante		

Written Practice 5

In the blanks provided, write the letter or letters of the phrases on the right that answer the questions on the left. Not all letters will be used, and some may be used more than once.

1. Wie oft bist du in Norwegen gewesen? _____

2. Ist Ihre Tante Ärztin geworden? _____

3. Womit seid ihr gefahren? _____

4. Haben Sie heute mit Herrn Bach gesprochen? _____

5. Wann ist der alte Musikant gestorben? _____

6. Ist der Flughafen hier in der Nähe? _____

7. Könnt ihr ihn verstehen? _____

8. Wann fängt das Konzert an? _____

9. Wird sie das Auto reparieren können? _____

10. Haben Sie das Geld gefunden? _____

a. Mit einem Freund.

b. Hoffentlich.

c. Ziemlich oft.

d. Leider nicht.

e. Von einer Kusine.

f. Nein, eine Tänzerin.

g. In einer Stunde.

h. Wegen des Wetters.

i. Mit dem Zug.

j. Vor einem Jahr.

k. Ja, sehr gut.

l. Nein, noch nicht.

m. Nein, er ist weit von hier.

More About Adverbs

Adverbs modify verbs, other adverbs, and adjectives. Let's look at the types of adverbs that function in each of these cases.

Some adverbs and adverbial phrases describe frequency or time. For example:

gewöhnlich	*usually*	oft	*often*
immer	*always*	selten	*seldom*
im Sommer	*in the summer*	vor einem Jahr	*a year ago*
manchmal	*sometimes*	wieder	*again*

In a sentence these adverbs may look like this:

Wir gehen **oft** ins Kino.   *We **often** go to the movies.*

Other adverbs describe a direction to a place or from a place:

| dorthin | *(to) there* | hierher | *(to) here* | nach Hause | *home(ward)* |

For example:

Die Jungen sind **dorthin** gelaufen.   *The boys ran **there**.*

Some adverbs or adverbial phrases describe the location where an action takes place:

dort (da)	*there*	oben	*above, overhead; upstairs*
draußen	*outside*	überall	*everywhere*
hier	*here*	unten	*below; downstairs*
in der Stadt	*in the city*	unter dem Tisch	*under the table*

For example:

Draußen ist es sehr kalt.   *It is very cold **outside**.*

Other adverbs describe an attitude toward someone or something:

| hoffentlich | *hopefully* | natürlich | *naturally* |
| leider | *unfortunately* | selbstverständlich | *of course, naturally* |

For example:

Der Mann ist **leider** gestorben.   ***Unfortunately**, the man died.*

Certain adverbs can modify other adverbs or adjectives. They tell to what degree the adverb functions. Let's look at some adverbs that can modify **langsam** (*slowly*, an adverb) or **kalt** (*cold*, an adjective).

außerordentlich kalt	*extraordinarily cold*	sehr kalt	*very cold*
außerordentlich langsam	*extraordinarily slowly*	sehr langsam	*very slowly*
relativ kalt	*relatively cold*	ziemlich kalt	*fairly cold*
relativ langsam	*relatively slowly*	ziemlich langsam	*fairly slowly*

Some adverbs are formed by adding the suffix **-erweise** to an adjective. A few such adverbs are:

Adjective	Adverb	
brutal	brutalerweise	*brutally*
erstaunlich	erstaunlicherweise	*astonishingly*
glücklich	glücklicherweise	*happily; fortunately*
möglich	möglicherweise	*possibly*
normal	normalerweise	*normally*

Remember that in German sentences there is a pattern of order for adverbs. They occur within sentences with time adverbs appearing first, adverbs of manner second, and adverbs of place third. For example:

Wir fahren **selten** (time) **mit dem**   *We **seldom** go **by bus** **to the city**.*
     Bus (manner) **in die Stadt** (place).

See Chapter 13 for details on adverbial word order.

Written Practice 6

Rewrite each sentence adding the adverbs in parentheses. Consider how the meaning is changed by these adverbs.

1. Ihre Tochter ist _____ intelligent.

   (sehr) _____.

   (außerordentlich) _____.

   (relativ) _____.

   (ziemlich) _____.

   (erstaunlicherweise) _____.

2. _____ sehen wir viele Probleme.

   (überall) _____.

   (hier) _____.

   (dort) _____.

   (in dieser Stadt) _____.

   (in Europa) _____.

3. Unsere Familie ist _____ in Griechenland gewesen.

(oft) _____.

(selten) _____.

(manchmal) _____.

(nie) _____.

(ziemlich oft) _____.

QUIZ

1. Write the correct forms of the relative pronouns.

	Masculine	Feminine	Neuter	Plural
nom	_____	_____	_____	_____
acc	_____	_____	_____	_____
dat	_____	_____	_____	_____
gen	_____	_____	_____	_____

2. Change the phrase in bold print to the ones in parentheses. Rewrite each sentence making any necessary changes to the relative pronouns and verbs used.

Das Buch, das ich kaufen will, ist ziemlich alt.

(der Wagen) _____.

(die Bluse) _____.

(die Handschuhe) _____.

(die Kleider) _____.

(das kleine Haus) _____.

3. Write the following verb phrases in the four tenses shown with the pronouns provided.

		hören sie lachen	**lassen das Auto waschen**
pres	er	_____	_____
past	wir	_____	_____
pres perf	ihr	_____	_____
fut	Sie	_____	_____

		lernen schwimmen	**sehen sie arbeiten**
pres	ich	_____	_____
past	du	_____	_____
pres perf	wir	_____	_____
fut	er	_____	_____

Complete each phrase with the sentences that follow. Make any necessary changes to the word order.

4. Wer sagt, dass…?

   Mein Vater hat nicht gut fahren können.

   _____?

   Der junge Reporter wird die Tänzerin interviewen wollen.

   _____?

   Ich interessiere mich nicht für Sport.

   _____?

   Herr Bach wird den alten VW wieder reparieren lassen.

   _____?

   Wir haben ihnen ein Paket geschickt.

   _____?

5. Jemand fragt, ob…

   Der Student ist gestern nach Amerika geflogen.

   _____.

Erik ließ seinen Wagen waschen.

_____.

Meine Schwester wird im Ausland wohnen müssen.

_____.

Diese Leute haben dorthin reisen dürfen.

_____.

Ich werde fleißig arbeiten.

_____.

Circle the letter of the word or phrase that best completes each sentence.

6. Die Leute, mit _____ ich gesprochen habe, kommen aus England.

   (a) damit   (c) denen

   (b) anstatt   (d) der

7. Wer hat diesen _____ verloren?

   (a) Regenschirm   (c) Krieg

   (b) Küche   (d) Besichtigung

8. Diese Schülerin, _____ sehr gut lernt, ist intelligent.

   (a) die   (c) der

   (b) den   (d) deren

9. Sie fragt, warum er es _____ lesen wollen.

   (a) wird   (c) gehabt

   (b) haben   (d) ist

10. Die Tänzerinnen, _____ der Reporter spricht, kommen aus Moskau.

   (a) darin   (c) von denen

   (b) womit   (d) deren

Write the present perfect tense conjugation for the following verbs with the pronouns provided.

1. helfen

    ich _____

    er _____

    wir _____

2. versprechen

    ich _____

    er _____

    wir _____

3. fliegen

    ich _____

    er _____

    wir _____

Write the past perfect tense conjugation for the following verbs with the pronouns provided.

4. mitgehen

    du _____

    ihr _____

    Sie _____

5. spazieren

    du _____

    ihr _____

    Sie _____

6. haben

    du _____

    ihr _____

    Sie _____

Provide the past participle for the following verbs.

   7. fragen _____

   8. studieren _____

   9. essen _____

 10. werden _____

Using the appropriate form of the dative case, complete each sentence with the words in parentheses.

 11. Warum glauben Sie _____ nicht?

     (Ihr Bruder) _____?

     (diese Dame) _____?

     (die Männer) _____?

 12. Ich werde morgen mit _____ sprechen.

     (er) _____.

     (sie *s.*) _____.

     (sie *pl.*) _____.

 13. Sie geben _____ die Fahrkarten.

     (ein Ausländer) _____.

     (du) _____.

     (ihr) _____.

In the blanks provided, write the auxiliary **haben** if the verb is transitive or write the auxiliary **sein** if the verb is intransitive or is a verb of motion.

 14. _____ gelaufen

 15. _____ gesprochen

 16. _____ mitgegangen

 17. _____ diskutiert

 18. _____ verstanden

Rewrite each sentence filling in the blank with the words in parentheses.

19. Sie sind vor _____ angekommen.

    (zwei Tage) _____ .

    (eine Woche) _____ .

    (ein Jahr) _____ .

20. Er hat drei Stunden auf _____ gewartet.

    (er) _____ .

    (du) _____ .

    (ich) _____ .

Write the accusative, dative, and genitive forms of the following words and phrases.

	Accusative	**Dative**	**Genitive**
21. ich	_____	_____	_____
22. du	_____	_____	_____
23. sie *pl.*	_____	_____	_____
24. diese Ausländer	_____	_____	_____
25. das Mädchen	_____	_____	_____
26. der Artikel	_____	_____	_____

Change the phrases conjugated in the present tense to the future tense with the pronouns provided. For example:

Ich komme mit.

Er *wird mitkommen.* _____

Wir *werden mitkommen.* _____

27. Wir bestellen ein Butterbrot.

    Du _____ .

    Er _____ .

    Sie *pl.* _____ .

28. Er geht mit.

   Sie *s.* _____.

   Ihr _____.

   Man _____.

29. Ihr wascht euch.

   Du _____.

   Er _____.

   Ich _____.

Rewrite the sentence with the pronouns provided in parentheses. Change the reflexive pronouns appropriately.

30. Er bestellt sich ein Glas Milch.

   (ich) _____.

   (du) _____.

   (wir) _____.

   (ihr) _____.

   (sie *pl.*) _____.

Conjugate the following verbs in the tenses shown with the pronouns provided.

	schicken	umsteigen	sich beeilen
31. **pres** ich	_____	_____	_____
32. **past** du	_____	_____	_____
33. **pres** perf er	_____	_____	_____
34. **past** perf wir	_____	_____	_____
35. **fut** ihr	_____	_____	_____
36. **fut** perf sie *pl.*	_____	_____	_____

Change each of the following present tense sentences to the present perfect and the future tenses.

37. Ich will es nicht hören.

   _____.

   _____.

38. Könnt ihr dieses Gedicht verstehen?

   _____?

   _____?

39. Du kannst Schach spielen.

   _____.

   _____.

Rewrite the sentence changing the words in bold print to the ones in parentheses. Make the appropriate changes to the relative clauses and verbs used.

40. **Das Kind**, dessen Mutter Diplomatin ist, wird in der Hauptstadt wohnen.
   (die Kinder)

   _____.

   (der Junge)

   _____.

   (das Mädchen)

   _____.

Complete the sentence with the phrases that follow. Make any necessary changes to the word order.

   Der Reporter schreibt, dass...

41. Der Diplomat hat nicht gut fahren können.

   _____.

42. Er wird den Helden interviewen wollen.

   _____.

Circle the letter of the word or phrase that best completes each sentence.

43. Ich habe dreißig Minuten _____ dich gewartet.

    (a) heute   (c) getan

    (b) vom   (d) auf

44. Habt ihr diesen Roman _____?

    (a) mit einem Freund   (c) schreibt

    (b) gelesen   (d) zu euren Eltern

45. Meine Wirtin hat mit meinem Sohn _____.

    (a) gespielt   (c) verstanden

    (b) aufgemacht   (d) erkannt

46. Es ist wieder kalt _____.

    (a) gehabt   (c) ausgesehen

    (b) gemacht   (d) geworden

47. Robert hat zu _____ gesprochen.

    (a) schnell   (c) beschrieben

    (b) beschreiben   (d) vor einer Woche

48. Ihre Schwester _____ sehr krank ausgesehen.

    (a) hat   (c) noch

    (b) ist   (d) war

49. Die Küche _____ ist sehr klein.

    (a) unserer Nachbarin   (c) diese Ausländer

    (b) meinem Enkel   (d) der Zeit

50. Du irrst _____ nicht.

    (a) schon   (c) ihn

    (b) dich   (d) jetzt

PART FOUR

SOME FINE POINTS

CHAPTER 16

Comparing Things

In this chapter you will learn:

More About Relative Pronouns

A Few Common Idioms

Comparative and Superlative of Adjectives and Adverbs

A Little German History

More About Relative Pronouns

There is still more to know about the use of German relative pronouns.

WELCHER AS A RELATIVE PRONOUN

It is possible to substitute a form of **welcher** for relative pronouns that take the form of the definite article. The genitive form is the only exception to this. Compare the following declensions of relative pronouns.

	Masculine	Feminine	Neuter	Plural
nom	der, welcher	die, welche	das, welches	die, welche
acc	den, welchen	die, welche	das, welches	die, welche
dat	dem, welchem	der, welcher	dem, welchem	denen, welchen
gen	dessen	deren	dessen	deren

Let's look at **welcher** as it appears in sentences.

Der Soldat, welcher im Irak war, ist wieder zu Hause.	*The soldier that was in Iraq is home again.*
Der Soldat, welchen Tina kennt, ist wieder zu Hause.	*The soldier that Tina knows is home again.*
Der Soldat, von welchem alle sprechen, ist wieder zu Hause.	*The soldier that everyone is speaking about is home again.*
Der Soldat, dessen Schwester Ärztin ist, ist wieder zu Hause.	*The soldier whose sister is a physician is home again.*

Written Practice 1

Rewrite each sentence, changing the phrase in bold print to the ones provided in parentheses. Use a form of **welcher** as the relative pronoun and make any necessary changes to the sentence. For example:

Das Haus, das er kaufen will, ist alt.

(das Auto) _Das Auto, welches er kaufen will, ist alt._

1. **Das Buch**, das sie gelesen hat, ist interessant.

   (der Brief) _____ .

   (die Zeitung) _____ .

   (der Roman) _____ .

   (die Romane) _____ .

2. **Das Mädchen**, mit dem Karl sprechen will, kommt aus Polen.

   (die Touristen) _____ .

   (der Matrose) _____ .

(die Tänzerin) _____ .

(das Kind) _____ .

WAS AS A RELATIVE PRONOUN

It is possible for an entire clause to be the antecedent of a relative pronoun. If this is the case, in German the relative pronoun becomes **was**. Let's look at some examples.

Er ist Zahnarzt geworden, was uns sehr erstaunte.	*He became a dentist, which astounded us very much.*
Es fing an zu regnen, was das Picknick schnell verdorben hat.	*It began to rain, which quickly spoiled the picnic.*
Es geht ihrem Mann jetzt gut, was uns sehr erfreute.	*Her husband is feeling well now, which made us very happy.*

Was also becomes the relative pronoun when the demonstrative **das** is the antecedent.

Ich verstehe das, was du sagen willst.	*I understand what you want to say.*
Verstehst du nichts von dem, was er sagt?	*Do you not understand anything of what he says?*

And **was** is the relative pronoun when the antecedent is either **alles**, **etwas**, **nichts**, **viel(es)**, or a neuter adjective used as a noun. For example:

Das ist alles, was ich geben kann.	*That is everything that I can give.*
Sie lesen etwas, was ziemlich interessant ist.	*They are reading something that is rather interesting.*
Der Lehrer versteht nichts, was das Kind schreibt.	*The teacher does not understand anything that the child writes.*
Es gibt vieles, was uns glücklich macht.	*There is much that makes us happy.*
Das war das Letzte, was er hörte.	*That was the last thing that he heard.*

Oral Practice

Practice saying the following list of sentences out loud.

German	English
Haben Sie etwas, was billig ist?	*Do you have something that is cheap?*
Nein, ich habe nichts, was billig ist.	*No, I have nothing that is cheap.*
Ist das alles, was Sie haben?	*Is that all that you have?*
Nein, ich habe viel mehr.	*No, I have a lot more.*
Haben Sie etwas, was nicht so teuer ist?	*Do you have something that is not so expensive?*
Ja, ich habe vieles, was nicht so teuer ist.	*Yes, I have a lot that is not so expensive.*
Karl hat den Preis gewonnen, was mich sehr erstaunte.	*Karl won the prize, which astounded me very much.*
Gudrun ist schnell gerannt, was uns sehr erstaunte.	*Gudrun ran fast, which astounded us very much.*
Erik wollte Geige spielen, was den Vater sehr erstaunte.	*Erik wanted to play the violin, which astounded the father very much.*

If a preposition is needed with **was**, a compound word with the prefix **wo-** is formed with that preposition, for example: **womit**, **wofür**. If the preposition begins with a vowel, the prefix is **wor-** is used: **worauf**, **worin**. Following are some example sentences:

German	English
Ich habe etwas, wofür du dich interessieren wirst.	*I have something that you will be interested in.*
Er schreibt nichts, worüber er nicht sprechen soll.	*He writes nothing that he should not speak about.*

Written Practice 2

Combine the first sentence with the sentences that follow. Form a relative clause with **was** or a **wo-/wor-** compound following the pattern of the example.

Ich habe nichts.

Nichts ist interessant.

Ich habe nichts, was interessant ist.

1. Ich habe etwas.

   Ich habe etwas im Park gefunden.

   _____.

   Meine Mutter hat mir etwas gegeben.

   _____.

   Du wirst dich über etwas freuen.

   _____.

   Die Kinder können mit etwas spielen.

   _____.

2. Ist das alles?

   Du kannst alles sagen.

   _____?

   Tina wollte alles kaufen.

   _____?

   Er interessiert sich für alles.

   _____?

   Sie wollen über alles sprechen.

   _____?

3. Ich lerne viel, …

   Viel steht nicht in Büchern.

   _____.

Goethe hatte über vieles geschrieben.

_____

Vieles ist interessant.

_____

4. Ich verstehe nichts, ...
   Die alte Frau sagt nichts.

_____

Du hast nichts in diesem Buch geschrieben.

_____

Man lernt nichts in dieser Klasse.

_____

A Few Common Idioms

Idioms are special phrases or special usages of words that are accepted in a language as an understandable concept, but when translated into another language, idioms most often make little or no sense. For example, the English idiom, _eat your heart out_, would sound absolutely ridiculous if translated literally into German. The same thing occurs when translating German idioms into English.

ES GIBT

German has a special idiomatic expression made up simply of the two words **es gibt**. Literally, those words mean _it gives_, but this expression is used when in English you say _there is_ or _there are_: _There are a lot of toys on the floor._ (**Es gibt viele Spielzeuge auf dem Boden.**) English has both a singular and plural form of this idiom: _there is_, _there are_. But German has only one form for both the singular and the plural: **es gibt**.

The German idiom functions much the same way as its English counterpart, except that the object that follows **es gibt** must be in the accusative case. You should recall that this means that all masculine nouns will make a declensional change. Let's look at some example sentences.

Es gibt viele Bücher in meiner Bibliothek.   _There are a lot of books in my library._

| Heute mittag gibt es Bratwurst und Suppe. | *For lunch today there are roast sausages and soup.* |
| Warum gibt es keinen Wein? | *Why is there no wine?* |

Oral Practice

Practice saying the following list of sentences out loud.

Was gibt es zum Abendessen?	*What is there for supper?*
Es gibt Gemüsesuppe zum Abendessen.	*There is vegetable soup for supper.*
Es gibt Rindfleisch und Kartoffeln.	*There is beef and potatoes.*
Es gibt Fisch und Reis.	*There is fish and rice.*
Was gibt es zu trinken?	*What is there to drink?*
Es gibt Kaffee oder Tee.	*There is coffee or tea.*
Es gibt Sprudel oder Mineralwasser.	*There is sparkling water or mineral water.*
Es gibt Bier oder Wein.	*There is beer or wine.*
Was gibt es zum Nachtisch?	*What is there for dessert?*
Es gibt Eis oder Pudding.	*There is ice cream or pudding.*
Es gibt einen Obstkuchen.	*There is a pie.*

WIE GEHT'S

You learned another German idiom early in this book: **Wie geht's?** (*How are you?*) Now that you've had a thorough look at the dative case, it's time to look again at this expression. This idiom uses the pronoun **es** as its subject (**Wie geht es?**), and its objects must be in the dative case.

The question **Wie geht's?** shows the pronoun **es** as a contraction. But when an object is added, the contraction is not used. Following are some examples:

Wie geht es dir?	*How are you?*
Es geht mir gut, danke. Und dir?	*I am fine, thanks. And you?*
Wie geht es Ihnen?	*How are you?*

Es geht mir sehr gut. Und Ihnen?	*I am very well. And you?*
Ziemlich gut.	*Fairly well.*
Wie geht es Ihrem Mann?	*How is your husband?*
Nicht so gut.	*Not so well.*
Es ging ihm letzte Woche viel besser.	*He was much better last week.*
Hoffentlich geht es ihm nächste Woche wieder besser.	*I hope he will be better again next week.*
Es wird mir auch besser gehen.	*I will feel better, too.*

The pronoun **es** is the subject of other common expressions, in which some mysterious *it* is the cause of meteorological conditions.

Es regnet.	*It is raining.*
Es schneit.	*It is snowing.*

Both **regnen** and **schneien** are regular verbs and use the auxiliary **haben** in the perfect tenses.

GERN HABEN

Another useful idiomatic expression is **gern haben**. Its translation is *to like* or *to be fond of*. The verb **haben** can be conjugated in any tense, and the object of that verb is then followed by **gern**. For example:

Hast du mich nicht gern?	*Don't you like me?*
Tina hatte den neuen Studenten gern.	*Tina liked the new student.*
Haben Sie sie gern gehabt?	*Did you like her?*
Ich werde diesen Mann nie gern haben.	*I will never like this man.*

GEBOREN

The infinitive **gebären** means *to bear* (*a child*). Its conjugation in the various tenses looks like this:

Present

ich gebäre	*I bear*	sie gebärt (*or* gebiert)	*she bears*

Past

ich gebar	*I bore*	sie gebar	*she bore*

Present Perfect

ich habe geboren	*I have bore*	sie hat geboren	*she has bore*

Future

ich werde gebären	*I will bear*	sie wird gebären	*she will bear*

The expression *to be born* is a common one: *I was born in July; She was born thirty years ago.* In German that expression is composed of the conjugation of the verb **sein** and the past participle **geboren**. In sentences it looks like this:

Mein Vater ist im Jahre 1970 geboren.	*My father was born in 1970.*
Wann bist du geboren?	*When were you born?*

Use **ist** with **geboren** when talking about people who are still alive. Use **wurde** with **geboren** when talking about people who are deceased.

Mein Sohn ist vor drei Wochen geboren.	*My son was born three weeks ago.*
Goethe wurde im Jahre 1749 geboren.	*Goethe was born in 1749.*

When giving the year that someone was born, you can use the phrase **im Jahre** with the year. It is also possible to use the year alone. In that case, do not use the preposition **in**.

Er ist im Jahre 1977 geboren.	*He was born in 1977.*
Er ist 1977 geboren.	*He was born in 1977.*

Do not use **im Jahre** with a month and a date.

Er ist im Oktober 1977 geboren.	*He was born in October 1977.*
Er ist am achten Oktober 1977 geboren.	*He was born on the eighth of October, 1977.*

Oral Practice

Practice saying the following list of sentences out loud.

Wann sind Sie geboren?	*When were you born?*
Ich bin im April geboren.	*I was born in April.*
In welchem Jahr bist du geboren?	*In what year were you born?*
Ich bin im Jahre 1988 geboren.	*I was born in 1988.*
Wo seid ihr geboren?	*Where were you born?*
Wir sind in Frankreich geboren.	*We were born in France.*
Wer ist in Deutschland geboren?	*Who was born in Germany?*
Professor Benz ist in Deutschland geboren.	*Professor Benz was born in Germany.*
Mozart wurde in Österreich geboren.	*Mozart was born in Austria.*
Wurde Bach in Deutschland geboren?	*Was Bach born in Germany?*
Ja, Bach wurde in Deutschland geboren.	*Yes, Bach was born in Germany.*
Wo wurde John F. Kennedy geboren?	*Where was John F. Kennedy born?*
Er wurde in den Vereinigten Staaten geboren.	*He was born in the United States.*

Written Practice 3

Using the names and years provided, write sentences that tell when someone was born and when someone died. For example:

Benjamin Franklin 1706–1790

Benjamin Frankin wurde 1706 geboren.

Er ist 1790 gestorben.

1. Wilhelm II. 1859–1941

_____.

_____.

2. Otto von Bismarck 1815–1898

_____.

_____.

3. mein Bruder 1995–2005

_____.

_____.

4. Karl der Große 742–814

_____.

_____.

5. meine Mutter 1966–1998

_____.

_____.

Comparative and Superlative of Adjectives and Adverbs

The basic form of an adjective or adverb is called the positive form. But two other forms exist that play significant roles in language: the comparative and the superlative.

The comparative of an adjective or adverb makes a comparison between two persons or things.

John is _bigger_ than Mary.   She runs _faster_ than her brother.

And like English, German forms a comparative by adding **-er** to the adjective or adverb.

klein	_small_	kleiner	_smaller_
schnell	_fast_	schneller	_faster_
weit	_far_	weiter	_farther_

Adjectives or adverbs with the vowels **a**, **o**, **u**, may require an umlaut in the comparative.

alt	*old*	älter	*older*
groß	*big*	größer	*bigger*
jung	*young*	jünger	*younger*

The word **als** (*than*) is used to identify the person or thing being compared to the subject: **Er ist älter als Erik.** (*He is older than Erik.*)

Comparatives have no ending when used as predicate adjectives or adverbs. But if the comparative is an adjective modifying a noun directly, it will have an adjective ending.

Adverb:

Er spricht schneller.	*He speaks faster.*
Sie läuft langsamer als Tanja.	*She runs slower than Tanja.*

Predicate Adjective:

Unser Haus ist größer.	*Our house is bigger.*
Mein Sohn ist kleiner als Ihr Sohn.	*My son is smaller than your son.*

Adjective Ending:

Der kleinere Junge ist mein Sohn.	*The smaller boy is my son.*
Das jüngere Mädchen ist meine Tochter.	*The younger girl is my daughter.*

The English superlative ends in -*est*: *tallest, funniest, biggest,* and so forth. German is similar but not identical—the ending **-sten** is added. A predicate adjective or adverb in the German superlative is formed using a prepositional phrase with **an**. Many adjectives and adverbs that contain the vowels **a, o, u** may require an umlaut in the superlative.

hart	*hard*	am härtesten	*(the) hardest*
jung	*young*	am jüngsten	*(the) youngest*
klein	*small*	am kleinsten	*(the) smallest*
rot	*red*	am rötesten	*(the) reddest*
schnell	*fast*	am schnellsten	*(the) fastest*
weit	*far*	am weitesten	*(the) farthest*

As you see from **hart**, **rot**, and **weit**, when an adjective or adverb ends in **-d, -t, -s, -ss, -ß,** or **-z,** the superlative suffix will be **-esten.**

am ältesten	*(the) oldest*
am blödesten	*(the) most*
am kürzesten	*(the) shortest idiotic*

If the superlative is an adjective modifying a noun directly, it will have an adjective ending and the preposition **an** is omitted.

Adverb:

| Er spricht am schnellsten. | *He speaks the fastest.* |
| Sie läuft am langsamsten. | *She runs the slowest.* |

Predicate Adjective:

| Unser Haus ist am größten. | *Our house is the biggest.* |
| Mein Sohn ist am kleinsten. | *My son is the smallest.* |

Adjective Ending:

| Der kleinste Junge ist mein Sohn. | *The smallest boy is my son.* |
| Das jüngste Mädchen ist meine Tochter. | *The youngest girl is my daughter.* |

Just as English has a few irregular forms in the comparative and superlative, so, too, does German.

Positive		Comparative		Superlative	
bald	*soon*	eher	*sooner*	am ehesten	*soonest*
groß	*big*	größer	*bigger*	am größten	*biggest*
gut	*good*	besser	*better*	am besten	*best*
hoch	*high*	höher	*higher*	am höchsten	*highest*
nah	*near*	näher	*nearer*	am nächsten	*nearest*

Written Practice 4

Form the comparative and superlative of the following adjectives.

	Comparative	**Superlative**
klein	*kleiner*	*am kleinsten*
1. kalt	_____	_____
2. interessant	_____	_____
3. gut	_____	_____
4. lang	_____	_____
5. dunkel	_____	_____
6. warm	_____	_____

7. schwarz   _____   _____

8. ruhig   _____   _____

9. weiß   _____   _____

10. arm   _____   _____

A Little German History

In the days of the Roman Empire, Tacitus wrote about the tribes of northern Europe—the Germanic tribes (**die germanischen Stämme**). They were fierce people who lived a more primitive existence than the Romans or other ethnic groups within the Roman Empire.

The Germanic people evolved over the centuries into the modern Germans who lived in a large number of small principalities. These principalities, as well as other larger states, were part of the Holy Roman Empire (**das heilige römische Reich deutscher Nation**), which in the beginning was ruled by Emperor Charlemagne (**Kaiser Karl der Große**). The word **Kaiser** is the German word for *Emperor* or *Caesar.*

The little German principalities were overseen by lesser nobles than Emperor Charlemagne in *Aix-la-Chapelle* (**Aachen**). These lesser nobles were called:

der Freiherr	*baron*	die Gräfin	*countess*
die Freifrau	*baroness*	der Herzog	*duke*
der Graf	*count*	die Herzogin	*duchess*

As Prussia (**Preußen**) grew more powerful and influential, it began to dominate the smaller principalities, and in the nineteenth century, under the leadership of Otto von Bismarck, a new united land emerged: Germany (**Deutschland**). At the same time, the Prussian king claimed the title **Kaiser** and was no longer referred to as **König**.

After World War I (**der erste Weltkrieg**), the monarchy collapsed, and Germany became a republic (**die Weimarer Republik**). In 1933 Adolf Hitler took over power and led the country with the title *leader* (**der Führer**). His political party was called the **Nazi** party, which is short for the National Socialistic German Workers' Party (**die Nationalsozialistische Deutsche Arbeiterpartei**). Soon after the end of the World War II (**der zweite Weltkrieg**), West Germany became a republic once again (**die Bundesrepublik Deutschland** or **BRD**), and East Germany became a separate republic (**die Deutsche Demokratische Republik** or **DDR**).

The new head of the West German republic was called the chancellor (**der Kanzler**) and the parliament was called the **Bundestag**. With the end of the Cold War (**der kalte Krieg**) in the late 1980s, Germany achieved the reunification (**die Wiedervereinigung**) it had sought since the end of World War II. The capital (**die Hauptstadt**) of West Germany at that time was Bonn. The capital of East Germany was East Berlin (**Ostberlin**). Today the capital of unified Germany is the historical capital, **Berlin**. Over the entrance to the parliament building in the capital city is the inscription **Dem Deutschen Volke** (*To the German people*).

Oral Practice

Practice saying the following list of sentences out loud.

Ich finde Geschichte sehr interessant.	*I find history very interesting.*
Weißt du etwas über die deutsche Geschichte?	*Do you know something about German history?*
Nein, ich weiß wenig über die deutsche Geschichte.	*No, I know little about German history.*
Der erste Kaiser des ersten Reiches war Karl der Große.	*The first emperor of the First Reich was Charlemagne.*
Der letzte Kaiser des zweiten Reiches war Wilhelm II. (der zweite).	*The last emperor of the Second Reich was Wilhelm II.*
Adolf Hitler war der Führer des dritten Reiches.	*Adolf Hitler was the leader of the Third Reich.*
Im Jahre 1989 endete der kalte Krieg.	*The Cold War ended in 1989.*
Die Mauer zwischen Ost- und Westberlin wurde abgerissen.	*The wall between East and West Berlin was pulled down.*
Deutschland ist jetzt eine Republik.	*Germany is a republic now.*
Hat Deutschland einen Kanzler oder eine Kanzlerin?	*Does Germany have a male or female chancellor?*
Was war die Hauptstadt der Bundesrepublik Deutschland?	*What was the capital of the Federal Republic of Germany?*
Die Hauptstadt der Bundesrepublik war Bonn.	*The capital of the Federal Republic was Bonn.*
Was war die Hauptstadt der DDR?	*What was the capital of the GDR?*

Die Hauptstadt der DDR war Ostberlin.	*The capital of the GDR was East Berlin.*
Was ist die heutige Hauptstadt Deutschlands?	*What is the present capital of Germany?*
Die heutige Hauptstadt ist Berlin.	*The present capital is Berlin.*
Wie heißt das deutsche Parlament?	*What is the name of the German parliament?*
Das deutsche Parlament heißt der Bundestag.	*The German parliament is called the Bundestag.*

Written Practice 5

Circle the letter of the word or phrase that best completes each sentence.

1. In welchem Jahr _____ er geboren?

    (a) wart   (c) sein

    (b) wurde   (d) kann

2. Alles, _____ sie sagte, war sehr interessant.

    (a) welches   (c) dass

    (b) das   (d) was

3. Hast du das schöne Mädchen _____?

    (a) gern   (c) sehr gut

    (b) welche   (d) gebären

4. Es gibt _____.

    (a) keinen Nachtisch   (c) kein Wein

    (b) noch   (d) wahrscheinlich

5. Unser Kind ist _____ geboren.

    (a) Dezember   (c) Donnerstag

    (b) 2001   (d) der zehnte Mai

6. Der Matrose, _____ ich gesprochen habe, ist ein Held.

    (a) für wen   (c) von welchem

    (b) darüber   (d) über ihn

7. Wir besichtigen _____, die mehr als 500 Jahre alt ist.

   (a) ein Schiff   (c) einer Stadt

   (b) eine Kirche   (d) der Stadtmauer

8. Ich _____ im Januar 1980 geboren.

   (a) bin   (c) konnte

   (b) wurde   (d) habe

9. Wann kommt der Zug, _____ wir dorthin fahren werden?

   (a) mit welchem   (c) darin

   (b) von dem   (d) worauf

10. Er gab mir etwas, _____ ich lange gewartet habe.

    (a) wann   (c) damit

    (b) worauf   (d) welche

11. Berlin ist die _____ Deutschlands.

    (a) Mauer   (c) Kaiser

    (b) Bundesrepublik   (d) Hauptstadt

12. Wilhelm II. war Kaiser des zweiten _____.

    (a) Republik   (c) Reiches

    (b) Weltkrieg   (d) Königs

13. Meine Tochter ist in Österreich _____.

    (a) gewohnt   (c) gegangen

    (b) gelebt   (d) geboren

14. Zu Hause sprechen wir _____ Deutsch.

    (a) gewöhnlich   (c) in einer Stunde

    (b) brutalerweise   (d) es gibt

15. Es gibt _____, was uns glücklich macht.

    (a) alle   (c) kein Nachtisch

    (b) vieles   (d) welches

16. Mein Vater ist _____ als mein Onkel.

    (a) schön   (c) älter

    (b) am schnellsten   (d) arm

17. Wer kann _____ laufen?

    (a) der langsame   (c) weite

    (b) am schnellsten   (d) hoch

18. Erik ist der _____ Student.

    (a) klein   (c) größer

    (b) am ärmsten   (d) beste

19. Meine Schwester spielt das Klavier _____ .

    (a) am schlechtesten   (c) kälter

    (b) bessere   (d) heißeste

20. Welche Stadt ist _____ ?

    (a) kleinere   (c) älteste

    (b) näher   (d) das größte

QUIZ

The definite article forms of relative pronouns are given below. Write in their **welcher** counterparts in the spaces provided.

1. **nom** der _____ die _____ das _____ die _____

2. **acc** den _____ die _____ das _____ die _____

3. **dat** dem _____ der _____ dem _____ denen _____

4. **gen** dessen _____ deren _____ dessen _____ deren _____

Combine the first sentence with the one that follows, making each one a relative clause with a definite article relative pronoun. Then rewrite the sentence using **welcher** as the relative pronoun. For example:

Er hat ein Auto.

Er wird das Auto reparieren lassen.

Er hat ein Auto, das er wird reparieren lassen.

Er hat ein Auto, welches er wird reparieren lassen.

5. Der Seemann fuhr auf einem Schiff.

   Das Schiff ging bei einer Insel unter.

   _____.

   _____.

Complete the following sentence with the ones that follow. Form each one as a relative clause.

6. Martin hat etwas, ...

   Du wirst dich über etwas freuen.

   _____.

   Etwas ist sehr teuer.

   _____.

   Er will etwas verkaufen.

   _____.

Write a statement using the example as a guide.

   Goethe 1749–1832

   Goethe wurde im Jahre 1749 geboren.

   Er ist im Jahre 1832 gestorben.

7. Thomas Jefferson 1743–1826

   _____.

   _____.

Rewrite each sentence filling in the blanks with the proper forms of the nouns or pronouns given.

8. Es geht _____ viel besser.

   (ich) _____.

   (er) _____.

   (sie _pl._) _____.

(meine Frau) _____ .

(der Soldat) _____ .

9. Gibt es _____?

(kein Wein) _____?

(eine Flasche Bier) _____?

(keine Milch) _____?

(keine Butter) _____?

(kein Sekt) _____?

10. Ich habe _____ gern.

(du) _____ .

(sie *s.*) _____ .

(ihr) _____ .

(der Junge) _____ .

(das Mädchen) _____ .

CHAPTER 17

Using Commands

In this chapter you will learn:

Passive Voice

Adjective Endings with Der- *Words*

Imperative

Plants

Animals

Passive Voice

Until now, you have dealt with verbs in the active voice. In the active voice, the subject is the doer of the action of the verb.

John kisses Mary.

John is the doer of the action, the one who does the kissing. But in the passive voice, the doer of the action is put in a passive position in the sentence. And the doer of the action can even be omitted from the sentence. For example:

Mary is being kissed by John.

The subject of this sentence is Mary. But she's not doing the kissing. Look at the same sentence with the doer of the action omitted.

Mary is being kissed.

The subject is still Mary, but the doer of the action isn't even mentioned. Another example:

The money was stolen from the bank.

Who took the money? A robber? The head of the bank? The doer of the action is not stated.

The German passive voice consists of a conjugation of **werden** followed by a past participle. Don't confuse this with the future tense, which is **werden** followed by an infinitive. Let's look at some examples of the German passive voice in the present tense.

das Geld wird gefunden	*the money is found*
Maria wird geküsst	*Maria is kissed*
es wird oft gesagt	*it is often said*
die Schüler werden unterrichtet	*the pupils are instructed*

The doer of the action, when added to the passive voice structure, becomes the object of the dative preposition **von**.

Das Geld wird von einem Jungen gefunden.	*The money is found by a boy.*
Was wird von ihr gesagt?	*What is said by her?*
Maria wird von Johannes geküsst.	*Maria is kissed by Johannes.*
Die Schüler werden von der Lehrerin unterrichtet.	*The pupils are instructed by the teacher.*

Naturally, a passive sentence can be stated in other tenses as well. The passive conjugation is simply the conjugation of **werden** in the various tenses with a past participle added:

Present: er wird

Past: er wurde

Present Perfect: er ist geworden

Past Perfect: er war geworden

Future: er wird werden

Future Perfect: er wird geworden sein

There is one significant difference: In the passive voice the participle **worden** is used in place of **geworden**. Let's look at some examples.

Present:
Sie wird von ihren Eltern geliebt.   *She is loved by her parents.*

Past:
Sie wurde von ihren Eltern geliebt.   *She was loved by her parents.*

Present Perfect:
Sie ist von ihren Eltern geliebt worden. *She was loved by her parents.*

Past Perfect:
Sie war von ihren Eltern geliebt worden. *She had been loved by her parents.*

Future:
Sie wird von ihren Eltern geliebt werden. *She will be loved by her parents.*

Future Perfect:
Sie wird von ihren Eltern geliebt   *She will have been loved by her*
    worden sein.   *parents.*

It is possible to change an active sentence into a passive sentence quite simply. First, determine the tense of the active sentence; that will be the tense of the passive sentence.

Mein Bruder fand den Regenschirm.   *My brother found the umbrella.*
    (past tense)

Then change the verb of the active sentence into a past participle.

fand → **gefunden**

Change the direct object (accusative case) of the active sentence into the subject (nominative case) of the passive sentence.

den Regenschirm → **Der Regenschirm**…gefunden.

Conjugate **werden** for the new subject in the tense of the original active sentence.

Der Regenschirm **wurde**…gefunden.

Make the subject of the active sentence the object of the preposition **von** in the passive sentence.

Der Regenschirm wurde **von meinem Bruder** gefunden.   *The umbrella was found by my brother.*

Let's try that again with another active sentence.

Die Studentin hat den Brief geschrieben.   *The student wrote the letter.*

Tense: present perfect

Past participle: geschrieben

New subject: der Brief

Conjugation of *werden*: ist…worden

Object of *von*: von der Studentin

And when all the elements are put together, the passive sentence looks like this:

Der Brief ist von der Studentin geschrieben worden.   *The letter was written by the student.*

Written Practice 1

Change the following present tense active sentences to present tense passive sentences. Consider how the meanings change.

1. Der Lehrer kauft zwei Bücher.

   _____.

2. Sie liest den Roman.

   _____.

3. Der Bäcker bäckt das Brot.

   _____.

4. Mein Vater ruft mich.

   _____.

5. Die Soldaten singen viele Lieder.

   _____.

Change the following past tense active sentences to past tense passive sentences.

6. Herr Bauer verkaufte das Haus.

   _____.

7. Meine Mutter rief Tante Gerda an.

   _____.

8. Sie tranken zwei Tassen Kaffee.

   _____.

9. Er lernte diese Gedichte.

   _____.

10. Die Wirtin brachte den Morgenkaffee.

    _____.

Change the following present perfect tense active sentences to present perfect tense passive sentences.

11. Er hat den Roman geschrieben.

   _____.

12. Die Kinder haben einen Hut gefunden.

   _____.

13. Meine Schwester hat das Eis gegessen.

   _____.

Change the following future tense active sentences to future tense passive sentences.

14. Der Reporter wird den Artikel schreiben.

   _____.

15. Die Ausländer werden das Museum besuchen.

   _____.

Oral Practice

Practice saying the following list of sentences out loud.

Die Lampe wurde gebrochen.	*The lamp was broken.*
Die Vase wurde auch gebrochen.	*The vase was broken, too.*
Was wurde repariert?	*What was repaired?*
Der Wagen wurde repariert.	*The car was repaired.*
Ist das Radio auch repariert worden?	*Was the radio repaired, too?*
Ja, es ist von Herrn Benz repariert worden.	*Yes, it was repaired by Mr. Benz.*
Was wird von Tina gebracht werden?	*What will be brought by Tina?*
Ein Obstkuchen wird von ihr gebracht werden.	*A fruit pie will be brought by Tina.*

Eine Flasche Wein wird von Thomas gebracht werden.	*A bottle of wine will be brought by Thomas.*
Von wem werden eure Kinder unterrichtet?	*By whom are your children taught?*
Unsere Kinder werden von Frau Keller unterrichtet.	*Our children are taught by Ms. Keller.*
Der Kuchen ist von meinem Sohn gebacken worden.	*The cake was baked by my son.*
Die Lieder sind von meiner Tochter gesungen worden.	*The songs were sung by my daughter.*
Die Kunsthalle ist von ihnen besucht worden.	*The art museum was visited by them.*
Der Artikel ist von ihr geschrieben worden.	*The article was written by her.*
Was ist passiert?	*What happened?*
Der Bahhof ist zerstört worden.	*The railroad station was destroyed.*
Was ist geschehen?	*What happened?*
Mein Pass ist gestohlen worden.	*My passport has been stolen.*

Adjective Endings with *Der-* Words

The definite articles (**der**, **die**, and **das**) are called **der-** words. But there are other **der-** words as well. It is important to identify them, because they act as signals for the adjective endings required. Following is a list of **der-** words to familiarize yourself with:

alle	*(plural only) all*	jeder	*each*
derselbe	*the same*	jener	*that*
dieser	*this*	welcher	*which*

When these **der-** words are used in the nominative case, the gender signal (**-r** for masculine, **-e** for feminine, and **-s** for neuter) appears in the **der-** word itself. The ending of the adjective that follows is then always an **-e**.

Nominative Case

masc	der gute Lehrer	dieser nette Mann	jeder kleine Junge
fem	die gute Frau	jene nette Dame	welche große Lampe
neut	das gute Kind	jedes nette Mädchen	dasselbe alte Schiff

In the remaining cases (excluding the feminine and neuter accusative, which are always identical to the nominative), the ending for all adjectives is **-en**. Let's look at a chart of these adjective endings.

	Masculine	Feminine	Neuter	Plural
nom	der gute Mann	die gute Frau	das gute Kind	die gut**en** Kinder
acc	den gut**en** Mann	die gute Frau	das gute Kind	die gut**en** Kinder
dat	dem gut**en** Mann	der gut**en** Frau	dem gut**en** Kind	den gut**en** Kindern
gen	des gut**en** Mannes	der gut**en** Frau	des gut**en** Kindes	der gut**en** Kinder

This pattern of adjective endings can be used for any **der-** word. For example, in the masculine:

nom	der gute Mann	dieser gute Mann	jeder gute Mann
acc	den gut**en** Mann	diesen gut**en** Mann	jeden gut**en** Mann
dat	dem gut**en** Mann	diesem gut**en** Mann	jedem gut**en** Mann
gen	des gut**en** Mannes	dieses gut**en** Mannes	jedes gut**en** Mannes

Written Practice 2

Write the following phrases in the accusative, dative, and genitive cases.

nom	**jener nette Wirt**	**diese kleine Bluse**	**welches rote Auto**
acc	_____	_____	_____
dat	_____	_____	_____
gen	_____	_____	_____

nom	**derselbe alte Wagen**	**jenes neue Haus**	**alle fremden Leute**
acc	_____	_____	_____
dat	_____	_____	_____
gen	_____	_____	_____

Oral Practice

Practice saying the following list of sentences out loud.

Kennen Sie den alten Herrn?	*Do you know the old gentleman?*
Nein, ich kenne ihn nicht.	*No, I do not know him.*
Hast du mit jener schönen Tänzerin gesprochen?	*Did you speak with that pretty dancer?*
Nein, ich habe mit dieser netten Schauspielerin gesprochen.	*No, I spoke with this nice actress.*
Ist das das Fahrrad dieses kleinen Kindes?	*Is that this little child's bike?*
Nein, das ist das Fahrrad jenes großen Jungen.	*No, that is that big boy's bike.*
Ist das der Fußball desselben großen Jungen?	*Is that the same big boy's soccer ball?*
Nein, das ist der Fußball dieses schönen Mädchens.	*No, that is this pretty girl's soccer ball.*
Hast du mit jenen interessanten Ausländern getanzt?	*Did you dance with those interesting foreigners?*
Ja, ich habe mit allen Ausländern getanzt.	*Yes, I danced with all the foreigners.*

Written Practice 3

Rewrite each sentence with the adjectives provided in parentheses. Supply the appropriate adjective endings. For example:

Kennst du die _____ Frau?

(alt) *Kennst du die alte Frau?*

1. Die Kinder dieses _____ Mannes lernen gut.

   (jung) _____ .

   (krank) _____ .

2. Sie hat mit demselben _____ Diplomaten gesprochen.

(neu) _____ .

(schlau) _____ .

3. Jede _____ Tanne ist mehr als zwanzig Jahre alt.

(grün) _____ .

(groß) _____ .

Imperative

An imperative is a command form of a verb. English imperatives are quite simple to form: the infinitive minus the particle *to*: *Go! Be quiet. Have a nice time.*

German has three imperative forms, because there are three forms of the word *you*: **du**, **ihr**, and **Sie**.

DU FORM

To form the **du** form of the imperative of most verbs, use the stem of the verb and add **-e** (in colloquial speech the **-e** is often dropped).

Infinitive	***Du* Form of Imperative**	
kommen	Komm(e)!	*Come.*
singen	Singe!	*Sing.*
fahren	Fahre!	*Drive.*

If the verb has an inseparable prefix, the imperative is not affected. But if the prefix is separable, the prefix appears at the end of the sentence as it does in the normal conjugation of the verb.

anrufen	Rufe an!	*Telephone.*
aussteigen	Steige aus!	*Get off!* (transportation)
erwarten	Erwarte!	*Expect.*
mitgehen	Gehe mit!	*Go along.*
verstehen	Verstehe!	*Understand.*
zerstören	Zerstöre!	*Destroy.*

If the verb is irregular in the present tense and has a vowel change from **-e-** to **-i-** or **-ie-**, that vowel change will also appear in the **du** form of the imperative.

Infinitive	Third Person	du Form	
ansehen	sieht an	Sieh an!	*Look at.*
helfen	hilft	Hilf!	*Help!*
stehlen	stiehlt	Stiehl!	*Steal.*

When this kind of irregularity occurs in the **du** form of the imperative, there is no **-e** ending.

THE *IHR* FORM

The **ihr** form of the imperative is the same as in the present tense.

Infinitive	Second Person Plural	ihr Form	
mitsingen	singt mit	Singt mit!	*Sing along.*
versprechen	versprecht	Versprecht!	*Promise.*
warten	wartet	Wartet!	*Wait!*

THE *SIE* FORM

The **Sie** form of the imperative is also the same as the present tense, but the imperative verb is followed by the pronoun **Sie**.

Infinitive	Third Person Formal	Sie Form	
ausgeben	geben aus	Geben Sie aus!	*Spend!*
kommen	kommen	Kommen Sie!	*Come!*
verstehen	verstehen	Verstehen Sie!	*Understand!*

It is important to consider the imperative forms of **haben**, **sein**, and **werden** separately. Take careful note of how these imperatives are formed.

	haben	sein	werden
du	Habe!	Sei!	Werde!
ihr	Habt!	Seid!	Werdet!
Sie	Haben Sie!	Seien Sie!	Werden Sie!

NOTICE: *All imperatives are punctuated with an exclamation point (!) in German.*

Use the three forms of the imperative in the same way that you use the three pronouns that mean *you*. **Du** is informal and singular. **Ihr** is informal and plural. And **Sie** is formal and either singular or plural. For example:

Erik, steh auf! Es ist schon spät.	*Erik, get up. It is already late.*
Kinder, esst langsam!	*Children, eat slowly.*
Frau Keller, bitte warten Sie hier!	*Ms. Keller, wait here, please.*

Oral Practice

Practice saying the following list of sentences out loud.

Thomas, warte! Ich komme schon.	*Thomas, wait. I am coming.*
Bleibt an der Ecke!	*Stay on the corner.*
Stehen Sie bitte auf!	*Please stand up.*
Bleiben Sie bitte sitzen!	*Please remain seated.*
Bleiben Sie bitte stehen!	*Please remain standing.*
Tina, rauche nicht so viel!	*Tina, do not smoke so much.*
Kinder, schreit nicht so laut!	*Children, do not yell so loudly.*
Herr Bauer, kommen Sie schnell!	*Mr. Bauer, come quickly.*
Rufen Sie die Polizei an!	*Call the police.*
Bringen Sie mir ein Glas Wasser!	*Bring me a glass of water.*
Bitte setzen Sie sich!	*Please sit down.*
Jungen, spielt nicht im Garten!	*Boys, do not play in the garden.*
Hilf mir!	*Help me.*
Vergiss nicht!	*Do not forget.*
Mach schnell!	*Hurry up.*
Sprich Deutsch!	*Speak German.*
Sei ruhig!	*Be quiet.*

Written Practice 4

Form the three types of imperative with the verbs provided.

	du	ihr	Sie
verkaufen	_____	_____	_____
versprechen	_____	_____	_____
trinken	_____	_____	_____
vorstellen	_____	_____	_____
tun	_____	_____	_____
zumachen	_____	_____	_____
lesen	_____	_____	_____
laufen	_____	_____	_____
sein	_____	_____	_____

USING *WIR*

There is another kind of imperative that is directed not only at another party but includes the speaker as well. In English this kind of imperative begins with *Let's* (*Let us*).

> Let's go to the show tonight.   Let's not argue anymore.

In German this kind of imperative is formed by conjugating a verb in the first person plural (**wir**) present tense and following that verb with the pronoun **wir**.

> Gehen wir nach Hause!   *Let's go home.*
> Stellen wir die Gäste vor!   *Let's introduce the guests.*

Written Practice 5

With the verbs provided, form both the **du** form of the imperative and the **wir** form that includes the speaker in the command. Consider the meaning of the two forms.

	du	**wir**
sprechen	_____	_____
sagen	_____	_____
reisen	_____	_____
aufmachen	_____	_____
zerstören	_____	_____
warten	_____	_____
essen	_____	_____
erhalten	_____	_____
ausge ben	_____	_____

A similar *Let's* expression is formed with the verb **lassen** and **uns**. With this expression, use the imperative form of lassen for **du**, **ihr**, or **Sie**.

du	Lass uns gehen!	*Let's go.*
ihr	Lasst uns darüber sprechen!	*Let's talk about it.*
Sie	Lassen Sie uns mitgehen!	*Let's go along.*

USING INFINITIVES

There is yet another imperative form that is used primarily for official commands to groups or unspecified people. The verb form is the infinitive, and no formal or informal relationship is implied. For example:

| Zurückbleiben! | *Stand back.* (Could be heard on a railway platform.) |
| Nicht rauchen! | *No smoking.* (Could be seen on a sign on a wall.) |

Plants

The following is a list of the names of plants that you will often hear in German. Let's get acquainted with these plant words.

das Gemüse	*vegetables*	der Mais	*maize, corn*
das Gras	*grass*	der Rasen	*lawn*
das Korn	*grain*	die Beere	*berry*
das Obst	*fruit*	die Blume	*flower*
der Baum	*tree*	die Nelke	*carnation*
der Blumenstrauß	*bouquet*	die Pflanze	*plant*
der Busch	*bush*	die Tanne	*fir, pine*

Oral Practice

Practice saying the following list of sentences out loud.

In diesem Garten wachsen viele Pflanzen.	*Many plants grow in this garden.*
Hier wachsen Rosen und Nelken.	*Roses and carnations grow here.*
Hier wächst nur Gemüse.	*Only vegetables grow here.*
Hier wurden viele Bäume gepflanzt.	*Many trees were planted here.*
Der Busch wurde neben dem Haus gepflanzt.	*The bush was planted next to the house.*
Zwischen den Tannen wachsen Tulpen.	*Tulips grow between the pines.*
Die Bauern haben Korn, Mais und Beeren gepflanzt.	*The farmers planted grain, corn, and berries.*
Die Obstbäume sind kleiner.	*The fruit trees are smaller.*

Animals

The following is a list of the names of animals that you will often hear in German.

das Huhn	*chicken*	der Fuchs	*fox*
das Kaninchen	*rabbit*	der Hase	*hare*
das Nilpferd	*hippo*	der Tiger	*tiger*
das Pferd	*horse*	der Wolf	*wolf*
das Schaf	*sheep*	die Katze	*cat*
das Schwein	*pig*	die Kuh	*cow*
der Bär	*bear*	die Schlange	*snake*

Oral Practice

Practice saying the following list of sentences out loud.

Ich bin nie auf einem Pferd geritten.	*I have never ridden a horse.*
Auf dem Bauernhof leben viele Tiere.	*Many animals live on the farm.*
Auf dem Bauernhof leben Kühe, Schafe und Schweine.	*Cows, sheep, and pigs live on the farm.*
Der Bauer füttert die Hühner, Pferde und Schweine.	*The farmer feeds the chickens, horses, and pigs.*
Lebt ein Bär oder ein Wolf im Walde?	*Does a bear or a wolf live in the woods?*
Ein Fuchs ist sehr schlau.	*A fox is very sly.*
Ein Nilpferd lebt an einem Fluss.	*A hippo lives near a river.*
Die Tiger leben in Asien.	*Tigers live in Asia.*
Nicht alle Schlangen sind gefährlich.	*Not all snakes are dangerous.*
Die Löwen sind auf der Jagd. Habt	*The lions are on the hunt.*
ihr Haustiere?	*Do you have pets?*
Ja, wir haben zwei Katzen und einen Igel.	*Yes, we have two cats and a hedgehog.*
Nein, wir dürfen keine Haustiere halten.	*No, we are not allowed to have pets.*

Written Practice 6

Circle the letter of the word or phrase that best completes each sentence.

1. _____ ruhig! Ich kann nichts hören.

   (a) Bleiben   (c) Schlau

   (b) Sei   (d) Liegen

2. Die alte Dame hat ihre Tasche _____ .

   (a) gefallen   (c) vergessen

   (b) aufgestanden   (d) verlieren

3. Hier darf man keine _____ halten.

   (a) Kaiser   (c) Haustiere

   (b) Busch   (d) Wohnungen

4. Warum musst du immer so laut _____?

   (a) schlafen   (c) Hunger haben

   (b) schreien   (d) gern haben

5. Im Garten _____ keine Nelken mehr.

   (a) wachsen   (c) rufen an

   (b) blieb   (d) angerufen

6. Wer hat die Pferde und _____ gefüttert?

   (a) Schafe   (c) Bäume

   (b) Busch   (d) Tulpen

7. Kinder, _____ bitte auf!

   (a) warten   (c) standen

   (b) steht   (d) erwartet

8. Diese grüne _____ ist sehr lang.

   (a) Schlange   (c) Igel

   (b) Flaschen   (d) Kuh

9. Es ist kalt und _____ wieder.

   (a) schneit   (c) bleibt

   (b) vergisst   (d) wächst

10. Ein Fuchs kann sehr ＿＿＿ sein.

    (a) schlau   (c) wahrscheinlich

    (b) letzte   (d) ruhigen

11. Nilpferde und Löwen leben in ＿＿＿.

    (a) Asien   (c) Afrika

    (b) Norddeutschland   (d) zu Hause

12. Herr Professor, ＿＿＿ mich bitte an!

    (a) rufen Sie   (c) sieh

    (b) seht   (d) bleiben Sie

13. Der ＿＿＿ hat hier viele Bäume gepflanzt.

    (a) Katze   (c) Wolf

    (b) Mais   (d) Bauer

14. Sein Sohn isst kein ＿＿＿.

    (a) Gemüse   (c) Igel

    (b) Nachtisch   (d) Obstbäume

15. Hast du diesen ＿＿＿ Artikel gelesen?

    (a) neue   (c) ruhig

    (b) interessanten   (d) schlaue

QUIZ

Rewrite each verb as a passive infinitive. For example:

    er singt *werden gesungen* ＿＿＿＿＿＿＿＿＿＿＿＿＿＿

1. er spielt ＿＿＿＿＿＿＿＿＿＿＿＿＿＿＿＿＿＿

    ich höre ＿＿＿＿＿＿＿＿＿＿＿＿＿＿＿＿＿＿

    man arbeitet ＿＿＿＿＿＿＿＿＿＿＿＿＿＿＿＿

    du machst zu ＿＿＿＿＿＿＿＿＿＿＿＿＿＿＿＿

    wir versprechen ＿＿＿＿＿＿＿＿＿＿＿＿＿＿

    sie pflanzt ＿＿＿＿＿＿＿＿＿＿＿＿＿＿＿＿＿

du erhältst _____

ich vergesse _____

ihr schreit _____

er nimmt mit _____

Write each of the following passive phrases in the tenses shown with the pronouns provided.

2.		werden gesehen	werden besucht	werden beschrieben
pres	ich	_____	_____	_____
past	du	_____	_____	_____
pres perf	er	_____	_____	_____
fut	wir	_____	_____	_____

		werden abgesandt	werden besessen	werden zerstört
pres	du	_____	_____	_____
past	er	_____	_____	_____
pres perf	ihr	_____	_____	_____
fut	Sie	_____	_____	_____

Change the following active voice sentences to the passive voice. Retain the tenses of the active voice sentences.

3. Die Lehrer diskutieren die Probleme.

   _____.

4. Sie haben das alte Haus abgerissen.

   _____.

5. Der Graf wird den neuen Kanzler vorstellen.

   _____.

Rewrite each sentence, adding the adjective provided in parentheses. For example:

Ich besuchte eine _____ Frau.

(alt) *Ich besuchte eine alte Frau.*

6. Hast du jenen _____ Bären gesehen?

(groß) _____?

(braun) _____?

7. Ist _____ alte Herr gestorben?

(diese) _____?

(jene) _____?

8. Wann kommt der _____ Bus?

(nächst) _____?

(letzt) _____?

9. Alle _____ Männer müssen ihnen helfen.

(jung) _____.

(deutsch) _____.

10. Form the three imperatives for the verbs provided.

	du	ihr	Sie
treffen	_____	_____	_____
pflanzen	_____	_____	_____
zumachen	_____	_____	_____
schlafen	_____	_____	_____
bleiben	_____	_____	_____
denken	_____	_____	_____
bekommen	_____	_____	_____
geben	_____	_____	_____
sein	_____	_____	_____
werden	_____	_____	_____

CHAPTER 18

Using the Passive Voice

In this chapter you will learn:

More About the Passive Voice

Modal Auxiliaries in the Passive Voice

Sich Lassen *and the Passive Voice*

Adjective Endings with Ein- *Words*

Professions

More About the Passive Voice

Learning about the passive voice is not over yet. For example, some active sentences have a dative object in them, and when such sentences are changed to the passive voice, the dative object, naturally, reappears in the passive sentence. Direct objects, which are in the accusative case, become nominative subjects in the passive, but dative case objects do not change their case when placed in a passive sentence. Compare the following two pairs of examples:

Accusative Case Direct Object Changed to Nominative Case in the Passive Voice

Das Kind findet **den Ball**. *The child finds **the ball**.*

Der Ball wird von dem Kind gefunden. ***The ball** is found by the child.*

Dative Case Object in the Passive Voice

Sie haben **dem Kind** geholfen. *They helped **the child**.*

Dem Kind ist von ihnen geholfen worden. ***The child** was helped by them.*

The dative object in the passive sentence cannot be the subject of the sentence, because it is in the dative case. Subjects are in the nominative case. Let's look at a few more examples, which show an active sentence changed to a passive sentence.

Die Lehrerin dankte allen Eltern. *The teacher thanked all the parents.*

Allen Eltern wurden von der Lehrerin gedankt. *All the parents were thanked by the teacher.*

Niemand wird ihm glauben. *No one will believe him.*

Ihm wird von niemandem geglaubt werden. *He will not be believed by anyone.*

Written Practice 1

Change each of the following present tense sentences to the past, present perfect, and future tenses.

1. Mir wird von ihm geholfen.

   _____ .

   _____ .

   _____ .

2. Der Lehrerin wird nicht geglaubt.

_____.

_____.

_____.

3. Ihm wird dafür gedankt.

_____.

_____.

_____.

4. Wird dem Professor imponiert?

_____?

_____?

_____?

Sometimes the subject of a sentence that contains a dative object is the pronoun **es**, which in most instances is elliptical, that is, it is understood but not spoken or written. However, the passive voice is sometimes expressed by beginning the main clause of the sentence with the pronoun **es**—but, in this case, **es** is not really the subject. The subject occurs after the conjugated verb and determines the kind of conjugation required. Let's look at a few examples.

Es wird hier nur Deutsch gesprochen.	*Only German is spoken here.*
Es wurden viele Häuser zerstört.	*Many houses were destroyed.*
Es wurde uns dafür gedankt.	*We were thanked for it.*

Modal Auxiliaries in the Passive Voice

Just as modal auxiliaries are used in the active voice together with an infinitive (**muss...trinken**), they can be used in the passive voice with a passive infinitive. A passive infinitive is a past participle followed by **werden** (**muss...gesehen werden**). Let's compare the two uses of modal auxiliaries.

Active Voice:

Ich kann die Musik nicht **hören**.   *I cannot **hear** the music.*

Sie wollte mit Hans **tanzen**.   *She wanted **to dance** with Hans.*

Passive Voice:

Mir kann nicht **geholfen werden**.   *I cannot **be helped**.*

Sie wollte von allen **bewundert werden**.   *She wanted **to be admired** by everyone.*

The modal auxiliaries in passive voice sentences can be conjugated in all the tenses except the future perfect, which becomes an awkward structure and is avoided. Even the present and past perfect tend to be replaced by the simple past tense. But for the purpose of illustration, let's look at a modal auxiliary in the passive voice in all the pertinent tenses.

Present:

Etwas muss gesagt werden.   *Something has to be said.*

Past:

Etwas musste gesagt werden.   *Something had to be said.*

Present Perfect:

Etwas hat gesagt werden müssen.   *Something had to be said.*

Past Perfect:

Etwas hatte gesagt werden müssen.   *Something had had to be said.*

Future:

Etwas wird gesagt werden müssen.   *Something will have to be said.*

Written Practice 2

Rewrite the following active voice sentences with the modals provided. Retain the tenses of the original sentences. For example:

> Er ging zur Schule.
> (müssen) *Er musste zur Schule gehen.* _____

1. Frau Schäfer wird nach Hannover fahren.

   (sollen) _____.

   (wollen) _____.

   (müssen) _____.

2. Haben Sie Ihre Nachbarn eingeladen?

   (können) _____?

   (müssen) _____?

   (dürfen) _____?

Follow the same directions, but notice that the original sentences are now in the passive voice.

3. Hans wird von seiner Schwester geküsst.

   (wollen) _____.

   (müssen) _____.

   (sollen) _____.

4. Ist der Wagen repariert worden?

   (können) _____?

   (müssen) _____?

   (sollen) _____?

5. Ihm wird sofort geholfen.

   (sollen) _____.

   (können) _____.

   (müssen) _____.

Written Practice 3

Rewrite each sentence replacing the original modal auxiliary with the ones provided in parentheses. Retain the original tense of the sentences.

1. Das Haus soll geräumt werden.

   (können) _____.

   (müssen) _____.

2. Es konnte nicht repariert werden.

   (dürfen) _____.

   (müssen) _____.

3. Das Kind wird fotografiert werden müssen.

   (wollen) _____.

   (können) _____.

Oral Practice

Practice saying the following list of sentences out loud.

Was muss gewaschen werden?	*What has to be washed?*
Der Wagen muss gewaschen werden.	*The car has to be washed.*
Wer kann eingeladen werden?	*Who can be invited?*
Unsere Verwandten können eingeladen werden.	*Our relatives can be invited.*
Herr Benz soll nicht eingeladen. werden	*Mr. Benz should not be invited.*
Was durfte nicht geschrieben werden?	*What was not allowed to be written?*
Diese Geschichte durfte nicht geschrieben werden.	*This story was not allowed to be written.*
Sein Lebenslauf durfte nicht geschrieben werden.	*His autobiography was not allowed to be written.*
Kann ihm nicht geholfen werden?	*Can he not be helped?*
Kann ihr nicht geglaubt werden?	*Can she not be believed?*
Kann dir nicht imponiert werden?	*Can you not be impressed?*

Written Practice 4

Rewrite each sentence with the new subjects provided in parentheses. Make any necessary changes.

1. Ist _____ abgeschleppt worden?

   (es) _____?

   (sie *pl.*) _____?

   (der Wagen) _____?

   (die Autos) _____?

   (der Bus) _____?

2. _____ konnte nicht verstanden werden.

   (sein Freund) _____.

   (die Kinder) _____.

   (ich) _____.

   (du) _____.

   (wir) _____.

3. _____ wird niemals geglaubt werden.

   (sie *pl.*) _____.

   (sie *s.*) _____.

   (er) _____.

   (meine Frau) _____.

   (der Physiker) _____.

Sich Lassen and the Passive Voice

It is possible to avoid passive structures by using a conjugation of **sich lassen** accompanied by an infinitive (**lässt sich...machen**). This pair of words is translated as *can be*. In English that's a form of passive voice with a modal auxiliary, but in German it's a reflexive verb used in place of a passive voice conjugation. Let's look at some examples.

Das alte Radio **lässt sich** nicht reparieren.	*The old radio **cannot be** repaired.*
Diese Probleme **ließen sich** leicht lösen.	*These problems **could be** solved easily.*

When this structure is conjugated in the various tenses, you will notice that a double-infinitive structure occurs in the perfect and future tenses. For example:

Present:

Das lässt sich nicht tun.	*That cannot be done.*

Past:

Das ließ sich nicht tun.	*That could not be done.*

Present Perfect:

Das hat sich nicht tun lassen.	*That could not be done.*

Future:

Das wird sich nicht tun lassen.	*That will not be able to be done.*

Written Practice 5

Rewrite each passive sentence with **sich lassen**. Keep the tense of the original sentences. Be aware of the change of meaning that occurs. For example:

Das lange Wort wird leicht geschrieben.
Das lange Wort lässt sich leicht schreiben.

1. Der Fernsehapparat wurde nicht repariert.

   _____.

2. Diese Romane sind schnell gelesen worden.

   _____.

3. Die Bären wurden nicht fotografiert.

   _____.

4. Das wird sehr leicht geändert.

   _____.

Written Practice 6

Rewrite the following passive sentences in the tenses shown.

1. **pres** _____.

   past Das ließ sich nicht verstehen.

   pres perf _____.

   fut _____.

2. **pres** Wird dem Gast gut gedient?

   past _____?

   pres perf _____?

   fut _____?

3. **pres** _____.

   past _____.

   pres perf _____.

   fut Du wirst gesehen werden.

4. **pres** _____.

   past Der kranken Katze konnte nicht geholfen werden.

   pres perf _____.

   fut _____.

5. **pres** Nichts kann getan werden.

   past _____.

   pres perf _____.

   fut _____.

Adjective Endings with *Ein-* Words

You have already learned about the adjective endings with **der-** words. Adjective endings with **ein-** words function slightly differently.

The **ein-** words are **ein** and **kein** plus the possessive adjectives (**mein, dein, sein, ihr, unser, euer, ihr, Ihr**). With **ein-** words, the identification of the gender of a noun is provided in the adjective in the nominative case. With **der-** words, gender is identified in the **der-** word itself. Let's compare the difference.

Der- Word Plus Adjective

Masculine	Feminine	Neuter	Plural
der nette Herr	die nette Frau	das nette Kind	die netten Frauen

Ein- Word Plus Adjective

Masculine	Feminine	Neuter	Plural
ein netter Herr	eine nette Frau	ein nettes Kind	keine netten Frauen

No matter which **ein-** word is used, the adjective endings function in the same way.

ihr guter Mann	ihr junger Mann
seine kleine Schwester	seine kranke Schwester
kein schönes Mädchen	kein intelligentes Mädchen

This difference between **der-** words and **ein-** words does not exist in the plural. With either kind of determiner, the adjective ending is always **-en** in all four cases.

nom	diese roten Autos
acc	unsere deutschen Verwandeten
dat	jenen alten Leuten
gen	Ihrer netten Kinder

The feminine and neuter are always identical in both the nominative and accusative, therefore the adjective endings with **ein-** words used in the nominative will also be used in the accusative.

nom	ihre kleine Schwester	sein neues Heft
acc	ihre kleine Schwester	sein neues Heft

In all other instances the adjective ending will always be **-en**.

	Masculine	Feminine	Neuter	Plural
nom	ein netter Herr	eine nette Frau	ein nettes Kind	keine netten Frauen
acc	einen netten Herrn	eine nette Frau	ein nettes Kind	keine netten Frauen
dat	einem netten Herrn	einer netten Frau	einem netten Kind	keinen netten Frauen
gen	eines netten Herrn	einer netten Frau	eines netten Kindes	keiner netten Frauen

Written Practice 7

Provide the appropriate adjective endings in all four cases for the nouns provided.

	mein jung Freund	unser alt Tante	ihr neu Fahrrad
nom	_____	_____	_____
acc	_____	_____	_____
dat	_____	_____	_____
gen	_____	_____	_____

	dein klein Haus	jed- groß Stuhl	dies- grau Katze
nom	_____	_____	_____
acc	_____	_____	_____
dat	_____	_____	_____
gen	_____	_____	_____

With the following phrases, provide the missing cases.

nom	_____	_____
acc	ihren kleinen Sohn	_____
dat	_____	deiner jungen Schwester
gen	_____	_____

nom	_____	_____
acc	_____	_____
dat	einer kranken Dame	unserem letzten Brief
gen	_____	_____

Oral Practice

Practice saying the following sentences out loud.

Wer hat meinen neuen Hut gefunden?	*Who found my new hat?*
Robert hat deinen neuen Hut gefunden.	*Robert found your new hat.*
Welches Auto hat sie verkauft?	*Which car did she sell?*
Sie hat ihr schwarzes Auto verkauft.	*She sold her black car.*
Sie hat ihr altes Auto verkauft.	*She sold her old car.*
Welchen Gürtel wollte er kaufen?	*Which belt did he want to buy?*
Er wollte einen braunen Gürtel kaufen.	*He wanted to buy a brown belt.*
Er wollte Ihren neuen Gürtel kaufen.	*He wanted to buy your new belt.*
Wessen Hund ist das?	*Whose dog is that?*
Das ist der Hund eines neuen Lehrers.	*That is a new teacher's dog.*
Das ist der Hund meiner amerikanischen Kusine.	*That is my American cousin's dog.*

Written Practice 8

Rewrite each sentence with the phrases provided in parentheses, making the necessary changes to adjective endings.

1. Ist das der Bruder _____?

   (dein amerikanischer Gast) _____?

   (Ihre nette Kusine) _____?

   (eure jungen Freunde) _____?

2. Kennen Sie _____?

   (meine neue Freundin) _____?

   (sein alter Onkel) _____?

   (ihr intelligenter Sohn) _____?

3. Hans wollte mit _____ spielen.

   (unser kleiner Hund) _____.

(jene netten Kinder) _____ .

(sein neuer Fußball) _____ .

Written Practice 9

Fill in the blanks with any appropriate adjective and its required ending.

1. Der _____ Rechtsanwalt ist ein Freund von mir.

2. Kennst du meine _____ Gärtnerin?

3. Thomas hat mit seinen _____ Geschwistern gearbeitet.

4. Gudrun will von allen _____ Jungen bewundert werden.

5. Ihre _____ Wohnung soll geräumt werden.

6. Sie haben sein _____ Auto abgeschleppt.

7. Habt ihr euren _____ Dolmetscher eingeladen?

8. Ist das ein _____ Gürtel?

9. Sie hatte keine _____ Flaschen gefunden.

10. Unser _____ Wohnzimmer ist dunkel.

Professions

When you inquire as to someone's profession, you ask:

Was sind Sie von Beruf?	*What is your occupation?*
Was bist du von Beruf?	*What is your occupation?*

The responses are numerous, because there are so many words that describe professions or occupations. When reading the following list, remember that the masculine version is shown. The feminine version is, in most cases, the same word but with **-in** added to the end of the word. Also, sometimes a vowel will be replaced by an umlaut vowel (**-ä-**, **-ö-**, or **-ü-**) for the feminine version.

der Arbeiter	*(blue-collar) worker*	der Mechaniker	*mechanic*
der Architekt	*architect*	der Pfleger	*(male) nurse; caretaker*

der Beamte	*government employee*	der Physiker	*physicist*
der Chemiker	*chemist*	der Politiker	*politician*
der Dichter	*poet*	der Rechtsanwalt	*lawyer*
der Dolmetscher	*translator*	der Schaffner	*conductor (transportation)*
der Erzieher	*nursery school teacher*	der Schriftsteller	*writer, author*
der Fotograf	*photographer*	der Sekretär	*secretary*
der Geschäftsmann (die -frau)	*businessman*	der Sportler	*athlete*
der Kaufmann (die -frau)	*merchant, businessman*	der Taxifahrer	*taxi driver*
der Maurer	*bricklayer*	der Trainer	*coach*

There are different ways to describe what you do for a profession. For example:

Ich arbeite als Pflegerin.	*I work as a nurse.*
Ich arbeite in der Firma als Dolmetscher.	*I work in the company as a translator.*
Ich bin in dieser Firma als Mechaniker beschäftigt.	*I am employed in the company as a mechanic.*
Ich bin Taxifahrer aber will Architekt werden.	*I am a taxi driver but want to become an architect.*

Written Practice 10

Circle the letter of the word or phrase that best completes each sentence.

1. Wen haben Sie _____?

    (a) abschleppen   (c) gepflanzt

    (b) änderten   (d) eingeladen

2. Wird _____ damit geholfen?

    (a) ihnen   (c) euren Rechtsanwalt

    (b) unsere   (d) keine Leute

3. Der kranke Mann _____ sofort nach Hause gebracht werden.

    (a) musste   (c) hat

    (b) ist   (d) gekonnt

4. Ist dein Wagen wieder _____ worden?

    (a) gewachsen

    (b) abgeschleppt

    (c) bewunderten

    (d) können

5. Die Geschäftsfrau kann nicht _____ werden.

    (a) soll

    (b) hat

    (c) gefunden

    (d) geglaubt

6. Ist deine Mutter Hausfrau oder _____?

    (a) Physikerin

    (b) Politiker

    (c) Gärtnerinnen

    (d) Erzieher

7. Werner hat ein neues _____ angezogen.

    (a) Ball

    (b) Pflanze

    (c) Affen

    (d) Hemd

8. Tanja hat _____ neues Auto.

    (a) diese

    (b) ein

    (c) welches

    (d) jenen

9. Was ist Ihr Vater von _____?

    (a) zu Hause

    (b) bewundert

    (c) Beruf

    (d) Arbeiter

10. Meine Tochter ist jetzt als Architektin _____.

    (a) gearbietet

    (b) beschäftigt

    (c) eingeladen

    (d) geändert

Oral Practice

Practice saying the following list of sentences out loud.

Was sind Sie von Beruf?	*What is your occupation?*
Ich bin Gärtner.	*I am a gardener.*
Ich arbeite als Dolmetscherin.	*I work as a translator.*
Ich bin als Maurer beschäftigt.	*I am employed as a bricklayer.*

Was ist deine Schwester von Beruf?	*What is your sister's occupation?*
Sie ist Geschäftsfrau.	*She is a businesswoman.*
Sie arbeitet als Chemikerin.	*She works as a chemist.*
Sie ist bei einer Firma als Sekretärin beschäftigt.	*She is employed in a company as a secretary.*
Mein Vater war Arbeiter.	*My father was a blue-collar worker.*
Jetzt arbeitet er als Beamter.	*Now he works as a government employee.*
Meine Mutter war Erzieherin.	*My mother was a nursery school teacher.*
Jetzt ist sie als Fotografin beschäftigt.	*Now she is employed as a photographer.*
Mein Sohn will Kaufmann werden.	*My son wants to become a merchant.*
Meine Tochter ist Sportlerin.	*My daughter is an athlete.*
Ist Ihr Onkel Rechtsanwalt?	*Is your uncle a lawyer?*
Nein, er ist Politiker.	*No, he is a politician.*
War Ihre Tante Schriftstellerin?	*Was your aunt a writer?*
Nein, sie war Dichterin.	*No, she was a poet.*
Dem Schaffner wurde gedankt.	*The conductor was thanked.*
Dem Taxifahrer konnte nicht geglaubt werden.	*The taxi driver could not be believed.*
Sein Wagen musste abgeschleppt werden.	*His car had to be towed away.*
Der neue Trainer war Mechaniker.	*The new coach was a mechanic.*

QUIZ

Rewrite the following sentences in the tenses shown.

1. **pres** Der Wagen muss abgeschleppt werden.

   past _____.

   pres perf _____.

   fut _____.

2. **pres** _____.

   past _____.

   pres perf Ihm ist dafür gedankt worden.

   fut _____.

Rewrite each passive sentence with the new subjects provided in parentheses.

3. _____ wurde von ihnen geholfen.

   (er) _____.

   (sie *s.*) _____.

   (der Beamte) _____.

   (mein Trainer) _____.

   (wir) _____.

4. _____ lässt sich nicht leicht ändern.

   (es) _____.

   (sie *pl.*) _____.

   (das Problem) _____.

   (die Probleme) _____.

   (das) _____.

Fill in the missing cases, providing the appropriate adjective endings.

5. **nom** *ein netter Mann* _____   _____

   acc _____   *seine neue Freundin*

   dat _____   _____

   gen _____   _____

6. **nom** *kein gutes Heft* _____   _____

   acc _____   _____

   dat _____   _____

   gen _____   *meiner alten Handschuhe*

Circle the letter of the word or phrase that best completes each sentence.

7. Meine Mutter ———— als Chemikerin.

    (a) lädt ein   (c) arbeitet

    (b) dienen   (d) folgte

8. Mein ———— Bruder konnte den Ball nicht fangen.

    (a) kleiner   (c) neues

    (b) alte   (d) ruhigen

9. Diese Frau ———— von allen Männern bewundert werden.

    (a) ist   (c) hatte

    (b) kannte   (d) wollte

10. Das ist ihr ———— Gedicht.

    (a) erstes   (c) ruhigen

    (b) letzte   (d) lang

CHAPTER 19

Using the Subjunctive Mood

In this chapter you will learn:

Subjunctive Mood

Indirect Discourse

Foreign Words in German

More Idioms

Subjunctive Mood

The subjunctive mood is a grammatical function that is losing ground in English. Many speakers avoid it, and some probably cannot identify it when they hear it or read it. Some examples of the English subjunctive conjugation are:

Long *live* the king!

I suggest you *be* on time tomorrow.

If only my husband *were* here.

345

The subjunctive mood plays a significant role in the German language, however. Let's look first at how the subjunctive conjugations are formed.

German has two subjunctive tenses: the present subjunctive (also called subjunctive I) and the past subjunctive (also called subjunctive II).

PRESENT SUBJUNCTIVE/SUBJUNCTIVE I

The present subjunctive has the appearance of a present tense verb, but there are small differences between the subjunctive conjugation and the indicative (the normal present tense conjugation). This is true even of the modal auxiliaries. The conjugational endings in the present subjunctive are: **-e**, **-est**, **-e**, **-en**, **-et**, and **-en**. To conjugate in the subjunctive, remove the infinitive ending from the stem of the verb and add these endings. For example:

	kommen	**versprechen**	**zumachen**	**können**
ich	komme	verspreche	mache zu	könne
du	kommest	versprechest	machest zu	könnest
er	komme	verspreche	mache zu	könne
wir	kommen	versprechen	machen zu	können
ihr	kommet	versprechet	machet zu	könnet
sie	kommen	versprechen	machen zu	können

There are some important things to note about this conjugation:

1. The first person and third person singular (**ich** and **er**) are always identical.

2. Present tense irregularities such as adding an umlaut (**ich fahre**, **du fährst**, **er fährt**) or by making a vowel change (**ich sehe**, **du siehst**, **er sieht**) do not occur.

3. The first person singular and plural (**ich** and **wir**) and the third person plural (**sie**) are often identical to the indicative conjugation. This is occasionally true with the **ihr** form with verb stems that end in **-t** or **-d**. This fact will become important later on.

4. Prefixes are not affected by the subjunctive conjugation and continue to follow the same rules as stated previously.

Of course, it is wise to look at the present subjunctive conjugation of **haben**, **sein**, and **werden** separately. They always play a special role in the conjugation of verbs.

	haben	**sein**	**werden**
ich	habe	sei	werde
du	habest	seiest	werdest
er	habe	sei	werde
wir	haben	seien	werden
ihr	habet	seiet	werdet
sie	haben	seien	werden

Written Practice 1

Conjugate the following verbs in the present subjunctive with the pronouns provided. Place an X after the verbs that are identical to the indicative present tense conjugation.

	schlafen	**vergessen**	**mitnehmen**
ich	_____	_____	_____
du	_____	_____	_____
er	_____	_____	_____
wir	_____	_____	_____
ihr	_____	_____	_____
sie	_____	_____	_____

	fragen	**aussehen**	**sein**
ich	_____	_____	_____
du	_____	_____	_____
er	_____	_____	_____
wir	_____	_____	_____
ihr	_____	_____	_____
sie	_____	_____	_____

PAST SUBJUNCTIVE/SUBJUNCTIVE II

The past subjunctive is formed from the past tense conjugation of verbs. If a verb is regular in the indicative past tense, it will have the same conjugation in the past subjunctive. Let's look at the past subjunctive of a few regular verbs.

	fragen	**aufmachen**	**besuchen**
ich	fragte	machte auf	besuchte
du	fragtest	machtest auf	besuchtest
er	fragte	machte auf	besuchte
wir	fragten	machten auf	besuchten
ihr	fragtet	machtet auf	besuchtet
sie	fragten	machten auf	besuchten

Irregular verbs are another story. The irregular past tense stem is used in the subjunctive conjugation, and the endings **-e**, **-est**, **-e**, **-en**, **-et**, and **-en** are added. You may have noticed that these are the same endings used in the present subjunctive. Also, irregular past tense verbs that have an **a**, **o**, **u** will add an umlaut in this conjugation. Some examples follow:

	verlieren	**sprechen**	**beschreiben**
ich	verlöre	spräche	beschriebe
du	verlörest	sprächest	beschriebest
er	verlöre	spräche	beschriebe
wir	verlören	sprächen	beschrieben
ihr	verlöret	sprächet	beschriebet
sie	verlören	sprächen	beschrieben

	mitgehen	**bleiben**	**fahren**
ich	ginge mit	bliebe	führe
du	gingest mit	bliebest	führest
er	ginge mit	bliebe	führe
wir	gingen mit	blieben	führen
ihr	ginget mit	bliebet	führet
sie	gingen mit	blieben	führen

And, of course, we have to isolate **haben**, **sein**, and **werden** for a special look.

	haben	**sein**	**werden**
ich	hätte	wäre	würde
du	hättest	wärest	würdest
er	hätte	wäre	würde

wir	hätten	wären	würden
ihr	hättet	wäret	würdet
sie	hätten	wären	würden

The modal auxiliaries in the past subjunctive look very much like their indicative past tense conjugations. However, those modals that have an umlaut in the infinitive add one in the past subjunctive.

	könnnen	**wollen**	**dürfen**
ich	könnte	wollte	dürfte
du	könntest	wolltest	dürftest
er	könnte	wollte	dürfte
wir	könnten	wollten	dürften
ihr	könntet	wolltet	dürftet
sie	könnten	wollten	dürften

Most irregular verbs that have a **-te** ending in the past tense do something special in the past subjunctive: The past tense vowel **-a-** is changed to **-e-**. Let's compare the past indicative with the past subjunctive of this category of verbs.

Past Indicative

	kennen	**senden**	**nennen**
ich	kannte	sandte	nannte
du	kanntest	sandtest	nanntest
er	kannte	sandte	nannte
wir	kannten	sandten	nannten
ihr	kanntet	sandtet	nanntet
sie	kannten	sandten	nannten

Past Subjunctive

	kennen	**senden**	**nennen**
ich	kennte	sendete	nennte
du	kenntest	sendetest	nenntest
er	kennte	sendete	nennte
wir	kennten	sendeten	nennten
ihr	kenntet	sendetet	nenntet
sie	kennten	sendeten	nennten

The verb **wissen**, which usually conforms to the conjugation type just illustrated (it adds the **-te** ending), does not use the vowel **-e-** in the past subjunctive. Let's compare this verb in both the present subjunctive and the past subjunctive.

	Present Subjunctive	**Past Subjunctive**
ich	wisse	wüsste
du	wissest	wüsstest
er	wisse	wüsste
wir	wissen	wüssten
ihr	wisset	wüsstet
sie	wissen	wüssten

Just as in the present subjunctive, the first and third person singular conjugations (**ich** and **er**) are always the same in the past subjunctive.

ich fragte	er fragte (*regular verb*)
ich käme	er käme (*irregular verb with umlaut*)
ich ginge	er ginge (*irregular verb*)
ich dürfte	er dürfte (*modal auxiliary*)

Indirect Discourse

Direct discourse is a direct quote of what someone has said: John said, "I like to drink black coffee." Indirect discourse is the retelling of what someone has said.

John said that he likes to drink black coffee.

German also has direct and indirect discourse. Direct quotes are handled the same as in English.

Johann sagte, „Ich trinke gern schwarzen Kaffee."

But indirect discourse is another matter. A German statement in indirect discourse requires the conjugated verb to be in the present subjunctive.

Johann sagte, dass er gern schwarzen Kaffee **trinke**.

The use of **dass** (*that*) can also be omitted in indirect discourse.

Johann sagte, er **trinke** gern schwarzen Kaffee.

It is not only the verb **sagen** that introduces a statement in indirect discourse. There are many others that do the same thing.

antworten	*to answer*	glauben	*to believe*
berichten	*to report*	meinen	*to think, to have the opinion, to mean*
denken	*to think*	mitteilen	*to inform*
erzählen	*to tell, relate*	schreiben	*to write*
fragen	*to ask*		

These verbs are in the past tense when used with indirect discourse.

Karl **antwortete**, er habe heute keine Zeit.

Karl answered that he has no time today.

Meine Tante **erzählte**, dass ein Unglück geschehen sei.

My aunt told (us) that an accident happened.

Written Practice 2

Change the direct quotes to indirect discourse using the phrases provided. For example:

Er sagte, dass...

„Karl ist krank gewesen.“

Er sagte, dass Karl krank gewesen sei.

_____

1. Er sagte, dass...

„Zwei Autos sind abgeschleppt worden.“

_____.

„Die Regierung wird den armen Menschen helfen.“

_____.

„Er geht nur selten ins Theater.“

_____.

2. Ein Freund schrieb uns, dass...

„Er kann nächste Woche kommen.“

_____.

„Sein Bruder ist in Gudrun verliebt.“

_____ .

„Seine Familie hat das Geld noch nicht erhalten.“

_____ .

Oral Practice

Practice saying the following list of sentences out loud.

Er sagte, dass das Wetter schlecht sei.	_He said that the weather is bad._
Er sagte, dass er wenig Zeit habe.	_He said that he has little time._
Sie sagte, Frau Benz sei wieder schwanger.	_She said Ms. Benz is pregnant again._
Sie sagte, Erik wolle Sportler werden.	_She said Erik wants to become an athlete._
Er berichtete, dass der Politiker gut angekommen sei.	_He reported that the politician arrived safely._
Er berichtete, die Kanzlerin reise morgen ab.	_He reported the chancellor is departing tomorrow._
Sie teilte uns mit, dass der alte Dichter sterbe.	_She informed us that the old poet is dying._
Sie teilte uns mit, der Fluss habe das Dorf überschwemmt.	_She informed us that the river flooded the village._

Consider the following examples carefully. They illustrate how the various tenses in direct discourse appear in indirect discourse. The simple past, the present perfect, and the past perfect all have the same form in indirect discourse.

Present:
„Er hat kein Geld.“   Er sagte, dass er kein Geld habe.

Past:
„Er hatte kein Geld.“   Er sagte, dass er kein Geld gehabt habe.

Present Perfect:
„Er hat kein Geld gehabt.“   Er sagte, dass er kein Geld gehabt habe.

Past Perfect:

„Er hatte kein Geld gehabt."   *Er sagte, dass er kein Geld gehabt habe.*

Future:

„Er wird kein Geld haben."   *Er sagte, dass er kein Geld haben werde.*

Written Practice 3

Rewrite the following direct quotes as indirect discourse using the phrases provided. Use the appropriate present subjunctive tense form.

1. Sie berichtete, ...

   „Die Regierung half dem alten König."

   _____.

   „Der Kanzler wird morgen ankommen."

   _____.

   „Es gibt nichts Schöneres als Wien."

   _____.

2. Martin schrieb mir, dass...

   „Seine Freundin war in Russland."

   _____.

   „Der Fluss hatte das Land überschwemmt."

   _____.

   „Die warme Sonne muss jeden Menschen gesund machen."

   _____.

INDIRECT QUESTIONS

An indirect question functions in the same way as indirect discourse. But indirect questions are introduced by the verb **fragen**. If there is no interrogative word (**was**, **warum**, **wo**, and so on) in the question, the conjunction **ob** (*whether*) begins the clause. For example:

Sie fragte, ob Hans noch krank sei.   *She asked whether Hans is still sick.*

Sie fragte, wohin der Gärtner
jetzt gehe.

*She asked where the gardener is going
now.*

Sie fragte, was der Schriftsteller
berichtet habe.

She asked what the writer reported.

Written Practice 4

Change the following direct questions to indirect questions using the phrases provided. Use the conjunction **ob** where there is no interrogative word.

1. Mein Mann fragte, ...

„Wo ist mein neuer Pullover?"

_____.

„Kann Erik den Wagen reparieren?"

_____.

„Wessen Tasche hat der Dieb gestohlen?"

_____.

„Waren sie schon in der Hauptstadt?"

_____.

„Wie viel wird Herr Bauer dafür ausgeben?"

_____.

So far, you have been using the present subjunctive conjugation only in indirect
discourse and indirect questions. But the past subjunctive plays a role here as well.
When the indicative present tense and the present subjunctive are identical, use the
past subjunctive. For example:

„Sie haben kein Geld."

They have no money.

The verb is the same in the present indicative (**haben**) as it is in the present subjunctive (**haben**). Therefore, the past subjunctive is used when this sentence is stated in
indirect discourse.

Herr Bauer erzählte, dass sie
kein Geld **hätten**.

Mr. Bauer said that they have no money.

Let's look at a few more examples.

„Die Kinder sollen zu Hause bleiben."	*The children should stay home.*
Herr Bauer erzählte, dass die Kinder zu Hause bleiben **sollten**.	*Mr. Bauer said that the children should stay at home.*
„Ihr werdet alles in der Küche finden."	*You will find everything in the kitchen.*
Herr Bauer erzählte, dass ihr alles in der Küche finden **würdet**.	*Mr. Bauer said that you will find everything in the kitchen.*
„Sie verkaufen das große Haus."	*They sell the large house.*
Herr Bauer erzählte, dass sie das große Hause **verkauften**.	*Mr. Bauer said that they are selling the large house.*

There is a tendency in the spoken language to avoid the present subjunctive conjugation and to use the past subjunctive exclusively. Compare the following examples:

Spoken German:

Sie sagte, dass ihr Mann wieder gesund **wäre**.	*She said that her husband **is** well again.*
Sie sagte, dass ihr Mann in England gearbeitet **hätte**.	*She said that her husband **had** worked in England.*

Written German:

Sie sagte, dass ihr Mann wieder gesund **sei**.	*She said that her husband is well again.*
Sie sagte, dass ihr Mann in England gearbeitet **habe**.	*She said that her husband had worked in England.*

Oral Practice

Practice saying the following list of sentences out loud.

Thomas sagte, dass Tina beim Arzt wäre.	*Thomas said that Tina is at the doctor's office.*
Er sagte, dass Tina beim Arzt gewesen wäre.	*He said that Tina was at the doctor's office.*

Er sagte, dass Tina nicht arbeiten könnte.	*He said that Tina cannot work.*
Er sagte, dass sie zu Hause bleiben müsste.	*He said that she has to stay home.*
Er sagte, dass sie sich den Arm gebrochen hätte.	*He said that she had broken her arm.*
Er sagte, dass sie nicht nach Bonn fahren würde.	*He said that she would not travel to Bonn.*
Sie fragte, ob Erik in Berlin arbeiten wollte.	*She asked whether Erik wants to work in Berlin.*
Sie fragte, ob Erik Jura studiert hätte.	*She asked whether Erik had studied law.*
Sie fragte, wo er früher gewohnt hätte.	*She asked where he had lived previously.*
Sie fragte, warum er nicht verheirat wäre.	*She asked why he is not married.*
Sie fragte, wie viel er in Berlin verdienen könnte.	*She asked how much he can earn in Berlin.*

Foreign Words in German

German is much like English in its willingness to adopt foreign words to enrich the language. There is a large category of German verbs of foreign origin that end in **-ieren**. You have already encountered several of them. The following list will familiarize you with a few more high-frequency verbs of this type.

delegieren	*to send as a delegate; to delegate*		
demonstrieren	*to demonstrate*	notieren	*to make a note of something*
faszinieren	*to fascinate*	produzieren	*to produce*
kontrollieren	*to control*	programmieren	*to program*
kopieren	*to copy*	protestieren	*to protest*
manifestieren	*to manifest*	restaurieren	*to restore*

These are only a few examples. This is a large category of verbs, and as you gain experience with German, you will encounter many more.

German has borrowed vocabulary from a variety of foreign sources including English. Here are a few of these words to consider.

anklicken	*to click (on an icon)*	die Farce	*farce*
chatten	*to chat (in a chat room)*	die Gala	*gala*
das Derby	*derby (horse race)*	die Hardware	*hardware (computer)*
das Design	*design*	die Software	*software*
das Happening	*happening*	faxen	*to fax*
das Internet	*Internet*	intuitiv	*intuitive*
das Motocross	*motocross*	invalid	*invalid (handicapped)*
der Browser	*browser*	nonchalant	*nonchalant*
der Computer	*computer*	posten	*to post*
der Favorit	*favorite*	surfen	*to surf*
der Manager	*manager*	updated	*updated*

Though this list of words and their definitions may seem obvious, it is always wise to consult a dictionary to find the precise meaning of a foreign word in German. There are often nuances of meaning or usages of the word that are not always immediately apparent.

The verb **fixieren**, for example, is an **-ieren** verb, which says that it most likely comes from a foreign source. And the stem **fix-** suggests that the verb means *to fix*. This is quite true, but the verb does not mean *to repair*. This verb means *to fix one's gaze* on someone or something. Rely on a dictionary for precision.

More Idioms

Idioms require a special explanation. Just as in English, German has a variety of idioms that cannot always be translated literally. Consider this English phrase: *Get a load of her.* Each of the words can be found separately in a dictionary, but the meaning (*Look at her*) will not be discovered that way.

Let's look at a few useful German idioms and special phrases with their English translations.

Das kommt darauf an.	*That depends.*
Du nimmst mich auf dem Arm.	*You are pulling my leg.*
Er erzählte mir ein Ammenmärchen.	*He told me a cock-and-bull story.*
Er hat schon lange ins Gras gebissen.	*He kicked the bucket long ago.*

Er kam vom Regen in die Traufe.	*He got out of the frying pan and into the fire.*
Er trägt sein Herz auf der Zunge.	*He wears his heart on his sleeve.*
Es tut mir leid.	*I am sorry.*
Gott sei Dank!	*Thank goodness.*
Hau ab!	*Get out! Knock it off!*
Ich brach das Schweigen, indem ich ihn zuerst anredete.	*I broke the ice by speaking to him first.*
Ich habe ein Hühnchen mit dir zu rupfen.	*I have a bone to pick with you.*
Stell dir mal vor!	*Just imagine.*
Was ist los?	*What is the matter?*
Wir wollen darum losen. Kopf oder Zahl?	*Let's flip for it. Heads or tails?*

QUIZ

Write the present and past subjunctive conjugations with the pronouns provided for each of the following verbs.

1.

	Present **berichten**	**Past**	**Present** **fahren**	**Past**
ich	_____	_____	_____	_____
du	_____	_____	_____	_____
er	_____	_____	_____	_____
wir	_____	_____	_____	_____
ihr	_____	_____	_____	_____
sie	_____	_____	_____	_____

2.

	mitgehen		**aussehen**	
ich	_____	_____	_____	_____
du	_____	_____	_____	_____

er	_____	_____	_____	_____
wir	_____	_____	_____	_____
ihr	_____	_____	_____	_____
sie	_____	_____	_____	_____

3. **werden**   **sein**

ich	_____	_____	_____	_____
du	_____	_____	_____	_____
er	_____	_____	_____	_____
wir	_____	_____	_____	_____
ihr	_____	_____	_____	_____
sie	_____	_____	_____	_____

Change each direct quote to indirect discourse using the phrases provided. For example:

> Erik sagte, dass…
>
> „Seine Mutter ist sehr krank."
>
> *Erik sagte, dass seine Mutter sehr krank sei.*

4. Erik sagte, dass…

„Seine Freundin will in Darmstadt arbeiten."

_____.

„Die Polizei erhielt einen interessanten Brief."

_____.

„Niemand hat ihm etwas über den Film erzählt."

_____.

„Er hat seine Freundin in Bremen kennen gelernt."

_____.

„Tina wird ein Geschenk für ihren Mann suchen."

_____.

„Unsere Freunde wollen ein Kind adoptieren."

_____.

„Die Touristen werden sich morgen mit Verwandten treffen."

_____.

5. Helga fragte,...

„Ist Herr Schneider bei euch zu Gast?"

_____.

„Wann wird der Wagen repariert werden?"

_____.

„Mit wem haben die Ausländer getanzt?"

_____.

„Haben Sie viele Geschenke zum Geburtstag bekommen?"

_____.

„Können die Jungen uns helfen?"

_____.

„Wo haben die Kinder sich die Hände gewaschen?"

_____.

„Lernten die Schüler lesen und schreiben?"

_____.

Circle the letter of the word or phrase that best completes each sentence.

6. Die Zeitung _____, dass die Dichterin gestorben sei.

(a) wollte   (c) berichtete

(b) sagt   (d) fragte

7. Martin hat uns gefragt, _____ wir seine Verwandten kennten.

(a) als   (c) wie viel

(b) ob   (d) wen

8. Er sagte zu der Wirtin, dass sein Zimmer zu klein _____.

(a) könne   (c) seien

(b) käme   (d) wäre

9. Meine Tante fragte mich, ob ich im Wald wandern _____.

   (a) habe   (c) warte

   (b) gehabt hätte   (d) wollte

10. Er sagte, dass die warme Sonne den Kranken gesund _____.

   (a) machen werde   (c) angekommen wäre

   (b) sollte   (d) würde

CHAPTER 20

Expressing Wishes and Conditions

In this chapter you will learn:

Expressing Wishes with the Subjunctive

The past subjunctive is used in more ways than just in indirect discourse. It is the conjugational form needed to express wishes. In such expressions it is often accompanied by the conjunction **wenn** (*if*). But a wish statement is still correct if **wenn** is omitted. Consider the following examples:

Wenn ich nur noch jung wäre!	
Wäre ich nur noch jung!	*If only I were still young.*

Wenn wir nur mehr Geld hätten!	
Hätten wir nur mehr Geld!	*If only we had more money.*

Oral Practice

Practice saying the following list of sentences out loud.

Wären wir doch in unserer Heimat!	*If we were just back in our homeland.*
Wenn wir doch in unserer Heimat wären!	

Hätte sie doch ihren Mann nie verlassen!	*If she had just never left her husband.*
Wenn sie doch ihren Mann nie velassen hätte!	

Hätte er doch mehr Mut!	*If he had just had more courage.*
Wenn er doch mehr Mut hätte!	

Könnte ich ihm doch helfen!	*If I could just help him.*
Wenn ich ihm doch helfen könnte!	

Wäret ihr nur bei mir!	*If only you were with me.*
Wenn ihr nur bei mir wäret!	

Wäre das Kind nur wieder gesund!	*If only the child were well again.*
Wenn das Kind nur wieder gesund wäre!	

Hätten wir doch mehr Glück gehabt!	*If we had just had more luck.*
Wenn wir doch mehr Glück gehabt hätten!	

Wäre er nur früher gekommen!	*If only he had come earlier.*
Wenn er nur früher gekommen wäre!	

You will notice that there are two tenses inferred by wishes like those just illustrated: a present tense wish and a past tense wish. For example:

Wenn er doch mehr Mut hätte!   *If he just had more courage.*

Wenn er doch mehr Mut gehabt hätte!   *If he had just had more courage.*

Wish expressions occur only in those two forms. Naturally, if the past tense wish uses a verb of motion or an intransitive verb, the auxiliary **sein** must be used.

Käme sie nur früher!   *If only she came earlier.*

Wäre sie nur früher gekommen!   *If only she had come earlier.*

Subjunctive with *Als Ob*

The conjunction **als ob** (*as if*) (sometimes stated as **als wenn**) introduces a subordinate clause that requires a verb in the past subjunctive. Since the clause is a subordinate clause, the conjugated verb is the last element in the clause.

Er tut so, als ob er alles wüsste.   *He acted as if he knew everything.*

Sie sprach, als ob sie viel   *She spoke as if she were much more*
    intelligenter wäre.   *intelligent.*

Written Practice 1

Complete each phrase with the sentences provided.

    1. Erik tat so, als ob…

       Er ist sehr klug. (**klug** = *smart*)

       _____.

       Er ist plötzlich reich geworden.

       _____.

       Er kann diese Probleme lösen.

       _____.

       Er hat den Kanzler schon kennen gelernt.

       _____.

2. Sie schrie, als ob...

Sie hat ein Ungeheuer gesehen. (**das Ungeheuer** = *monster*)

_____.

Sie muss sterben.

_____.

Sie ist wahnsinnig. (**wahnsinnig** = *insane*)

_____.

Sie kann nicht schwimmen.

_____.

Expressing Conditions with the Subjunctive

The conjunction **wenn** is used to express a condition (the conditional subjunctive). It states that if a certain condition is met, a certain result will occur. For example:

Condition: →	**Result:**
Wenn Bonn nicht so weit wäre,	führen wir dorthin.
Condition: *If Bonn were not so far.*	Result: *We'd drive there.*

In the clause that shows the result (the non-**wenn** clause), it is common to use **würde** plus an infinitive in place of the past subjunctive verb. In such an instance, the previous example will look like this:

Wenn Bonn nicht so weit wäre, **würden** wir dorthin **fahren**.

If Bonn were not so far, we would drive there.

The structure of **würde** plus an infinitive is widely used in the non-**wenn** clause. However, if the tense of the verb is a perfect tense or if the conjugated verb is a modal, the **würde**-plus-infinitive structure can be avoided. For example:

A Single Verb: brauchen
Wenn ich gesund wäre, würde ich den Arzt nicht brauchen.

If I were well, I would not need the doctor.

Future Tense:

Wenn ich gesund wäre, würde ich
morgen nach Spanien reisen.

*If I were well, I would travel to Spain
tomorrow.*

Modal Auxiliary:

Wenn ich gesund wäre, könnte ich
ins Kino gehen.

If I were well, I could go to the movies.

A Perfect Tense:

Wenn ich gesund gewesen wäre, hätte
ich meinen Onkel in Bonn besucht.

*If I had been well, I would have
visited my uncle in Bonn.*

Written Practice 2

Using **wenn** in the first clause, combine the following pairs of sentences. For
example:

Wir haben mehr Zeit. Wir gehen ins Kino.
Wenn wir mehr Zeit hätten, würden wir ins Kino gehen.

1. Ich verstehe Deutsch. Ich lese diese Bücher.

   _____.

2. Wir können ihm helfen. Er ist glücklich.

   _____.

3. Sie haben ihm mehr Geld gegeben. Er hat das neue Haus gekauft.

   _____.

4. Ich habe im Lotto gewonnen. Ich bin nach Amerika geflogen.

   _____.

5. Der Schüler ist fleißiger gewesen. Er hat das Gedicht auswendig gelernt.

   _____.

Irregular Verbs in the Subjunctive

A few verbs do not form the past subjunctive in the regular manner. Examine the list that follows and take note of these exceptions of past subjunctive forms.

Infinitive		Past Subjunctive
empfehlen	*to recommend*	empföhle
gelten	*to be valid; worth*	gölte *or* gälte
helfen	*to help*	hülfe
schwimmen	*to swim*	schwömme
schwören	*to swear, curse*	schwüre
stehen	*to stand*	stünde *or* stände
sterben	*to die*	stürbe
verderben	*to ruin, spoil*	verdürbe
verstehen	*to understand*	verstünde *or* verstände
werben	*to recruit; court*	würbe
werfen	*to throw, hurl*	würfe

Oral Practice

Practice saying the following list of sentences out loud.

Wenn ich älter wäre, würde ich in Frankreich arbeiten.	*If I were older, I would work in France.*
Wenn ich älter wäre, könnte ich in Berlin studieren.	*If I were older, I could study in Berlin.*
Wenn ich älter wäre, würde ich bei meinem Onkel wohnen.	*If I were older, I would live at my uncle's house.*
Wenn ich älter wäre, müsste ich meinen eigenen Wagen kaufen.	*If I were older, I would have to buy my own car.*
Sie hätte mir geholfen, wenn sie mehr Zeit gehabt hätte.	*She would have helped me, if she had had more time.*
Sie hätte mir geholfen, wenn sie in der Nähe gewohnt hätte.	*She would have helped me, if she had lived in the area.*
Sie hätte mir geholfen, wenn sie nicht so krank gewesen wäre.	*She would have helped me, if she had not been so sick.*
Sie hätte mir geholfen, wenn ihr Wagen repariert worden wäre.	*She would have helped me, if her car had been repaired.*

Being Polite in the Subjunctive

In order to sound more polite, it is common to use the past subjunctive **möchte** (*would like*) in place of **wollen** (*to want*).

Ich will ein Stück Kuchen.	*I want a piece of cake.*
Ich **möchte** ein Stück Kuchen.	*I **would like** a piece of cake.*
Was wollen Sie essen?	*What do you want to eat?*
Was **möchten** Sie essen?	*What **would** you **like** to eat?*

Infinitive Clauses

There are times in German when **zu** is added to an infinitive. That combination is called an infinitive clause. Infinitive clauses are frequently used following **viel(es)**, **etwas**, and **nichts**. For example:

Es gibt viel zu tun.	*There is a lot to do.*
Ich habe etwas zu sagen.	*I have something to say.*
Gibt es nichts zu trinken?	*Is there nothing to drink?*

If an infinitive has a inseparable prefix (**be-**, **emp-**, **ent-**, **er-**, **ge-**, **ver-**, or **zer-**), **zu** in an infinitive phrase will precede the verb.

Er hatte etwas zu verkaufen.	*He had something to sell.*

If the infinitive has a separable prefix (**an-**, **ein-**, **durch-**, **mit-**, **vor-**, or **zu-**), **zu** will stand between the prefix and the infinitive, and the phrase will be written as one word.

Er findet etwas anzuziehen.	*He finds something to put on.*

You must also use an infinitive phrase after **etwas** and **nichts** when they are followed by an adjective used as a noun.

Der Soldat hat nichts **Neues** zu berichten.	*The soldier has nothing **new** to report.*
Der Künstler fand etwas **Interessantes** zu malen.	*The artist found something **interesting** to paint.*

ES AS A SIGNAL FOR AN INFINITIVE CLAUSE

Sentences that use the pronoun **es** as their subject can signal the need for an infinitive clause.

Es ist wichtig sich jeden Tag zu duschen.	*It is important to shower every day.*
Es war schwer mit dem alten Mann zu reden.	*It was hard to talk with the old man.*
Es fiel mir nicht ein, Geld von ihm zu borgen.	*It did not occur to me to borrow money from him.*

Written Practice 3

Change the sentences in parentheses to infinitive clauses, attaching them to the sentence provided. For example:

Es war schwer…

(Sie tanzt mit Erik.)

Es war schwer mit Erik zu tanzen.

1. Es ist sehr wichtig…

(Die Kinder trinken genug Milch.)

_____.

(Er arbeitet fleißig.)

_____.

(Wir kommen pünktlich an.)

_____.

(Sie helfen alten Menschen.)

_____.

(Sie hat gute Freunde.)

_____.

(Wir sind höflich. [**höflich** = *polite*])

_____.

PHRASES THAT REQUIRE AN INFINITIVE CLAUSE

There are some specific phrases that always require an infinitive clause. They begin with a preposition and end with the infinitive clause.

anstatt...zu *instead of*   ohne...zu *without* (*doing something*)   um...zu *in order to*

Clauses formed with these three structures can precede or follow the main clause of the sentence.

Helga borgte Geld, anstatt Arbeit zu suchen.	*Helga borrowed money instead of looking for work.*
Er fuhr nach Hause, ohne uns zu helfen.	*He went home without helping us.*
Um Geld zu verdienen, musste Erik nach Leipzig ziehen.	*In order to earn money, Erik had to move to Leipzig.*

Written Practice 4

Change the sentences in parentheses to infinitive clauses, attaching them to the sentences provided. For example:

Er kam in die Küche, ohne...

(Er wäscht sich die Hände.)

Er kam in die Küche, ohne sich die Hände zu waschen.
_____

1. Er kam in die Küche, ohne...

(Er grüsst seine Mutter.)

_____.

(Er hilft seiner Mutter.)

_____.

(Er macht die Tür zu.)

_____.

2. Karin arbeitet in Berlin, um...

(Sie verdient mehr Geld.)

_____.

(Sie wohnt bei einer Tante.)

_____.

(Sie besucht die großen Museen.)

_____.

3. Die Kinder stehen an der Ecke, anstatt…
   (Sie gehen zur Schule.)

_____.

(Sie besuchen ihren kranken Onkel.)

_____.

(Sie beeilen sich nach Hause zu kommen.)

_____.

OTHER VERBAL STRUCTURES WITH INFINITIVE CLAUSES

Thus far, you have dealt with infinitive clauses that consist of **zu** and a single verb: **zu gehen**, **anzuziehen**, **zu besuchen**, and so forth. But other verbal structures can also occur in infinitive clauses.

Modals:

Er **kann** seinen Onkel **besuchen**.	_He **can visit** his uncle._
Er spart sein Geld, um seinen Onkel **besuchen zu können**.	_He saves his money in order **to be able to visit** his uncle._

Perfect Tense:

Er **hat** einen Schatz **gefunden**.	_He **found** a treasure._
Er glaubt einen Schatz **gefunden zu haben**.	_He believes **to have found** a treasure._
Er **ist** in die Hauptstadt **geflogen**.	_He **flew** to the capital._
Er behauptet in die Hauptstadt **geflogen zu sein.**	_He claims **to have flown** to the capital._

Passive:

Er **wird** von einem Freund **besucht**.	_He **is visited** by a friend._
Er behauptet von einem Freund **besucht zu werden**.	_He claims **to be visited** by a friend._
Er **ist verhaftet worden**.	_He **was arrested**._

Er schämte sich **verhaftet**   *He was ashamed **to have been arrested**.*
   worden zu sein.

In each of the previous examples, the conjugated verb of the first sentence becomes the infinitive preceded by **zu** in the infinitive clause. This occurs whether the conjugated verb is a modal auxiliary, the auxiliary in a perfect tense, or the auxiliary of a passive structure.

kann besuchen	→	*besuchen zu können*
hat gefunden	→	*gefunden zu haben*
ist geflogen	→	*geflogen zu sein*
wird besucht	→	*besucht zu werden*
ist besucht worden	→	*besucht worden zu sein*

Written Practice 5

Rewrite each of the following verb phrases as an infinitive clause with **zu**. Consider what each infinitive clause means.

1. muss arbeiten _____

2. soll vergessen _____

3. will sprechen _____

4. hat gelernt _____

5. hat verstanden _____

6. ist gewesen _____

7. ist mitgegangen _____

8. wird zerstört _____

9. wurde aufgemacht _____

10. ist bewundert worden _____

Written Practice 6

Circle the letter of the word or phrase that best completes each sentence.

1. Das Kind schrie, _____ es ein Ungeheuer gesehen hätte.

   (a) wenn   (c) ob

   (b) wohin   (d) als ob

2. Karl hilft Karin, _____ uns zu helfen.

   (a) anstatt   (c) von ihm

   (b) als wenn   (d) von ihnen

3. Der Dieb wäre glücklich gewesen, wenn ihn niemand _____ .

   (a) geblieben wäre   (c) gesehen hätte

   (b) ankommen würde   (d) geglaubt würde

4. _____ du mir glaubtest, könnte ich dir damit helfen.

   (a) Als ob   (c) Anstatt

   (b) Wenn   (d) Ohne zu

5. Thomas ging zur Schule, _____ sich die Haare zu kämmen.

   (a) ohne   (c) wenn

   (b) als ob   (d) denn

6. Wenn er dich kennte, _____ er dich einladen.

   (a) soll   (c) würde

   (b) möchten   (d) hätte

7. _____ mein Mann nur hier!

   (a) Wäre   (c) Möchte

   (b) Könnte   (d) Hätte

8. Wenn der alte Mann _____ , würde seine Frau weinen.

   (a) verstand   (c) gehabt habe

   (b) müsste   (d) stürbe

9. Die Schauspielerin lächelte, als ob ich etwas Dummes _____ .

   (a) gesagt hätte   (c) verkaufen werde

   (b) geflogen wäre   (d) bewundert worden wäre

10. Wenn ich doch bei meinen Eltern _____!

    (a) hülfe   (c) müsste

    (b) wäre   (d) möchte

11. Wenn ich plötzlich reich würde, dann _____ ich viele neue Freunde.

    (a) fände   (c) gegeben hätte

    (b) gäbe   (d) gefunden worden wäre

12. Felix _____, als ob er nicht verstanden hätte.

    (a) machte zu   (c) tat so

    (b) sprecht   (d) glaubte

13. Gudrun redete, als ob sie alles _____.

    (a) wüsste   (c) geschrieben würde

    (b) erwartet   (d) fahren möchte

14. Es ist wichtig gut fahren _____ können.

    (a) hätte   (c) ob

    (b) wäre   (d) zu

15. Wenn ich das Geld gefunden hätte, hätte ich es Ihnen _____.

    (a) verloren   (c) geben können

    (b) verhaftet worden   (d) vorgestellt

QUIZ

Write the past subjunctive and the present conditional of the following verbs in the third person singular. For example:

    gehen   *ginge* _____   *würde gehen* _____

  1. tragen   _____   _____

     bringen   _____   _____

     zumachen   _____   _____

     werden   _____   _____

     vergessen   _____   _____

sprechen	_____	_____
verstehen	_____	_____
lassen	_____	_____
ankommen	_____	_____
vorstellen	_____	_____
kennen	_____	_____
wissen	_____	_____
haben	_____	_____
einladen	_____	_____
sein	_____	_____

Complete each sentence with the phrases in parentheses, making them the result of a conditional statement. For example:

Wenn er hier wäre, _____.

(Er hilft mir.)

Wenn er hier wäre, würde er mir helfen.

2. Wenn er hier wäre, _____.

(Er spricht mit Onkel Peter.)

_____.

(Ich kann mit ihm tanzen.)

_____.

(Wir gehen zusammen in die Bibliothek.)

_____.

(Er muss auf dem Sofa schlafen.)

_____.

3. Wenn das Wetter besser gewesen wäre, _____.

(Wir sind in die Stadt gefahren.)

_____.

(Wir haben im Garten spielen können.)

_____.

(Der Wagen ist repariert worden.)

_____.

(Thomas hat die Kinder zum Stadtpark gebracht.)

_____.

4. Wenn _____, würde sie uns Eis kaufen.

(Sie hat mehr Geld.)

_____.

(Unsere Tante ist hier.)

_____.

(Wir arbeiten fleißíg.)

_____.

(Es wird heiß.)

_____.

Complete each sentence with the phrases in parentheses. For example:

Er lacht, als ob…

(Die Geschichte ist dumm.)

Er lacht, als ob die Geschichte dumm wäre.

5. Er tat so, als ob…

(Er hat alles verstanden.)

_____.

(Er ist so klug.)

_____.

(Ich bin nicht sein Freund.)

_____.

(Er hat uns gar nicht gesehen.)

_____.

(Wir werden ihm kein Geschenk geben.)

_____.

6. Karin spricht, als ob…

(Sie ist sehr klug.)

_____.

(Sie hat die Lösung gefunden.)

_____.

(Wir wollen ihr nicht helfen.)

_____.

(Sie hat ein Ungeheuer gesehen.)

_____.

(Martin ist nur ein Bekannter.)

_____.

Complete each sentence given by forming infinitive clauses from the sentences in parentheses. For example:

Es ist wichtig…

(Wir verstehen das Problem.)

Es ist wichtig das Problem zu verstehen.

7. Es ist oft schwer…

(Wir glauben einem Dieb.)

_____.

(Ich finde interessante Bücher.)

_____.

(Er arbeitet für einen bösen Mann.)

_____.

(Wir bleiben zu Hause, wenn das Wetter schön ist.)

_____.

8. Er möchte nach Wien reisen, um…

(Er besucht einen Freund.)

_____.

(Er sucht da Arbeit.)

_____ .

(Er vergisst seine Probleme in Freiburg.)

_____ .

(Er kann an der Universität studieren.)

_____ .

9. Tanja behauptet...

(Sie hat eine Freundin im Kaufhaus gesehen.)

_____ .

(Sie hat dem neuen Chef damit geholfen.)

_____ .

(Sie ist nach Asien geflogen.)

_____ .

(Sie ist von allen Jungen bewundert worden.)

_____ .

Rewrite the following phrase as an infinitive clause with **um...zu**, **ohne...zu**, and **anstatt...zu**. For example:

sich die Hände waschen

um sich die Hände zu waschen

ohne sich die Hände zu waschen

anstatt sich die Hände zu waschen.

10. lassen den Wagen reparieren

_____ .

_____ .

_____ .

PART FOUR TEST

Combine each first sentence with the one that follows, making each sentence a relative clause with a definite article relative pronoun. Then, rewrite the new sentences using **welcher** as the relative pronoun. For example:

> Er hat ein Auto.
>
> Er wird das Auto reparieren lassen.
>
> *Er hat ein Auto, das er wird reparieren lassen.*
> _____
> *Er hat ein Auto, welches er wird reparieren lassen.*
> _____

1. Die Studentin ist die Tochter meiner Wirtin.

   Erik tanzte mit der Studentin.

   _____.

   _____.

2. Die Männer haben wenig Freizeit.

   Ich arbeite mit den Männern in einer Fabrik.

   _____.

   _____.

3. Sie haben das Dorf besichtigt.

   Mein Onkel ist in dem Dorf geboren.

   _____.

   _____.

Complete each sentence with the sentences that follow, forming them as relative clauses.

4. Meine Freundin hat etwas, …

   Du wirst dich über etwas freuen.

   _____.

   Etwas ist sehr teuer.

   _____.

   5. Der Physiker findet alles, ...

      Seine Frau hat alles verloren.

      _____ .

      Er kann alles verkaufen.

      _____ .

Write each of the following passive phrases in the tenses shown with the pronouns provided.

   6. werden gefunden

pres	ich	_____
past	du	_____
pres perf	er	_____
fut	wir	_____

   7. muss verhaftet werden

pres	ich	_____
past	du	_____
pres perf	er	_____
fut	wir	_____

Rewrite the following active voice sentences in the passive voice. Retain the tenses of the active voice sentences.

   8. Die Lehrer diskutierten das Examen.

      _____ .

   9. Wir haben das alte Haus verkauft.

      _____ .

  10. Unsere Wirtin wird den neuen Mieter vorstellen.

      _____ .

Rewrite each sentence, adding the adjectives provided in parentheses. For example:

    Ich besuchte eine _____ Frau.

    (alt) *Ich besuchte eine alte Frau.*

11. Habt ihr einen _____ Bären gesehen?

    (groß) _____?

12. Die Töchter dieses _____ Mannes arbeiten in Kiel.

    (alt) _____.

13. Sie hat mit dem _____ Diplomaten gesprochen.

    (jung) _____.

14. Alle _____ Kinder müssen zu Hause bleiben.

    (krank) _____.

Form the three imperatives for the verbs provided.

	du	ihr	Sie
15. treffen	_____	_____	_____
16. vorstellen	_____	_____	_____
17. aufmachen	_____	_____	_____
18. sehen	_____	_____	_____
19. sein	_____	_____	_____
20. geben	_____	_____	_____
21. werden	_____	_____	_____

Rewrite each passive sentence with the new subjects provided in parentheses, making any necessary changes.

22. _____ wurde von ihnen geholfen.

    (er) _____.

    (die Jungen) _____.

    (wir) _____.

23. _____ musste nicht verkauft werden.

    (die Bücher) _____ .

    (es) _____ .

    (die Wohnung) _____ .

Provide the appropriate adjective endings for each blank in the cases given.

24. **nom**   *ein guter Mann* _____   _____

    acc   _____   *seine letzte Frage* _____

    dat   _____   _____

    acc   *sein neues Heft* _____   _____

    dat   _____   _____

    gen   _____   *meiner alten Handschuhe* __

Write the present and past subjunctive conjugations with the pronouns provided for each of the following verbs.

	Present Subj.	**Past Subj.**
25. trinken		
ich	_____	_____
du	_____	_____
er	_____	_____
wir	_____	_____
ihr	_____	_____
sie	_____	_____
26. zumachen		
ich	_____	_____
du	_____	_____
er	_____	_____
wir	_____	_____
ihr	_____	_____
sie	_____	_____

	Present Subj.	Past Subj.
27. werden		
ich	_____	_____
du	_____	_____
er	_____	_____
wir	_____	_____
ihr	_____	_____
sie	_____	_____
28. sein		
ich	_____	_____
du	_____	_____
er	_____	_____
wir	_____	_____
ihr	_____	_____
sie	_____	_____

Rewrite each sentence with the direct quotes provided, forming a statement in indirect discourse. For example:

Erik sagte, dass…

„Seine Mutter ist sehr krank."

Erik sagte, dass seine Mutter sehr krank sei.

29. Frau Schneider sagte, dass…

„Ihre Freundin will in Darmstadt wohnen."

_____.

„Niemand wird ihr darüber erzählen."

_____.

„Die Besucher werden sich morgen mit einer Physikerin treffen."

_____.

30. Der Beamte fragte, ...

„Ist Herr Schneider ein Freund von Ihnen?"

_____.

„Wann ist der Wagen repariert worden?"

_____.

„Haben Sie Ihre Fahrkarten bekommen?"

_____.

Complete each sentence with the phrases in parentheses, using them as the result of a conditional statement. For example:

Wenn er hier wäre, _____ .

(Er hilft mir.)

Wenn er hier wäre, würde er mir helfen.

31. Wenn er hier wäre, _____ .

(Tina kann mit ihm sprechen.)

_____.

(Wir gehen zusammen ins Kino.)

_____.

32. Wenn das Wetter besser gewesen wäre, _____ .

(Sie sind in die Berge gefahren.)

_____.

(Ich habe im Garten sitzen können.)

_____.

Complete each sentence with the phrases in parentheses. For example:

Er lacht, als ob...

(Die Geschichte ist dumm.)

Er lacht, als ob die Geschichte dumm wäre.

33. Er tat so, als ob...

(Er hat alles verstanden.)

_____.

(Tanja ist seine Freundin.)

_____.

(Er hat uns gar nicht gesehen.)

_____.

34. Das Mädchen spricht, als ob...

(Sie ist sehr klug.)

_____.

(Die Jungen wollen ihr nicht helfen.)

_____.

(Sie hat einen Wolf gesehen.)

_____.

Complete each sentence given by forming infinitive clauses from the sentences in parentheses. For example:

Es ist wichtig...

(Wir verstehen das Problem.)

Es ist wichtig das Problem zu verstehen.

35. Es ist schwer...

(Wir helfen alten Menschen.)

_____.

(Ich finde interessante Bücher.)

_____.

(Sie wohnen in einem neuen Haus.)

_____.

36. Sie fahren nach Italien, um...

(Sie besuchen Freunde.)

_____.

(Sie fotografieren die alten Städte.)

_____ .

(Sie können an der Universität studieren.)

_____ .

Circle the letter of the word or phrase that best completes each sentence.

37. In welchem Jahr _____ er geboren?

   (a) wart   (c) sein

   (b) wurde   (d) kann

38. Hast du das schöne Mädchen _____?

   (a) gern   (c) sehr gut

   (b) welche   (d) gebären

39. Es gibt _____.

   (a) keinen Nachtisch   (c) kein Wein

   (b) noch   (d) wahrscheinlich

40. Berlin ist die _____ Deutschlands.

   (a) Mauer   (c) Kaiser

   (b) Bundesrepublik   (d) Hauptstadt

41. Die alte Dame hat ihre Tasche _____.

   (a) gefallen   (c) vergessen

   (b) aufgestanden   (d) verlieren

42. Unsere Familie kann keine _____ halten.

   (a) Kaiser   (c) Haustiere

   (b) Busch   (d) Wohnungen

43. Im Garten _____ viele Blumen.

   (a) wachsen   (c) rufen an

   (b) blieb   (d) angerufen

44. Herr Professor, _____ mich bitte an!

   (a) rufen Sie   (c) sieh

   (b) seht   (d) bleiben Sie

45. Meine Kusine _____ als Sekretärin.

    (a) lädt ein   (c) arbeitet

    (b) dienen   (d) folgte

46. Wird _____ damit geholfen?

    (a) ihr   (c) einen Ausländer

    (b) unsere   (d) keine Leute

47. Die alte Dame _____ ins Krankenhaus gebracht werden.

    (a) musste   (c) hat

    (b) ist   (d) gekonnt

48. Herr Bauer will ein neues _____ anziehen.

    (a) Ball   (c) Affen

    (b) Pflanze   (d) Hemd

49. Die Zeitung _____, dass der alte Schriftsteller gestorben sei.

    (a) wollte   (c) berichtete

    (b) sagt   (d) fragte

50. Der Lehrer hat uns gefragt, _____ wir den Roman gelesen hätten.

    (a) als   (c) wie viel

    (b) ob   (d) wen

Circle the letter of the word or phrase that best completes each sentence.

1. _____ ist das?
   - (a) Herr Keller
   - (b) Wer
   - (c) Name
   - (d) Heißt

2. Das Mädchen heißt _____.
   - (a) Herr
   - (b) Frau
   - (c) Angela
   - (d) Erik Schäfer

3. _____ Name ist Tina.
   - (a) Das
   - (b) Wer
   - (c) Junge
   - (d) Mein

4. Mein Bruder ist nicht _____.
   - (a) die Schweiz
   - (b) zu Hause
   - (c) die Lehrerin
   - (d) Österreicherin

5. Nein, die Hauptstadt ist _____ weit von hier.
   - (a) in
   - (b) nicht
   - (c) was
   - (d) ja

6. _____ ist die Professorin?
   - (a) Wo
   - (b) Der
   - (c) Wie
   - (d) Nein

7. Es _____ sehr warm.
   - (a) sind
   - (b) hat
   - (c) wird
   - (d) wieder

8. _____ ist die Party?
   - (a) Warum
   - (b) Wann
   - (c) Gestern
   - (d) Sommer

9. Ist die Frau Ihre Mutter _____ Ihre Tante?
   - (a) oder
   - (b) wenn
   - (c) trotz
   - (d) sehr

10. Wie _____ CDs habt ihr?

   (a) keine

   (b) lange

   (c) viele

   (d) mehr

11. Meine Schwester will Lehrerin _____.

   (a) haben

   (b) werden

   (c) bekommen

   (d) lernen

12. _____ wird heiß.

   (a) Diese Uhr

   (b) Der Ofen

   (c) Seine Briefe

   (d) Unsere Blumen

13. Doktor Bauer ist _____.

   (a) nach Hause

   (b) gestern

   (c) nicht heute

   (d) Zahnarzt

14. Meine Tochter _____ eine Freundin.

   (a) sieht

   (b) besuchen

   (c) bekamt

   (d) wurden

15. Warum _____ du ein Sweatshirt?

   (a) kommst

   (b) gingst

   (c) trägst

   (d) gekauft

16. Das Kind nimmt ein _____ Milch.

   (a) groß

   (b) kleine

   (c) Dorf

   (d) Glas

17. Robert Bensen kommt _____ Amerika.

   (a) aus

   (b) in der

   (c) davon

   (d) wegen

18. Ich _____ einen Freund, wo das neue Restaurant ist.

   (a) frage

   (b) spiele

   (c) werde

   (d) wird

19. _____ fahren Sie morgen?

   (a) Heute

   (b) Wohin

   (c) Wer

   (d) Zu Hause

20. _____ siehst du in der Kunsthalle?

    (a) Wen   (c) Eine junge Frau

    (b) Der alte Mann   (d) Ein Bus

21. Ich _____ meine Eltern vor.

    (a) gehe   (c) bin geblieben

    (b) kam   (d) stellte

22. Das _____ ist nicht sehr groß.

    (a) Lehrer   (c) Haus

    (b) Kinder   (d) Brief

23. Meine Eltern sind _____ gefahren.

    (a) mit dem Zug   (c) nächste Woche

    (b) zu Hause   (d) Berlin

24. Das _____ Glas war ein Geschenk von meiner Tante.

    (a) neuen   (c) schwarz und weiß

    (b) schlechtes   (d) kleine

25. Sehen Sie _____ Bruder?

    (a) Ihren   (c) eure

    (b) meiner   (d) unser

26. Man kommt _____ nach Berlin.

    (a) mit dem Zug   (c) in Hamburg

    (b) zu Hause   (d) bei meinen Eltern

27. Peter kommt _____ spät zur Party.

    (a) gestern   (c) keine

    (b) sehr   (d) warum

28. Wir wohnen _____ in der Schweiz.

    (a) jetzt   (c) mit dem Auto

    (b) neu   (d) vom Bahnhof

29. Kommst du _____?

    (a) schön   (c) spaziert

    (b) zu Fuß   (d) sehr kalt

30. Ich gab zu viel Geld _____.

    (a) davon   (c) aus

    (b) wovon   (d) in

31. Meine Tante trägt _____.

    (a) den Bahnhof   (c) das Flugzeug

    (b) einen Brief   (d) eine Bluse

32. _____ Sie den jungen Amerikaner?

    (a) Kennen   (c) Bekommen

    (b) Laufen   (d) Lesen

33. Ich _____, wer da wohnt.

    (a) wohnte   (c) weiß

    (b) stelle   (d) will

34. Er hat seine Bücher _____.

    (a) verloren   (c) haben

    (b) gesungen   (d) sein

35. Sie kann _____ Montag bleiben.

    (a) bis   (c) an

    (b) mit   (d) aus

36. Seine Kinder _____ kein Brot.

    (a) hatte   (c) aßen

    (b) gingen mit   (d) verstanden

37. Sie hatten nur vier _____.

    (a) Affe   (c) Bleistifte

    (b) Wohnung   (d) Schwester

38. Bist du vom Theater _____ Bahnhof gefahren?

    (a) im   (c) ohne

    (b) zum   (d) wider

39. Ich habe mehr als eine Stunde _____ sie gewartet.

    (a) heute   (c) getan

    (b) vom   (d) auf

40. Habt ihr diesen Roman _____?

    (a) mit einem Freund   (c) schreibt

    (b) gelesen   (d) zu euren Eltern

41. Die Schauspielerin hat mit meinem Sohn _____.

    (a) gespielt   (c) verstanden

    (b) aufgemacht   (d) erkannt

42. Es ist sehr heiß _____.

    (a) gehabt   (c) ausgesehen

    (b) gemacht   (d) geworden

43. Robert hat _____ gespielt.

    (a) besser   (c) beschrieben

    (b) wovon   (d) schlechte

44. Ihre Großmutter _____ sehr krank ausgesehen.

    (a) hat   (c) noch

    (b) ist   (d) war

45. Die neue Wohnung _____ ist sehr klein.

    (a) unserer Nachbarin   (c) diese Ausländer

    (b) meinem Enkel   (d) der Zeit

46. Er hatte ein Geschenk für _____.

    (a) diesem Herrn   (c) ihr

    (b) seinen Sohn   (d) dir

47. _____ Bücher hat er gefunden?

    (a) Mein   (c) Wessen

    (b) Unserer   (d) Etwas

48. Morgen fliegen wir _____ London.

    (a) nach   (c) im

    (b) in   (d) ohne

49. Unser Sohn studiert _____ einer Universität in Kanada.

    (a) vor   (c) durch

    (b) an   (d) vom

50. Der Metzger _____ das Fleisch.

   (a) schnitt   (c) kaufen

   (b) genommen   (d) ging

51. Sie senden _____ Freund einen Brief.

   (a) ihrem   (c) ihr

   (b) seine   (d) seinen

52. Es ist fünfzehn _____ nach elf.

   (a) Jahre   (c) Monate

   (b) Tage   (d) Minuten

53. Wann sind die Zwillinge _____?

   (a) getan   (c) gern

   (b) geboren   (d) geschrieben

54. Dieses Buch gehört meiner _____ .

   (a) Bruder   (c) Kusine

   (b) Eltern   (d) Freundinnen

55. Der Ausländer wohnt _____ .

   (a) bei uns   (c) aus Amerika

   (b) mit der Straßenbahn   (d) nach ihr

56. Du irrst _____ nicht.

   (a) schon   (c) ihn

   (b) dich   (d) jetzt

57. Um wie viel Uhr _____ Ihre Kusine nach Hause kommen?

   (a) wird   (c) ist

   (b) hat   (d) war

58. Der kranke Student hat das Examen nicht _____ können.

   (a) werden   (c) sein

   (b) machen   (d) müssen

59. Hat sie sich _____ geputzt?

   (a) die Zähne   (c) die Handschuhe

   (b) die Haare   (d) die Flasche

60. Ziehst du _____ ein neues Hemd an?

    (a) sich   (c) dir

    (b) ihn   (d) mich

61. Die Touristen, mit _____ er gesprochen hat, kommen aus Italien.

    (a) damit   (c) denen

    (b) anstatt   (d) der

62. Wer hat diesen Regenschirm kaufen _____?

    (a) gekonnt   (c) wollen

    (b) hören   (d) verloren

63. Der Junge, _____ Klavier spielt, ist mein Enkel.

    (a) die   (c) deren

    (b) den   (d) der

64. Hans fragt, wann sie den Artikel _____ lesen wollen.

    (a) wird   (c) gehabt

    (b) haben   (d) ist

65. Hast du Robert schwimmen _____?

    (a) gelernt   (c) gewusst

    (b) wollen   (d) sehen

66. Deutschland liegt in _____.

    (a) Europa   (c) Winter

    (b) April   (d) Berlin

67. Die _____ Italiens ist Rom.

    (a) Leute   (c) Länder

    (b) Hauptstadt   (d) Osten

68. Ich kann dir nicht _____.

    (a) helfen   (c) gesehen

    (b) sehen   (d) geholfen

69. Wann _____ Sie angekommen?

    (a) hat   (c) seien

    (b) haben   (d) sind

70. Meine Schwester ist _____ als mein Bruder.

    (a) älter   (c) am schnellsten

    (b) klein   (d) junge

71. Während des _____ wohnte er in Paris.

    (a) Haus   (c) Sommer

    (b) Krieges   (d) Wagens

72. Ich zog _____ ein blaues Hemd an.

    (a) unser   (c) mir

    (b) dich   (d) seines

73. Die Männer, _____ in einer Fabrik arbeiten, sind meine Freunde.

    (a) der   (c) denen

    (b) die   (d) deren

74. Angela hatte etwas, _____ sehr teuer war.

    (a) was   (c) welche

    (b) womit   (d) der

75. Der Kaiser ist im _____ 1941 gestorben.

    (a) Berlin   (c) Jahre

    (b) geboren   (d) jünger

76. Meine Frau kommt _____ um sieben Uhr von der Arbeit.

    (a) ziemlich   (c) vor einer Woche

    (b) gestern   (d) gewöhnlich

77. _____ Blusen hat sie gekauft?

    (a) Welche   (c) Was

    (b) Wer   (d) Während

78. Der Polizist _____ ihm damit helfen können.

    (a) mussten   (c) werdet

    (b) hat   (d) sollt

79. Der Film fängt um _____ Uhr an.

    (a) neunzehn   (c) zweiundzwanzigsten

    (b) einundzwanzigste   (d) spät

80. Der Manager _____ sie um vierzehn Uhr an.

    (a) schnitt   (c) rennt

    (b) rief   (d) rannte

81. Er tut so, als ob er krank _____ .

    (a) hatte   (c) wurde

    (b) hätte   (d) wäre

82. Tina sagte, dass ihr Mann nach Frankreich reisen _____ .

    (a) hätte   (c) braucht

    (b) müsse   (d) sei

83. Warum musste die alte Kirche zerstört _____ ?

    (a) sollen   (c) haben

    (b) werden   (d) gewesen

84. _____ wurde dafür gedankt.

    (a) Ihm   (c) Die Pflegerin

    (b) Der Gärtner   (d) Ich

85. Sind sie _____ Schweiz gewesen?

    (a) von   (c) in der

    (b) vom   (d) im

86. Zehn weniger acht ist _____ .

    (a) eins   (c) minus

    (b) zwei   (d) plus

87. Karl ging nach Hause, ohne uns _____ danken.

    (a) dafür   (c) hätte

    (b) zu   (d) würde

88. Nein, wir haben _____ Fahrkarten.

    (a) eine   (c) keine

    (b) meines   (d) deinen

89. Die Tochter des Lehrers tanzt _____ .

    (a) am besten   (c) konnte

    (b) spät   (d) längere

90. _____ er mehr Geld hätte, könnte er eine Afrikareise machen.

    (a) Als   (c) Als ob

    (b) Weil   (d) Wenn

91. _____ ist abgerissen worden.

    (a) Ihm   (c) Mir

    (b) Es   (d) Mich

92. Deine Kusine läuft _____.

    (a) sehr   (c) langsame

    (b) am schnellsten   (d) den Garten

93. Frau Keller erzählte, _____ der alte Mann kein Geld habe.

    (a) wo   (c) als

    (b) wohin   (d) dass

94. Martin fragte, _____ Helga bei euch zu Gast wäre.

    (a) ob   (c) dass

    (b) als ob   (d) wessen

95. Wenn ich in Bonn wäre, _____ ich bei meiner Tante wohnen.

    (a) kann   (c) würde

    (b) könne   (d) worden

96. Es ist wichtig genug Milch _____ trinken.

    (a) hat   (c) hatte

    (b) zu   (d) ist

97. Der Kanzler hat etwas _____ zu sagen.

    (a) Wichtiges   (c) neu

    (b) was   (d) intelligent

98. Der Sohn dieses _____ Mannes arbeitet in Freiburg.

    (a) junge   (c) alten

    (b) netter   (d) gestorben

99. Thomas hat die neue Studentin _____.

    (a) lesen   (c) studieren

    (b) etwas   (d) gern

100. Wir fahren nach Leipzig, _____ Freunde zu besuchen.

    (a) ob   (c) wegen

    (b) um   (d) trotz

APPENDIX A

Principal Parts of Irregular Verbs

The second person singular and third person singular are shown in the present tense throughout the list below. In the past tense and subjunctive imperfect, only the third person singular is illustrated. You will see, however, that in the present tense conjugations of **sein** and **tun**, all persons are illustrated.

Indicative				Subjunctive
Infinitive	**Present**	**Past**	**Past Participle**	**Imperfect**
backen	bäckst bäckt	buk *or* backte	gebacken	büke *or* backte
befehlen	befiehlst befiehlt	befahl	befohlen	beföhle
beginnen	beginnst beginnt	begann	begonnen	begönne
beißen	beißt beißt	biss	gebissen	bisse
bergen	birgst birgt	barg	geborgen	bürge
bersten	birst birst	barst	geborsten	börste
betrügen	betrügst betrügt	betrog	betrogen	betröge
bewegen	bewegst bewegt	bewog	bewogen	bewöge

Indicative				Subjunctive
Infinitive	Present	Past	Past Participle	Imperfect
biegen	biegst biegt	bog	gebogen	böge
bieten	bietest bietet	bot	geboten	böte
binden	bindest bindet	band	gebunden	bände
bitten	bittest bittet	bat	gebeten	bäte
blasen	bläst bläst	blies	geblasen	bliese
bleiben	bleibst bleibt	blieb	geblieben	bliebe
bleichen	bleichst bleicht	blich	geblichen	bliche
braten	brätst brät	briet	gebraten	briete
brechen	brichst bricht	brach	gebrochen	bräche
brennen	brennst brennt	brannte	gebrannt	brennte
bringen	bringst bringt	brachte	gebracht	brächte
denken	denkst denkt	dachte	gedacht	dächte
dingen	dingst dingt	dingte *or* dang	gedungen	dingte
dreschen	drischst drischt	drosch	gedroschen	drösche
dringen	dringst dringt	drang	gedrungen	dränge
dürfen	darfst darf	durfte	gedurft	dürfte
empfangen	empfängst empfängt	empfing	empfangen	empfinge
empfehlen	empfiehlst empfiehlt	empfahl	empfohlen	empföhle

Indicative				Subjunctive
Infinitive	**Present**	**Past**	**Past Participle**	**Imperfect**
empfinden	empfindest empfindet	empfand	empfunden	empfände
erlöschen	erlischst erlischt	erlosch	erloschen	erlösche
erschrecken	erschrickst erschrickt	erschrak	erschrocken	erschäke
erwägen	erwägst erwägt	erwog	erwogen	erwöge
essen	isst isst	aß	gegessen	ässe
fahren	fährst fährt	fuhr	gefahren	führe
fallen	fällst fällt	fiel	gefallen	fiele
fangen	fängst fängt	fing	gefangen	finge
fechten	fichtest ficht	focht	gefochten	föchte
finden	findest findet	fand	gefunden	fände
flechten	flichtst flicht	flocht	geflochten	flöchte
fliegen	fliegst fliegt	flog	geflogen	flöge
fliehen	fliehst flieht	floh	geflohen	flöhe
fließen	fließt fließt	floss	geflossen	flösse
fressen	frisst frisst	fraß	gefressen	frässe
frieren	frierst friert	fror	gefroren	fröre
gären	gärst gärt	gor	gegoren	göre
gebären	gebierst gebiert	gebar	geboren	gebäre

Indicative				Subjunctive
Infinitive	Present	Past	Past Participle	Imperfect
geben	gibst gibt	gab	gegeben	gäbe
gedeihen	gedeihst gedeiht	gedieh	gediehen	gediehe
gehen	gehst geht	ging	gegangen	ginge
gelten	giltst gilt	galt	gegolten	gälte *or* gölte
genesen	genest genest	genas	genesen	genäse
genießen	genießt genießt	genoss	genossen	genösse
geraten	gerätst gerät	geriet	geraten	geriete
gewinnen	gewinnst gewinnt	gewann	gewonnen	gewänne *or* gewönne
gießen	gießt gießt	goss	gegossen	gösse
gleichen	gleichst gleicht	glich	geglichen	gliche
gleiten	gleitest gleitet	glitt	geglitten	glitte
glimmen	glimmst glimmt	glomm *or* glimmte	geglommen *or* geglimmt	glömme
graben	gräbst gräbt	grub	gegraben	grübe
greifen	greifst greift	griff	gegriffen	griffe
haben	hast hat	hatte	gehabt	hätte
halten	hältst hält	hielt	gehalten	hielte
hängen	hängst hängt	hing	gehangen	hinge
hauen	haust haut	hieb	gehauen	hiebe

Indicative				Subjunctive
Infinitive	**Present**	**Past**	**Past Participle**	**Imperfect**
heben	hebst hebt	hob	gehoben	höbe
heißen	heißt heißt	hieß	geheißen	hieße
helfen	hilfst hilft	half	geholfen	hülfe
kennen	kennst kennt	kannte	gekannt	kennte
klimmen	klimmst klimmt	klomm *or* klimmte	geklommen *or* geklimmt	klömme
klingen	klingst klingt	klang	geklungen	klänge
kneifen	kneifst kneift	kniff	gekniffen	kniffe
kommen	kommst kommt	kam	gekommen	käme
können	kannst kann	konnte	gekonnt	könnte
kriechen	kriechst kriecht	kroch	gekrochen	kröche
laden	lädst *or* ladest lädt *or* ladet	lud *or* ladete	geladen *or* geladet	lüde *or* ladete
lassen	lässt lässt	ließ	gelassen	ließe
laufen	läufst läuft	lief	gelaufen	liefe
leiden	leidest leidet	litt	gelitten	litte
leihen	leihst leiht	lieh	geliehen	liehe
lesen	liest liest	las	gelesen	läse
liegen	liegst liegt	lag	gelegen	läge
lügen	lügst lügt	log	gelogen	löge

	Indicative			**Subjunctive**
Infinitive	**Present**	**Past**	**Past Participle**	**Imperfect**
mahlen	mahlst mahlt	mahlte	gemahlen	mahlte
meiden	meidest meidet	mied	gemieden	miede
melken	melkst melkt	melkte	gemelkt *or* gemolken (*adj.*)	mölke
messen	misst misst	maß	gemessen	mässe
mögen	magst mag	mochte	gemocht	möchte
müssen	musst muss	musste	gemusst	müsste
nehmen	nimmst nimmt	nahm	genommen	nähme
nennen	nennst nennt	nannte	genannt	nennte
pfeifen	pfeifst pfeift	pfiff	gepfiffen	pfiffe
pflegen	pflegst pflegt	pflegte *or* pflog	gepflegt *or* gepflogen	pflegte *or* pflöge
preisen	preist preist	pries	gepriesen	priese
quellen	quillst quillt	quoll	gequollen	quölle
raten	rätst rät	riet	geraten	riete
reiben	reibst reibt	rieb	gerieben	riebe
reißen	reißt reißt	riss	gerissen	risse
reiten	reitest reitet	ritt	geritten	ritte
rennen	rennst rennt	rannte	gerannt	rennte
riechen	riechst riecht	roch	gerochen	röche

Indicative

Subjunctive

Infinitive	Present	Past	Past Participle	Imperfect
ringen	ringst ringt	rang	gerungen	ränge
rinnen	rinnst rinnt	rann	geronnen	rönne
rufen	rufst ruft	rief	gerufen	riefe
salzen	salzst salzt	salzte	gesalzt *or* gesalzen (*fig.*)	salzte
saufen	säufst säuft	soff	gesoffen	söffe
saugen	saugst saugt	sog	gesogen	söge
schaffen	schaffst schafft	schuf	geschaffen	schüfe
schallen	schallst schallt	scholl	geschallt	schölle
scheiden	scheidest scheidet	schied	geschieden	schiede
scheinen	scheinst scheint	schien	geschienen	schiene
schelten	schiltst schilt	schalt	gescholten	schölte
scheren	schierst schiert	schor	geschoren	schöre
schieben	schiebst schiebt	schob	geschoben	schöbe
schießen	schießt schießt	schoss	geschossen	schösse
schinden	schindest schindet	schund	geschunden	schünde
schlafen	schläfst schläft	schlief	geschlafen	schliefe
schlagen	schlägst schlägt	schlug	geschlagen	schlüge
schleichen	schleichst schleicht	schlich	geschlichen	schliche

Indicative				Subjunctive
Infinitive	**Present**	**Past**	**Past Participle**	**Imperfect**
schleifen	schleifst schleift	schliff	geschliffen	schliffe
schleißen	schleißt schleißt	schliss	geschlissen	schlisse
schliefen	schliefst schlieft	schloff	geschloffen	schlöffe
schließen	schließt schließt	schloss	geschlossen	schlösse
schlingen	schlingst schlingt	schlang	geschlungen	schlänge
schmeißen	schmeißt schmeißt	schmiss	geschmissen	schmisse
schmelzen	schmilzt schmilzt	schmolz	geschmolzen	schmölze
schneiden	schneidest schneidet	schnitt	geschnitten	schnitte
schrecken	schrickst schrickt	schrak	geschrocken	schräke
schreiben	schreibst schreibt	schrieb	geschrieben	schriebe
schreien	schreist schreit	schrie	geschrien	schriee
schreiten	schreitest schreitet	schritt	geschritten	schritte
schweigen	schweigst schweigt	schwieg	geschwiegen	schwiege
schwellen	schwillst schwillt	schwoll	geschwollen	schwölle
schwimmen	schwimmst schwimmt	schwamm	geschwommen	schwömme
schwinden	schwindest schwindet	schwand	geschwunden	schwände
schwingen	schwingst schwingt	schwang	geschwungen	schwänge
schwören	schwörst schwört	schwur	geschworen	schwüre

Indicative				Subjunctive
Infinitive	**Present**	**Past**	**Past Participle**	**Imperfect**
sehen	siehst sieht	sah	gesehen	sähe
sein	bin bist ist sind seid sind	war	gewesen	wäre
senden	sendest sendet	sandte *or* sendete	gesandt *or* gesendet	sendete
sieden	siedest siedet	sott *or* siedete	gesotten	sötte *or* siedete
singen	singst singt	sang	gesungen	sänge
sinken	sinkst sinkt	sank	gesunken	sänke
sinnen	sinnst sinnt	sann	gesonnen	sänne
sitzen	sitzt sitzt	saß	gesessen	säße
sollen	sollst soll	sollte	gesollt	sollte
spalten	spaltest spaltet	spaltete	gespalten *or* gespaltet	spaltete
speien	speist speit	spie	gespien	spie
spinnen	spinnst spinnt	spann	gesponnen	spönne
spleißen	spleißt spleißt	spliss	gesplissen	splisse
sprechen	sprichst spricht	sprach	gesprochen	spräche
sprießen	sprießt sprießt	spross	gesprossen	sprösse
springen	springst springt	sprang	gesprungen	spränge
stechen	stichst sticht	stach	gestochen	stäche
stecken	steckst steckt	steckte *or* stak	gesteckt	steckte *or* stäke

Indicative				**Subjunctive**
Infinitive	**Present**	**Past**	**Past Participle**	**Imperfect**
stehen	stehst steht	stand	gestanden	stünde *or* stände
stehlen	stiehlst stiehlt	stahl	gestohlen	stöhle *or* stähle
steigen	steigst steigt	stieg	gestiegen	stiege
sterben	stirbst stirbt	starb	gestorben	stürbe
stieben	stiebst stiebt	stob *or* stiebte	gestoben *or* gestiebt	stöbe *or* stiebte
stinken	stinkst stinkt	stank	gestunken	stänke
stoßen	stößt stößt	stieß	gestoßen	stieße
streichen	streichst streicht	strich	gestrichen	striche
streiten	streitest streitet	stritt	gestritten	stritte
tragen	trägst trägt	trug	getragen	trüge
treffen	triffst trifft	traf	getroffen	träfe
treiben	treibst treibt	trieb	getrieben	triebe
treten	trittst tritt	trat	getreten	träte
triefen	triefst trieft	troff	getrieft *or* getroffen	tröffe
trinken	trinkst trinkt	trank	getrunken	tränke
tun	tue tust tut tun tut tun	tat	getan	täte
verderben	verdirbst verdirbt	verdarb	verdorben	verdürbe
verdrießen	verdrießt verdrießt	verdross	verdrossen	verdrösse

Indicative				Subjunctive
Infinitive	**Present**	**Past**	**Past Participle**	**Imperfect**
vergessen	vergisst vergisst	vergaß	vergessen	vergäße
verhehlen	verhehlst verhehlt	verhehlte	verhehlt *or* verhohlen	verhehlte
verlieren	verlierst verliert	verlor	verloren	verlöre
verwirren	verwirrst verwirrt	verwirrte	verwirrt *or* verworren (*adj.*)	verwirrte
wachsen	wächst wächst	wuchs	gewachsen	wüchse
wägen	wägst wägt	wog *or* wägte	gewogen	wöge *or* wägte
waschen	wäschst wäscht	wusch	gewaschen	wüsche
weichen	weichst weicht	wich	gewichen	wiche
weisen	weist weist	wies	gewiesen	wiese
wenden	wendest wendet	wandte *or* wendete	gewandt *or* gewendet	wendete
werben	wirbst wirbt	warb	geworben	würbe
werden	wirst wird	wurde	geworden	würde
werfen	wirfst wirft	warf	geworfen	würfe
wiegen	wiegst wiegt	wog	gewogen	wöge
winden	windest windet	wand	gewunden	wände
wissen	weißt weiß	wusste	gewusst	wüsste
wollen	willst will	wollte	gewollt	wollte
zeihen	zeihst zeiht	zieh	geziehen	ziehe

Indicative				Subjunctive
Infinitive	**Present**	**Past**	**Past Participle**	**Imperfect**
ziehen	ziehst	zog	gezogen	zöge
	zieht			
zwingen	zwingst	zwang	gezwungen	zwänge
	zwingt			

Some irregular verbs are used in impersonal expressions and are conjugated only in the third person singular.

Indicative				Subjunctive
Infinitive	**Present**	**Past**	**Past Participle**	**Imperfect**
dünken	dünkt	dünkte *or*	gedünkt *or*	dünkte *or*
	deucht	deuchte	gedeucht	deuchte
gelingen	gelingt	gelang	gelungen	gelänge
geschehen	geschieht	geschah	geschehen	geschähe
misslingen	misslingt	misslang	misslungen	misslänge

APPENDIX B

Prepositions and Their Required Cases

Accusative	Dative	Accusative-Dative	Genitive
bis	aus	an	(an)statt
durch	außer	auf	angesichts
für	bei	hinter	anlässlich
gegen	gegenüber	in	außerhalb
ohne	mit	neben	beiderseits
um	nach	über	bezüglich
wider	seit	unter	diesseits
	trotz	vor	hinsichtlich
	von	zwischen	jenseits
	wegen		trotz
	zu		unterhalb
			während
			wegen

ENGLISH-GERMAN DICTIONARY

a, an ein, eine
address Adresse (*f.*)
to admire bewundern
to adopt adoptieren
after nach
afterward nachdem
against gegen
against wider
airplane Flugzeug (*n.*)
airport Flughafen (*m.*)
all alle
alone allein
along entlang
Alps Alpen (*pl.*)
already schon
always immer
America Amerika
American Amerikaner (*m.*)
and und
angry, mad böse
to annoy, irritate reizen
to answer antworten
apartment Wohnung (*f.*)
apothecary Apotheke (*f.*)
April April (*m.*)

Arabic arabisch
architect Architekt (*m.*)
arm Arm (*m.*)
around um
to arrange arrangieren
to arrest verhaften
to arrive ankommen
as als
to ask fragen
to astound erstaunen
at an
at home zu Hause
athlete Sportler (*m.*)
attractive attraktiv
August August (*m.*)
aunt Tante (*f.*)
Australia Australien
Austria Österreich
autumn Herbst (*m.*)
bad schlecht
to bake backen
baker Bäcker (*m.*)
ball Ball (*m.*)
ballpoint pen Kuli (*m.*)
bank Bank (*f.*)

baron Freiherr (*m.*)
baroness Freifrau (*f.*)
to be sein
to be acquainted with kennen
to be called, named heißen
to be pleased, glad sich freuen
to be valid, worth gelten
to be wrong sich irren
to bear (a child) gebären
bear Bär (*m.*)
because denn, weil
because of wegen
to become, get; shall/will werden
bed Bett (*n.*)
beef Rindfleisch (*n.*)
beer Bier (*n.*)
before, in front of vor
behind hinter
to believe glauben
to belong to gehören
belt Gürtel (*m.*)
berry Beere (*f.*)
between zwischen
beverage Getränk (*n.*)
bicycle Fahrrad (*n.*)
big groß
billion Milliarde (*f.*)
black schwarz
blind blind
blouse Bluse (*f.*)
book Buch (*n.*)
boss Chef (*m.*)
bottle Flasche (*f.*)
bouquet Blumenstrauß (*m.*)
boy Junge (*m.*)
bread Brot (*n.*)
to break brechen
bricklayer Maurer (*m.*)
bridge Brücke (*f.*)
bright hell
to bring bringen

brother Bruder (*m.*)
brown braun
bus Bus (*m.*)
bush Busch (*m.*)
businessman Geschäftsmann (*m.*)
businesswoman Geschäftsfrau (*f.*)
but aber
butcher Metzger (*m.*)
to buy kaufen
by bei
by heart auswendig
cabbage Kohl (*m.*)
to call up, telephone anrufen
calm, quiet ruhig
Canada Kanada
capital city Hauptstadt (*f.*)
capitalist Kapitalist (*m.*)
car Auto (*n.*)
car Wagen (*m.*)
carnation Nelke (*f.*)
carpet Teppich (*m.*)
castle Burg (*f.*)
cat Katze (*f.*)
cathedral Dom (*m.*)
CD CD (*f.*)
chair Stuhl (*m.*)
chalk Kreide (*f.*)
chancellor Kanzler (*m.*)
to change ändern
cheap billig
cheese Käse (*m.*)
chemist Chemiker (*m.*)
chess Schach (*n.*)
chicken Hühnchen (*n.*)
chicken Huhn (*n.*)
child Kind (*n.*)
church Kirche (*f.*)
circus Zirkus (*m.*)
city center, downtown Stadtzentrum (*n.*)

city excursion Stadtrundfahrt (*f.*)
city hall Rathaus (*n.*)
city Stadt (*f.*)
city wall Stadtmauer (*f.*)
to clear away, vacate räumen
climate Klima (*n.*)
clock; hour; watch Uhr (*f.*)
to close zumachen
clothes Kleider (*pl.*)
coach (athletic), trainer Trainer (*m.*)
coat Mantel (*m.*)
cock-and-bull story Ammen-märchen (*n.*)
coffee Kaffee (*m.*)
coke (Coca-Cola) Coca (*f.*), Cola (*f.*)
cold Erkältung (*f.*)
cold kalt
to collect sammeln
Cologne Köln
to come kommen
communist Kommunist (*m.*)
computer Computer (*m.*)
concert Konzert (*n.*)
conductor (transportation) Schaffner (*m.*)
conflict Konflikt (*m.*)
constitution Konstitution (*f.*)
continent Erdteil (*m.*)
to control kontrollieren
cool kühl
to copy kopieren
corn Mais (*m.*)
corner Ecke (*f.*)
count Graf (*m.*)
cow Kuh (*f.*)
to cry weinen
cupboard Schrank (*m.*)
to cut schneiden
to dance tanzen
dangerous gefährlich

dark dunkel
daughter Tochter (*f.*)
day Tag (*m.*)
death Tod (*m.*)
December Dezember (*m.*)
to delegate, send as a delegate delegieren
to demonstrate demonstrieren
Denmark Dänemark
dentist Zahnarzt (*m.*)
department store Kaufhaus (*n.*)
to describe beschreiben
desk Schreibtisch (*m.*)
dessert Nachtisch (*m.*)
to destroy zerstören
dialect Dialekt (*m.*)
dictionary Wörterbuch (*n.*)
difficult schwer
diligent fleißig
diplomat Diplomat (*m.*)
to dispatch absenden
to do tun
to do handicrafts basteln
door Tür (*f.*)
to drink trinken
to drive, travel fahren
drugstore Drogerie (*f.*)
duke Herzog (*m.*)
during während
each jeder
early früh
earth, Earth Erde (*f.*)
east Osten (*m.*)
easy leicht
eat essen
eat (used for animals) fressen
effective effektiv
eight acht
eighteen achtzehn
eighty achtzig
eleven elf
emperor Kaiser (*m.*)

empire Reich (*n.*)
entire, whole ganz
evening Abend (*m.*)
examination Examen (*n.*)
except außer
to expect, await erwarten
expensive teuer
to fall fallen
to fall in love sich verlieben
family Familie (*f.*)
far weit
farmer Bauer (*m.*)
to fascinate faszinieren
fast schnell
father Vater (*m.*)
February Februar (*m.*)
federal parliament Bundestag (*m.*)
to feel empfinden
to feel fühlen
fifteen fünfzehn
fifty fünfzig
to find finden
fir, pine tree Tanne (*f.*)
fish Fisch (*m.*)
to fit passen
five fünf
to flood überschwemmen
floor Boden (*m.*)
floor lamp Stehlampe (*f.*)
flower Blume (*f.*)
to fly fliegen
to follow folgen
fondly gern
food Essen (*n.*)
for für
foreigner Ausländer (*m.*)
to forget vergessen
forty vierzig
four vier
fourteen vierzehn
fox Fuchs (*m.*)

Friday Freitag (*m.*)
friend Freund (*m.*)
from, of von
from where woher
fruit Obst (*n.*)
fruit pie Obstkuchen (*m.*)
funny komisch
to gather, collect sammeln
German Deutsche (*m./f.*)
German champagne Sekt (*m.*)
Germanic germanisch
Germany Deutschland
get off (transportation) aussteigen
get on (transportation) einsteigen
gift Geschenk (*n.*)
girl Mädchen (*n.*)
girlfriend Freundin (*f.*)
to give geben
glass Glas (*n.*)
glove Handschuh (*m.*)
to go gehen
to go along mitgehen
to go cycling Rad fahren
to go in for, pursue; participate in; drive treiben
go skiing Ski laufen
God Gott (*m.*)
good gut
good-bye auf Wiederschauen, auf Wiedersehen
good day, hello guten Tag
good evening guten Abend
good morning guten Morgen
good night gute Nacht
government Regierung (*f.*)
grain Korn (*n.*)
grandchild Enkel (*m.*)
grandfather Großvater (*m.*)
grandmother Großmutter (*f.*)
grass Gras (*n.*)

gray grau
green grün
to greet grüssen
to grow wachsen
guest Gast (*m.*)
half halb
hallway Flur (*m.*)
ham Schinken (*m.*)
to hang hängen
to happen geschehen
to happen passieren
happy, lucky glücklich
harbor Hafen (*m.*)
harbor excursion Hafenrundfahrt (*f.*)
hare Hase (*m.*)
hat Hut (*m.*)
to have haben
to have the opinion,
   mean meinen
heads or tails Kopf oder Zahl
healthy gesund
to hear hören
heart Herz (*n.*)
heavy schwer
hedgehog Igel (*m.*)
hell Hölle (*f.*)
to help helfen
her ihr
here hier
high hoch
to hike, wander wandern
hippo Nilpferd (*n.*)
his sein
history Geschichte (*f.*)
hockey Eishockey (*n.*)
to hold halten
holy heilig
home(ward) nach Hause
to horrify entsetzen
horse Pferd (*n.*)
hospital Krankenhaus (*n.*)

hot heiß
hour Stunde (*f.*)
house Haus (*n.*)
how, as wie
human, person Mensch (*m.*)
hundred hundert
hungry hungrig
hunt Jagd (*f.*)
hurry sich beeilen
ice, ice cream Eis (*n.*)
if wenn
to imagine sich vorstellen
to imitate imitieren
to immigrate immigrieren
to impress imponieren
in in
to inform, notify mitteilen
insane wahnsinnig
inspite of trotz
instead of anstatt (statt)
to instruct, teach unterrichten
interesting interessant
to interrupt unterbrechen
to introduce vorstellen
to invite einladen
Italy Italien
jacket Jacke (*f.*)
January Januar (*m.*)
job Job (*m.*)
July Juli (*m.*)
June Juni (*m.*)
key Schlüssel (*m.*)
to kick, shove stoßen
king König (*m.*)
to kiss küssen
kitchen Küche (*f.*)
to knock klopfen
to know, be acquainted
   with kennen
to know wissen
lady Dame (*f.*)
lager beer Pils (*n.*)

lamp Lampe (*f.*)
landlady Wirtin (*f.*)
last letzte
late spät
to laugh lachen
law Jura (*n./pl.*)
lawn Rasen (*m.*)
lawyer Rechtsanwalt (*m.*)
to lay legen
leader Führer (*m.*)
to learn lernen
left link
less; minus weniger
to let lassen
library Bibliothek (*f.*)
to lie, recline lügen
to lie (omit the truth) lügen
light, easy leicht
light Licht (*n.*)
to like, please gefallen
little, small klein
little, few wenig
little bit bisschen
living room Wohnzimmer (*n.*)
long lang
to look at ansehen
to look for suchen
to look like aussehen
to lose verlieren
loud laut
to love lieben
main railroad station Hauptbahnhof (*m.*)
male nurse Pfleger (*m.*)
to manifest manifestieren
many, much viel(e)
to march marschieren
March März (*m.*)
market square Marktplatz (*m.*)
married verheiratet
May Mai (*m.*)
meat Fleisch (*n.*)

mechanic Mechaniker (*m.*)
merchant Kaufmann (*m.*)
milk Milch (*f.*)
million Million (*f.*)
mineral water Mineralwasser
   (*n.*)
minus minus
Monday Montag (*m.*)
monster Ungeheuer (*n.*)
month Monat (*m.*)
more mehr
morning Morgen (*m.*)
mother Mutter (*f.*)
motorcycle Motorrad (*n.*)
movie Film (*m.*)
movie theater Kino (*n.*)
Munich München
music Musik (*f.*)
my mein
name Name (*m.*)
to name nennen
nation Nation (*f.*)
near nah
to need brauchen
neighbor Nachbar (*m.*)
never nie
new neu
newspaper Zeitung (*f.*)
next to, near neben
nice nett
night Nacht (*f.*)
nine neun
nineteen neunzehn
ninety neunzig
no one niemand
north Norden (*m.*)
North America Nordamerika
not nicht
not any, none kein
to note, make a note of
   something notieren
notebook Heft (*n.*)

nothing nichts
novel Roman (*m.*)
November November (*m.*)
now jetzt
nurse Krankenschwester (*f.*)
nursery school teacher Erzieher
   (*m.*)
October Oktober (*m.*)
official, government employee
   Beamte (*m.*)
often oft
old alt
on auf
on foot zu Fuß
one eins
one man
to open aufmachen
opposite gegenüber
or oder
to order bestellen
to organize organisieren
our unser
out aus
outing Ausflug (*m.*)
oven Ofen (*m.*)
over, above über
package Paket (*n.*)
pain Schmerz (*m.*)
parents Eltern (*pl.*)
park Park (*m.*)
parliament Parlament (*n.*)
party Party (*f.*)
party (political) Partei (*f.*)
passport Pass (*m.*)
patient Kranke (*m.*)
peas Erbsen (*pl.*)
pencil Bleistift (*m.*)
people Leute (*pl.*)
people, nation Volk (*n.*)
person Mensch (*m.*)
pessimist Pessimist (*m.*)
pet Haustier (*n.*)

to photograph fotografieren
photographer Fotograf (*m.*)
physician Arzt (*m.*)
physicist Physiker (*m.*)
piano Klavier (*n.*)
picnic Picknick (*n.*)
picture Bild (*n.*)
picture postcard Ansichtskarte
   (*f.*)
pig Schwein (*n.*)
pilot Pilot (*m.*)
pink rosa
plant Pflanze (*f.*)
to plant pflanzen
to play spielen
please bitte
to please, make happy erfreuen
to pluck rupfen
plus plus
pocket Tasche (*f.*)
poet Dichter (*m.*)
police Polizei (*f.*)
polite höflich
politician Politiker (*m.*)
poor arm
position Position (*f.*)
to possess, own besitzen
postcard Postkarte (*f.*)
post office Post (*f.*)
postage stamp Briefmarke (*f.*)
poster Poster (*n.*)
potato Kartoffel (*f.*)
pregnant schwanger
prep school Gymnasium (*n.*)
president Präsident (*m.*)
pretty schön
probably wahrscheinlich
problem Problem (*n.*)
to produce produzieren
professor Professor (*m.*)
to program programmieren
to promise versprechen

to pronounce aussprechen
to protect schützen
to protest protestieren
to push schieben
to put, place stellen
quarter Viertel (*n.*)
queen Königin (*f.*)
rabbit Kaninchen (*n.*)
radio Radio (*n.*)
railroad station Bahnhof (*m.*)
rain Regen (*m.*)
to rain regnen
to read lesen
to receive bekommen
to recommend empfehlen
to recruit werben
red rot
to reflect widerspiegeln
to relate erzählen
relative Verwandte (*m.*)
to report berichten
republic Republik (*f.*)
to request bitten
to restore restaurieren
reunification Wiedervereinigung (*f.*)
rice Reis (*m.*)
to ride reiten
right recht
to rinse spülen
river Fluss (*m.*)
roast sausage Bratwurst (*f.*)
Roman römisch
room Zimmer (*n.*)
rose Rose (*f.*)
to run laufen, rennen
to run away weglaufen
Russian russisch
same derselbe
sandwich Butterbrot (*n.*)
Saturday Samstag, Sonnabend (*m.*)

to say sagen
schedule Fahrplan (*m.*)
school Schule (*f.*)
scientist Wissenschaftler (*m.*)
to scratch kratzen
season Jahreszeit (*f.*)
to seat oneself sich setzen
second zweite
secretary Sekretär (*m.*)
to see sehen
to sell verkaufen
to send schicken
to send senden
September September (*m.*)
to serve dienen
to set setzen
seven sieben
seventeen siebzehn
seventy siebzig
shall, will werden
to shave rasieren
sheep Schaf (*n.*)
ship Schiff (*n.*)
shop, store Laden (*m.*)
short kurz
to shout schreien
siblings Geschwister (*pl.*)
sick krank
sights Sehenswürdigkeiten (*pl.*)
sightseeing tour Besichtigung (*f.*)
since seit
to sing singen
singer Sänger (*m.*)
sister Schwester (*f.*)
to sit sitzen
six sechs
sixteen sechzehn
sixty sechzig
sky Himmel (*m.*)
to sleep schlafen
slow langsam

smart klug
to smoke rauchen
snake Schlange (*f.*)
snow Schnee (*m.*)
to snow schneien
soccer Fußball (*m.*)
soccer player Fußballspieler (*m.*)
sofa Sofa (*n.*)
someone jemand
son Sohn (*m.*)
song Lied (*n.*)
Sunday Sonntag (*m.*)
soon bald
south Süden (*m.*)
South America Südamerika
sparkling water Sprudel (*m.*)
sparkling wine Sekt (*m.*)
to speak sprechen
to speak to anreden
to spend ausgeben
to spoil, rot verderben
sport (form of) Sportart (*f.*)
spring Frühling (*m.*)
to stand stehen
to stand back, remain
    behind zurückbleiben
to start, begin anfangen
to stay, remain bleiben
to steal stehlen
stairs, staircase Treppe (*f.*)
still noch
story, history Geschichte (*f.*)
street Straße (*f.*)
streetcar Straßenbahn (*f.*)
to stroll spazieren
to study studieren
summer Sommer (*m.*)
Sunday Sonntag (*m.*)
supper Abendessen (*n.*)
to swear schwören
sweater Pullover (*m.*)
sweatshirt Sweatshirt (*n.*)

Sweden Schweden
to swim schwimmen
table Tisch (*m.*)
table tennis Tischtennis (*m.*)
to take along/with mitnehmen
to talk reden
taxi driver Taxifahrer (*m.*)
tea Tee (*m.*)
teacher Lehrer (*m.*)
telegram Telegramm (*n.*)
ten zehn
to thank danken
that dass (*conj.*)
that jener
there da, dort
there is/are es gibt
thief Dieb (*m.*)
to think denken
third dritte
thirst Durst (*m.*)
thirteen dreizehn
thirty dreißig
this dieser
thousand tausend
three drei
through durch
Thursday Donnerstag (*m.*)
ticket Fahrkarte (*f.*)
tiger Tiger (*m.*)
time Zeit (*f.*)
tired müde
to zu
today heute
today's (*adj.*) heutig
tomorrow morgen
tongue Zunge (*f.*)
too zu
tour Tour (*f.*)
tourist Tourist (*m.*)
to tow away abschleppen
traffic Verkehr (*m.*)
train Zug (*m.*)

to transfer umsteigen
to travel reisen
tree Baum (*m.*)
tribe Stamm (*m.*)
trillion Billion (*f.*)
trip Reise (*f.*)
to try probieren
Tuesday Dienstag (*m.*)
tulip Tulpe (*f.*)
tunnel Tunnel (*m.*)
twelve zwölf
twenty zwanzig
twins Zwillinge (*pl.*)
two zwei
umbrella Regenschirm (*m.*)
uncle Onkel (*m.*)
under unter
to understand verstehen
unfortunately leider
university Universität (*f.*)
until, as far as bis
vase Vase (*f.*)
vegetable soup Gemüsesuppe (*f.*)
vegetables Gemüse (*n.*)
very sehr
vicinity Nähe (*f.*)
Vienna Wien
village Dorf (*n.*)
violin Geige (*f.*)
to visit besuchen
to wait warten
wall Wand (*f.*)
war Krieg (*m.*)
warm warm
to wash waschen
water Wasser (*n.*)
to wear tragen
weather Wetter (*n.*)

Wednesday Mittwoch (*m.*)
week Woche (*f.*)
weekend Wochenende (*n.*)
west Westen (*m.*)
what was
when wann
whenever wenn
where wo
where to wohin
whether ob
which welcher
white weiß
who wer
whose wessen
why warum
wife, woman Frau (*f.*)
to win, gain gewinnen
window Fenster (*n.*)
wine Wein (*m.*)
wing Flügel (*m.*)
winter Winter (*m.*)
with mit
without ohne
wolf Wolf (*m.*)
woman, wife Frau (*f.*)
word Wort (*n.*)
to work arbeiten
worker Arbeiter (*m.*)
world war Weltkrieg (*m.*)
to write schreiben
writer Schriftsteller (*m.*)
year Jahr (*n.*)
yellow gelb
yesterday gestern
you du, ihr, Sie
young jung
your dein, euer, Ihr
zoo Zoo (*m.*)

GERMAN-ENGLISH DICTIONARY

Abend (*m.*) evening
Abendessen (*n.*) dinner, supper
aber but
abschleppen to tow away
absenden to dispatch, send off
acht eight
achtzehn eighteen
achtzig eighty
adoptieren to adopt
Adresse (*f.*) address
alle all, everyone
allein alone
Alpen (*pl.*) Alps
als as, when
alt old
Amerika America
Amerikaner (*m.*) American
Ammenmärchen (*n.*) cock-and-bull story
an at
ändern to change
anfangen to start
ankommen to arrive
anreden to address, speak to
anrufen to call up, telephone
ansehen to look at
Ansichtskarte (*f.*) picture postcard

anstatt (statt) instead of
antworten to answer
Apotheke (*f.*) drugstore, apothecary
April (*m.*) April
arabisch Arabic
arbeiten to work
Arbeiter (*m.*) worker
Architekt (*m.*) architect
arm poor
Arm (*m.*) arm
arrangieren to arrange
Arzt (*m.*) physician
attraktiv attractive
auf on
auf Wiederschauen good-bye
auf Wiedersehen good-bye
aufmachen to open
August (*m.*) August
aus out
Ausflug (*m.*) outing
ausgeben to spend
Ausländer (*m.*) foreigner
aussehen to look like
außer except
aussprechen to pronounce
aussteigen to get off (transportation)

Australien Australia
auswendig by heart
Auto (*n.*) car
backen to bake
Bäcker (*m.*) baker
Bahnhof (*m.*) railroad station
bald soon
Ball (*m.*) ball
Bank (*f.*) bank
Bär (*m.*) bear
basteln to do handicrafts
Bauer (*m.*) farmer
Baum (*m.*) tree
Beamte (*m.*) official, government
  employee
sich **beeilen** hurry
Beere (*f.*) berry
bei by, at
bekommen to receive, get
berichten to report
beschreiben to describe
Besichtigung (*f.*) sightseeing
  tour
besitzen to possess, own
bestellen to order
besuchen to visit
Bett (*n.*) bed
bewundern to admire
Bibliothek (*f.*) library
Bier (*n.*) beer
Bild (*n.*) picture
billig cheap
Billion (*f.*) trillion
bis until, as far as
bisschen little bit
bitte please
bitten to request
bleiben to remain, stay
Bleistift (*m.*) pencil
blind blind
Blume (*f.*) flower
Blumenstrauß (*m.*) bouquet

Bluse (*f.*) blouse
Boden (*m.*) floor
böse angry, mad
Bratwurst (*f.*) roast sausage
brauchen to need
braun brown
brechen to break
Briefmarke (*f.*) postage stamp
bringen to bring
Brot (*n.*) bread
Brücke (*f.*) bridge
Bruder (*m.*) brother
Buch (*n.*) book
Bundestag (*m.*) federal
  parliament
Burg (*f.*) castle
Bus (*m.*) bus
Busch (*m.*) bush
Butterbrot (*n.*) sandwich
CD (*f.*) CD
Chef (*m.*) boss
Chemiker (*m.*) chemist
Coca (*f.*) Coca-Cola
Cola (*f.*) Coca-Cola
Computer (*m.*) computer
da there
Dame (*f.*) lady
Dänemark Denmark
danken to thank
dass that (*conj.*)
dein your
delegieren to delegate, send as a
  delegate
demonstrieren to demonstrate
denken to think
denn because
derselbe same
Deutsche (*m./f.*) German
Deutschland Germany
Dezember (*m.*) December
Dialekt (*m.*) dialect
Dichter (*m.*) poet

Dieb (*m.*) thief
dienen to serve
Dienstag (*m.*) Tuesday
dieser this
Diplomat (*m.*) diplomat
Dom (*m.*) cathedral
Donnerstag (*m.*) Thursday
Dorf (*n.*) village
dort there
drei three
dreißig thirty
dreizehn thirteen
dritte third
Drogerie (*f.*) drugstore
dunkel dark
durch through
Durst (*m.*) thirst
Ecke (*f.*) corner
effektiv effective
einladen to invite
eins one
einsteigen to get on
  (transportation)
Eis (*n.*) ice, ice cream
Eishockey (*n.*) hockey
elf eleven
Eltern (*pl.*) parents
empfehlen to recommend
empfinden to feel
Enkel (*m.*) grandchild
entlang along
entsetzen to horrify
Erbsen (*pl.*) peas
Erde (*f.*) earth, Earth
Erdteil (*m.*) continent
erfreuen to please, make happy
Erkältung (*f.*) cold
erstaunen to astound
erwarten to expect, await
erzählen to relate, tell
Erzieher (*m.*) nursery school
  teacher

es gibt there is/are
essen to eat
Essen (*n.*) food
euer your
Examen (*n.*) examination
fahren to drive, travel
Fahrkarte (*f.*) ticket
Fahrplan (*m.*) schedule
Fahrrad (*n.*) bicycle
fallen to fall
Familie (*f.*) family
faszinieren to fascinate
Februar (*m.*) February
Fenster (*n.*) window
Film (*m.*) film, movie
finden to find
Fisch (*m.*) fish
Flasche (*f.*) bottle
Fleisch (*n.*) meat
fleißig diligent
fliegen to fly
Flügel (*m.*) wing
Flughafen (*m.*) airport
Flugzeug (*n.*) airplane
Flur (*m.*) hallway
Fluss (*m.*) river
folgen to follow
Fotograf (*m.*) photographer
fotografieren to photograph
fragen to ask
Frau (*f.*) woman, wife
Freifrau (*f.*) baroness
Freiherr (*m.*) baron
Freitag (*m.*) Friday
fressen to eat (used for animals)
sich **freuen** to be glad, pleased
Freund (*m.*) friend
Freundin (*f.*) girlfriend
früh early
Frühling (*m.*) spring
Fuchs (*m.*) fox
fühlen to feel

Führer (*m.*) leader
fünf five
fünfzehn fifteen
fünfzig fifty
für for
Fußball (*m.*) soccer
Fußballspieler (*m.*) soccer
   player
ganz whole, entire
Gast (*m.*) guest
gebären to bear (a child)
geben to give
gefährlich dangerous
gefallen to like, please
gegen against
gegenüber opposite
gehen to go
gehören to belong to
Geige (*f.*) violin
gelb yellow
gelten to be valid, worth
Gemüse (*n.*) vegetables
Gemüsesuppe (*f.*) vegetable
   soup
germanisch Germanic
gern fondly
Geschäftsfrau (*f.*) businesswoman
Geschäftsmann (*m.*) businessman
geschehen to happen
Geschenk (*n.*) gift
Geschichte (*f.*) history, story
Geschwister (*pl.*) siblings
gestern yesterday
gesund healthy
Getränk (*n.*) beverage
gewinnen to win, gain
Glas (*n.*) glass
glauben to believe
glücklich happy, lucky
Gott (*m.*) God
Graf (*m.*) count
Gras (*n.*) grass

grau gray
groß big
Großmutter (*f.*) grandmother
Großvater (*m.*) grandfather
grün green
grüssen to greet
Gürtel (*m.*) belt
gut good
gute Nacht good night
guten Abend good evening
guten Morgen good morning
guten Tag good day, hello
Gymnasium (*n.*) prep school
haben to have
Hafen (*m.*) harbor
Hafenrundfahrt (*f.*) harbor
   excursion
halb half
halten to hold
Handschuh (*m.*) glove
hängen to hang
Hase (*m.*) hare
Hauptbahnhof (*m.*) main
   railroad station
Hauptstadt (*f.*) capital city
Haus (*n.*) house
Haustier (*n.*) pet
Heft (*n.*) notebook
heilig holy
heiß hot
heißen to be called, named
helfen to help
hell bright
Herbst (*m.*) fall, autumn
Herz (*n.*) heart
Herzog (*m.*) duke
heute today
heutig today's (*adj.*)
hier here
Himmel (*m.*) sky
hinter behind
hoch high

höflich polite
Hölle (f.) hell
hören to hear
Huhn (n.) chicken
Hühnchen (n.) chicken
hundert hundred
hungrig hungry
Hut (m.) hat
Igel (m.) hedgehog
ihr you, her, their
Ihr your
imitieren to imitate
immer always
immigrieren to immigrate
imponieren to impress
in in
interessant interesting
sich irren to be wrong
Italien Italy
Jacke (f.) jacket
Jagd (f.) hunt
Jahr (n.) year
Jahreszeit (f.) season
Januar (m.) January
jeder each
jemand someone
jener that
jetzt now
Job (m.) job
Juli (m.) July
jung young
Junge (m.) boy
Juni (m.) June
Jura (pl.) law
Kaffee (m.) coffee
Kaiser (m.) emperor
kalt cold
Kanada Canada
Kaninchen (n.) rabbit
Kanzler (m.) chancellor
Kapitalist (m.) capitalist
Kartoffel (f.) potato

Käse (m.) cheese
Katze (f.) cat
kaufen to buy
Kaufhaus (n.) department store
Kaufmann (m.) merchant
kein none, not any
kennen to know, be acquainted
  with
Kind (n.) child
Kino (n.) movie theater
Kirche (f.) church
Klavier (n.) piano
Kleider (pl.) clothes
klein little
Klima (n.) climate
klopfen to knock
klug smart
Kohl (m.) cabbage
Köln Cologne
komisch funny
kommen to come
Kommunist (m.) communist
Konflikt (m.) conflict
König (m.) king
Königin (f.) queen
Konstitution (f.) constitution
kontrollieren to control
Konzert (n.) concert
Kopf oder Zahl heads or tails
kopieren to copy
Korn (n.) grain
krank sick
Kranke (m.) patient
Krankenhaus (n.) hospital
Krankenschwester (f.) nurse
kratzen to scratch
Kreide (f.) chalk
Krieg (m.) war
Küche (f.) kitchen
Kuh (f.) cow
kühl cool
Kuli (m.) ballpoint pen

kurz short
küssen to kiss
lachen to laugh
Laden (*m.*) store, shop
Lampe (*f.*) lamp
lang long
langsam slow
lassen to let
laufen to run
laut loud
legen to lay
Lehrer (*m.*) teacher
leicht light, easy
leider unfortunately
lernen to learn
lesen to read
letzte last
Leute (*pl.*) people
Licht (*n.*) light
lieben to love
Lied (*n.*) song
liegen to lie, recline
link left
lügen to lie (omit the truth)
Mädchen (*n.*) girl
Mai (*m.*) May
Mais (*m.*) corn
man one
manifestieren to manifest
Mantel (*m.*) coat
Marktplatz (*m.*) market square
marschieren to march
März (*m.*) March
Maurer (*m.*) bricklayer
Mechaniker (*m.*) mechanic
mehr more
mein my
meinen to have the opinion, mean
Mensch (*m.*) person, human
Metzger (*m.*) butcher
Milch (*f.*) milk
Milliarde (*f.*) billion

Million (*f.*) million
Mineralwasser (*n.*) mineral water
minus minus
mit with
mitgehen to go along/with
mitnehmen to take along/with
mitteilen to inform
Mittwoch (*m.*) Wednesday
Monat (*m.*) month
Montag (*m.*) Monday
morgen tomorrow
Morgen (*m.*) morning
Motorrad (*n.*) motorcycle
müde tired
München Munich
Musik (*f.*) music
Mutter (*f.*) mother
nach after
nach Hause home(ward)
Nachbar (*m.*) neighbor
nachdem afterward
Nachtisch (*m.*) dessert
nah near
Nähe (*f.*) vicinity
Name (*m.*) name
Nation (*f.*) nation
neben near, next to
Nelke (*f.*) carnation
nennen to name
nett nice
neu new
neun nine
neunzehn nineteen
neunzig ninety
nicht not
nichts nothing
nie never
niemand no one
Nilpferd (*n.*) hippo
noch still
Nordamerika North America

Norden north
notieren to note, make a note of something
November (*m.*) November
ob whether
Obst (*n.*) fruit
Obstkuchen (*m.*) fruit pie
oder or
Ofen (*m.*) oven
oft often
ohne without
Oktober (*m.*) October
Onkel (*m.*) uncle
organisieren to organize
Osten east
Österreich Austria
Paket (*n.*) package
Park (*m.*) park
Parlament (*n.*) parliament
Partei (*f.*) party (political)
Party (*f.*) party
Pass (*m.*) passport
passen to fit
passieren to happen
Pessimist (*m.*) pessimist
Pferd (*n.*) horse
Pflanze (*f.*) plant
pflanzen to plant
Pfleger (*m.*) male nurse
Physiker (*m.*) physicist
Picknick (*n.*) picnic
Pilot (*m.*) pilot
Pils (*n.*) lager beer
plus plus
Politiker (*m.*) politician
Polizei (*f.*) police
Position (*f.*) position
Post (*f.*) post office
Poster (*n.*) poster
Postkarte (*f.*) postcard
Präsident (*m.*) president
probieren to try, taste

Problem (*n.*) problem
produzieren to produce
Professor (*m.*) professor
programmieren to program
protestieren to protest
Pullover (*m.*) sweater
Rad fahren to go cycling
Radio (*n.*) radio
Rasen (*m.*) lawn
rasieren to shave
Rathaus (*n.*) city hall
rauchen to smoke
räumen to clear away
recht right
Rechtsanwalt (*m.*) lawyer
reden to talk
Regen (*m.*) rain
Regenschirm (*m.*) umbrella
Regierung (*f.*) government
regnen to rain
Reich (*n.*) empire
Reis (*m.*) rice
Reise (*f.*) trip
reisen to travel
reiten to ride
reizen to annoy, irritate
rennen to run
Republik (*f.*) republic
restaurieren to restore
Rindfleisch (*n.*) beef
Roman (*m.*) novel
römisch Roman
rosa pink
Rose (*f.*) rose
rot red
ruhig quiet, calm
rupfen to pluck
russisch Russian
sagen to say
sammeln to gather, collect
Samstag (*m.*) Saturday
Sänger (*m.*) singer

Schach (*n.*) chess
Schaf (*n.*) sheep
Schaffner (*m.*) conductor
  (transportation)
schicken to send
schieben to push
Schiff (*n.*) ship
Schinken (*m.*) ham
schlafen to sleep
Schlange (*f.*) snake
schlecht bad
Schlüssel (*m.*) key
Schmerz (*m.*) pain
Schnee (*m.*) snow
schneiden to cut
schneien to snow
schnell fast
schon already
schön pretty
Schrank (*m.*) cupboard
schreiben to write
Schreibtisch (*m.*) desk
schreien to shout
Schriftsteller (*m.*) writer
Schule (*f.*) school
schützen to protect
schwanger pregnant
schwarz black
Schweden Sweden
Schwein (*n.*) pig
schwer heavy, difficult
Schwester (*f.*) sister
schwimmen to swim
schwören to swear
sechs six
sechzehn sixteen
sechzig sixty
sehen to see
Sehenswürdigkeiten (*pl.*) sights
sehr very
sein his
sein to be

seit since
Sekretär (*m.*) secretary
Sekt (*m.*) sparkling wine,
  German champagne
senden to send
September (*m.*) September
setzen to set
sich setzen to sit down
sieben seven
siebzehn seventeen
siebzig seventy
singen to sing
sitzen to sit
Ski laufen to go skiing
Sofa (*n.*) sofa
Sohn (*m.*) son
Sommer (*m.*) summer
Sonnabend (*m.*) Saturday
Sonntag (*m.*) Sunday
spät late
spazieren to stroll
spielen to play
Sportart (*f.*) (form of) sport
Sportler (*m.*) athlete
sprechen to speak
Sprudel (*m.*) sparkling water
spülen to rinse
Stadt (*f.*) city
Stadtmauer (*f.*) city wall
Stadtrundfahrt (*f.*) city
  excursion
Stadtzentrum (*n.*) city center
Stamm (*m.*) tribe
stehen to stand
Stehlampe (*f.*) floor lamp
stehlen to steal
stellen to put, place
stoßen to kick, shove
Straße (*f.*) street
Straßenbahn (*f.*) streetcar
studieren to study
Stuhl (*m.*) chair

Stunde (*f.*) hour
suchen to seek, look for
Südamerika South America
Süden south
Sweatshirt (*n.*) sweatshirt
Tag (*m.*) day
Tanne (*f.*) fir, pine tree
Tante (*f.*) aunt
tanzen to dance
Tasche (*f.*) pocket
tausend thousand
Taxifahrer (*m.*) taxi driver
Tee (*m.*) tea
Telegramm (*n.*) telegram
Teppich (*m.*) carpet
teuer expensive
Tiger (*m.*) tiger
Tisch (*m.*) table
Tischtennis (*m.*) table tennis
Tochter (*f.*) daughter
Tod (*m.*) death
Tour (*f.*) tour
Tourist (*m.*) tourist
tragen to wear
Trainer (*m.*) trainer, coach
treiben to drive; go in for; pursue; participate in
Treppe (*f.*) stairs, staircase
trinken to drink
trotz inspite of
Tulpe (*f.*) tulip
tun to do
Tunnel (*m.*) tunnel
Tür (*f.*) door
über over, above
überschwemmen to flood
Uhr (*f.*) clock; hour; watch
um around
umsteigen to transfer
und and
Ungeheuer (*n.*) monster
Universität (*f.*) university

unser our
unter under
unterbrechen to interrupt
unterrichten to teach, instruct
Vase (*f.*) vase
Vater (*m.*) father
verderben to spoil, rot
vergessen to forget
verhaften to arrest
verheiratet married
verkaufen to sell
Verkehr (*m.*) traffic
sich **verlieben** to fall in love
verlieren to lose
versprechen to promise
verstehen to understand
Verwandte (*m.*) relative
viel(e) much, many
vier four
Viertel (*n.*) quarter
vierzehn fourteen
vierzig forty
Volk (*n.*) people, nation
von from, of
vor before, in front of
vorstellen to introduce
sich **vorstellen** to imagine
wachsen to grow
Wagen (*m.*) car
wahnsinnig insane
während during
wahrscheinlich probably
Wand (*f.*) wall
wandern to hike, wander
wann when
warm warm
warten to wait
warum why
was what
waschen to wash
Wasser (*n.*) water
wegen because of

weglaufen to run away
Wein (*m.*) wine
weinen to cry
weiß white
weit far
welcher which
Weltkrieg (*m.*) world war
wenig little, few
weniger less; minus
wenn whenever, if
wer who
werben to recruit
werden to become, get; shall/will
wessen whose
Westen west
Wetter (*n.*) weather
wider against
widerspiegeln to reflect
wie how, as
Wiedervereinigung (*f.*) reunification
Winter (*m.*) winter
Wirtin (*f.*) landlady
wissen to know
Wissenschaftler (*m.*) scientist
wo where
Woche (*f.*) week
Wochenende (*n.*) weekend
woher from where

wohin where to
Wohnung (*f.*) apartment
Wohnzimmer (*n.*) living room
Wolf (*m.*) wolf
Wort (*n.*) word
Wörterbuch (*n.*) dictionary
Zahnarzt (*m.*) dentist
zehn ten
Zeit (*f.*) time
Zeitung (*f.*) newspaper
zerstören to destroy
Zimmer (*n.*) room
Zirkus (*m.*) circus
Zoo (*m.*) zoo
zu to, too
zu Fuß on foot
zu Hause at home
Zug (*m.*) train
zumachen to close
Zunge (*f.*) tongue
zurückbleiben to stand back,
    remain behind
zwanzig twenty
zwei two
zweite second
Zwillinge (*pl.*) twins
zwischen between
zwölf twelve

ANSWER KEY

CHAPTER 1

QUIZ

1. (fah-ren)   2. (shpee-len)   3. (koh-moo-nist)   4. (frow)   5. (kry-deh)
6. (boo*ch*)   7. (uh-line)   8. (sh**ue**-len)   9. (tahnt-zen)   10. (moo-tuh)

CHAPTER 2

Written Practice 1

1. Ich heiße Martin. / Mein Name ist Martin.   2. Ich heiße Tina. / Mein Name ist Tina.   3. Ich heiße Herr Schäfer. / Mein Name ist Herr Schäfer.   4. Ich heiße Frau Kamps. / Mein Name ist Frau Kamps.   5. Ich heiße Boris Becker. / Mein Name ist Boris Becker.   6. Ich heiße Maria Schell. / Mein Name ist Maria Schell.   7. Ich heiße Professor Bach. / Mein Name ist Professor Bach.   8. Ich heiße Doktor Berg. / Mein Name ist Doktor Berg.   9. Ich heiße Iris. / Mein Name ist Iris.   10. Ich heiße _____. / Mein Name ist _____.

Written Practice 2

1. die Diplomatin   2. die Studentin   3. die Artistin   4. die Kommunistin
5. die Mechanikerin   6. die Optimistin   7. die Pilotin   8. die Managerin

Written Practice 3

1. Wie heißen Sie? / Ich heiße Angela.   2. Wie heißen Sie? / Ich heiße Herr Bauer.
3. Wie heißen Sie? / Ich heiße Thomas.   4. Wie heißen Sie? / Ich heiße Frau Kamps.   5. Wie heißen Sie? / Ich heiße Gudrun Klein.

Written Practice 4

1. Wo ist das Kind? / Das Kind ist hier.   2. Wo ist mein Vater? / Mein Vater ist dort.   3. Wo ist Erik? / Erik ist in Deutschland.   4. Wo ist Thomas? / Thomas ist da.   5. Wo ist Iris? / Iris ist in München.

Written Practice 5

1. Guten Morgen, Onkel Peter.   2. Guten Abend, Herr Schneider.   3. Guten Tag, Frau Keller.   4. Gute Nacht, Martin.

Written Practice 6

1. Guten Tag, Helga. / Wie geht's?   2. Guten Morgen, Thomas. / Wie geht's?
3. Guten Abend, Tanja. / Wie geht's?   4. Guten Tag, Herr Bach. / Wie geht's?
5. Guten Morgen, Rita. / Wie geht's?   6. Guten Abend, Frau Kamps. / Wie geht's?

QUIZ

1. die Lehrerin   2. die Reporterin   3. Mein Name ist Gudrun. / Ich heiße Gudrun.   4. Mein Name ist Felix. / Ich heiße Felix.   5. Wer ist das? / Das ist Tanja.   6. Wo ist der Pilot? / Der Pilot ist in Polen.   7. Wo ist die Frau? / Die Frau ist in Rom.   8. b   9. c   10. b

CHAPTER 3

Written Practice 1

1. Nein, Werner ist nicht in der Schweiz.   2. Nein, der Junge ist nicht mein Bruder.   3. Nein, das Mädchen ist nicht meine Schwester.   4. Nein, die Bibliothek ist nicht hier.   5. Nein, der Park ist nicht weit von hier.

Written Practice 2

1. Ist das ein Professor oder ein Lehrer? / Das ist ein Professor/Lehrer.   2. Ist das der Vater oder der Großvater? / Das ist der Vater/Großvater.   3. Ist das eine Lampe oder eine Vase? / Das ist eine Lampe/Vase.   4. Ist das Frau Bauer oder Frau Schäfer? / Das ist Frau Bauer/Frau Schäfer.

Written Practice 3

1. Wer ist das?   2. Wer ist das?   3. Was ist das?   4. Wer ist das?
5. Wo ist München?

Written Practice 4

1. Ist Ihre Schwester hier?   2. Ist Ihr Vater hier?   3. Ist Ihre Tante hier?
4. Ist Ihr Wagen hier?   5. Ist Ihre Schule hier?

Written Practice 5

Sample answers are given.   1. Ist das ein Museum oder eine Bibliothek?
2. Wo ist Ihr Vater?   3. Der Mann ist mein Onkel.   4. Was ist das?   5. Ist die Frau Ihre Mutter oder Ihre Tante?   6. Die Dame ist eine Lehrerin.

7. Mein Bruder ist in der Schweiz.   8. Der Park ist nicht weit von hier.
9. Der Herr heißt Professor Schmidt.   10. Ist das Ihre Tochter?

QUIZ

1. ein Auto / mein Auto / Ihr Auto   2. eine Bibliothek / meine Bibliothek /
Ihre Bibliothek   3. ein Mädchen / mein Mädchen / Ihr Mädchen   4. Ja, mein
Professor ist in Deutschland. / Nein, mein Professor ist nicht in Deutschland.
5. Ja, meine Freundin ist Österreicherin. / Nein, meine Freundin ist keine
Österreicherin.   6. Wo ist Ihr Onkel?   7. Was ist das?   8. d   9. a
10. a

CHAPTER 4

Written Practice 1

1. bin   2. sind   3. bist   4. ist   5. seid   6. ist   7. ist   8. ist
9. ist   10. sind

Written Practice 2

1. Er ist hier.   2. Ist sie da?   3. Es ist weit von hier.   4. Wo ist es?
5. Sie sind zu Hause.   6. Wo ist sie?   7. sie   8. es   9. er   10. er
11. er   12. sie *s.*   13. es   14. es   15. sie *pl.*

Written Practice 3

1. Ist Ihr Vater jung? / Ist Ihr Vater krank? / Ist Ihr Vater gesund?   2. Das Buch
ist interessant. / Das Buch ist neu. / Das Buch ist schwarz.   3. Wir sind klein. /
Wir sind groß. / Wir sind krank.

Written Practice 4

1. neu / alt   2. krank / gesund   3. schlecht / gut   4. kurz / lang
5. jung / alt   6. groß / klein   7. weiß / schwarz   8. gesund / krank
9. lang / kurz   10. klein / groß

Written Practice 5

1. Wann ist das Examen?   2. Wer ist in der Schweiz?   3. Wann ist die Party?
4. Warum sind Thomas und Helga in Bonn   5. Warum ist Ihr Großvater zu
Hause?   6. Wer ist morgen in Deutschland?   7. Wann sind wir in Leipzig?
8. Wer ist gesund?   9. Wann ist das Examen?   10. Warum ist das Kind zu
Hause?

Written Practice 6

1. Tanja und Maria sind in Berlin, denn sie sind krank.   2. Das Examen ist
nächste Woche.   3. Ich bin zu Hause, denn ich bin krank.   4. Das Konzert ist
am Montag.

Written Practice 7

1. Vier und/plus fünf ist neun.   2. Wie viel ist acht minus/weniger sechs?
3. Zehn minus/weniger drei ist sieben.

QUIZ

1. heißen / heiße   2. heißt / heißt   3. bin / seid   4. ist / bist   5. sie *s.*
6. es   7. er   8. b   9. b   10. d

CHAPTER 5

Written Practice 1

1. haben   2. hat   3. haben   4. habt   5. hat   6. hast   7. haben
8. haben   9. hat   10. hat

Written Practice 2

1. Hast du die CDs? / Hast du das Geld? / Hast du ein Heft?   2. Ich habe die
Fahrkarten. / Ich habe den Fahrplan. / Ich habe das Brot.

Written Practice 3

1. Was hast du?   2. Was hast du?   3. Was habt ihr?   4. Was haben Sie?
5. Was hast du?   6. Was haben Sie?

Written Practice 4

1. Doktor Keller, ist das Ihr Schreibtisch?   2. Tanja, ist das dein Schreibtisch?
3. Tante Gerda, ist das dein Schreibtisch?   4. Albert und Tina, ist das euer
Schreibtisch?   5. Frau Schäfer, ist das Ihr Schreibtisch?

Written Practice 5

1. dein / euer / Ihr   2. deine / eure / Ihre   3. dein / euer / Ihr   4. deine /
eure / Ihre   5. dein / euer / Ihr

Written Practice 6

1. Wie viel Milch habt ihr? / Wir haben viel Milch.   2. Wie viele CDs habt
ihr? / Wir haben viele CDs.   3. Wie viel Geld habt ihr? / Wir haben viel Geld.
4. Wie viele Fahrkarten habt ihr? / Wir haben viele Fahrkarten.   5. Wie viele
Schlüssel habt ihr? / Wir haben viele Schlüssel.

Written Practice 7

1. Wer hat mein Geld? / Wer hat viel Geld? / Wer hat kein Geld?   2. Martin hat
eure Schlüssel. / Martin hat viele Schlüssel. / Martin hat keine Schlüssel.
3. Wo ist deine Freundin? / Wo is Ihre Freundin? / Wo ist eure Freundin?

Written Practice 8

1. Nein, wir haben kein Brot.   2. Nein, Frau Keller hat keine Schlüssel.
3. Nein, ich habe kein Geld.   4. Nein, das Kind hat keine Milch.   5. Nein,
meine Schwester hat keine Bluse.   6. Nein, wir haben keine Zimmer.
7. Nein, Robert hat keine CDs.   8. Nein, mein Vater hat kein Bier.

Written Practice 9

1. Wo ist das Sofa? / Wo sind der Stuhl und der Schreibtisch?   2. Die Zimmer haben ein Fenster. / Die Zimmer haben kein Fenster.   3. Der Tisch ist sehr klein. / Die Zimmer sind sehr klein.

QUIZ

1. haben / habe   2. hat / hast   3. deine / eure / Ihre / keine / *sing.*   4. dein / euer / Ihr kein / *sing.*   5. deine / eure / Ihre /keine / *plur.*   6. Nein, ich habe kein Sofa.   7. Nein, Herr Bauer hat keine Tochter.   8. c   9. d   10. a

PART ONE TEST

1. (flook-tsoik)   2. (hye-sen)   3. (eer zite)   4. (mine-eh taw*ch*-tuh)   5. (frow shay-fuh)   6. heißt   7. heißen   8. heiße   9. heißt   10. heißt   11. Was ist das?   12. Wo ist Onkel Peter?   13. Wer hat kein Geld?   14. Warum ist sie zu Hause?   15. Wann ist das Examen?   16. Wer ist sehr jung?   17. Wo ist deine Freundin?   18. Was hat Robert?   19. Wann ist das Konzert?   20. Wo sind Tina und Marianne?   21. ein / Ihr / kein   22. eine / Ihre / keine   23. ein / Ihr / kein   24. ein / Ihr / kein   25. eine / Ihre / keine   26. Nein, das ist nicht meine Schwester.   27. Nein, das Fenster ist nicht groß.   28. Nein, meine Tante ist nicht in Berlin.   29. er   30. sie *pl.*   31. sie *s.*   32. es   33. sie *pl.*   34. Ist das Haus klein oder groß?   35. Ist das Auto neu oder alt?   36. Nein, Erik hat kein Geld.   37. Nein, wir haben keine Fahrkarten.   38. Nein, ich habe kein Brot.   39. b   40. c   41. d   42. b   43. b   44. a   45. a   46. d   47. a   48. c   49. b   50. a

CHAPTER 6

Written Practice 1

1. Deine Tochter wird Lehrerin. / Meine Schwester wird auch Lehrerin.
2. Erik wird Zahnarzt. / Sie werden auch Zahnarzt.   3. Die Kinder werden Fußballspieler. / Er wird auch Fußballspieler.

Written Practice 2

1. d   2. a   3. k   4. f   5. h   6. j   7. g   8. e   9. c   10. i

Written Practice 3

1. Es wird wieder kalt.   2. Es wird wieder kühl.   3. Es wird wieder hell.
4. Es wird wieder dunkel.   5. Es wird wieder heiß.

Written Practice 4

horen: ich höre / du hörst / er hört / wir hören / ihr hört / sie hören / Tina hört;
suchen: ich suche / du suchst / er sucht / wir suchen / ihr sucht / sie suchen / Tina

sucht; **fragen:** ich frage / du fragst / er fragt / wir fragen / ihr fragt / sie fragen / Tina fragt

Written Practice 5

1. Fährst du mit dem Bus oder mit dem Zug?   2. Fährt sie mit dem Bus oder mit dem Zug?   3. Fahren Sie mit dem Bus oder mit dem Zug?   4. Fährt Herr Weber mit dem Bus oder mit dem Zug?   5. Fahren sie mit dem Bus oder mit dem Zug?   6. Fährt er mit dem Bus oder mit dem Zug?   7. Fahren die Kinder mit dem Bus oder mit dem Zug?

Written Practice 6

1. Ja, Herr Mann schreibt ein Buch.   2. Ja, wir hören die Musik.   3. Ja, ich trage einen Hut.   4. Ja, wir sind in Österreich. / Nein, wir sind nicht in Österreich.   5. Ja, ich fahre mit dem Bus. / Nein, ich fahre nicht mit dem Bus. 6. Ja, Onkel Peter schläft im Park. / Nein, Onkel Peter schläft nicht im Park. 7. Ja, die Kinder fallen ins Bett. / Nein, die Kinder fallen nicht ins Bett.   8. Ja, wir kommen nach Hause. / Nein, wir kommen nicht nach Hause.

Written Practice 7

1. Die Kinder sind dreizehn Jahre alt.   2. Das Museum ist fünfzehn Jahre alt. 3. Du bist zwanzig Jahre alt.

QUIZ

1. **werden:** ich werde / du wirst / er wird / wir werden / ihr werdet / Sie werden / die Kinder werden;   **suchen:** ich suche / du suchst / er sucht / wir suchen / ihr sucht / Sie suchen / die Kinder suchen;   **spielen:** ich spiele / du spielst / er spielt / wir spielen / ihr spielt / Sie spielen / die Kinder spielen   2. Mein Bruder wird Arzt. / Du wirst auch Arzt.   3. Sie werden Krankenschwester. / Ich werde auch Krankenschwester.   4. **fahren:** ich fahre / du fährst / er fährt / ihr fahrt / die Kinder fahren;   **schlafen:** ich schlafe / du schläfst / er schläft / ihr schlaft / die Kinder schlafen;   **tragen:** ich trage / du trägst / er trägt / ihr tragt / die Kinder tragen   5. Ja, ich trage eine Bluse. / Nein, ich trage keine Bluse. 6. Ja, ich kaufe die Fahrkarten. / Nein, ich kaufe keine Fahrkarten.   7. Wie alt ist Iris? / Iris ist zwölf Jahre alt.   8. Wie alt ist dein Sohn? / Mein Sohn ist neunzehn Jahre alt.   9. c   10. c

CHAPTER 7

Written Practice 1

sprechen: ich spreche / du sprichst / er spricht / wir sprechen / ihr sprecht / sie sprechen;   **sehen:** ich sehe / du siehst / er sieht / wir sehen / ihr seht / sie sehen

Written Practice 2

1. Er besucht meine Freundin. / Er erwartet meine Freundin. / Er versteht meine Freundin. / Er findet meine Freundin.   2. Eric sieht die Schlüssel. / Eric sucht die Schlüssel. / Eric stiehlt die Schlüssel. / Eric verkauft die Schlüssel.

Written Practice 3

1. kleine   2. weiße   3. dunkel   4. jung   5. neue   6. graue
7. deutsche

Written Practice 4

1. c   2. e   3. h   4. j   5. l   6. g   7. f   8. k   9. d   10. b

Written Practice 5

Sample answers are given.   1. Meine Mutter liest eine Zeitung.   2. Die Kinder spielen im Park.   3. Der alte Mann spricht Englisch und Deutsch.
4. Ich habe kein Geld. Ich kann es nicht kaufen.   5. Der Dieb stiehlt meine Tasche.   6. Ist der Kaffee heiß oder kalt?   7. Es ist dunkel. Wo ist die Lampe?   8. Siehst du die Bibliothek?   9. Guten Abend, Frau Doktor.
10. Der braune Hut ist sehr alt.   11. Ist euer Vater wieder gesund?   12. Ist der neue Wagen braun oder rot?   13. Ich finde meine Schlüssel.   14. Martin bestellt ein Butterbrot und ein Glas Milch.   15. Die Schlüssel gehören Tina.

Written Practice 6

1. Wer besucht eine Freundin in Berlin?   2. Wohin fährt dein/Ihr Vater?
3. Was finden die Kinder?   4. Warum trägt sie ein Sweatshirt?   5. Wie alt ist deine Tochter?   6. Wann gehst du in die Stadt?   7. Wo spielen zwei Jungen Tennis?   8. Wie viele Schlüssel hat der Professor?   9. Wohin fährt er mit dem Bus?   10. Was liest Karin?   11. Wer wartet im Park?   12. Wie viel Geld hat Erik?   13. Was versteht Sonja?   14. Warum liest du das Buch?
15. Was trägt Onkel Heinz?

QUIZ

1. **reisen:** ich reise / du reist / er reist / wir reisen / ihr reist / sie reisen;
sehen: ich sehe / du siehst / er sieht / wir sehen / ihr seht / sie sehen;
sprechen: ich spreche / du sprichst / er spricht / wir sprechen / ihr sprecht / sie sprechen;   **verstehen:** ich verstehe / du verstehst / er versteht / wir verstehen / ihr versteht / sie verstehen   2. Andrea sucht eine neue Bluse. / Andrea verkauft eine neue Bluse. / Andrea findet eine neue Bluse. / Andrea sieht eine neue Bluse.
3. Verstehst du das Buch? / Liest du das Buch? / Findest du das Buch? / Stiehlst du das Buch? Sample answers are given for 4–6:   4. Die Kinder kaufen Eis.
5. Ich reise nach Leipzig.   6. Denn es ist sehr kalt.   7. c   8. a   9. d
10. a

CHAPTER 8

Written Practice 1

1. Warum fährt man mit der Straßenbahn?   2. Wie kommt man vom Rathaus zum Bahnhof?   3. Weiß man, wohin Gudrun reist?   4. Hier spricht man Deutsch.

Written Practice 2

kommen: ich komme / wir kommen / du kommst / ihr kommt / er kommt / sie kommen / man kommt / dieser Herr kommt / die Kinder kommen / diese Dame kommt

Written Practice 3

1. Herr Braun/Er kommt aus London.   2. Der Amerikaner/Er kommt aus New York.   3. Die Österreicherin/Sie kommt aus Wien.   4. Frau Benz/Sie kommt aus Deutschland.   5. Diese Dame/Sie kommt aus Italien.

Written Practice 4

1. Morgen reisen die Touristen nach Italien.   2. Im Park sehen wir viele Kinder.   3. Im Restaurant bestelle ich ein Glas Bier.   4. Vom Rathaus zur Schule fahren sie mit dem Auto.   5. Heute fliegt mein Vater nach Australien.

Written Practice 5

1. Meine Eltern wohnen jetzt in Freiburg.   2. Lebt Ihre Großmutter noch?
3. Wir kennen den Mann nicht. Wie heißt er?   4. Er fährt mit dem Zug nach Rom.   5. Herr Benz wohnt in der Schillerstraße.   6. Wohin fährst/gehst du?
7. Wissen Sie, wo Frau Schneider wohnt?   8. Ich gehe zum Rathaus. Es ist nicht weit von hier.   9. Warum geht ihr zu Fuß?   10. Kennen Sie meine Eltern nicht?

Written Practice 6

1. Wir fotografieren das Rathaus.   2. Martin verliert das Geld.   3. Ich studiere Deutsch und Russisch.   4. Die Kinder probieren den Pudding.
5. Diese Leute spazieren im Park.

Written Practice 7

ankommen: ich komme an / du kommst an / er kommt an / wir kommen an / ihr kommt an / sie kommen an;   **einsteigen:** ich steige ein / du steigst ein / er steigt ein/ wir steigen ein / ihr steigt ein / sie steigen ein;   **vorstellen:** ich stelle vor / du stellst vor / er stellt vor / wir stellen vor / ihr stellt vor / sie stellen vor

Written Practice 8

1. Kennen Sie meinen Onkel? / Kennen Sie diese Dame? / Kennen Sie den Professor? / Kennen Sie das Mädchen?   2. Dieser Mann kauft einen Wagen. / Dieser Mann kauft mein Haus. / Dieser Mann kauft Ihre CDs. / Dieser Mann kauft den Teppich.

Written Practice 9

1. Wer verkauft meinen Wagen? / Wer verkauft einen Hut? / Wer verkauft die Fahrkarten? / Wer verkauft das Auto? / Wer verkauft es?   2. Kennt ihr meine Eltern? / Kennt ihr den Lehrer? / Kennt ihr die Leute? / Kennt ihr meinen Freund? / Kennt ihr ihn?

QUIZ

1. Wo spielen die Kinder?   2. Woher kommt dein Onkel?   3. Wohin fahren die Touristen morgen?   4. Meine Eltern fotografieren die Kinder. / Meine Eltern fotografieren diesen Mann. / Meine Eltern fotografieren Ihren Bruder. / Meine Eltern fotografieren diese Frau. / Meine Eltern fotografieren uns.   5. meinen Vater / mich / dich / Ihren Zahnarzt / ihn / sie / keine Schule / uns / euch / diese Leute   6. b   7. a   8. c   9. a   10. d

CHAPTER 9

Written Practice 1

1. Ich finde seine Kleider.   2. Ich kenne ihre Freundin.   3. Wir kaufen euren Wagen.   4. Ich sehe mein Kind.   5. Er nimmt deine Milch.   6. Ihre Eltern wohnen in Leipzig.   7. Unser Chef weiß nichts.

Written Practice 2

1. Ich besuche Ihre Eltern in München. / Ich besuche eure Eltern in München. / Ich besuche unsere Eltern in München.   2. Wer findet meinen Bleistift? / Wer findet seinen Bleistift? / Wer findet unseren Bleistift?

Written Practice 3

fragen: ich fragte / du fragtest / er fragte / wir fragten / ihr fragtet / sie fragten / wer fragte;   **gehören:** ich gehörte / du gehörtest / er gehörte / wir gehörten / ihr gehörtet / sie gehörten / wer gehörte;   **vorstellen:** ich stellte vor / du stelltest vor / er stellte vor / wir stellten vor / ihr stelltet vor / sie stellten vor / wer stellte vor

Written Practice 4

1.   **fahren:** ich fuhr / du fuhrst / er fuhr / wir fuhren / ihr fuhrt / sie fuhren / dieser Mann fuhr;   **kommen:** ich kam / du kamst / er kam / wir kamen / ihr kamt / sie kamen / dieser Mann kam;   **fliegen:** ich flog / du flogst / er flog / wir flogen / ihr flogt / sie flogen / dieser Mann flog

Written Practice 5

essen: aß; **lesen:** las; **sagen:** sagte; **sprechen:** sprach; **bleiben:** blieb; **heißen:** hieß; **haben:** hatte; **gehen:** ging; **sein:** war; **warten:** wartete; **arbeiten:** arbeitete; **werden:** wurde; **finden:** fand; **wissen:** wusste; **verstehen:** verstand; **ankommen:** kam an

Written Practice 6

1. Ich kam mit dem Bus.   2. Es wurde heute sehr kalt.   3. Warum aßt ihr im Wohnzimmer?   4. Meine Tochter studierte an einer Universität in Amerika. 5. Wo stiegen wir um?   6. Die Männer zerstörten das alte Haus.   7. Wen sahst du im Wohnzimmer?   8. Der Chef diskutierte die Probleme.   9. Ich war immer krank.   10. Wusstest du, wer die Bücher verkaufte?

Written Practice 7

1. Ich fand eine neue Lampe für dich. / Ich fand eine neue Lampe für meinen Freund. / Ich fand eine neue Lampe für sie. / Ich fand eine neue Lampe für Ihren Chef.   2. Diese Frau hatte nichts gegen mich. / Diese Frau hatte nichts gegen uns. / Diese Frau hatte nichts gegen Ihre Chefin. / Diese Frau hatte nichts gegen Sie.   3. Robert kam ohne das Geld. / Robert kam ohne ihn. / Robert kam ohne sie. / Robert kam ohne seinen Vater.   4. Er ging ohne seinen Freund zum Park. / Er ging ohne dich zum Park. / Er ging ohne uns zum Park. / Er ging ohne ihren Onkel zum Park. / Er ging ohne euch zum Park. / Er ging ohne seine Kinder zum Park.   5. Die Amerikaner fuhren bis Hamburg. / Die Amerikaner fuhren bis München. / Die Amerikaner fuhren bis Polen. / Die Amerikaner fuhren bis gestern Abend. / Die Amerikaner fuhren bis elf Uhr.

Written Practice 8

1. die Bücher   2. die Arme   3. die Väter   4. die Schwestern   5. die Böden   6. die Rathäuser   7. die Himmel   8. die Ärztinnen   9. die Kleider   10. die Tanten   11. die Brüder   12. die Hefte   13. die Zeitungen   14. die Tische   15. die Teppiche   16. die Lampen

QUIZ

1. Ich habe unsere Fahrkarten.   2. Gudrun las meine Zeitung.   3. Erik besuchte seinen Freund.   4. Herr Schmidt verkaufte meinen Wagen. / Herr Schmidt verkaufte deinen Wagen. / Herr Schmidt verkaufte ihren Wagen. / Herr Schmidt verkaufte euren Wagen. / Herr Schmidt verkaufte unseren Wagen. 5. **bestellen:** ich bestellte / du bestelltest / er bestellte / wir bestellten / ihr bestelltet / sie bestellten / die Leute bestellten;   **ausgeben:** ich gab aus / du gabst aus / er gab aus / wir gaben aus / ihr gabt aus / sie gaben aus / die Leute gaben aus;   **sein:** ich war / du warst / er war / wir waren / ihr wart / sie waren / die Leute waren   6. Wer machte die Tür auf?   7. Verstandest du, was er sagte?   8. Die Touristen hatten ein Geschenk für mich. / Die Touristen hatten ein Geschenk für ihn. / Die Touristen hatten ein Geschenk für meine Tante. / Die Touristen hatten ein Geschenk für deinen Sohn. / Die Touristen hatten ein Geschenk für sie. / Die Touristen hatten ein Geschenk für ihre Eltern. 9. b   10. a

CHAPTER 10

Written Practice 1

denken: ich denke / du denkst / er denkt; **anfangen:** ich fange an / du fängst an / er fängt an; **helfen:** ich helfe / du hilfst / er hilft; **brechen:** du brichst / er bricht / wir brechen; **fallen:** du fällst / er fällt / wir fallen; **vergessen:** du vergisst / er vergisst / wir vergessen; **fallen:** ich fiel / er fiel / wir fielen; **bringen:** ich brachte / er brachte / wir brachten; **stehen:** ich stand / er stand / wir standen; **rennen:** ich rannte / du ranntest / ihr ranntet; **anrufen:** ich rief an / du riefst an / ihr rieft an; **schneiden:** ich schnitt / du schnittest / ihr schnittet

Written Practice 2

der Metzger: ihrem Metzger / meinem Metzger / diesem Metzger; **die Wohnung:** ihrer Wohnung / meiner Wohnung / dieser Wohnung; **das Land:** ihrem Land / meinem Land / diesem Land; **die Bücher:** ihren Büchern / meinen Büchern / diesen Büchern; **die Uhr:** ihrer Uhr / meiner Uhr / dieser Uhr

Written Practice 3

1. Der Metzger gab mir ein Geschenk. / Der Metzger gab dir ein Geschenk. / Der Metzger gab ihnen ein Geschenk. / Der Metzger gab meinem Sohn ein Geschenk. / Der Metzger gab meinen Söhnen ein Geschenk. / Der Metzger gab der Ausländerin ein Geschenk. 2. Wer schreibt ihr einen Brief? / Wer schreibt uns einen Brief? / Wer schreibt Ihnen einen Brief? / Wer schreibt euch einen Brief? / Wer schreibt der Polizei einen Brief? / Wer schreibt Ihren Kindern einen Brief? 3. Was sendet er uns? / Was sendet er ihnen? / Was sendet er euch? / Was sendet er Ihnen? / Was sendet er mir?

Written Practice 4

1. Robert schrieb ihr einen Brief. / Robert schrieb ihn ihr. 2. Ich kaufte ihm ein Auto. / Ich kaufte es ihm. 3. Senden Sie ihnen neue Bücher? / Senden Sie sie ihnen? 4. Gudrun brachte ihr ein Heft. / Gudrun brachte es ihr. 5. Wir verkauften ihnen die Kleider. / Wir verkauften sie ihnen.

Written Practice 5

1. halb 2. fünfunddreißig 3. eins 4. Viertel 5. zwölf 6. fünfundvierzig 7. vor / vier

Written Practice 6

1. Er besuchte uns am ersten März. / Er besuchte uns am dritten März. / Er besuchte uns am neunten März. / Er besuchte uns am fünfzehnten März. / Er besuchte uns am siebenundzwanzigsten März. 2. Ihr Sohn ist am dreißigsten Juli geboren. / Ihr Sohn ist am einunddreißigsten Juli geboren. / Ihr Sohn ist am zweiten Juli geboren. / Ihr Sohn ist am siebten Juli geboren. / Ihr Sohn ist am zwölften Juli geboren.

Written Practice 7

1. Ich spiele gern Schach.   2. Ich wandere gern.   3. Ich schwimme gern.
4. Ich spiele gern Golf.   5. Ich fahre gern Rad.   6. Ich laufe gern Ski.
7. Ich lese gern.

QUIZ

1. **laufen:** ich laufe / du läufst / er läuft;   **fressen:** ich fresse / du frisst / er frisst;   **geben:** ich gebe / du gibst / er gibt;   **denken:** ich dachte / du dachtest / er dachte;   **anfangen:** ich fing an / du fingst an / er fing an;
helfen: ich half / du halfst / er half   2. **das Fenster: kein**em Fenster / **Ihr**em Fenster / **dies**em Fenster;   **die Kinder: kein**en Kindern / **Ihr**en Kindern / **dies**en Kindern;   **die Treppe: kein**er Treppe / **Ihr**er Treppe / **dies**er Treppe;   **der Besuch: kein**em Besuch / **Ihr**em Besuch / **dies**em Besuch;   **die Leute: kein**en Leuten / **Ihr**en Leuten / **dies**en Leuten   3. Sie geben mir drei Fahrkarten. / Sie geben dir drei Fahrkarten. / Sie geben ihm drei Fahrkarten. / Sie geben ihr drei Fahrkarten. / Sie geben euch drei Fahrkarten.   4. Iris schrieb ihm einen Brief. Iris schrieb ihn ihm. / Sie gaben ihnen neue Kulis. Sie gaben sie ihnen.   5. Es ist halb eins.   6. Es ist neun Uhr fünfundvierzig.   7. Es ist Viertel nach eins.   8. Ich bin am ersten Februar geboren. / Ich bin am dritten Februar geboren. / Ich bin am siebten Februar geboren. / Ich bin am sechzehnten Februar geboren. / Ich bin am achtundzwanzigsten Februar geboren.   9. a
10. d

PART TWO TEST

1. **werden:** werde / wirst / wird / werden   2. **anfangen:** fange an / fängst an / fängt an / fangen an   3. **sehen:** sehe / siehst / sieht / sehen   4. **fahren:** fahre / fährst / fährt / fahrt   5. **stehlen:** stehle / stiehlst / stiehlt / stehlt
6. **mitgehen:** gehe mit / gehst mit / geht mit / geht mit   7. **fahren:** fuhr / fuhrst / fuhr / fuhren   8. **besuchen:** besuchte / besuchtest / besuchte / besuchten
9. **helfen:** half / halfst / half / halfen   10. **gehen:** ging / gingst / gingen / gingt
11. **sein:** war / warst / waren / wart   12. **haben:** hatte / hattest / hatten / hattet
13. Wen besuchte Erik in Berlin?   14. Wohin fahren Ihre/deine Eltern?
15. Was fand sie?   16. Wann gehst du nach Hause?   17. Wem gab Tina einen Kuli?   18. Wohin fährt er mit dem Bus?   19. Was liest Karin?   20. Wo warten die Kinder?   21. kenne   22. fahren   23. gehst   24. Wissen
25. Kennen   26. Seine Freunde fotografieren die Kinder. / Seine Freunde fotografieren diesen Mann. / Seine Freunde fotografieren uns.   27. Wer verkauft einen Hut? / Wer verkauft das Auto? / Wer verkauft es?   28. Kennen Sie meine Eltern? / Kennen Sie den Lehrer? / Kennen Sie ihn?   29. meine Mutter / meiner Mutter   30. den Zahnarzt / dem Zahnarzt   31. die Kinder / den Kindern

32. sein Heft / seinem Heft   33. diese Bücher / diesen Büchern   34. Wer machte das Fenster auf?   35. Sie flogen nach Asien.   36. Verstandest du, was sie fragte?   37. Sie gab mir drei Zeitungen. / Sie gab dir drei Zeitungen. / Sie gab ihm drei Zeitungen. / Sie gab ihr drei Zeitungen.   38. Was sandten sie uns? / Was sandten sie euch? / Was sandten sie Ihnen? / Was sandten sie ihnen?   39. Gibst du ihm eine Zeitung? / Gibst du sie ihm?   40. Thomas sandte ihnen einen Brief. / Thomas sandte ihn ihnen.   41. Ich kaufte ihr eine Blume. / Ich kaufte sie ihr.   42. Das Kind ist am ersten März geboren. / Das Kind ist am dritten März geboren. / Das Kind ist am siebten März geboren. / Das Kind ist am neunten März geboren. / Das Kind ist am siebenundzwanzigsten März geboren. / Das Kind ist am dreißigsten März geboren.   43. c   44. a   45. b   46. a   47. d   48. c   49. a   50. d

CHAPTER 11

Written Practice 1

lachen: ich habe gelacht / du hast gelacht / er hat gelacht / wir haben gelacht / ihr habt gelacht / sie haben gelacht;   **versuchen:** ich habe versucht / du hast versucht / er hat versucht / wir haben versucht / ihr habt versucht / sie haben versucht;   **vorstellen:** ich habe vorgestellt / du hast vorgestellt / er hat vorgestellt / wir haben vorgestellt / ihr habt vorgestellt / sie haben vorgestellt

Written Practice 2

sprechen: ich habe gesprochen / du hast gesprochen / er hat gesprochen / wir haben gesprochen / ihr habt gesprochen / sie haben gesprochen;   **versprechen:** ich habe versprochen / du hast versprochen / er hat versprochen / wir haben versprochen / ihr habt versprochen / sie haben versprochen;   **aussprechen:** ich habe ausgesprochen / du hast ausgesprochen / er hat ausgesprochen / wir haben ausgesprochen / ihr habt ausgesprochen / sie haben ausgesprochen;   **wissen:** ich habe gewusst / du hast gewusst / er hat gewusst / wir haben gewusst / ihr habt gewusst / sie haben gewusst;   **beschreiben:** ich habe beschrieben / du hast beschrieben / er hat beschrieben / wir haben beschrieben / ihr habt beschrieben / sie haben beschrieben;   **aussehen:** ich habe ausgesehen / du hast ausgesehen / er hat ausgesehen / wir haben ausgesehen / ihr habt ausgesehen / sie haben ausgesehen

Written Practice 3

1. Was hast du gesagt?   2. Wir haben Deutsch gelernt.   3. Die Kinder haben gern im Park gespielt.   4. Haben Sie meinen Sohn gesehen?   5. Wir haben drei Briefe von ihnen erhalten.   6. Robert hat in der Hauptstadt gewohnt.   7. Habt ihr die schöne Musik gehört?   8. Die Männer haben das alte Haus zerstört.   9. Ich habe euch ein kleines Paket gesandt.   10. Wer hat die Musik

arrangiert?   11. Er hat es versprochen.   12. Was hast du gelesen?
13. Gudrun hat mein Fahrrad genommen.   14. Was hat der Dieb gestohlen?
15. Niemand hat dich verstanden.

Written Practice 4

1. Der Ausländer hat mit den Kindern gesprochen. / Der Ausländer hat mit meiner
Tante gesprochen. / Der Ausländer hat mit dem König gesprochen. / Der
Ausländer hat mit mir gesprochen. / Der Ausländer hat mit uns gesprochen. / Der
Ausländer hat mit ihnen gesprochen.   2. Gudrun wohnt seit April bei ihren
Eltern. / Gudrun wohnt seit April bei meiner Schwester. / Gudrun wohnt seit April
bei einem Freund. / Gudrun wohnt seit April bei ihm. / Gudrun wohnt seit April
bei ihr. / Gudrun wohnt seit April bei mir.   3. Sie bekommt einen Brief von
ihren Eltern. / Sie bekommt einen Brief von einem Ausländer. / Sie bekommt
einen Brief von deinem Bruder. / Sie bekommt einen Brief von dir. / Sie bekommt
einen Brief von euch.

Written Practice 5

1. Die Hauptstadt Frankreichs ist Paris.   2. Die Hauptstadt Italiens ist Rom.
3. Die Hauptstadt Russlands ist Moskau.   4. Die Hauptstadt Norwegens ist
Oslo.   5. Die Hauptstadt Polens ist Warschau.   6. Die Hauptstadt Spaniens ist
Madrid.   7. Die Hauptstadt Tschechiens ist Prag.   8. Die Hauptstadt
Griechenlands ist Athen.   9. Die Hauptstadt Japans ist Tokio.   10. Die
Hauptstadt Österreichs ist Wien.

QUIZ

1. **dienen:** ich habe gedient / du hast gedient / er hat gedient / wir haben gedient /
ihr habt gedient / sie haben gedient;   **verkaufen:** ich habe verkauft / du hast
verkauft / er hat verkauft / wir haben verkauft / ihr habt verkauft / sie haben
verkauft;   **vorstellen:** ich habe vorgestellt / du hast vorgestellt / er hat
vorgestellt / wir haben vorgestellt / ihr habt vorgestellt / sie haben vorgestellt
2. **sagen:** gesagt; **trinken:** getrunken; **imponieren:** imponiert; **erkennen:**
erkannt; **gehören:** gehört; **aussehen:** ausgesehen; **schreiben:** geschrieben; **helfen:**
geholfen; **essen:** gegessen; **glauben:** geglaubt; **tun:** getan; **stehlen:** gestohlen;
lesen: gelesen; **besitzen:** besessen   3. **finden:** ich finde / ich fand / ich habe
gefunden; du findest / du fandest / du hast gefunden;   **ausgeben:** du gibst aus /
du gabst aus / du hast ausgegeben; er gibt aus / er gab aus / er hat ausgegeben
4. Warum glaubt er seinem Bruder nicht? / Warum glaubt er dieser Dame nicht? /
Warum glaubt er den Männern nicht? / Warum glaubt er mir nicht? / Warum
glaubt er uns nicht?   5. Ich habe gestern mit deiner Kusine gesprochen. / Ich
habe gestern mit dem König gesprochen. / Ich habe gestern mit ihm gesprochen. /
Ich habe gestern mit ihr gesprochen. / Ich habe gestern mit ihnen gesprochen.
6. b   7. d   8. b   9. a   10. a

CHAPTER 12

Written Practice 1

spazieren: ich bin spaziert / du bist spaziert / er ist spaziert / wir sind spaziert / ihr seid spaziert / sie sind spaziert; **kommen:** ich bin gekommen / du bist gekommen / er ist gekommen / wir sind gekommen / ihr seid gekommen / sie sind gekommen; **umsteigen:** ich bin umgestiegen / du bist umgestiegen / er ist umgestiegen / wir sind umgestiegen / ihr seid umgestiegen / sie sind umgestiegen; **bleiben:** ich bin geblieben / du bist geblieben / er ist geblieben / wir sind geblieben / ihr seid geblieben / sie sind geblieben; **sterben:** ich bin gestorben / du bist gestorben / er ist gestorben / wir sind gestorben / ihr seid gestorben / sie sind gestorben; **folgen:** ich bin gefolgt / du bist gefolgt / er ist gefolgt / wir sind gefolgt / ihr seid gefolgt / sie sind gefolgt

Written Practice 2

1. Ich bin sehr müde gewesen.   2. Ist deine Schwester wieder gesund geworden?   3. Der Zug ist um elf Uhr zehn angekommen.   4. Die Kinder sind in der Stadt geblieben.   5. Die Touristen sind zum Rathaus gegangen. 6. Meine Eltern sind im Park spazieren gegangen.   7. Wir haben Hunger gehabt.   8. Wohin bist du gefahren?   9. Die Jungen sind zum Marktplatz gelaufen.   10. Sie haben kein Geld gehabt.

Written Practice 3

1. Wir haben eine Stunde auf ihn gewartet. / Wir haben eine Stunde auf dich gewartet. / Wir haben eine Stunde auf diesen Ausländer gewartet. / Wir haben eine Stunde auf unsere Wirtin gewartet. / Wir haben eine Stunde auf die Diplomaten gewartet. / Wir haben eine Stunde auf euch gewartet.   2. Ich denke niemals an diese Probleme. / Ich denke niemals an meine Arbeit. / Ich denke niemals an unseren König. / Ich denke niemals an sie. / Ich denke niemals an Sie. / Ich denke niemals an sie.

Written Practice 4

1. **unterbrechen:** ich unterbreche / ich unterbrach / ich habe unterbrochen; du unterbrichst / du unterbrachst / du hast unterbrochen; ihr unterbrecht / ihr unterbracht / ihr habt unterbrochen   2. **widerspiegeln:** er spiegelt wider / er spiegelte wider / er hat widergespiegelt; wir spiegeln wider / wir spiegelten wider / wir haben widergespiegelt; du spiegelst wider / du spiegeltest wider / du hast widergespiegelt

Written Practice 5

1. Sie wissen nicht, dass es wieder sehr kalt geworden ist. / Sie wissen nicht, dass Onkel Peter vor zwei Tagen gestorben ist.   2. Niemand fragt, ob sie noch in Freiburg wohnen. / Niemand fragt, ob wir ihnen glauben.   3. Sie hat ihre Tasche verloren, während sie in Schweden gewesen ist. / Sie hat ihre Tasche verloren, während sie mit den Kindern gespielt hat.   4. Die Königin fragt, ob

der König noch in Frankreich ist. / Die Königin fragt, ob ihre Kinder schon nach Italien gereist sind. / Die Königin fragt, ob die alte Frau Hunger gehabt hat. / Die Königin fragt, ob der Wissenschaftler den Leuten geholfen hat.

QUIZ

1. **gehen:** ich bin gegangen / du bist gegangen / er ist gegangen / wir sind gegangen;   **marschieren:** ich bin marschiert / du bist marschiert / er ist marschiert / wir sind marschiert;   **umsteigen:** ich bin umgestiegen / du bist umgestiegen / er ist umgestiegen / wir sind umgestiegen;   **ankommen:** ich bin angekommen / du bist angekommen / ihr seid angekommen / sie sind angekommen;   **reisen:** ich bin gereist / du bist gereist / ihr seid gereist / sie sind gereist;   **folgen:** ich bin gefolgt / du bist gefolgt / ihr seid gefolgt / sie sind gefolgt   2. **sein:** gelaufen; **haben:** gesehen / **haben:** gesprochen; **haben:** gelernt / **sein:** mitgegangen; **sein:** gekommen / **haben:** diskutiert; **sein:** gestorben / **haben:** verstanden; **haben:** gewusst / **haben:** geschrieben; **haben:** versprochen / **sein:** geworden; **sein:** gewesen / **haben:** gehabt; **haben:** getrunken / **sein:** geblieben; **haben:** abgesandt   3. **acc:** mich / dich / ihn / sie / uns / euch / sie / diesen Ausländer / das Mädchen / die Musik / viele Romane; **dat:** mir / dir / ihm / ihr / uns / euch / ihnen / diesem Ausländer / dem Mädchen / der Musik / vielen Romanen   4. Er ist vor einem Tag angekommen. / Er ist vor drei Wochen angekommen. / Er ist vor einer Woche angekommen. / Er ist vor einer Minute angekommen. / Er ist vor einem Jahr angekommen. / Er ist vor zwei Jahren angekommen.   5. Mein Bruder schreibt, dass seine Frau Ärztin geworden ist. / Mein Bruder schreibt, dass er ein Haus in der Hauptstadt gekauft hat. / Mein Bruder schreibt, dass unser Onkel im Februar zu Besuch kommt. / Mein Bruder schreibt, dass niemand seinen neuen Roman gelesen hat.   6. b   7. a   8. d   9. d   10. a

CHAPTER 13

Written Practice 1

fahren: ich werde fahren / du wirst fahren / er wird fahren / wir werden fahren; **aufmachen:** ich werde aufmachen / du wirst aufmachen / er wird aufmachen / wir werden aufmachen;   **beschreiben:** ich werde beschreiben / du wirst beschreiben / er wird beschreiben / wir werden beschreiben;   **haben:** ich werde haben / er wird haben / ihr werdet haben / sie werden haben;   **sein:** ich werde sein / er wird sein / ihr werdet sein / sie werden sein;   **werden:** ich werde werden / er wird werden / ihr werdet werden / sie werden werden

Written Practice 2

1. Morgen bestellt sie ein Glas Rotwein.   2. Morgen erhält die Familie drei Briefe.   3. Morgen weint der Vater wieder.   4. Morgen steigen die Ausländer

am Marktplatz um.   5. Morgen fliegst du wieder nach Portugal?   6. Morgen liest er den interessanten Roman.   7. Morgen spielen die Kinder unter dem Tisch.

Written Practice 3

1. Ich komme mit der Straßenbahn nach Hause. / Ich komme heute mit der Straßenbahn nach Hause.   2. Wir sind mit dem Zug in die Schweiz gereist. / Wir sind vor einer Woche mit dem Zug in die Schweiz gereist.

Written Practice 4

dat: dem Fahrrad / den Leuten / meinem Schrank / seiner Nachbarin / unseren Gästen / dem Handschuh / den Handschuhen / einem Roman / einer Bratwurst / dem Turm / der Burg / den Kaufhäusern / deinen Geschwistern / dem Dom; **gen:** des Fahrrads / der Leute / meines Schranks / seiner Nachbarin / unserer Gäste / des Handschuhs / der Handschuhe / eines Romans / einer Bratwurst / des Turms / der Burg / der Kaufhäuser / deiner Geschwister / des Doms

Written Practice 5

1. Robert hatte mir ein Geschenk gegeben.   2. Wir waren zum Park gegangen.
3. Hattest du mit dem kleinen Hund gespielt?   4. Warum warst du so böse gewesen?   5. Unsere Gäste waren in der Stadt geblieben.

Written Practice 6

1. Ich werde mich in einer Stunde rasieren. / Du wirst dich in einer Stunde rasieren. / Wir werden uns in einer Stunde rasieren. / Ihr werdet euch in einer Stunde rasieren. / Sie werden sich in einer Stunde rasieren.

Written Practice 7

sich beeilen: Ich beeile mich. / Du beeilst dich. / Er beeilt sich. / Wir beeilen uns. / Wer beeilt sich?   **sich rasieren schnell:** Ich rasiere mich schnell. / Du rasierst dich schnell. / Er rasiert sich schnell. / Wir rasieren uns schnell. / Wer rasiert sich schnell?   **sich irren:** Ich irre mich. / Sie irrt sich. / Sie irren sich. / Ihr irrt euch. / Man irrt sich.   **sich freuen über das Buch:** Ich freue mich über das Buch. / Sie freut sich über das Buch. / Sie freuen sich über das Buch. / Ihr freut euch über das Buch. / Man freut sich über das Buch.

Written Practice 8

1. Du wirst dich waschen. / Er wird sich waschen. / Ich werde mich waschen.
2. Er wird hier aussteigen. / Ihr werdet hier aussteigen. / Sie werden hier aussteigen.   3. Ich werde in Bonn arbeiten. / Du wirst in Bonn arbeiten. / Wer wird in Bonn arbeiten?

QUIZ

1. Du wirst ein Bier bestellen. / Wir werden ein Bier bestellen. / Sie werden ein Bier bestellen.   2. Sie wird nichts versprechen. / Ihr werdet nichts versprechen. / Man wird nichts versprechen.   3. **acc:** meine Gäste / ihren Handschuh / seine Enkelin / das Kaufhaus; **dat:** meinen Gästen / ihrem Handschuh / seiner Enkelin /

dem Kaufhaus; **gen:** meiner Gäste / ihres Handschuhs / seiner Enkelin / des Kaufhauses   4. Wann hast du dich gewaschen? / Wann hat sie sich gewaschen? / Wann haben wir uns gewaschen? / Wann habt ihr euch gewaschen? / Wann haben Sie sich gewaschen?   5. Ich weiß nicht, wo meine Verwandten gearbeitet haben. / Ich weiß nicht, warum die Jungen vor der Bank warten. / Ich weiß nicht, wie lange sie noch arbeiten wird. / Ich weiß nicht, woher diese Ausländer kommen. / Ich weiß nicht, wie diese Gäste heißen.   6. **sich beeilen: pres perf** sie hat sich beeilt, **past perf** sie hatte sich beeilt / **pres perf** wir haben uns beeilt, **past perf** wir hatten uns beeilt / **pres perf** ihr habt euch beeilt, **past perf** ihr hattet euch beeilt; **aussteigen: pres perf** sie ist ausgestiegen, **past perf** sie war ausgestiegen / **pres perf** wir sind ausgestiegen, **past perf** wir waren ausgestiegen / **pres perf** ihr seid ausgestiegen, **past perf** ihr wart ausgestiegen; **arbeiten: pres perf** sie hat gearbeitet, **past perf** sie hatte gearbeitet / **pres perf** wir haben gearbeitet, **past perf** wir hatten gearbeitet / **pres perf** ihr habt gearbeitet, **past perf** ihr hattet gearbeitet   7. c   8. a   9. a   10. a

CHAPTER 14

Written Practice 1
aussteigen: pres er steigt aus / **past** er stieg aus / **pres perf** er ist ausgestiegen / **past perf** er war ausgestiegen / **fut** er wird aussteigen / **fut perf** er wird ausgestiegen sein;   **versprechen: pres** wir versprechen / **past** wir versprachen / **pres perf** wir haben versprochen / **past perf** wir hatten versprochen / **fut** wir werden versprechen / **fut perf** wir werden versprochen haben;   **besuchen: pres** du besuchst / **past** du besuchtest / **pres perf** du hast besucht / **past perf** du hattest besucht / **fut** du wirst besuchen / **fut perf** du wirst besucht haben;   **sich rasieren: pres** ich rasiere mich / **past** ich rasierte mich / **pres perf** ich habe mich rasiert / **past perf** ich hatte mich rasiert / **fut** ich werde mich rasieren / **fut perf** ich werde mich rasiert haben;   **wohnen: pres** ich wohne / **past** du wohntest / **pres perf** er hat gewohnt / **past perf** wir hatten gewohnt / **fut** ihr werdet wohnen / **fut perf** sie werden gewohnt haben;   **verstehen: pres** ich verstehe / **past** du verstandest / **pres perf** er hat verstanden / **past perf** wir hatten verstanden / **fut** ihr werdet verstehen / **fut perf** sie werden verstanden haben

Written Practice 2
1. wegen des Examens / wegen dieser Besichtigung / wegen der Touristen
2. während eines Krieges / während des Gewitters / während des Tages
3. trotz des Schnees / trotz seiner Geschwister / trotz einer Nachbarin
4. anstatt der Handschuhe / anstatt einer Küche / anstatt dieser Flaschen

Written Practice 3

1. Sie zieht sich die Jacke an. / Ich ziehe mir den Regenmantel an. / Du ziehst dir das Sweatshirt an.   2. Wir haben uns eine Flasche Wein gekauft. / Ihr habt euch die Handschuhe gekauft. / Sie haben sich einen Roman gekauft.   3. Ich habe mir den Finger gebrochen. / Sie haben sich die Finger gebrochen. / Du hast dir die Beine gebrochen.

Written Practice 4

1. Er hat sich die Hände gewaschen. / Ihr habt euch die Hände gewaschen. / Die Männer haben sich die Hände gewaschen. / Wir haben uns die Hände gewaschen. / Du hast dir die Hände gewaschen.

Written Practice 5

1. **acc:** den Helden / den Jungen / den Soldaten; **dat:** dem Helden / dem Jungen / dem Soldaten; **gen:** des Helden / des Jungen / des Soldaten   2. **acc:** den Affen / den Prinzen / den Diplomaten; **dat:** dem Affen / dem Prinzen / dem Diplomaten; **gen:** des Affen / des Prinzen / des Diplomaten

Written Practice 6

1. Ich will einen Roman lesen. / Ich wollte einen Roman lesen. / Wir haben einen Roman lesen wollen. / Wir werden einen Roman lesen wollen.   2. Du kannst sehr gut Schach spielen. / Du konntest sehr gut Schach spielen. / Ihr habt sehr gut Schach spielen können. / Ihr werdet sehr gut Schach spielen können.   3. Sie muss ein bisschen warten. / Sie musste ein bisschen warten. / Sie haben ein bisschen warten müssen. / Sie werden ein bisschen warten müssen.   4. Ich soll fleißig arbeiten. / Er sollte fleißig arbeiten. / Wir haben fleißig arbeiten sollen. / Man wird fleißig arbeiten sollen.

Written Practice 7

1. Die Kinder konnten gut Klavier spielen. / Die Kinder haben gut Klavier spielen können.   2. Ich musste jeden Tag fleißig arbeiten. / Ich habe jeden Tag fleißig arbeiten müssen.   3. Du solltest dir die Hände waschen. / Du hast dir die Hände waschen sollen.   4. Sie mochte kein Eis. / Sie hat kein Eis gemocht.   5. Hier konnte man umsteigen. / Hier hat man umsteigen können.   6. Ihr musstet den Nachbarn helfen. / Ihr habt den Nachbarn helfen müssen.

QUIZ

1. **schicken: pres** ich schicke / **past** du schicktest / **pres perf** er hat geschickt / **past perf** wir hatten geschickt / **fut** ihr werdet schicken / **fut perf** sie werdet geschickt haben;   **waschen: pres** ich wasche / **past** du wuschst / **pres perf** er hat gewaschen / **past perf** wir hatten gewaschen / **fut** ihr werdet waschen / **fut perf** sie werden gewaschen haben;   **aussteigen: pres** ich steige aus / **past** du stiegst aus / **pres perf** er ist ausgestiegen / **past perf** wir waren ausgestiegen / **fut** ihr werdet aussteigen / **fut perf** sie werden ausgestiegen sein   2. **mit:** d; **von:** d; **wegen:** g; **zu:** d; **in:** a–d; **trotz:** g; **anstatt:** g; **auf:** a–d; **während:** g; **durch:** a;

für: a; **statt:** g; **gegen:** a; **bis:** a; **neben:** a–d   3. Wegen des Gewitters mussten wir zu Hause bleiben. / Wegen des Regens mussten wir zu Hause bleiben. / Wegen dieser Arbeit mussten wir zu Hause bleiben.   4. Statt meines Bruders hat Erik uns helfen müssen. / Statt unserer Geschwister hat Erik uns helfen müssen. / Statt dieses Matrosen hat Erik uns helfen müssen.   5. Man putzt sich die Zähne. / Die Kinder putzen sich die Zähne. / Meine Tochter putzt sich die Zähne. / Wir putzen uns die Zähne. / Du putzt dir die Zähne.   6. Du hast dir einen warmen Mantel angezogen. / Sie hat sich einen warmen Mantel angezogen. / Sie haben sich einen warmen Mantel angezogen. / Niemand hat sich einen warmen Mantel angezogen. / Tina hat sich einen warmen Mantel angezogen.   7. **acc:** die Kirche / einen Helden / die Gäste; **dat:** der Kirche / einem Helden / den Gästen; **gen:** der Kirche / eines Helden / der Gäste   8. **dürfen: pres** ich darf / **past** ihr durftet; **können: pres** ich kann / **past** ihr konntet;   **mögen: pres** ich mag / **past** ihr mochtet;   **wollen: pres** er will / **past** wir wollten; **sollen: pres** er soll / **past** wir sollten;   **müssen: pres** er muss / **past** wir mussten   9. Hast du dieses Gedicht verstehen können? / Wirst du dieses Gedicht verstehen können?   10. Meine Nachbarin hat ihre Pflicht tun sollen. / Meine Nachbarin wird ihre Pflicht tun sollen.

CHAPTER 15

Written Practice 1

1. Ich habe das Heft, das du verloren hast. / Ich habe einen Regenschirm, den du verloren hast. / Ich habe die Flasche, die du verloren hast. / Ich habe den Artikel, den du verloren hast.   2. Robert besucht den Matrosen, dessen Vater Diplomat gewesen ist. / Robert besucht die Ausländer, deren Vater Diplomat gewesen ist. / Robert besucht eine Dame, deren Vater Diplomat gewesen ist. / Robert besucht das Mädchen, dessen Vater Diplomat gewesen ist.   3. Wo fandest du die Schlüssel, nach denen der Polizist fragte? / Wo fandest du den Wagen, nach dem der Polizist fragte? / Wo fandest du den Ausländer, nach dem der Polizist fragte? / Wo fandest du das Mädchen, nach dem der Polizist fragte? / Wo fandest du die Tasche, nach der der Polizist fragte?   4. Der Soldat, den ich in Freiburg traf, wohnt jetzt in Wien. / Die Touristen, die ich in Freiburg traf, wohnen jetzt in Wien. / Die Tänzerin, die ich in Freiburg traf, wohnt jetzt in Wien. / Das Kind, das ich in Freiburg traf, wohnt jetzt in Wien. / Der Polizist, den ich in Freiburg traf, wohnt jetzt in Wien.   5. Die Kinder, deren Schwester gestorben ist, wollen nicht mitgehen. / Der Junge, dessen Schwester gestorben ist, will nicht mitgehen. / Die Tänzerin, deren Schwester gestorben ist, will nicht mitgehen. / Das Mädchen, dessen Schwester gestorben ist, will nicht mitgehen. / Der Student, dessen Schwester gestorben ist, will nicht mitgehen.

Written Practice 2

1. Die Mutter sagt, dass sie die Kinder gut hat erziehen wollen. / Die Mutter sagt, dass ihr Sohn Soldat wird werden müssen. / Die Mutter sagt, dass die Kinder kein Bier haben trinken dürfen.   2. Ich weiß nicht, warum Tina das Klavier nicht hat spielen können. / Ich weiß nicht, warum du nach Belgien wirst reisen sollen. / Ich weiß nicht, warum die Tänzerin in Bremen wird tanzen wollen.

Written Practice 3

können es reparieren: pres ich kann es reparieren / **past** ich konnte es reparieren / **pres perf** wir haben es reparieren können / **fut** wir werden es reparieren können; **hören sie sprechen: pres** ich höre sie sprechen / **past** ich hörte sie sprechen / **pres perf** wir haben sie sprechen hören / **fut** wir werden sie sprechen hören; **lassen ein Hemd machen: pres** Sie lassen ein Hemd machen / **past** Sie ließen ein Hemd machen / **pres perf** er hat ein Hemd machen lassen / **fut** er wird ein Hemd machen lassen; **wollen ihn interviewen: pres** Sie wollen ihn interviewen / **past** Sie wollten ihn interviewen / **pres perf** er hat ihn interviewen wollen / **fut** er wird ihn interviewen wollen

Written Practice 4

1. mit ihm / mit wem   2. damit / womit   3. davon / wovon   4. in sie / in wen   5. darin / worin   6. daran / woran   7. gegen sie / gegen wen   8. dagegen / wogegen   9. daraus / woraus   10. nach ihr / nach wem

Written Practice 5

1. c   2. b, d, f, l   3. i   4. d, l   5. j   6. b, d, m   7. d, k   8. g   9. b, d, l   10. d, l

Written Practice 6

1. Ihre Tochter ist sehr intelligent. / Ihre Tochter ist außerordentlich intelligent. / Ihre Tochter ist relativ intelligent. / Ihre Tochter ist ziemlich intelligent. / Ihre Tochter ist erstaunlicherweise intelligent.   2. Überall sehen wir viele Probleme. / Hier sehen wir viele Probleme. / Dort sehen wir viele Probleme. / In dieser Stadt sehen wir viele Probleme. / In Europa sehen wir viele Probleme. 3. Unsere Familie ist oft in Griechenland gewesen. / Unsere Familie ist selten in Griechenland gewesen. / Unsere Familie ist manchmal in Griechenland gewesen. / Unsere Familie ist nie in Griechenland gewesen. / Unsere Familie ist ziemlich oft in Griechenland gewesen.

QUIZ

1. **nom:** der / die / das / die; **acc:** den / die / das / die; **dat:** dem / der / dem / denen; **gen:** dessen / deren / dessen / deren   2. Der Wagen, den ich kaufen will, ist ziemlich alt. / Die Bluse, die ich kaufen will, ist ziemlich alt. / Die Handschuhe, die ich kaufen will, sind ziemlich alt. / Die Kleider, die ich kaufen will, sind ziemlich alt. / Das kleine Haus, das ich kaufen will, ist ziemlich alt.   3. **hören sie lachen: pres** er hört sie lachen / **past** wir hörten sie lachen / **pres perf** ihr habt

sie lachen hören / **fut** Sie werden sie lachen hören; **lassen das Auto waschen: pres** er lässt das Auto waschen / **past** wir ließen das Auto waschen / **pres perf** ihr habt das Auto waschen lassen / **fut** Sie werden das Auto waschen lassen; **lernen schwimmen: pres** ich lerne schwimmen / **past** du lerntest schwimmen / **pres perf** wir haben schwimmen lernen / **fut** er wird schwimmen lernen; **sehen sie arbeiten: pres** ich sehe sie arbeiten / **past** du sahst sie arbeiten / **pres perf** wir haben sie arbeiten sehen / **fut** er wird sie arbeiten sehen

4. Wer sagt, dass mein Vater nicht gut hat fahren können? / Wer sagt, dass der junge Reporter die Tänzerin wird interviewen wollen? / Wer sagt, dass ich mich nicht für Sport interessiere? / Wer sagt, dass Herr Bach den alten VW wieder wird reparieren lassen? / Wer sagt, dass wir ihnen ein Paket geschickt haben?   5. Jemand fragt, ob der Student gestern nach Amerika geflogen ist. / Jemand fragt, ob Erik seinen Wagen waschen ließ. / Jemand fragt, ob meine Schwester im Ausland wird wohnen müssen. / Jemand fragt, ob diese Leute dorthin haben reisen dürfen. / Jemand fragt, ob ich fleißig arbeiten werde.

6. c   7. a   8. a   9. a   10. c

PART THREE TEST

1. **helfen:** ich habe geholfen / er hat geholfen / wir haben geholfen
2. **versprechen:** ich habe versprochen / er hat versprochen / wir haben versprochen   3. **fliegen:** ich bin geflogen / er ist geflogen / wir sind geflogen
4. **mitgehen:** du warst mitgegangen / ihr wart mitgegangen / Sie waren mitgegangen   5. **spazieren:** du warst spaziert / ihr wart spaziert / Sie waren spaziert   6. **haben:** du hattest gehabt / ihr hattet gehabt / Sie hatten gehabt
7. gefragt   8. studiert   9. gegessen   10. geworden   11. Warum glauben Sie Ihrem Bruder nicht? / Warum glauben Sie dieser Dame nicht? / Warum glauben Sie den Männern nicht?   12. Ich werde morgen mit ihm sprechen. / Ich werde morgen mit ihr sprechen. / Ich werde morgen mit ihnen sprechen.
13. Sie geben einem Ausländer die Fahrkarten. / Sie geben dir die Fahrkarten. / Sie geben euch die Fahrkarten.   14. sein   15. haben   16. sein   17. haben
18. haben   19. Sie sind vor zwei Tagen angekommen. / Sie sind vor einer Woche angekommen. / Sie sind vor einem Jahr angekommen.   20. Er hat drei Stunden auf ihn gewartet. / Er hat drei Stunden auf dich gewartet. / Er hat drei Stunden auf mich gewartet.   21. mich / mir / mein   22. dich / dir / dein   23. sie / ihnen / ihr   24. diese Ausländer / diesen Ausländern / dieser Ausländer
25. das Mädchen / dem Mädchen / des Mädchens   26. den Artikel / dem Artikel / des Artikels   27. Du wirst ein Butterbrot bestellen. / Er wird ein Butterbrot bestellen. / Sie werden ein Butterbrot bestellen.   28. Sie wird mitgehen. / Ihr werdet mitgehen. / Man wird mitgehen.   29. Du wirst dich

waschen. / Er wird sich waschen. / Ich werde mich waschen.   30. Ich bestelle mir ein Glas Milch. / Du bestellst dir ein Glas Milch. / Wir bestellen uns ein Glas Milch. / Ihr bestellt euch ein Glas Milch. / Sie bestellen sich ein Glas Milch.
31. **pres:** ich schicke / ich steige um / ich beeile mich   32. **past:** du schicktest / du stiegst um / du beeiltest dich   33. **pres perf:** er hat geschickt / er ist umgestiegen / er hat sich beeilt   34. **past perf:** wir hatten geschickt / wir waren umgestiegen / wir hatten uns beeilt   35. **fut:** ihr werdet schicken / ihr werdet umsteigen / ihr werdet euch beeilen   36. **fut perf:** sie werden geschickt haben / sie werden gestiegen sein / sie werden sich beeilt haben   37. Ich habe es nicht hören wollen. / Ich werde es nicht hören wollen.   38. Habt ihr dieses Gedicht verstehen können? / Werdet ihr dieses Gedicht verstehen können?   39. Du hast Schach spielen können. / Du wirst Schach spielen können.   40. Die Kinder, deren Mutter Diplomatin ist, werden in der Hauptstadt wohnen. / Der Junge, dessen Mutter Diplomatin ist, wird in der Hauptstadt wohnen. / Das Mädchen, dessen Mutter Diplomatin ist, wird in der Hauptstadt wohnen.   41. Der Reporter schreibt, dass der Diplomat nicht gut hat fahren können.   42. Der Reporter schreibt, dass er den Helden wird interviewen wollen.   43. d   44. b
45. a   46. d   47. a   48. a   49. a   50. b

CHAPTER 16

Written Practice 1
1. Der Brief, welchen sie gelesen hat, ist interessant. / Die Zeitung, welche sie gelesen hat, ist interessant. / Der Roman, welchen sie gelesen hat, ist interessant. / Die Romane, welche sie gelesen hat, sind interessant.   2. Die Touristen, mit welchen Karl sprechen will, kommen aus Polen. / Der Matrose, mit welchem Karl sprechen will, kommt aus Polen. / Die Tänzerin, mit welcher Karl sprechen will, kommt aus Polen. / Das Kind, mit welchem Karl sprechen will, kommt aus Polen.

Written Practice 2
1. Ich habe etwas, was ich im Park gefunden habe. / Ich habe etwas, was meine Mutter mir gegeben hat. / Ich habe etwas, worüber du dich freuen wirst. / Ich habe etwas, womit die Kinder spielen können.   2. Ist das alles, was du sagen kannst? / Ist das alles, was Tina kaufen wollte? / Ist das alles, wofür er sich interessiert? / Ist das alles, worüber Sie sprechen wollen?   3. Ich lerne viel, was nicht in Büchern steht. / Ich lerne viel, worüber Goethe geschrieben hatte. / Ich lerne viel, was interessant ist.   4. Ich verstehe nichts, was die alte Frau sagt. / Ich verstehe nichts, was du in diesem Buch geschrieben hast. / Ich verstehe nichts, was man in dieser Klasse lernt.

Written Practice 3

1. Wilhelm II. wurde 1859 geboren. / Er ist 1941 gestorben.   2. Otto von Bismarck wurde 1815 geboren. / Er ist 1898 gestorben.   3. Mein Bruder wurde 1995 geboren. / Er ist 2005 gestorben.   4. Karl der Große wurde 742 geboren. / Er ist 814 gestorben.   5. Meine Mutter wurde 1966 geboren. / Sie ist 1998 gestorben.

Written Practice 4

1. kälter / am kältesten   2. interessanter / am interessantesten   3. besser / am besten   4. länger / am längsten   5. dunkler / am dunkelsten   6. wärmer / am wärmsten   7. schwärzer / am schwärzesten   8. ruhiger / am ruhigsten   9. weißer / am weißesten   10. ärmer / am ärmsten

Written Practice 5

1. b   2. d   3. a   4. a   5. b   6. c   7. b   8. a   9. a   10. b   11. d   12. c   13. d   14. a   15. b   16. c   17. b   18. d   19. a   20. b

QUIZ

1. **nom:** welcher / welche / welches / welche   2. **acc:** welchen / welche / welches / welche   3. **dat:** welchem / welcher / welchem / welchen   4. **gen:** dessen / deren / dessen / deren   5. Der Seemann fuhr auf einem Schiff, das bei einer Insel unterging. / Der Seemann fuhr auf einem Schiff, welches bei einer Insel unterging.   6. Martin hat etwas, worüber du dich freuen wirst. Martin hat etwas, was sehr teuer ist. Martin hat etwas, was er verkaufen will.   7. Thomas Jefferson wurde im Jahre 1743 geboren. Er ist im Jahre 1826 gestorben.   8. Es geht mir viel besser. / Es geht ihm viel besser. / Es geht ihnen viel besser. / Es geht meiner Frau viel besser. / Es geht dem Soldaten viel besser.   9. Gibt es keinen Wein? / Gibt es eine Flasche Bier? / Gibt es keine Milch? / Gibt es keine Butter? / Gibt es keinen Sekt?   10. Ich habe dich gern. / Ich habe sie gern. / Ich habe euch gern. / Ich habe den Jungen gern. / Ich habe das Mädchen gern.

CHAPTER 17

Written Practice 1

1. Zwei Bücher werden von dem Lehrer gekauft.   2. Der Roman wird von ihr gelesen.   3. Das Brot wird von dem Bäcker gebacken.   4. Ich werde von meinem Vater gerufen.   5. Viele Lieder werden von den Soldaten gesungen.   6. Das Haus wurde von Herrn Bauer verkauft.   7. Tante Gerda wurde von meiner Mutter angerufen.   8. Zwei Tassen Kaffee wurden von ihnen getrunken.   9. Diese Gedichte wurden von ihm gelernt.   10. Der Morgenkaffee wurde von der Wirtin gebracht.   11. Der Roman ist von ihm geschrieben worden.   12. Ein Hut ist von den Kindern gefunden worden.   13. Das Eis ist von meiner

Schwester gegessen worden.   14. Der Artikel wird von dem Reporter geschrieben werden.   15. Das Museum wird von den Ausländern besucht werden.

Written Practice 2

acc: jenen netten Wirt / diese kleine Bluse / welches rote Auto; **dat:** jenem netten Wirt / dieser kleinen Bluse / welchem roten Auto; **gen:** jenes netten Wirts / dieser kleinen Bluse / welches roten Autos; **acc:** denselben alten Wagen / jenes neue Haus / alle fremden Leute; **dat:** demselben alten Wagen / jenem neuen Haus / allen fremden Leuten; **gen:** desselben alten Wagens / jenes neuen Hauses / aller fremden Leute

Written Practice 3

1. Die Kinder dieses jungen Mannes lernen gut. / Die Kinder dieses kranken Mannes lernen gut.   2. Sie hat mit demselben neuen Diplomaten gesprochen. / Sie hat mit demselben schlauen Diplomaten gesprochen.   3. Jede grüne Tanne is mehr als zwanzig Jahre alt. / Jede große Tanne is mehr als zwanzig Jahre alt.

Written Practice 4

verkaufen: Verkaufe! / Verkauft! / Verkaufen Sie!   **versprechen:** Versprich! / Versprecht! / Versprechen Sie!   **trinken:** Trinke! / Trinkt! / Trinken Sie! **vorstellen:** Stelle vor! / Stellt vor! / Stellen Sie vor!   **tun:** Tue! / Tut! / Tun Sie! **zumachen:** Mache zu! / Macht zu! / Machen Sie zu!   **lesen:** Lies! / Lest! / Lesen Sie!   **laufen:** Laufe! / Lauft! / Laufen Sie!   **sein:** Sei! / Seid! / Seien Sie!

Written Practice 5

sprechen: Sprich! / Sprechen wir!   **sagen:** Sage! / Sagen wir! **reisen:** Reise! / Reisen wir!   **aufmachen:** Mache auf! / Machen wir auf! **zerstören:** Zerstöre! / Zerstören wir!   **warten:** Warte! / Warten wir! **essen:** Iss! Essen wir!   **erhalten:** Erhalte! / Erhalten wir!   **ausgeben:** Gib aus! / Geben wir aus!

Written Practice 6

1. b   2. c   3. c   4. b   5. a   6. a   7. b   8. a   9. a   10. a 11. c   12. a   13. d   14. a   15. b

QUIZ

1. **er spielt:** werden gespielt; **ich höre:** werden gehört; **man arbeitet:** werden gearbeitet; **du machst zu:** werden zugemacht; **wir versprechen:** werden versprochen; **sie pflanzt:** werden gepflanzt; **du erhältst:** werden erhalten; **ich vergesse:** werden vergessen; **ihr schreit:** werden geschrien; **er nimmt mit:** werden mitgenommen   2. **werden gesehen: pres** ich werde gesehen / **past** du wurdest gesehen / **pres perf** er ist gesehen worden / **fut** wir werden gesehen werden;   **werden besucht: pres** ich werde besucht / **past** du wurdest besucht / **pres perf** er ist besucht worden / **fut** wir werden besucht werden;   **werden**

beschrieben: pres ich werde beschrieben / **past** du wurdest beschrieben / **pres perf** er ist beschrieben worden / **fut** wir werden beschrieben werden; **werden abgesandt: pres** du wirst abgesandt / **past** er wurde abgesandt / **pres perf** ihr seid abgesandt worden / **fut** Sie werden abgesandt werden; **werden besessen: pres** du wirst besessen / **past** er wurde besessen / **pres perf** ihr seid besessen worden / **fut** Sie werden besessen werden; **werden zerstört: pres** du wirst zerstört / **past** er wurde zerstört / **pres perf** ihr seid zerstört worden / **fut** Sie werden zerstört werden 3. Die Probleme werden von den Lehrern diskutiert. 4. Das alte Haus ist von ihnen abgerissen worden. 5. Der neue Kanzler wird von dem Grafen vorgestellt werden. 6. Hast du jenen großen Bären gesehen? / Hast du jenen braunen Bären gesehen? 7. Ist dieser alte Herr gestorben? / Ist jener alte Herr gestorben? 8. Wann kommt der nächste Bus? Wann kommt der letzte Bus? 9. Alle jungen Männer müssen ihnen helfen. / Alle deutschen Männer müssen ihnen helfen. 10. **treffen:** Triff! / Trefft! / Treffen Sie! **pflanzen:** Planze! / Pflanzt! / Pflanzen Sie! **zumachen:** Mache zu! / Macht zu! / Machen Sie zu! **schlafen:** Schlafe! / Schlaft! / Schlafen Sie! **bleiben:** Bleibe! / Bleibt! / Bleiben Sie! **denken:** Denke! / Denkt! / Denken Sie! **bekommen:** Bekomme! / Bekommt! / Bekommen Sie! **geben:** Gib! / Gebt! / Geben Sie! **sein:** Sei! / Seid! / Seien Sie! **werden:** Werde! / Werdet! / Werden Sie!

CHAPTER 18

Written Practice 1

1. Mir wurde von ihm geholfen. / Mir ist von ihm geholfen worden. / Mir wird von ihm geholfen werden. 2. Der Lehrerin wurde nicht geglaubt. / Der Lehrerin ist nicht geglaubt worden. / Der Lehrerin wird nicht geglaubt werden. 3. Ihm wurde dafür gedankt. / Ihm ist dafür gedankt worden. / Ihm wird dafür gedankt werden. 4. Wurde dem Professor imponiert? / Ist dem Professor imponiert worden? / Wird dem Professor imponiert werden?

Written Practice 2

1. Frau Schäfer wird nach Hannover fahren sollen. / Frau Schäfer wird nach Hannover fahren wollen. / Frau Schäfer wird nach Hannover fahren müssen. 2. Haben Sie Ihre Nachbarn einladen können? / Haben Sie Ihre Nachbarn einladen müssen? / Haben Sie Ihre Nachbarn einladen dürfen? 3. Hans wird von seiner Schwester geküsst werden wollen. / Hans wird von seiner Schwester geküsst werden müssen. / Hans wird von seiner Schwester geküsst werden sollen. 4. Hat der Wagen repariert werden können? / Hat der Wagen repariert werden müssen? / Hat der Wagen repariert werden sollen? 5. Ihm soll sofort geholfen werden. / Ihm kann sofort geholfen werden. / Ihm muss sofort geholfen werden.

Written Practice 3

1. Das Haus kann geräumt werden. / Das Haus muss geräumt werden.   2. Es durfte nicht repariert werden. / Es musste nicht repariert werden.   3. Das Kind wird fotografiert werden wollen. / Das Kind wird fotografiert werden können.

Written Practice 4

1. Ist es abgeschleppt worden? / Sind sie abgeschleppt worden? / Ist der Wagen abgeschleppt worden? / Sind die Autos abgeschleppt worden? / Ist der Bus abgeschleppt worden?   2. Sein Freund konnte nicht verstanden werden. / Die Kinder konnten nicht verstanden werden. / Ich konnte nicht verstanden werden. / Du konntest nicht verstanden werden. / Wir konnten nicht verstanden werden. 3. Ihnen wird niemals geglaubt werden. / Ihr wird niemals geglaubt werden. / Ihm wird niemals geglaubt werden. / Meiner Frau wird niemals geglaubt werden. / Dem Physiker wird niemals geglaubt werden.

Written Practice 5

1. Der Fernsehapparat ließ sich nicht reparieren.   2. Diese Romane haben sich schnell lesen lassen.   3. Die Bären ließen sich nicht fotografieren.   4. Das lässt sich sehr leicht ändern.

Written Practice 6

1. **pres** Das lässt sich nicht verstehen. / **pres perf** Das hat sich nicht verstehen lassen. / **fut** Das wird sich nicht verstehen lassen.   2. **past** Wurde dem Gast gut gedient? / **pres perf** Ist dem Gast gut gedient worden? / **fut** Wird dem Gast gut gedient werden?   3. **pres** Du wirst gesehen. / **past** Du wurdest gesehen. / **pres perf** Du bist gesehen worden.   4. **pres** Der kranken Katze kann nicht geholfen werden. / **pres perf** Der kranken Katze hat nicht geholfen werden können. / **fut** Der kranken Katze wird nicht geholfen werden können.   5. **past** Nichts konnte getan werden. / **pres perf** Nichts hat getan werden können. / **fut** Nichts wird getan werden können.

Written Practice 7

nom: mein junger Freund / unsere alte Tante / ihr neues Fahrrad; **acc:** meinen jungen Freund / unsere alte Tante / ihr neues Fahrrad; **dat:** meinem jungen Freund / unserer alten Tante / ihrem neuen Fahrrad; **gen:** meines jungen Freundes / unserer alten Tante / ihres neuen Fahrrads; **nom:** dein kleines Haus / jeder große Stuhl / diese graue Katze; **acc:** dein kleines Haus / jeden großen Stuhl / diese graue Katze; **dat:** deinem kleinen Haus / jedem großen Stuhl / dieser grauen Katze; **gen:** deines kleinen Hauses / jedes großen Stuhls / dieser grauen Katze; **nom:** ihr kleiner Sohn / deine junge Schwester; **acc:** deine junge Schwester; **dat:** ihrem kleinen Sohn; **gen:** ihres kleinen Sohns / deiner jungen Schwester; **nom:** eine kranke Dame / unser letzter Brief; **acc:** eine kranke Dame / unseren letzten Brief; **gen:** einer kranken Dame / unseres letzten Briefes

Written Practice 8

1. Ist das der Bruder deines amerikanischen Gasts? / Ist das der Bruder Ihrer netten Kusine? / Ist das der Bruder eurer jungen Freunde?   2. Kennen Sie meine neue Freundin? / Kennen Sie seinen alten Onkel? / Kennen Sie ihren intelligenten Sohn?   3. Hans wollte mit unserem kleinen Hund spielen. / Hans wollte mit jenen netten Kindern spielen. / Hans wollte mit seinem neuen Fußball spielen.

Written Practice 9

Sample answers are given.   1. alte   2. neue   3. jüngeren   4. hübschen
5. neue   6. kaputtes   7. deutschen   8. brauner   9. reinen   10. kleines

Written Practice 10

1. d   2. a   3. a   4. b   5. d   6. a   7. d   8. b   9. c   10. b

QUIZ

1. **past** Der Wagen musste abgeschleppt werden. / **pres perf** Der Wagen hat abgeschleppt werden müssen. / **fut** Der Wagen wird abgeschleppt werden müssen.
2. **pres** Ihm wird dafür gedankt. / **past** Ihm wurde dafür gedankt. / **fut** Ihm wird dafür gedankt werden.   3. Ihm wurde von ihnen geholfen. / Ihr wurde von ihnen geholfen. / Dem Beamten wurde von ihnen geholfen. / Meinem Trainer wurde von ihnen geholfen. / Uns wurde von ihnen geholfen.   4. Es lässt sich nicht leicht ändern. / Sie lassen sich nicht leicht ändern. / Das Problem lässt sich nicht leicht ändern. / Die Probleme lassen sich nicht leicht ändern. / Das lässt sich nicht leicht ändern.   5. **nom:** ein netter Mann; **acc:** einen netten Mann; **dat:** einem netten Mann / seiner neuen Freundin; **gen:** eines netten Mannes / seiner neuen Freundin   6. **nom:** kein gutes Heft / meine alten Handschuhe; **acc:** kein gutes Heft / meine alten Handschuhe; **dat:** keinem guten Heft / meinen alten Handschuhen; **gen:** eines guten Hefts / meiner alten Handschuhe   7. c   8. a
9. d   10. a

CHAPTER 19

Written Practice 1

schlafen: ich schlafe X / du schlafest / er schlafe / wir schlafen X / ihr schlafet / sie schlafen X;   **vergessen:** ich vergesse X / du vergessest / er vergesse / wir vergessen X / ihr vergesset / sie vergessen X;   **mitnehmen:** ich nehme mit X / du nehmest mit / er nehme mit / wir nehmen mit X / ihr nehmet mit / sie nehmen mit X;   **fragen:** ich frage X / du fragest / er frage / wir fragen X / ihr fraget / sie fragen X;   **aussehen:** ich sehe aus X / du sehest aus / er sehe aus / wir sehen aus X / ihr sehet aus / sie sehen aus X;   **sein:** ich sei / du seiest / er sei / wir seien / ihr seiet / sie seien

Written Practice 2

1. Er sagte, dass zwei Autos abgeschleppt worden seien. / Er sagte, dass die Regierung den armen Menschen helfen werde. / Er sagte, dass er nur selten ins Theater gehe.   2. Ein Freund schrieb uns, dass er nächste Woche kommen könne. / Ein Freund schrieb uns, dass sein Bruder in Gudrun verliebt sei. / Ein Freund schrieb uns, dass seine Familie das Geld noch nicht erhalten habe.

Written Practice 3

1. Sie berichtete, die Regierung habe dem alten König geholfen. / Sie berichtete, der Kanzler werde morgen ankommen. / Sie berichtete, es gebe nichts Schöneres als Wien.   2. Martin schrieb mir, dass seine Freundin in Russland gewesen sei. / Martin schrieb mir, dass der Fluss das Land überschwemmt habe. / Martin schrieb mir, dass die warme Sonne jeden Menschen gesund machen müsse.

Written Practice 4

1. Mein Mann fragte, wo sein neuer Pullover sei. / Mein Mann fragte, ob Erik den Wagen reparieren könne. / Mein Mann fragte, wessen Tasche der Dieb gestohlen habe. / Mein Mann fragte, ob sie schon in der Hauptstadt gewesen seien. / Mein Mann fragte, wie viel Herr Bauer dafür ausgeben werde.

QUIZ

1. **berichten: pres** ich berichte; **past** ich berichtete / **pres** du berichtest; **past** du berichtetest / **pres** er berichte; **past** er berichtete / **pres** wir berichten; **past** wir berichteten / **pres** ihr berichtet; **past** ihr berichtetet / **pres** sie berichten; **past** sie berichteten; **fahren: pres** ich fahre; **past** ich führe / **pres** du fahrest; **past** du führest / **pres** er fahre; **past** er führe / **pres** wir fahren; **past** wir führen / **pres** ihr fahret; **past** ihr führet / **pres** sie fahren; **past** sie führen   2. **mitgehen: pres** ich gehe mit; **past** ich ginge mit / **pres** du gehest mit; **past** du gingest mit / **pres** er gehe mit; **past** er ginge mit / **pres** wir gehen mit; **past** wir gingen mit / **pres** ihr gehet mit; **past** ihr ginget mit / **pres** sie gehen mit; **past** sie gingen mit; **aussehen: pres** ich sehe aus; **past** ich sähe aus / **pres** du sehest aus; **past** du sähest aus / **pres** er sehe aus; **past** er sähe aus/ **pres** wir sehen aus; **past** wir sähen aus / **pres** ihr sehet aus; **past** ihr sähet aus / **pres** sie sehen aus; **past** sie sähen aus

3. **werden: pres** ich werde; **past** ich würde / **pres** du werdest; **past** du würdest / **pres** er werde; **past** er würde / **pres** wir werden; **past** wir würden / **pres** ihr werdet; **past** ihr würdet / **pres** sie werden; **past** sie würden; **sein: pres** ich sei; **past** ich wäre / **pres** du seiest; **past** du wärest / **pres** er sei; **past** er wäre / **pres** wir seien; **past** wir wären / **pres** ihr seiet; **past** ihr wäret / **pres** sie seien; **past** sie wären   4. Erik sagte, dass seine Freundin in Darmstadt arbeiten wolle/wollte. / Erik sagte, dass die Polizei einen interessanten Brief erhalten habe/hätte. / Erik sagte, dass niemand ihm etwas über den Film erzähle/erzählte. / Erik sagte, dass er seine Freundin in Bremen kennen gelernt habe/hätte. / Erik sagte, dass Tina ein Geschenk für ihren Mann suchen werde/würde. / Erik sagte, dass unsere Freunde

ein Kind adoptieren wollten. / Erik sagte, dass die Touristen sich morgen mit Verwandten treffen würden.   5. Helga fragte, ob Herr Schneider bei euch zu Gast sei/wäre. / Helga fragte, wann der Wagen repariert werden werde/würde. / Helga fragte, mit wem die Ausländer getanzt hätten. / Helga fragte, ob Sie viele Geschenke zum Geburtstag bekommen hätten. / Helga fragte, ob die Jungen uns helfen könnten. / Helga fragte, wo die Kinder sich die Hände gewaschen hätten. / Helga fragte, ob die Schüler lesen und schreiben gelernt hätten.   6. c   7. b   8. d   9. d   10. a

CHAPTER 20

Written Practice 1

1. Erik tat so, als ob er sehr klug wäre. / Erik tat so, als ob er plötzlich reich geworden wäre. / Erik tat so, als ob er diese Probleme lösen könnte. / Erik tat so, als ob er den Kanzler schon kennen gelernt hätte.   2. Sie schrie, als ob sie ein Ungeheuer gesehen hätte. / Sie schrie, als ob sie sterben müsste. / Sie schrie, als ob sie wahnsinnig wäre. / Sie schrie, als ob sie nicht schwimmen könnte.

Written Practice 2

1. Wenn ich Deutsch verstünde, würde ich diese Bücher lesen.   2. Wenn wir ihm helfen könnten, würde er glücklich sein.   3. Wenn sie ihm mehr Geld gegeben hätten, hätte er das neue Haus gekauft.   4. Wenn ich im Lotto gewonnen hätte, wäre ich nach Amerika geflogen.   5. Wenn der Schüler fleißiger gewesen wäre, hätte er das Gedicht auswendig gelernt.

Written Practice 3

1. Es ist sehr wichtig genug Milch zu trinken. / Es ist sehr wichtig fleißig zu arbeiten. / Es ist sehr wichtig pünktlich anzukommen. / Es ist sehr wichtig alten Menschen zu helfen. / Es ist sehr wichtig gute Freunde zu haben. / Es ist sehr wichtig höflich zu sein.

Written Practice 4

1. Er kam in die Küche, ohne seine Mutter zu grüssen. / Er kam in die Küche, ohne seiner Mutter zu helfen. / Er kam in die Küche, ohne die Tür zuzumachen. 2. Karin arbeitet in Berlin, um mehr Geld zu verdienen. / Karin arbeitet in Berlin, um bei einer Tante zu wohnen. / Karin arbeitet in Berlin, um die großen Museen zu besuchen.   3. Die Kinder stehen an der Ecke, anstatt zur Schule zu gehen. / Die Kinder stehen an der Ecke, anstatt ihren kranken Onkel zu besuchen. / Die Kinder stehen an der Ecke, anstatt sich zu beeilen nach Hause zu kommen.

Written Practice 5

1. arbeiten zu müssen   2. vergessen zu sollen   3. sprechen zu wollen
4. gelernt zu haben   5. verstanden zu haben   6. gewesen zu sein

7. mitgegangen zu sein   8. zerstört zu werden   9. aufgemacht zu werden
10. bewundert worden zu sein

Written Practice 6

1. d   2. a   3. c   4. b   5. a   6. c   7. a   8. d   9. a   10. b
11. a   12. c   13. a   14. d   15. c

QUIZ

1. **tragen:** trüge / würde tragen;   **bringen:** brächte / würde bringen;
zumachen: machte zu / würde zumachen;   **werden:** würde / würde werden;
vergessen: vergässe / würde vergessen;   **sprechen:** spräche / würde sprechen;
verstehen: verstünde / würde verstehen;   **lassen:** ließe / würde lassen;
ankommen: käme an / würde ankommen;   **vorstellen:** stellte vor / würde
vorstellen;   **kennen:** kennte / würde kennen;   **wissen:** wüsste / würde
wissen;   **haben:** hätte / würde haben;   **einladen:** lüde ein / würde einladen;
sein: wäre / würde sein   2. Wenn er hier wäre, würde er mit Onkel Peter
sprechen. / Wenn er hier wäre, könnte ich mit ihm tanzen. / Wenn er hier wäre,
würden wir zusammen in die Bibliothek gehen. / Wenn er hier wäre, müsste er auf
dem Sofa schlafen.   3. Wenn das Wetter besser gewesen wäre, wären wir in die
Stadt gefahren. / Wenn das Wetter besser gewesen wäre, hätten wir im Garten
spielen können. / Wenn das Wetter besser gewesen wäre, wäre der Wagen repariert
worden. / Wenn das Wetter besser gewesen wäre, hätte Thomas die Kinder zum
Stadtpark gebracht.   4. Wenn sie mehr Geld hätte, würde sie uns Eis kaufen. /
Wenn unsere Tante hier wäre, würde sie uns Eis kaufen. / Wenn wir fleißig
arbeiteten, würde sie uns Eis kaufen. / Wenn es heiß würde, würde sie uns Eis
kaufen.   5. Er tat so, als ob er alles verstanden hätte. / Er tat so, als ob er so klug
wäre. / Er tat so, als ob ich nicht sein Freund wäre. / Er tat so, als ob er uns gar
nicht gesehen hätte. / Er tat so, als ob wir ihm kein Geschenk geben würden.
6. Karin spricht, als ob sie sehr klug wäre. / Karin spricht, als ob sie die Lösung
gefunden hätte. / Karin spricht, als ob wir ihr nicht helfen wollten. / Karin spricht,
als ob sie ein Ungeheuer gesehen hätte. / Karin spricht, als ob Martin nur ein
Bekannter wäre.   7. Es ist oft schwer einem Dieb zu glauben. / Es ist oft schwer
interessante Bücher zu finden. / Es ist oft schwer für einen bösen Mann zu
arbeiten. / Es ist oft schwer zu Hause zu bleiben, wenn das Wetter schön ist.
8. Er möchte nach Wien reisen, um einen Freund zu besuchen. / Er möchte nach
Wien reisen, um da Arbeit zu suchen. / Er möchte nach Wien reisen, um seine
Probleme in Freiburg zu vergessen. / Er möchte nach Wien reisen, um an der
Universität zu studieren.   9. Tanja behauptet eine Freundin im Kaufhaus
gesehen zu haben. / Tanja behauptet dem neuen Chef damit geholfen zu haben. /
Tanja behauptet nach Asien geflogen zu sein. / Tanja behauptet von allen Jungen
bewundert worden zu sein.   10. um den Wagen reparieren zu lassen / ohne den
Wagen reparieren zu lassen / anstatt den Wagen reparieren zu lassen

PART FOUR TEST

1. Die Studentin, mit der Erik tanzte, ist die Tochter meiner Wirtin. / Die Studentin, mit welcher Erik tanzte, ist die Tochter meiner Wirtin. 2. Die Männer, mit denen ich in einer Fabrik arbeite, haben wenig Freizeit. / Die Männer, mit welchen ich in einer Fabrik arbeite, haben wenig Freizeit. 3. Sie haben das Dorf, in dem mein Onkel geboren ist, besichtigt. / Sie haben das Dorf, in welchem mein Onkel geboren ist, besichtigt. 4. Meine Freundin hat etwas, worüber du dich freuen wirst. / Meine Freundin hat etwas, was sehr teuer ist. 5. Der Physiker findet alles, was seine Frau verloren hat. / Der Physiker findet alles, was er verkaufen kann. 6. **werden gefunden: pres** ich werde gefunden / **past** du wurdest gefunden / **pres perf** er ist gefunden worden / **fut** wir werden gefunden werden 7. **muss verhaftet werden: pres** ich muss verhaftet werden / **past** du musstest verhaftet werden / **pres perf** er hat verhaftet werden müssen / **fut** wir werden verhaftet werden müssen 8. Das Examen wurde von den Lehrern diskutiert. 9. Das alte Haus ist von uns verkauft worden. 10. Der neue Mieter wird von unserer Wirtin vorgestellt werden. 11. Habt ihr einen großen Bären gesehen? 12. Die Töchter dieses alten Mannes arbeiten in Kiel. 13. Sie hat mit dem jungen Diplomaten gesprochen. 14. Alle kranken Kinder müssen zu Hause bleiben. 15. **treffen:** Triff! / Trefft! / Treffen Sie! 16. **vorstellen:** Stelle vor! / Stellt vor! / Stellen Sie vor! 17. **aufmachen:** Mache auf! / Macht auf! / Machen Sie auf! 18. **sehen:** Sieh! / Seht! / Sehen Sie! 19. **sein:** Sei! / Seid! / Seien Sie! 20. **geben:** Gib! / Gebt! / Geben Sie! 21. **werden:** Werde! / Werdet! / Werden Sie! 22. Ihm wurde von ihnen geholfen. / Den Jungen wurden von ihnen geholfen. / Uns wurden von ihnen geholfen. 23. Die Bücher mussten nicht verkauft werden. / Es musste nicht verkauft werden. / Die Wohnung musste nicht verkauft werden. 24. **nom:** ein guter Mann / seine letzte Frage; **acc:** einen guten Mann / seine letzte Frage; **dat:** einem guten Mann / seiner letzten Frage; **acc:** sein neues Heft / meine alten Handschuhe; **dat:** seinem neuen Heft / meinen alten Handschuhen / **gen:** seines neuen Hefts / meiner alten Handschuhe 25. **trinken: pres** ich trinke; **past** ich tränke / **pres** du trinkest; **past** du tränkest / **pres** er trinke; **past** er tränke / **pres** wir trinken; **past** wir tränken / **pres** ihr trinket; **past** ihr tränket / **pres** sie trinken; **past** sie tränken 26. **zumachen: pres** ich mache zu; **past** ich machte zu / **pres** du machest zu; **past** du machtest zu / **pres** er mache zu; **past** er machte zu / **pres** wir machen zu; **past** wir machten zu / **pres** ihr machet zu / **past** ihr machtet zu / **pres** sie machen zu; **past** sie machten zu 27. **werden: pres** ich werde; **past** ich würde / **pres** du werdest; **past** du würdest / **pres** er werde; **past** er würde / **pres** wir werden; **past** wir würden / **pres** ihr werdet; **past** ihr würdet / **pres** sie werden; **past** sie würden 28. **sein: pres** ich sei; **past** ich wäre / **pres** du seiest; **past** du wärest / **pres** er sei; **past** er wäre / **pres** wir seien; **past** wir wären / **pres** ihr seiet; **past** ihr wäret / **pres** sie seien; **past** sie wären 29. Frau Schneider sagte, dass

ihre Freundin in Darmstadt wohnen wolle. / Frau Schneider sagte, dass niemand ihr darüber erzählen werde. / Frau Schneider sagte, dass die Besucher sich morgen mit einer Physikerin treffen würden. 30. Der Beamte fragte, ob Herr Schneider ein Freund von Ihnen sei. / Der Beamte fragte, wann der Wagen repariert worden sei. / Der Beamte fragte, ob Sie Ihre Fahrkarten bekommen hätten. 31. Wenn er hier wäre, könnte Tina mit ihm sprechen. / Wenn er hier wäre, würden wir zusammen ins Kino gehen. 32. Wenn das Wetter besser gewesen wäre, wären sie in die Berge gefahren. / Wenn das Wetter besser gewesen wäre, hätte ich im Garten sitzen können. 33. Er tat so, als ob er alles verstanden hätte. / Er tat so, als ob Tanja seine Freundin wäre. / Er tat so, als ob er uns gar nicht gesehen hätte. 34. Das Mädchen spricht, als ob sie sehr klug wäre. / Das Mädchen spricht, als ob die Jungen ihr nicht helfen wollten. / Das Mädchen spricht, als ob sie einen Wolf gesehen hätte. 35. Es ist schwer alten Menschen zu helfen. / Es ist schwer interessante Bücher zu finden. / Es ist schwer in einem neuen Haus zu wohnen. 36. Sie fahren nach Italien, um Freunde zu besuchen. / Sie fahren nach Italien, um die alten Städte zu fotografieren. / Sie fahren nach Italien, um an der Universität studieren zu können. 37. b 38. a 39. a 40. d 41. c 42. c 43. a 44. a 45. c 46. a 47. a 48. d 49. c 50. b

FINAL EXAM

1. b 2. c 3. d 4. b 5. b 6. a 7. c 8. b 9. a 10. c
11. b 12. b 13. d 14. a 15. c 16. d 17. a 18. a 19. b
20. a 21. d 22. c 23. a 24. d 25. a 26. a 27. b 28. a
29. b 30. c 31. d 32. a 33. c 34. a 35. a 36. c 37. c
38. b 39. d 40. b 41. a 42. d 43. a 44. a 45. a 46. b
47. c 48. a 49. b 50. a 51. a 52. d 53. b 54. c 55. a
56. b 57. a 58. b 59. a 60. c 61. c 62. c 63. d 64. a
65. d 66. a 67. b 68. a 69. d 70. a 71. b 72. c 73. b
74. a 75. c 76. d 77. a 78. b 79. a 80. b 81. d 82. b
83. b 84. a 85. c 86. b 87. b 88. c 89. a 90. d 91. b
92. b 93. d 94. a 95. c 96. b 97. a 98. c 99. d 100. b

INDEX